THE
DIVINE
SARAH

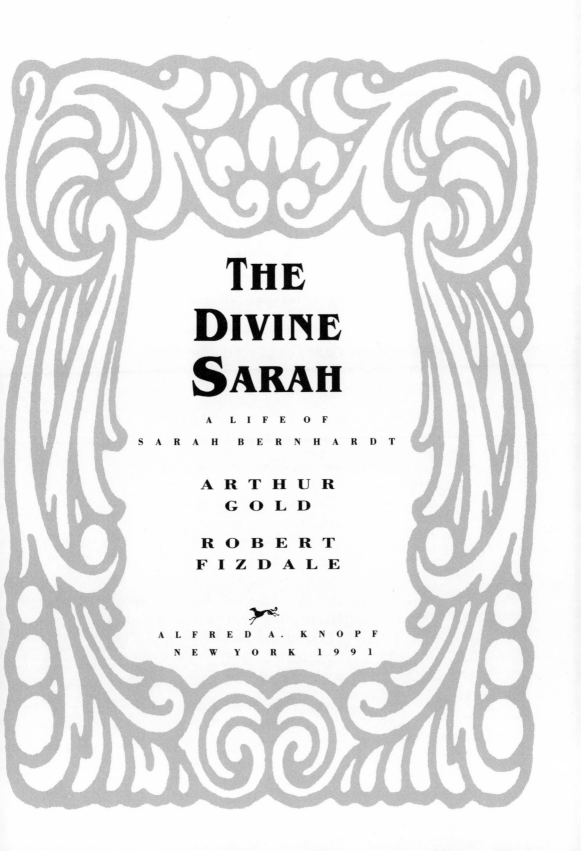

THE DIVINE SARAH

A LIFE OF
SARAH BERNHARDT

ARTHUR GOLD

ROBERT FIZDALE

ALFRED A. KNOPF
NEW YORK 1991

THIS IS A BORZOI BOOK
PUBLISHED BY ALFRED A. KNOPF, INC.

Owing to limitations of space, all acknowledgments for permission to
reprint previous material may be found on pages 351–2.

Library of Congress Cataloging-in-Publication Data
Gold, Arthur.
The Divine Sarah : a life of Sarah Bernhardt / Arthur Gold and
Robert Fizdale.—1st ed.
p.   cm.
Includes bibliographical references (p.   ) and index.
ISBN 0-394-52879-4
1. Bernhardt, Sarah, 1844–1923.   2. Actors—France—Biography.
I. Fizdale, Robert.   II. Title.
PN2638.B5G6   1991
792'.028'092—dc20
[B]   89-45361   CIP

Manufactured in the United States of America
FIRST EDITION

TO MICHEL DE BRY

who devoted his time, his energy, and his thought to the creation of a panoply to celebrate to the fullest the art of Sarah Bernhardt and keep her alive in the world's memory. Monsieur de Bry generously gave us the opportunity to study and to quote from the letters and documents in his collection of Bernhardtiana, and—even more generously—shared with us his profound knowledge of our subject.

AND TO THIERRY BODIN

who not only pointed out the paths that would lead us to Sarah Bernhardt, but to the people of her world. His erudition was dazzling, his enthusiasm overwhelming, and the hospitality he and his wife, Pierrette, showed us heartwarming.

CONTENTS

Illustrations follow pages 20, 52, 148, 180, 244, and 308.

ACKNOWLEDGMENTS

We are extremely grateful to the following people and institutions for the invaluable help they gave us: the Bibliothèque Nationale and its *conservateur en chef*, in the department of manuscripts, Mme. Callut; the Bibliothèque de l'Arsenal and its *conservateur en chef de la Bibliothèque des Arts et du Spectacle*, Mlle. Giteau and her staff: Mme. Faure, Mlle. Tourniac, and Mlle. Drouin; the Bibliothèque de la Comédie Française and its *conservateur*, Mlle. Noelle Guibert; the Musée d'Orsay and its director, Françoise Cachin; the Musée du Petit Palais and its conservateur en chef, Mme. Thérèse Burollet; the Bibliothèque Historique de la Ville de Paris, the Musée de l'Armée and M. Vergnaud in the Secretariat ECPA. We also wish to thank Fonds Zola Bibliothèque Nationale de Paris (for Bernhardt's letter to Zola), the Musée Rodin in Paris, and the Musée des Beaux-Arts in Dijon, as well as the Musée du Petit Palais in Geneva, the Victoria and Albert Theatre Museum in London and its director Sir Roy Strong, the Harvard Theatre Collection in Cambridge and its directrice Dr. Jeanne Newland, and the New York Public Library of the Performing Arts.

We cannot thank all the people who were helpful, but among the many who contributed to this book we must give special thanks to the Prince and Princess de Ligne La Trémoïlle, the Baroness Elie de Rothschild, the Prince Amyn Aga Khan, Jane Lady Abdy, Anka Muhlstein and Louis Begley, Sydney and Marit Gruson, Paul and Lucille Audouy, Mr. and Mrs. Angelo Torricini, Charles Oulmont, the late Henri Sauguet, Giorgio Strehler, Daniel Stes, Giacchino Lanza, Georges Liebert, Mlle. Annette Vaillant, Denise Blum, Nanos Valaoritis (who gave us a picture of his great uncle, Damala), brothers Pierre and Jacques Loti-Viaud (not only for permission to quote from the letters and voluminous journals of Pierre Loti, but for the trouble they took to find them for us), the Princess Mario de Ruspoli (for her kindness in letting us quote from the letters her grandfather, Charles Haas, received from Sarah Bernhardt), Mme. Claudine Loste, Alan Lesieutre (for allowing us to reproduce the photographs of Bernhardt in his archives, as well as the Clairin paintings of Sarah as Sardou's Théodora, as Saint Teresa in his *Vierge D'Avila*, and Clairin's affiche for La Tosca), Mme. Colette Monceau (who analyzed Sarah's handwriting), Bernard Minoret (for sharing his encyclopedic knowledge of French theatre history), the late Madame Terka Reichenbach (Sarah's great-granddaughter, who so kindly gave us the photograph of Maurice Bernhardt "grown up") and *her* son, the photographer Georges P. Clemençeau (who, through the courtesy of his cousin, Mlle. Marie-Louise Barberot, rephotographed for us the early family photographs in her collection), Jean-Pierre Richepin (for the photograph of his illustrious grandfather, the poet-playwright Jean Richepin, one of the great loves of Sarah's life), the Morgan Library in New York (for permission to quote the passionate letters she sent Richepin), and the great actress Irene Worth (who told us they were there).

We must also thank Sir John Gielgud, who shared his memories of seeing Bernhardt perform when he was fifteen. His impressions were as sensitive and as vivid as Proust's response to Bernhardt as "Berma." Sir John sent us to his colleague, Richard Bebb, who earned our undying gratitude by playing all of Bernhardt's recordings for us.

We thank Dario Cecchi, Count Ghislain de Diesbach, Jean-Claude Eger, Philippe Gand, Paul Lorenz, Countess Guy de Beaumont, Claude and Ida Bourdet (who put their archives on Sarah's beloved Doctor Pozzi at our disposal), the late André Bernheim, André Rieupeyrout (who invited us to a screening of Sacha Guitry's early silent documentary film, *Ceux de Nos Jours*, in which one sees Sarah declaiming and looking radiant a few weeks after the amputation of her leg), Maitre Claudine Herrmann, Raymond Mander and Joe Mitchenson, the late Delphine Seyrig, Annette Vaillant, Mme. Suzanne Fessart, Maitre Claudine Herrmann, and William Weaver. All of these (and countless others) have contributed immeasurably to our book.

We have very special thanks to offer our publisher, Sonny Mehta, his staff, and our editors Bob Gottlieb and Carol Janeway, and her associate, Robin Swados, production editor Kevin Bourke, and designer Iris Weinstein. They all made working with them at Knopf a great pleasure. Last, but very far from least, we owe a debt of gratitude to our photographers, Phillippe Doumic, Jean-Loupe Charmet, and Jakob Mydtskov, and to two brilliant Frenchwomen who helped us with research, Liliane Ziegel and Claude Nabokoff, without whom this book would not exist.

THE
DIVINE
SARAH

Mark Twain said: "There are five kinds of actresses: bad actresses, fair actresses, good actresses, great actresses—and then there is Sarah Bernhardt." If it pleased Mark Twain to place a crown on Bernhardt's head, it gave George Bernard Shaw equal pleasure to send it flying when he wrote of "the childishly egotistical character of her acting, which is not the art of making you think more highly or feel more deeply, but the art of making you admire her, pity her, champion her, weep with her, laugh at her jokes, follow her fortunes breathlessly, and applaud her wildly when the curtain falls. It is the art of finding out all your weaknesses and practicing on them— cajoling you, harrowing you, exciting you—on the whole fooling you. . . ."

To fool the customer is part of the actor's business. But Shaw was not made to be fooled. A crusader in knickerbockers, his mission was to shed light on a misguided world. Bernhardt was of another persuasion. She lived to mesmerize, to dazzle, to lure the public into the mysteries of sensuality and poetic illusion. He was the rock of truth; she, the siren on the rock, her tail in the treacherous waters that surround it, her face turned to the moon.

D. H. Lawrence did not share Shaw's feelings when he saw Bernhardt play *La Dame aux Camélias* at the Theatre Royal in Nottingham. The novelist was twenty-three at the time, the actress forty years older than he.

> There she is [he wrote], the incarnation of wild emotion which we share with all live things, but which is gathered in us in all complexity and inscrutable fury. She represents the primeval passions of woman, and she is fascinating to an extraordinary degree. I could love such a woman myself, love her to madness; all for the pure wild passion of it. Take care about

3

going to see Bernhardt. Unless you are very sound, do not go. When I think of her now I can still feel the weight hanging in my chest as it hung there for days after I saw her. Her winsome, sweet playful ways; her sad, plaintive little murmurs; her terrible panther cries; and then the awful, inarticulate sounds, the little sobs that fairly sear one, and the despair and death; it is too much in one evening.

In 1885 the young Sigmund Freud was in Paris studying hypnotism and neurology with Jean-Martin Charcot. While there he saw Bernhardt in Sardou's *Théodora*, a melodramatic spectacle of lust, sadism, and sin, subjects the future psychoanalyst was to examine in ways the playwright could not have imagined. But, like Lawrence, the student of hypnosis succumbed, unresisting, to the actress's mesmeric gifts:

I can't say anything good about the piece itself. . . . But how that Sarah plays! After the first words of her lovely, vibrant voice I felt I had known her for years. Nothing she could have said would have surprised me; I believed at once everything she said. . . . I have never seen a more comical figure than Sarah in the second act, where she appears in a simple dress, and yet one soon stops laughing, for every inch of that little figure lives and bewitches. Then her flattering and imploring and embracing; it is incredible what postures she can assume and how every limb and joint acts with her. A curious being: I can imagine that she needn't be any different in life than on the stage.

Freud's feelings for Sarah went deeper than a student crush. For years a photograph of Bernhardt greeted his troubled patients as they entered his office. We do not know whether he displayed the likeness because he thought it a symbol of the eternal woman, or of the eternally neurotic woman, or because he was interested in the connection between acting and life. If it was the last, he was not alone. The fascination of celebrated tragediennes— from Rachel to Garbo, from Bernhardt to Callas—lies in the suggestive power, not only of their art, but of the lives they lead. We wish to know the secrets of these hallucinatory creatures who play on our emotions, arouse our desires, and act out our fantasies. Intimates for an evening, they reach out and touch us with an immediacy that makes our lives seem drab in comparison. Like the mythic queens they portray, their egotism intrigues us and their tyrannical caprices—intolerable in ordinary mortals—are forgiven with the indulgence given to shameless dreams.

The poet-playwright Edmond Rostand caught the actress at her volcanic best in his preface to Jules Huret's biography of Sarah Bernhardt, written when she was in her middle fifties:

1899: A brougham stops at the door. A woman enveloped in furs jumps out, threads her way through the crowd . . . and mounts a winding stairway; plunges into a dressing room bursting with flowers and as overheated as a hothouse; throws her little beribboned handbag with its inexhaustible contents into one corner, her bewinged hat into another; takes off her furs, and instantaneously dwindles into a mere scabbard of white silk; rushes onto a dimly lit stage and immediately animates a crowd of listless, yawning, loitering folk; dashes backward and forward, inspiring everyone with her own feverish energy; goes into the prompter's box, directs her scenes; points out the proper gesture and intonation, rises up in wrath and insists everything be done again; shouts with fury; sits down, smiles, drinks tea, and begins to rehearse her own part; draws tears from hardened actors who thrust their enraptured heads out of the wings to watch her; returns to her room, where the set designers are waiting, demolishes their plans and reconstructs them; collapses, wipes her brow with a lace handkerchief and thinks of fainting; returns to her dressing room and teaches the extras how to do their hair; listens to hundreds of letters, weeps over some tale of misfortune and opens the inexhaustible little clinking handbag; returns to the stage to superintend the lighting of a scene and reduces the electrician to a state of temporary insanity; scolds a super who blundered the day before; returns to her room for dinner, sits down to table, splendidly pale with fatigue; thinks over her plans; eats with peals of bohemian laughter; has no time to finish; dresses for the evening performance; acts with all her heart and soul; discusses business between the acts; remains at the theatre to make arrangements until three in the morning; gets into her carriage; snuggles into her furs and anticipates the delights of lying down at last; bursts out laughing on remembering that someone is waiting to read a five act play to her; goes home, listens to the play, becomes excited, weeps, accepts it, finds she cannot sleep and takes advantage of the opportunity to study a role!

PART ONE

YOUTH

Sarah at twelve with her mother, 1856

D E S P I T E her chaotic existence, Bernhardt found time to write a volume of memoirs called *Ma Double Vie* (*My Double Life*), a title that suggests revelations about her private life as well as her acting career. It promises more than it fulfills for while it seems to present a woman of disarming frankness, a closer reading reveals the prototypical actress impersonating—and consummately—a character called Myself. In self-portraits, written or painted, the artist is free to choose his pose. Bernhardt chose a three-quarter view, a protective device designed to conceal that portion of herself which her adoring public might find questionable or sordid. As the most celebrated woman of her day, she was wary of the prying public and resolved not to expose more of herself than she thought proper. And so she omitted the darker passages of her life, censored many of her lovers out of existence, and rarely mentioned the illegitimate son she adored. Yet it was her complexity, her promiscuity, her neurasthenic passions and sufferings, combined with her beauty, charm, and limitless ambition that contributed to her genius. With all her discretion, Bernhardt could not resist beginning her story with a broadside against her mother, the beloved villainess of her memoirs. Her opening words, despite their air of detachment, breathe rancor, and—since the wounds of childhood never quite heal—a lasting resentment:

My mother adored travelling. She went from Spain to England, from London to Paris, from Paris to Berlin. From there she went to Christiania; then she came back, gave me a kiss and left for Holland, her native land. She sent clothes to my nurse, cakes to me. She wrote to one of my aunts: "Look in on little Sarah, I'll be back in a month." Then a month later she wrote to another of her sisters: "Go to see the child at her nurse's. I'll be back in a few weeks." My grandmother was blind. And my father had been in China for two years. Why I don't know.

With these words Bernhardt rang up the curtain on Act I, Scene 1 of her life. She had found a tone, a rhythm, and a provocative attitude for her entrance. Deftly she juggled, as actors must, with truth as illusion, illusion as truth. In the pages that follow, she focusses a spotlight on certain figures. Others are hidden in shadow. These were her intimates whose secrets, like her own, she held inaccessible. And when she embellishes, or falsifies the facts, at least she gives her readers a fascinating dream image, a picture of what she would have liked her life to be.

The biographer's task would be simpler had Sarah first appeared, Venus-like, floating down the Seine aboard a pearly shell. Tales about her origins are unreliable at best. Some she invented; others were the fantasies of journalists bent on revealing "the truth about Sarah Bernhardt" whether they knew it or not. It was said she was German, Hungarian, Algerian, even American; that she was found on a park bench in the Tuileries; that her grandfather was an animal trainer in a Bavarian circus; that her father was a French aristocrat. Among the addresses thought to be her birthplace are 32 rue Saint Honoré and 22 rue de la Michodière. But only a handsome eighteenth-century house at 5 rue de l'Ecole de Médecine bears an official plaque proclaiming that distinction.

The one certainty in Sarah's background is her mother, Julie Bernard (*sic*). A Jewish girl from Amsterdam, Julie arrived in Paris in a roundabout way. The story goes that she and her sister Rosine fled their middle-class home after their mother died and their father remarried. Young and in search of adventure, they stopped in Baden, Hamburg, and London, cities, it seems, where they learned more than German and English. The only authentic record of Julie's flight is in Le Havre, where two birth certificates attest to her activities abroad. They tell of twin girls born on 22 April 1843 to "Julie Bernard, *artiste musicale*, the daughter of Maurice Bernard, oculist, and of the late Jeannette Hart." Within two weeks both infants had died, and Julie went on to try her luck in Paris. Some months later she found herself in an "interesting condition" once again. This time her condition was of lasting interest, for the child she bore on 23 October 1844 was to become known as Sarah Bernhardt. (Her birth certificate would disappear along with countless others during the Paris Commune when the Hôtel de Ville was destroyed by fire.)

Whether out of tact, shame, or resentment, Sarah never revealed her father's identity, if, in fact, she knew it. Others were not so hesitant. It is generally thought that he was a native of Le Havre, but whether he was a highborn naval officer named Morel or a brilliant young law student named Bernhardt is a question still discussed in Paris. Certain descendants of Sarah's uncle, Edouard Ker-Bernhardt, who took the Breton form of the name and emigrated to Chile, are convinced that he was really her father, not her uncle. Sarah herself added to the mystery in her memoirs and in *The Idol of Paris*, an autobiographical novel she wrote late in life in which the father she describes is too good to be true: too kind, too understanding, too saintly to be the parent of anyone on this earth.

On the other hand, Julie, or Youle (as she called herself in the Dutch fashion), was of this earth, earthy. Short, blond, and pretty, she worked as a seamstress by day and led what was euphemistically called *la vie galante* by night. But she was far too ambitious to settle for the rough-and-tumble of a midinette's life. Her goal was to find a key, any key that would open the doors of bourgeois Paris. It was a dangerous game. One false move would find her in an underworld from which there was little hope of escape. The prospect of marriage was dim. She was a "fallen woman," and, worse still, one with no dowry to offer a husband. To her, work was insulting, unthinkable. She had not come to Paris to slave twelve hours a day for the pitiful wages working girls received in the days of Louis-Philippe.

Her desire to rise in the world is readily understood when one considers the life she saw about her. The poor districts of Paris were in a state of medieval decay. Houses and shacks leaned on one another like drunken derelicts. Tenements clung to the Louvre itself. Notre Dame was a ruin, the Seine a sewer. Brackish water was delivered by peasants who trudged from house to house with buckets suspended from their straining shoulders. The people, laid low by disease, were often hunchbacked, clubfooted, syphilitic, or tubercular. Ten thousand thieves and as many prostitutes prowled the city. Two hundred brothels welcomed those who could afford their pleasures. Yet Paris was a Catherine wheel of excitement. Actors and magicians, singers and dancers, jugglers, acrobats, and high-wire artists entertained the passersby in the hope of picking up a few sous. Knife grinders and organ-grinders, glaziers and coal vendors elbowed their way through the narrow streets. Pedestrians hugged the walls as horsemen muscled their way through the crowds.

There was no need to go indoors to dictate a letter, have a haircut, or a tooth pulled, as public scribes, barbers, and dentists worked away on the bridges and quais. Dr. Thomas Evans, Napoleon III's American dentist, and the man who mercifully introduced dental anesthesia to France, described his "colleagues" at work: "extractions were . . . performed by mountebanks at street corners . . . where the howls of the victims were drowned by the beating of drums, the clash of cymbals, and the laughter and applause of the delighted and admiring crowd." To add to the bedlam, food vendors and outdoor cooks hawked their wares with hoarse street cries and the ringing of bells. As one English traveller said: "It was all rough, filthy fun."*

When night fell the city was drowned in cave-like darkness, relieved only by the flicker of an occasional street lamp. When the moon shone, the lamps remained unlit and the city was awash in still country light, and in the light, too, of those artists who were to nourish the imagination of Youle's daughter. There were the painters Ingres and Delacroix, Daumier and Constantin Guys, to mirror the way their countrymen looked and lived, thought and felt. There was Baudelaire, the poet laureate of darkness, whose lines Sarah was to declaim with chilling effect. There were her future friends, George Sand and Victor Hugo, who were to provide her with her early triumphs. And there was Rachel, the frail little Jewish girl who at seventeen revealed to the French—as Sarah would—the glories of a dramatic literature that had fallen into neglect.

There is no account, accurate or inaccurate, of Youle's first years in Paris. The very fact of her existence would be forgotten had she not been Sarah's mother. Yet, faced with what Balzac called "the splendors and miseries of courtesans," she managed, with a single-mindedness born of desperation, to storm the enclaves of the rich, that top-hatted, corsetted, and crinolined world she longed to enter, if only through the back door. By 1850, the squalor of her apprentice days behind her, she had arrived, a courtesan in good standing; a position not to be dismissed since courtesans had a proud lineage of their own. To this day, the French roll their names

---

*In 1836, Frances Trollope (the novelist's mother) wrote in her *Paris and the Parisians*: "In a city where everything intended to meet the eye is converted into graceful ornament; where the shops and coffee houses have the air of fairy palaces—in such a city as this, you are shocked and disgusted at every step you take, or at every gyration that the wheels of your chariot can make, by sights and smells that may not be described." Even the fastidious Mrs. Trollope could not help overhear a man who muttered: "What luck!" as he escaped the "ejectments" that came flying out of doors and windows.

on the tongue like vintage wine. Ninon de Lenclos and Marion Delorme, Liane de Pougy and Marie Duplessis are more than random threads in France's history, they are figures woven into its fabric. Admiration for their gifts may have been grudging, but it was admiration all the same, for it was no simple feat to persuade sound, thrifty men to part with extravagant, even ruinous sums in exchange for sensual pleasures and the excitement of infidelity. To indulge the caprices and satisfy the greed of an opulent mistress was conspicuous proof of a gentleman's wealth and position. Had not kings and emperors set an impressive example? Writers too were drawn to courtesans. Not only Balzac, but Stendhal, Zola, Flaubert, and Proust enliven their pages with the rise and fall of those women who were the bubbling foam on the dark wave of prostitution that engulfed Paris.

If Youle was not a legendary courtesan, she was a very successful one in her own way. By the time Sarah was six, Dumas *père*, Rossini, the Duc de Morny, and the Baron Hippolyte Larrey, Napoleon III's doctor (whose father, the Baron Dominique, was the military surgeon who had accompanied Napoleon on all his campaigns), were regulars at her salon. A clever parvenue, she had picked up a smattering of smart talk, a certain cultivation, and a sense of luxury, all with startling speed.

That Youle was Jewish did nothing to hinder her career. On the contrary, it was a promise of carnal pleasure in a city where every self-respecting bordello offered at least one Jewish girl and one black girl for connoisseurs of exotica. It was more than sexual allure that won Youle her place. She played the piano, sang with charm, dressed becomingly, and, as she could tell a risqué story with a modest blush, was more entertaining than the usual run of bourgeois ladies with their cult of purity. At a time when the writer Droz urged women to allow their husbands to ruffle their dresses and steal a kiss, to overcome their prudishness and meet passion with passion, Youle knew that she could become a commodity in demand. Unfortunately for Sarah, she was selfish and neurasthenic, hardly surprising as hers was a hazardous profession. She realized that her only capital was herself, that there was no guarantee of permanence in her liaisons, that her lovers would provide generous monthly allowances only as long as she continued to please them.

If Youle rose high in the ranks of kept women, her lively sister Rosine rose even higher. Together the Bernard girls were a piquant sister act. Arm in arm, Rosine, all charm and rowdy laughter, and Youle, all sighs and genteel airs, made the rounds of theatres and public balls where assignations were easily arranged and where their beauty and high-toned availability spelt comfort and satisfaction. For Youle, a lesser comfort than Rosine was their sister Henriette, who kept a concerned but censorious eye on them. Henriette married a pious gentleman named Félicien Faure and lived in a pleasant villa on the outskirts of Paris. It was the only proper house Sarah knew as a child. Certainly it was unlike her mother's apartments, where all was lechery, laughter, and greed. Sarah knew nothing of this in her early childhood, for soon after she was born she was shipped off to a farm near Quimperlé on the Brittany coast to be cared for by a peasant wet nurse. Sarah's nurse was a kind woman who called her "Milk Blossom" and loved her "the way the poor love: when they find the time."

Brittany provided a splendid backdrop for the actress-to-be. Days from Paris by carriage, it was centuries away in time. The natives, Celts by origin, spoke Breton, the only language Sarah said she knew in her early childhood. Low, thatched farmhouses dotted the bleak, windswept landscape. It was in such a house that Sarah spent winter evenings listening to terrifying stories of ghosts and witches. In the long summer days, she was free to run about, play with the farm animals, and pick wildflowers. Fittingly enough, Sarah's earliest memory was charged with drama. One evening Nurse went out to gather potatoes while her invalid husband lay dozing in his trundle bed. Sarah sat in a high chair, a fire flickering in the hearth at her feet. In her nurse's absence, she unfastened the narrow tray that held her in place and fell into the flames. In a matter of seconds, Nurse's husband snatched Sarah up, dipped her into a pail of milk, and coated her with butter.

A week later, according to Sarah, "carriages began rolling in from all parts of the world." The first to arrive was Youle with her lover, Baron Larrey, and two of his doctor friends. Then Rosine and Henriette appeared, to cluck over their niece, and cover the martyred Youle with sisterly effusions. To complete the picture, neighboring peasants sidled in to offer pigs' bladders stuffed with butter for Sarah's burns and to gape at the city folk: the ladies in trailing dresses and poke bonnets, the gentlemen decked out in smart English tweeds for their country outing.

Nothing could have been prettier than Youle's despair. "She was as sincere in her grief," Sarah recalled, "as she had been in her forgetful neglect. She would have sacrificed her golden locks, her tapering fingers, her tiny feet, to save the child to whom she had not given a moment's thought a week before."

T H E S E   bitter words were written in retrospect. Youle stayed on until her daughter recovered, then moved her and her nurse to a dreary little house in Neuilly. A year or two later Youle took an apartment in the rue de Provence. Neither was a happy arrangement. Sarah longed for her mother, whose prolonged absences meant dullness and neglect as her aunts never came to see her. But then, how could the child know that for Youle out of sight meant out of mind, that transient love was her mother's profession? During one of Youle's trips abroad with a lover, Nurse's husband died. Nurse soon married the concierge in the rue de Provence and moved Sarah to the concierge's loge, with its one *oeil-de-boeuf* window over the entryway. Sarah did not hesitate to pull out all the stops when she described her windowless room and the prison-like walls that lined the street.

"I could not eat," she wrote. "I grew pale and anemic, and should certainly have died of consumption had it not been for a most unexpected incident."

One day when she was playing in the courtyard her Aunt Rosine appeared.

"I buried my face in her furs," she remembered. "I stamped with rage, I sobbed, I laughed, and in my frenzy I tore her lace sleeves."

Embarrassed by the scene, Rosine asked to be taken to the concierge's loge. There Nurse explained that she did not know how to reach Youle to tell her where Sarah was. Her explanations meant nothing to Sarah, who begged to be taken to her mother. Rosine's response was a kiss, "a thousand affected gestures, frivolous, charming, and cold," and a promise to come for her the following day. But Sarah did not believe her. Instinct told her she was about to be abandoned as, gently but firmly, Rosine extricated herself from her grasp, smoothed her rumpled dress, emptied her purse into

Nurse's hand, and closed the door, leaving only the scent of perfume in her wake.

"My poor nurse was in tears," Sarah remembered. "Taking me in her arms, she opened the window. 'Don't cry any more,' she said. 'Look at your pretty aunt. She'll come back for you.' In a fit of despair, I hurled myself towards my aunt who was about to step into her carriage. And then there was nothing but darkness—darkness, and the muffled sound of voices—far away—far away—"

In effect, if one is to believe Sarah, she had thrown herself out the window. The fall, she claimed, cost her a broken arm and a shattered kneecap—relatively slight damage for a girl who might not have lived to tell the tale. It is quite possible that Bernhardt was indulging in one of her splendid fantasies. She was, after all, a woman for whom a scratch was a festering wound, an illness a fatal disease, a poor review an act of treason. Yet, for all her exaggeration, the girl she depicts in her memoirs bears a striking resemblance to the woman she became. Like many an actor, she could not resist adding excitement and drama to the story of her life. Perhaps she felt as Laurence Olivier did when he wrote, "In my heart of hearts I only know that I am far from sure when I am acting and when I am not, or should I more frankly put it, when I am lying and when I am not."

Broken limbs or no, Sarah's fall brought her what she wanted most: a life with her mother. But it was not in Youle's nature to provide the love Sarah dreamt of. She was bitterly disappointed. Half a century later she would write in *My Double Life*: "I shall pass over those two years of my life which left me with nothing but confused memories of broken promises and lassitude."

A photograph of mother and daughter taken at the time tells something of their story. Youle is wearing a silk dress, a fur-trimmed cape, and a "*style Renaissance*" turban. One gloved hand hangs elegantly at her side, the other rests on her daughter's shoulder. She appears to be a respectable woman of means. Indeed, it may have been that ambiguous, cocotte-as-lady pose which made for her success with the gentlemen. But it is the tiny Sarah who draws our attention as she stares resolutely into the glass eye of the camera. In a military reefer, a ribboned hat on her pretty blond head, she strikes a Napoleonic pose with her hand tucked into her coat like the Man of Destiny himself. Clearly this self-willed seraph was born to command, not to obey.

As the months went by, Sarah found that she was in the way, that

Youle's attentions were more dutiful than loving. Her lifelong attempt to gain her mother's approval was under way. Disillusion, as is often the case, played its part. Young as she was, she had known rejection. Now she suffered the pangs of unrequited love. She courted Youle with a child's passionate innocence, only to find that nothing could make her as radiant as her lovers' attentions or their extravagant gifts. It was a futile battle in which neither would emerge the winner.

Extravagant gifts were not the courtesan's sole reward. A nice plump baby sitting in a tulip was on its way, she told Sarah coyly. Her Dutch coquetry was quite unnecessary, for at seven Sarah was rather knowing about the men who visited her mother. Under these circumstances Sarah's presence was a problem. For Youle to play the madonna with a newborn infant might lend her a certain charm in her admirers' eyes, but to be seen arguing with her unmanageable daughter would be awkward indeed.

In the fall of 1851, shortly before Sarah's seventh birthday, Youle solved the problem by enrolling her in the Institution Fressard, a fashionable girls' boarding school in nearby Auteuil. Youle announced her decision with misgivings, but instead of the explosion she had anticipated, there was her unpredictable child jumping for joy.

Sarah described her trip to school as though it were a happy yesterday:

How proud I was of my blue velvet frock and how impatiently I waited for Aunt Rosine who was to take us to Auteuil! . . . First *maman*, calm and dignified, climbed into my aunt's magnificent carriage. Then it was my turn, and I must say I gave myself some pretty grand airs for the benefit of the concierge and the shopkeepers who were looking on. My aunt jumped in, boisterously giving orders in English to her ridiculously stiff coachman.

We were followed by another carriage with three men: my godfather Régis, General de Polhes, and a M Fleury, a popular painter of horses and hunting scenes. On the way I learned that they were all to dine with friends at a fashionable cabaret near Auteuil. I did not pay much attention to my mother and my aunt as they usually spoke English or German when they talked about me. What tender loving smiles they cast in my direction! The trip was intoxicating. My nose pressed against the window, I gazed eagerly at the gray, muddy road bordered with ugly houses and a few scattered trees. I thought it beautiful simply because it was always changing. At last the carriage stopped at 18 rue Boileau. On the gate was a long, black, iron plaque with gold lettering. I looked up. "You'll soon be able to read that," *Maman* said. My aunt whispered in my ear, "Madame Fressard's Pension." Pretending to read the sign, I called out, "Madame Fressard's Pension!" As we entered the school everyone was laughing at my cleverness.

The festive party was welcomed by Madame Fressard herself. With her practiced eye she could see that the simpering cocottes in their unwieldy crinolines made a fuss over Sarah chiefly to impress their escorts, who, despite their air of polite amusement, were anxious to be off. But Youle could not leave without giving last-minute instructions. Sarah's unruly hair was to be brushed a hundred times before it was combed. Then she produced a large supply of jams and chocolates which Sarah was to eat on alternate days for her "delicate stomach." Finally, Youle entrusted a large jar of cold cream to the schoolmistress. Her own concoction, she confided, it was to be applied liberally to Sarah's face, neck, and elbows at bedtime. Of course she would pay double for laundry, she added grandly. "Ah, my poor mother," Sarah wrote. "I remember perfectly well that my sheets were changed once a month just as they were for everyone else."

Sarah spent two years at Madame Fressard's. There she learned to read, write, and embroider. But she had not left her demonic temper behind. She had tantrums, she proudly remembered, that came "close to madness" and was exiled to the infirmary, where she seethed in solitary grandeur.

A visit of Stella Colas, an ingénue from the Comédie Française, was a high point for Sarah.

"I couldn't close my eyes all night," she recalled. "In the morning I combed my hair carefully and, with pounding heart, prepared myself to listen to something I didn't understand but which held me spellbound."

The actress's throaty rendition of the Dream from Racine's *Athalie* moved her so that she could not wait to try it herself. That night in the dormitory, she sat up in bed, dug her head into her shoulders, drew a deep breath, and in the deepest voice she could muster croaked: "*Tremble, fille digne de moi! Tremble, trem-ble, trem-em-em-ble,*" while her schoolmates shrieked with laughter. It was Sarah's first histrionic effort—and her first failure. Never one to accept defeat, she did what she often longed to do in the years to come: she struck her critics down, pummelled them, and tried to make them pay in blood. But just as she would be punished when she attacked the critics—who, in any case, tend to have the last word—now Mademoiselle Caroline, one of the teachers, came running, ruler in hand, to whack Sarah over the knuckles. The indignities of childhood are not easily forgotten. When they met again many years later, Sarah instinctively hid her hands behind her back.

After her years at the Institution Fressard, Sarah spoke like a little lady and knew good manners from bad. The next step, Youle decided, was to send her to a convent school where she could acquire the refinements that would attract a rich husband or lover. Sarah knew nothing of her mother's plans when Rosine appeared to break the news and bring her home. But Sarah's family had overestimated Madame Fressard's civilizing influence.

> The idea [Sarah wrote] of not asking me what I would like to do, of upsetting my routine, threw me into a rage. I rolled on the ground, I screamed at the top of my voice, I hurled reproaches at my mother, my aunt, and the faithless Mme Fressard. For two hours I fought everyone off, I ran into the garden, escaped up a tree, threw myself into a muddy pond. Finally, at the end of my strength, I was captured like a wild animal and thrust, sobbing, into my aunt's carriage. I remained with my aunt for three days with such a high fever that it was feared I was dying.

To regain her "calm," the invalid was sent to stay at her Aunt Henriette Faure's villa, where, Sarah wrote, she saw her father for the last time. There, on a park bench, seated on her father's knee, she heard—so she said— things she had never been told, confidences she understood despite her tender age, confessions that made her weep. "My poor father. I was never to see him again, never, never. . . ."

Whether this melancholy vignette was pure invention, or a passage in her life which moved her so profoundly that she could not bring herself to be more explicit, remains a mystery. Certainly if she met a real father who chose to divulge the circumstances of her birth and his reasons for abandoning her, she never broke his trust. More than likely, the man on the park bench was a phantom figure, conjured up to satisfy her longing for a father's love.

S A R A H was almost nine when, in the autumn of 1853, she entered Grandchamp, an Augustine convent school near Versailles, founded in 1768 under the patronage of Louis XV's consort, Queen Marie Leszczyńska, for daughters of the nobility. Run by the Sisters of Notre Dame de Sion (Our Lady of Zion), it kept its head aristocratically high and its educational standards girlishly low—hardly surprising at a time when universities were not yet open to women.

Grandchamp offered its students a handsome eighteenth-century building, commodious, well-ventilated classrooms and dormitories, large gardens, three wooded parks, an infirmary, a chapel for daily religious services, and rooms for weekly baths. The school's prospectus promised "to form the students by inspiring them to a solid, enlightened piety; to develop their intelligence and good judgment; to embellish their minds with all useful knowledge; to contribute, as much as possible, toward making their company agreeable and their virtues sweet."

Sarah did not always live up to these goals, but she was to write about her school days with warmth and charm. As described in *My Double Life*, her first memory of Grandchamp was of a cavernous entrance hall where portraits of Saint Augustine, Pope Pius IX, and Henri V stared down at her.* It was there that she was welcomed by the mother superior, Mère Sainte-Sophie, her mentor-to-be.

Many years later Bernhardt would write:

On seeing me pale with terror, my eyes filled with tears, she gently took my hand, and when she lifted her veil, I saw the sweetest, merriest face

*Devout royalists, the Sisters of Our Lady of Zion believed that the Comte de Chambord, claimant to the throne as Henri V, was the rightful king and refused to acknowledge the fact that France was ruled by the prince-president Louis-Napoleon, who on 2 December 1852 had crowned himself Emperor Napoleon III.

1. At sixteen, when Sarah entered the Conservatoire

2. Sarah and her mother

3. Sarah's Aunt Rosine,
Youle's lively sister

4. Youle (left) with her daughters, Sarah
(center) and Jeanne

5. Youle (left) and Sarah

6. In her late teens, in Nadar's atelier

7. From a different sitting in Nadar's atelier: a three-quarter view

8. The Belgian Prince de Ligne, Sarah's first great love, and the father of her only child, Maurice

9, 10. ABOVE: Sarah, age twenty-eight, with Maurice, age eight. RIGHT: Sarah, age thirty-five, with Maurice, age fifteen

11, 12. LEFT: Maurice grown up. BELOW: (Standing, left to right) Saryta, Jacques, and Sarah; (seated) Terka and Maurice

imaginable. She had such an air of kindness, strength, and gaiety that I flung myself into her arms.

What secret instinct did this woman possess? this woman who, without coquetry, without troubling about her beauty, with never a glance in the mirror, knew that her face was made to charm, that her bright smile could transform the somber convent into a radiant place. I think I understand now what a unique and shining soul existed in that smiling, stout, and saintly creature who awakened all that was noble in me.

Just as she had at Madame Fressard's, Youle recited her cocotte's litany of fruit preserves, chocolate, face creams, and the training of her daughter's unruly hair. Then, with vague promises of a speedy return, and a quick tear, she was gone. "But I," Sarah wrote, "I had no desire to cry."

It was not long before Sarah set Grandchamp on its ear. Always agitated, always eager to attract attention, she was the troublemaker of the school. She sat on the convent wall and imitated the bishop of Versailles while he delivered a funeral oration in the square below. She shocked the nuns with her foul language, slapped one sister who forced a comb through her tangled hair, and cursed another who doused her with holy water in the hope of exorcising the young heathen's evil spirits. She tried to run away from school more than once and was sent back to her mother for a time.

Fortunately, Mère Sainte-Sophie was there to look after her. Patiently, step by tactful step, she set out to win her over. She gave her a garden plot of her own, and when the flowers bloomed and the creatures Sarah found revealed their secrets, she was spellbound. Proudly, she showed her pet crickets, grass snakes, lizards, and spiders to those girls daring enough to peek into the cages the gardener made for her. She naughtily fattened her spiders with flies, and when one of her friends cut herself, she made a bandage of a spider's web.

Of course there were studies as well. Sarah had a gift for drawing, and geography, with its glimpses of far-off places, set the future world traveller to dreaming. Spelling bored her, arithmetic drove her "wild," piano lessons filled her with "profound contempt," and lessons in deportment reduced her to helpless giggles. She did not realize that being taught the proper way to stifle a cough, carry a handkerchief, remove a glove, curtsy, or cross a room gracefully were, in effect, her first lessons in the art of acting.

Sarah saw very little of her mother during her six years at Grandchamp. Vacations, broken only by a brief stay with Aunt Henriette or a flying visit from Aunt Rosine, were spent trailing listlessly about the deserted school. On the rare occasions when she was allowed to come home, she was overwhelmed by an oppressive loneliness. Youle, who had always favored Jeanne, Sarah's beautiful younger sister, was now devoted to her to the exclusion of all else. To complicate matters further, another baby girl in yet another tulip had been delivered to her mother's door. Unfortunately Régine, the new arrival, was to be victimized in more appalling ways than Sarah herself.

Under the circumstances, it is quite understandable that Sarah was drawn to the tranquil routine of convent life. Mystic reveries and shapeless longings possessed her. She dreamed of casting herself before the altar, reverent and sacrificial, a sufferer for Christ and the Holy Virgin. A heavy black cloak emblazoned with a white cross would cover her prostrate body. Around her, flaming candles—lustrous as stars—would find their reflections in the polished floor:

I decided to die under that cloak. How, I do not know. I knew I must not kill myself as that would be a crime. But that is how I would die. Carried away by my dream, I imagined the Sisters' fright and the students' horrified cries. The thought of the commotion I might create made me very happy.

(It is curious to think that Bernhardt's childish wish to make a public show of death would be brilliantly fulfilled, again and again, by her famous "death scenes" in theatres throughout the world.)

When Sarah was thirteen, it was announced in chapel that the archbishop of Paris, Monseigneur Sibour, was to honor the school with his presence. A visit from the archangel Gabriel could not have created a greater stir. Servants waxed the already gleaming floors, the gardener trimmed the trimmest of gardens, and chandeliers acquired a new luster. The massive armchair reserved for such occasions was reverently uncovered, and a crimson carpet was rolled out for the illustrious feet. To add to the excitement, a program was arranged to honor the archbishop. A welcoming speech followed by songs and piano pieces would begin the proceedings. And then, Sarah learned, would come the great event of the day: a student performance of *Tobias Regains His Sight*. A biblical play in three tableaux, it was written by the convent's literary light, Mère Sainte-Thérèse, who read it aloud amid such snuffles and stifled sobs from the assembled girls that the author, Sarah tells us,

> had to make a great effort not to be guilty, even for a moment, of the sin of pride. Anxiously, I asked what role I would perform since I had no doubt, given my little personality, that I would be in the play. I trembled in advance, my hands were icy, my heart beat furiously, and beads of perspiration dampened my brow.

Despite, or perhaps because of, Sarah's "little personality," she was not included in the cast. The coveted role of the angel Raphael had been given to her timid friend Louise. But Sarah was not easily discouraged. She offered to play the sea monster, but no, Caesar, the convent dog, had been given that honor. She made a costume for him with cardboard fins and scales, but another girl's costume was chosen instead. Humiliated, yet unable to stay away, she watched all the rehearsals.

At the final run-through, Louise made a trembling entrance, sank down on the nearest bench, and tearfully confessed that she could not go on. At this Sarah leapt onto the stage, shouting that she knew the part from memory, and, please, could she take Louise's place. Of course Sarah sailed through her lines; of course she was surrounded and praised; and of course Caesar, clever dog that he was, played dead on cue and brought down the house. Sarah felt every inch a heroine, as if she had saved the day.

The following morning the archbishop arrived to the pealing of chapel bells. When he stepped down from his gilded carriage, Mère Sainte-Sophie kissed the episcopal ring, and the girls, all in white, knelt to receive his blessing. After a short mass the entertainment began. The play was warmly applauded. In her first public performance, Sarah, in a long white robe that sprouted paper wings and a halo, covered herself with glory. Nonetheless, she was troubled. Monseigneur Sibour was about to present holy medals, and she was afraid that she would not be given one. Indeed, when her turn came, the archbishop asked if she had been baptized. No, *Mon Père*, I mean *Monseigneur*, she stammered. Her embarrassment was eased when Mère Sainte-Sophie explained that she would be baptized in the spring. At this, the kindly prelate gave Sarah a medal and said he would try to return for the ceremony.

But a few weeks later it was announced at chapel that Monseigneur

Sibour had been assassinated by a mad priest whom he had excommunicated.

"I sobbed," Sarah wrote with characteristic abandon, "and the swelling organ notes that accompanied the prayer for the dead only made me weep more bitterly. It was at that moment that I was seized by a mystic love, an ardor for religious practice and the theatrical grandeur of the church."

The nuns who moved about the altar in stately progression now became her idols. The cross and the tabernacle moved her to ecstasy. She lost all interest in food. She had always been thin; now she was a wraith. In her search for spiritual nourishment, Sarah felt she had found her vocation. She would be a nun.

That spring, Sarah and her sisters, Jeanne and Régine, were baptized at Grandchamp in somewhat bizarre circumstances. In her usual fashion, Youle arrived with a coterie: Aunt Rosine, Aunt Henriette and Uncle Faure with their children, and three godfathers-to-be. Of real fathers there were none. Sarah was deeply ashamed. How sinful, how vulgar her mother seemed to the new devotee of the Holy Spirit! "I adored *maman*," she wrote, "but with a fervent desire to leave her, never to see her again, to sacrifice her to God." It was a classic example of the courtesan's daughter who, given the advantages of a fashionable education, despises the mother who made it possible. (George Bernard Shaw, who was never to approve of Bernhardt, was to explore the subject in *Mrs. Warren's Profession*.)

Sarah had found God, but the devil was still in her. One day she staged a funeral procession for her pet lizard. Twenty giggling schoolmates chanting a mock *de profundis* followed her to the tiny grave. A cluster of nuns watched the irreverent procession. Suddenly, a soldier's shako sailed into the garden and landed at Sarah's feet.

"Has anyone seen my hat?" cried a soldier astride the convent wall. At the sight of him, Sarah ran to the large outdoor gymnasium, climbed to the highest platform, and pulled the rope ladder up behind her. "Here it is! You'll never get it," she shouted, putting the shako squarely on her head. By this time the soldier was in the garden, pushing the girls aside as he made for Sarah. All eyes were on her, a perverse Juliet taunting a puzzled Romeo from her gymnast's balcony. Her first impulse had been pure mischief, but the chance to play to an audience was irresistible, and she could not stop her teasing. At last, she threw the shako to the ground. Terrified of punishment, she refused to come down until everyone had gone.

Night closed in before Sarah lowered the ladder. As she started down, she heard a fierce growl. It was Caesar. Frightened of the dark, but even more frightened by her canine co-star, she scurried back up. "I began to feel like a martyr," Sarah remembered, "abandoned by everyone, with a dog who threatened to eat me alive. They should have known how frightened I was. I had a weak chest and they had left me to shiver in the cold. I lay on the platform, sobbing, calling for my mother and for Mère Sainte-Sophie. I wanted to die." Finally, the mother superior appeared. But it was too late. Sarah contracted pleurisy and lay in bed, "between life and death," for weeks. These were her final days at Grandchamp. When at last she could be moved, a resigned Youle came to collect her and her trunks. After a long, tearful parting with Mère Sainte-Sophie, Youle and Sarah, courtesan and would-be nun, stepped into their carriage and set off on the road to Paris. As they rolled along, neither could have imagined that more than a hundred years later visitors who came to Grandchamp would be shown Sarah's little garden, the dormitory where she slept, the chapel where she said her prayers, and the Salle des Fêtes, where the school's most celebrated pupil had enjoyed her first theatrical triumph.

At fifteen, theatrical success, indeed success of any kind, was as far from Sarah's mind as the theatre itself. Ambition was in her but only as a nameless longing, a formidable energy. Her fierce concentration on herself, her hysterical rages and insatiable hunger for attention, combined with a reckless gaiety and a striving for the life of the spirit were forces that, mysteriously harnessed, would one day shape her life and her art. As yet, these aspects of her "little personality" were more a burden than a pleasure, both to her mother and to herself.

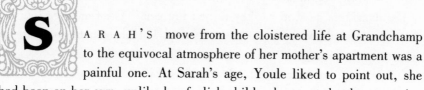

S A R A H ' S   move from the cloistered life at Grandchamp to the equivocal atmosphere of her mother's apartment was a painful one. At Sarah's age, Youle liked to point out, she had been on her own, unlike her foolish child, who spent the days mooning about the apartment, dreaming of spiritual salvation. Youle could be an unpleasant woman, and an even more unpleasant mother, yet she was ambitious for her eldest daughter. She provided her with drawing lessons and pretty clothes, which Sarah loved, and piano lessons, which she hated. She engaged Mademoiselle de Brabender, the pious, gentle spinster who was to be Sarah's tutor and friend in the next years. Mademoiselle had lived at the Imperial Russian court as the tutor of a grand duchess—a detail Bernhardt proudly included in her memoirs—and was well equipped to act as Sarah's finishing school. Sarah worked hard for her, not so much because she liked to study, but because she was determined to go back to Grandchamp with enough learning to qualify as a teaching sister. Fond as she was of Brabender, her real affection was reserved for Madame Guérard, their upstairs neighbor. *"Mon p'tit dame"* (as Sarah would always call her in ungrammatical baby talk) doted on the girl from the moment they met. A gentle, indulgent widow, "My li'l lady" was to worship Sarah with that blind devotion that seems to be one of the rewards of celebrity—a reward that the celebrated, in their infinite self-absorption, accept as their due.

Madame Guérard did not stand in judgment of Youle's morals or Sarah's moods. On the contrary, she found them an endless source of fascination. She was everyone's confidante, made a good fourth at whist, and had a calming influence when shrill and stormy bickerings shook the walls of the second floor. It was she who tried to reason with Youle about her painfully obvious preference for Jeanne and her heartless neglect of Régine. And it was she who came to Sarah's defense when Youle spoke of the future. It was a delicate subject. Sarah was fifteen, the legal age for marriage, and the men who hung about the Bernhardt apartment had begun to show a more than fatherly interest in her. They had had the mother, why should they not have the daughter as well? That Youle did everything to encourage them was common knowledge, so common, in fact, that she was given dishonorable mention in that vast inventory of Parisian life, the *Journal* of Jules and Edmond Goncourt. "Overheard in Brébant's restaurant," one entry reads: "The Sarah Bernhardt family, now *there's* a family! The mother made whores of her daughters as soon as they turned thirteen." The Goncourt *Journal*, dependably vindictive, was repeating gossip, but like much gossip it was surprisingly accurate.

Marie Colombier, Sarah's bosom friend in the days when they were both aspiring young actresses, was to go much further than the Goncourts in her *Memoirs of Sarah Barnum*, a thinly disguised account of Bernhardt's

life. It was to be published many years later, in 1883, but still well before
the publication of Sarah's own memoirs.

Colombier's book is cruel, envious, sensational, anti-Semitic, and—
to Sarah's lasting regret—both witty and revealing. It tells much that Sarah
preferred to leave untold. In self-defense, she pronounced it a pack of lies.
Others saw a good deal of truth in it. Oddly enough, it is Sarah's adored
and adoring grandchild, Lysiane Bernhardt, who inadvertently gave the game
away in her sentimental biography of her grandmother published in 1945.
A telltale passage shows that Colombier, like the Goncourts, was not far
from the truth. Lysiane speaks of Marie as

> a jealous, spiteful, hypocritical actress who divulged all the secrets of the
> woman who had been her intimate friend. When one has to deal with a
> bitterly envious woman, one must either get rid of her or try to convert
> her. Sarah did neither but allowed her to go on nursing her hatred, to
> collect tales about her, to invent rumors, and even to buy up her letters.

What Lysiane was saying, in effect, was that Marie Colombier, in refusing
to whitewash Bernhardt, had betrayed her friend's confidence.

Several *romans-à-clef* about Sarah's life, almost as lubricious as
Barnum, were to be published, among them Edmond de Goncourt's *La
Faustin*, Félicien Champsaur's *Dinah Samuel*, and Jean Lorrain's *Le Tréteau*.
They dealt with Bernhardt the celebrated actress out of necessity, as none
of the writers had known her in her early years. Colombier was the only one
who was privileged, if one can call it that, to be in and out of Youle's
apartment when Sarah was sixteen.

Here is her firsthand account of an evening *chez* Youle in 1860, with
real names substituted for Colombier's all-too-transparent pseudonyms:

> The salon was a fairly large room that gave onto the street. . . . At first
> glance it seemed extremely elegant but on closer inspection it revealed
> that tasteless hodge-podge typical of kept women. A profusion of showy
> imitation objets d'art and furniture made for a vulgar ensemble. There
> were undeniable signs of dirt and disorder. Dripping oil lamps had left
> rings on the piano and tables, the carpets and draperies were stained, the
> backs of the sofas and chairs revealed grease marks left by pomaded hair.
> A bottle of Parfait d'Amour lay forgotten on the mantlepiece. . . . A torn

corset lay spread out on a card table. Through the open doors one saw the same slovenly neglect in the adjoining rooms. . . .

When Sarah arrived, she took off her hat, cloak, and gloves and arranged her hair in front of the mirror. . . . Tall and thin, ridiculously thin, the young girl had an extraordinary head. Her profile had a purity of line that was a softer, more refined version of her mother's Jewish features. . . .

The unforgettable thing about her face was her flashing eyes, those superbly long eyes that borrowed color from the changing light: old gold when she dreamed, cat's-eye green when she frowned, cobalt blue when she smiled. . . .

Suddenly her mother appeared on the arm of an old gentleman whom everyone fussed over. At an imperious glance from Youle, Sarah fell into his arms, murmuring: *Cher Monsieur Régis, cher bon ami.* Then, half-coaxing, half-mocking, Sarah began to flirt with the visitor. [Although Colombier does not mention it, most of her readers knew that Monsieur Régis Lavolée was Sarah's godfather and, gossip had it, the father of her sister Régine as well.] As her young hands touched his sagging cheeks, his head began to droop, his half-closed eyes melted in lust, and his slack lips quivered as he slobbered over his young friend.

Meanwhile Aunt Rosine, always busy when at her sister's, lit the dining room candles. Dinner was announced. Youle, on Régis's arm, led the family into the dining room, reproaching the old fellow all the while. Coarse language issued from her lips, but her face remained oddly virginal. He was a dirty old man who had deceived her, she complained. Why did he never come to see her? How could he be so mean about money? Had he forgotten how long they'd been together? Twice the name of Régine was heard. "But really now, Youle, I assure you—" Régis muttered lamely. Impatiently Sarah lifted the lid of the soup tureen and said: "You two over there! Save your squabbling for tomorrow. Everything's getting cold." . . .

When Régis began a sermon on the shocking state of theatrical morals, Youle gave Sarah a kick under the table and a meaningful look. Sarah obediently rose to embrace her *bon ami.* Her "dear friend's" eyes brightened at once. Hypnotized by her mother's unwavering stare, Sarah, despite her aversion, allowed Monsieur Régis to fondle her although she shuddered each time his lips touched her lovely neck. . . . Her docility was rewarded with a banknote from Régis and a smile of approval from her mother. Emboldened by his generosity, the old man put Sarah on his lap with his arm around her waist. Sensuously he stroked her dress, warming himself at the altar of young flesh beneath the silk. Sarah stared at the ceiling but her pinched lips and flaring nostrils betrayed her mortification.

At ten o'clock he left, but Sarah was still not free. As soon as Youle pocketed the money her daughter had received, she launched into a familiar tirade. She had spent a fortune on her, made endless sacrifices. But that was over. From now on Sarah would have to fend for herself. Then Aunt Rosine chimed in: "You're pretty and you're talented. You must make your own way. No sentimental foolishness either. If someone takes a shine to you, you can't let his age or his white hair stop you. Have a heart. Your mother has worked long enough. Now it's up to you to repay her for all she's done." Sarah remained silent, but when they scolded her for not getting more money out of the old man, she lost her temper. "Surely," she shouted, "you can't expect me to sleep with your lovers!" Youle rose to strike her, but Rosine intervened. Jeanne and Régine listened without saying a word. Half an hour later the entire household was in bed.

As scenes of this kind multiplied, Sarah's choices narrowed. In her exalted moments, she longed for the safety of the convent. Mère Sainte-Sophie had shown her the way to spiritual advancement through the love of God. Youle, her own mother, was showing her the way to worldly advancement through the love of men. Sarah felt she must follow the way of Mère Sainte-Sophie. Now that she was being urged to become a junior partner in the firm of Bernhardt Soeurs, she saw the venality of their lives more clearly than before. The struggle between mother and daughter took a new turn. Sarah had always been envious of the love Youle lavished on Jeanne; now she felt a perverse satisfaction in knowing that Régis's attentions had aroused Youle's jealousy. It was obvious that Monsieur Régis of the sagging cheeks preferred the budding daughter to the full-blown mother. It was all very well for Youle to encourage her child to flirt with her old lover, but she felt her age when she saw that it was for Sarah that he emptied his pockets—and for nothing but a hug and a kiss.

It was the Duc de Morny, an infinitely more distinguished habitué of Youle's salon, who helped clear the air. The scion of a glittering dynasty of illegitimacy, the duke was the illegitimate grandson of Talleyrand through his father, Comte Charles de Flahaut, and of the Empress Josephine through his mother, Queen Hortense of Holland. And, as the son of Queen Hortense, he was the illegitimate half brother of Napoleon III. He had, in fact, helped to hoist him onto an emperor's throne. Morny, the very spirit of the enterprising Second Empire, had a hand in everything. He made millions developing new railroads and mines, transformed the sleepy fishing village of Deauville into a fashionable watering place, provided Paris with Longchamp, its first modern racecourse, and inaugurated the Grand Prix. As though that were not enough, he dabbled in playwrighting, collaborated with Offenbach on librettos, and even wrote a few airs for that composer's delightful operettas. (Offenbach was to say that "no one promoted his protégés with greater charm than the duc de Morny.")

In 1854, Morny had been made president of the Corps Législatif, a position he occupied with distinction for the rest of his life. In 1855 Napoleon III sent him as a special envoy to the coronation of Tsar Alexander II of Russia. There he married the beautiful young Princess Trubetskoi, herself the illegitimate half sister of the newly crowned Tsar. It would almost seem the frisky duke took a bride in order to enjoy the pleasures of infidelity, for along with his splendid collection of paintings, he acquired an equally splendid collection of mistresses, Rosine and Youle among them.

One day Youle invited Morny to a family council to discuss Sarah's future. Why not make an actress of the child, Morny said in his offhand way. Sarah, somewhat intimidated by the mighty duke, and careful to avoid her mother's eye, announced that she had decided to take the veil:

> I threw my arms around my mother. "You'd like me to be a nun, wouldn't you?" I said. "It wouldn't make you unhappy, would it?"
>
> *Maman* stroked my hair, saying: "Of course it would. You know perfectly well that after your sister Jeanne I love you more than anyone in the world." Her voice was as pure as a mountain stream, and she said these words in her slow sweet drawl. But I recoiled, shattered by the unconscious cruelty of her remark.

By now the duke was bored and rose to go, but not before he told Youle that she would make a terrible diplomat. Then, with a pat on Sarah's cheek, he added: "Take my advice. Send her to the Conservatoire!"

In the end everyone agreed that marriage was the only sensible solution—everyone except Sarah, who announced that, were she to be a bride, she would be the bride of Jesus and of no one else. But even as she spoke, the duke's "Send her to the Conservatoire!" echoed in her ears, although she did not realize that his words were to be the guidepost to her future—as fateful as the three resounding thuds that, in France, herald the rise of the theatre curtain.

One unalterable fact had not been mentioned: to be an actress was to be a kept woman, high or low. Everyone present knew that the stage was a parade ground for pretty girls, a steppingstone to silk sheets and the kept life—just as they knew that even for the most talented a rich protector was a necessity, as salaries were abysmally low and actresses were required to provide their own costumes and jewels, even at the Comédie Française. Sarah was aware of all this, since she had overheard a good deal of gossip about actresses and courtesans. They were, after all, the principal subject of conversation at Youle's apartment.

It would not be long before she learned that the distinction between an actress's dressing room and a courtesan's bedroom was blurred at best. That both actress and courtesan were in the business of passion, pleasure, and make-believe. Both performed nightly and gave matinées. Both hoped for long runs and good pay and lived in dread of unemployment and old age. Without work neither actress nor courtesan could afford the finery that attracted the paying customer. Finally, both actress and courtesan had an "I-don't-give-a-damn" attitude to a world made uneasy by their libertine ways and their contempt for middle-class standards. The only exceptions were those rare women fortunate enough to be the stars of their respective domains. Then, and only then, would they be rewarded with the respect, the adulation, and the envy that success inevitably attracts.

Before leaving Youle's, Morny suggested that Sarah might change her mind about taking holy orders were she to sniff the air of the Comédie Française. Their mutual friend Alexandre Dumas had a box and would be happy to have Youle and her friends join him.

That Tuesday, *the* night at the House of Molière, Sarah settled into Dumas' loge.

When the curtain went up I thought I would faint [Sarah wrote]. It was the curtain of my life that rose before me. Those columns would be my palaces. That frieze of painted clouds would be my sky. And those boards would yield beneath my frail weight. Large tears rolled down my cheeks, tears without sobs, tears I felt would never cease. *Maman* was exasperated, and scoured the theatre through her opera-glass. Mademoiselle de Brabender gave me her handkerchief, as mine had fallen and I did not dare to pick it up. I remember only one thing about *Amphytrion.* I felt so sorry for Alcmène that I burst into wild sobs. The audience, much amused, stared at our loge. "Good God, what an idiot that child is," I heard my godfather mutter. "They'd better stick her back in the convent and leave her there!"

Such was the beginning of my artistic career.

On the way home, Sarah fell asleep in Dumas' carriage. As impetuous as his own D'Artagnan, the author swept her into his arms and carried her up to her room. As he helped Youle unbutton her daughter's dress, he gave Sarah a gift she was always to treasure: three shining words, *"Bonsoir, petite étoile."* Like Morny, Dumas saw the possibility of talent in his "little star." Certainly Sarah's tearful response to Molière had moved him more than her mother's relentless inspection of the audience.

J U S T as Morny predicted, Sarah was eager to go to the Conservatoire after her evening at the Comédie Française. But it was not easy to enter that venerable institution; one had to compete with dozens of budding young actors who had been coached in the traditional tragic and comic scenes. Youle did not bother with such formalities. Instead she asked Morny to use his influence with the director of the Conservatoire, the composer Daniel Auber. Auber agreed to look out for the little Bernhardt girl. In the meantime, Sarah was subjected to the dubious wisdom of Youle's theatre-loving friends—all connoisseurs—or so they thought. The result was utter confusion: Sarah must prepare scenes from Corneille, Molière, Racine, and Voltaire. . . . She must be fattened up; her diction must be improved, her voice strengthened.

Monsieur Meydieu, or l'Odieux ("The Odious One"), as Sarah called him, took charge and wrote out a regime of tongue twisters to be repeated forty times before meals and twenty times before bedtime. The poor girl was made to rehearse such phrases as *"Le plus petit papa, petit pipi, petit popo, petit pupu,"* a racy equivalent of "Peter Piper picked a peck of pickled peppers." It was Dumas who straightened Sarah out in one memorable lesson. Tongue twisters were all very well, he told her, but classic texts were more to the point. Why not try Racine's *Phèdre?* She could be Aricie, the virgin princess who loved Hippolyte. He would take all the other roles. As Dumas paced the floor of Sarah's room, he warmed to his task. He caressed the words, lent them unexpected meaning, shouted, whispered, swooned, commanded, and struck poses which, despite his frock coat and his paunch, seemed all of Ancient Greece to Sarah. When she responded in her pure, sweet voice, the old veteran felt that she might well become an actress.

Dumas' encouraging smile, like the prince's kiss in *The Sleeping Beauty*, brought Sarah to life. It was a historic moment: a pioneer of the Romantic movement was passing the torch to the girl who was to become the last of the Romantic actresses. Dumas could not have predicted that his young protégée would perform in his *Mademoiselle de Belle-Ile* and in *Kean*, the play in which he defined actors and acting so brilliantly. As for Sarah, only much later would she learn that the man who coached her had written a penetrating essay on *Phèdre*, that his dramatic readings were the envy of great actors, that his son, Dumas *fils*, was the author of *La Dame aux Camélias*, the play she would be more closely identified with than any other.

Dumas was proclaiming, "You turn pale and seem speechless, Madame,"* when Youle opened the door. She always forgot that her daughter wanted to act, she sighed, adding that Dumas was an angel to bother, but couldn't he teach her a fable instead? It would be so much less noisy. In any case, Sarah must comb her hair and come to the salon. A nice gentleman from Holland was waiting to have a word with her. Sarah, like Aricie, turned pale, knowing that her mother considered the Dutchman a great catch while she found him disgusting. Black hairs sprouted from his cheeks and chin, his nose and ears. His hands were like furry paws. Yet, there he stood, sick with love. Behind him Jeanne aped his bear-like stance. Sarah could barely contain her giggles. Monsieur B. proposed. Sarah disposed. She had no time for marriage; she was going to be an actress. At the thought of all that money slipping through her fingers, Youle pleaded with her daughter to accept, but to no avail. Sarah's hour with Dumas had transported her to another world,

---

"Vous changez de couleur et semblez interdite, Madame."

a world, she felt, that neither her ambitious mother nor her rich suitor could understand. Theirs was an age-old argument: the mother urging financial security, the daughter willing to risk everything for Art. Sarah thought of acting as an ascent to success and fame. Youle saw it as a descent into obscurity and squalor. At her wit's end, she asked Meydieu to bring Sarah down to earth.

She was a romantic idiot, The Odious One told her. Marriage was a business. She would be wealthy when the Dutchman's parents died. Sarah shuddered. She couldn't possibly marry a man she didn't love. A few days later, Madame Guérard asked Sarah to come upstairs. To her surprise, there was her shaggy suitor, lying in wait. Years later she would write in her memoirs:

> Monsieur B. begged me to change my mind. It was very painful. The poor man was crying. "Do you want a better settlement?" he asked. "I can offer more money if you like." But it wasn't that at all. "Monsieur, I don't love you," I said quietly. "I'll die of pain if you refuse me," he answered. I looked at the man. "Die of pain!" I was confused, saddened, and—delighted! He loved me the way people love in a play! I uttered some stupid phrases I had heard or read somewhere. Monsieur B. did not die. On the contrary, he is still alive and richer than ever.

The Conservatoire de Musique et Déclamation, Paris's historic Conservatory of Music and Drama, which Sarah was about to enter, had its origins in the reign of Louis XVI. At that time it trained singers and trumpeters to provide the fanfares at court ceremonies and the music at royal entertainments. Acting was added by Napoleon Bonaparte in 1808. Deportment and Dance followed. Actors, it was wisely thought, could benefit from classes in gesture and movement, while singers, especially those destined for the Opéra-Comique, where spoken recitative was required—would profit from lessons in diction, acting, and the dance. By 1860, when Sarah came to the Conservatoire, it was considered the finest drama school in the world—just as its teachers, the leading players of the Comédie Française—were considered the finest actors in the world. Although, as Henry James put it, they were "prodigiously great," their names have faded with time. Like the stars to which they were compared, they shone, flickered, and, with the birth of new stars, disappeared. There are exceptions of course. Rachel and Bernhardt left images that linger in the mind like memories of people we have known, even though we have never seen them. On the other hand, the names of Provost and Samson, Regnier and Edmond Got say little or nothing to us, yet they were the John Gielguds and Laurence Oliviers of their day. Surely we can trust Henry James when he writes that one of the most perfect things he ever saw was a scene played by François Regnier or that Edmond Got was "the finest living actor."

Acting, like style, does not improve, it merely changes. Whenever splendid new actors appear they are thought more convincing, more "natural," than their predecessors. Is it not because they reflect the manners of their contemporaries and, in so doing, make the public more comfortable, more receptive? A Vanessa Redgrave or a Laurence Olivier can indulge in histrionics, but were they to tear the scenery to shreds à la Sarah Siddons or Edmund Kean, they would be laughed off the stage. To be caught up in an actor's art we must believe that his behavior could be ours and that our behavior could be his.

Yet all acting, from the grandest to the most familiar, from the high classic to low vaudeville, is unnatural. Bernhardt was considered more natural than Rachel, Duse more natural than Bernhardt, for naturalism presents a different image to each succeeding generation. It is all done with mirrors, as it were. Sarah herself was to invent a style that mirrored the sentiments, humors, anxieties, gestures, and social inflections of her time. If she wept and fainted, it was because women of her day were given to weeping and fainting. And so it was nineteenth-century Paris, Victor Hugo's "rouged and terrible city," that shaped her dramatic gifts. Degas once said: "Painting a picture is something that requires as much cunning, treachery, and deceit as the preparation of a crime." The same could be said of acting.

In Sarah's early days, everything from high drama to low comedy was available in the forty theatres and innumerable *café-concerts* which dotted the theatre-mad capital. Ludovic Halévy, the librettist for Offenbach's *La Belle Hélène* and *La Vie Parisienne*, described a performance at one of the city's most popular music halls, the kind of theatre Youle was afraid her daughter might end up in:

One evening I took Flaubert to the *Délassements Comiques*. He had never been, though he lived close by in the boulevard du Temple. We enjoyed it to our heart's content. There was a frightful racket. As we entered we were deafened by wild applause. A beginner was on stage—pretty, gay, funny. She sang so deliciously out of tune that the audience kept asking for more. She must have repeated the same song three or four times. At last, gloriously happy, she pleaded for mercy. The public obviously wanted her to sing all night. Flaubert was madly exhilarated. "It's marvellous," he shouted above the din. "I've never heard such applause, or anyone so wonderfully off pitch." Then, along with the others, he called out: "Encore! Encore!"

At the other end of the theatrical spectrum stood Rachel, the greatest actress of the first half of the century. Perhaps it is fortunate that no mechanical recordings of her performances exist, for we should have to borrow nine-teenth-century spectacles—and mentalities—to appreciate her genius in the way that Delacroix, Chopin, and Liszt did.

There are compelling accounts of her acting, however. One of the most vivid is by Charlotte Brontë, who saw her *Phèdre* in Brussels in 1843 (the year before Sarah was born) and described it ten years later in the novel *Villette*. The passage is a brilliant evocation of the actress's uncanny genius, a genius strangely akin to Brontë's own. The shy spinster from a remote wind-swept English parsonage and the *grande amoureuse* from the teeming slums of Paris had similar gifts. Both inspired their audiences to marvel at their way with words, to weep with pity for the heroines they portrayed, and to shiver with fear at their Gothic travails.

I longed to see a being of whose powers I had heard reports which made me conceive peculiar anticipations . . . [Brontë wrote]. She was a study of such nature as had not encountered my eyes yet: a great and new planet she was: but in what shape? I waited her rising.

She rose at nine that December night: above the horizon I saw her come. She could shine yet with pale grandeur and steady might; but that star verged already on its judgment-day. Seen near, it was a chaos—hollow, half-consumed: an orb perished or perishing—half lava, half glow. . . .

For a while—a long while—I thought it was only a woman, though an unique woman, who moved in might and grace before this multitude. By and by I recognized my mistake. Behold! I found upon her something neither of woman nor of man: in each of her eyes sat a devil. These evil forces bore her through the tragedy, kept up her feeble strength—for she was but a frail creature; and as the action rose and the stir deepened, how wildly they shook her with their passions of the pit! They wrote HELL on her straight, haughty brow. They tuned her voice to the note of torment. They writhed her regal face to a demoniac mask. Hate and Murder and Madness incarnate, she stood.

It was a marvellous sight: a mighty revelation.

It was a spectacle low, horrible, immoral.

Sarah was a child when these words were published. By the time she entered the Conservatoire, Rachel was dead. Yet her demonic image haunted those who had thrilled to her art. She was the point of comparison, the gauge by which Sarah would be measured again and again. If she inherited Rachel's mantle, and many thought she did, she wore it in her own fashion. Rachel ignored the works of Hugo, Dumas, and Musset and revived the neglected glories of Racine and Corneille. Sarah worshipped the Romantics and saw the classics through their eyes. In spite of their differences, Sarah was cut from the same starry cloth as Rachel, whose style of declamation and of "making points" was taught at the Conservatoire as if it were holy writ.

To know something of Rachel is to understand Bernhardt more fully. She was born in 1821 in a Swiss village near Basel, one of the six children of Jacob and Esther Félix, itinerant Jewish peddlers. At ten she was in Paris, singing and reciting in cheap cafés for a few sous. Then a miracle—the theatre seems to be the last refuge of miracles—occurred. Rachel was discovered by a man named Saint-Aulaire, who took her into his School of Acting. At thirteen she was on the stage. In the next two years she played thirty-two roles: soubrettes, *confidentes*, heroines. At fifteen she was the talk of theatrical Paris, and—another miracle—was put into the hands of one of the greatest actors of the Comédie Française, Joseph-Isidore Samson, who arranged for her to study at the Conservatoire. At seventeen she made her debut at the Comédie Française.

In no time, the pale, studious-looking girl with the dark, haunted eyes gained a place among the geniuses of the French theatre. *Le Tout-Paris*, Madame Récamier and Chateaubriand among them, came to applaud the miraculous Rachel, who towered above all other actresses—all four feet, ten inches of her. But then who was to say that Phèdre herself was any taller? As soon as Rachel was recognized as the undisputed queen of tragedy, a typical Parisian comedy began. France, the country of measure and reason, accused her of calculation and concern for her future, accusations that could safely be applied to Louis-Philippe himself. The thrifty French joked about her Jewish avarice. The gentlemen of the stock exchange, after a day of cutthroat money-making, frowned disapprovingly at the actress's demands for high fees. Public reaction to her promiscuity was provincial. Grand ladies who came to throw bouquets at her feet held on to them grimly when they heard she was having affairs with her betters. Aristocrats who adorned their salons with her fascinating presence snubbed her when they found that her indiscretions were uncomfortably similar to theirs. And, of course, they felt that her love of grandeur was a sign of Jewish ostentation when she decorated her house with an extravagance which equalled their own. That the house was a gift from her lover, Comte Colonna-Walewski (the natural son of Napoleon) only intensified their feelings. Thrilled to see her display larger-than-life emotions on the stage, they thought she should leave her temperament behind like a castoff costume when she went into society. They did not recognize scandal as the divine right of actresses. As Balzac said of another artist, not long dead: "One cannot expect the pleasures, ideas, and morality of a Byron to be those of a haberdasher."

Scandal embroidered with wit is one of the actress's most beguiling cloaks. One day Louis-Philippe's son the Prince de Joinville sent his card to Rachel with the message: "Where? When? How much?" Her reply: "At your place. This evening. No charge," tickled her admirers. That the affair lasted seven years tickled them less. One of her last lovers was Prince Jérôme, Napoleon's nephew and a cousin of Napoleon III. She was past thirty and in failing health.

"I am coming home to die," she wrote from Havana, "and like Napoleon, I shall go to the Invalides to demand a stone on which to lay my head. . . ." Rachel died at thirty-six. A few days before her death, an admirer asked for an autograph. "A week from now," she wrote, "I shall begin to be devoured by worms and biographers." Among the mourners at her funeral were the Dumases, father and son, Sainte-Beuve, Scribe, Théophile Gautier, Alfred de Vigny, and Prosper Mérimée.

Sarah was to learn all this and more at the Conservatoire. She always kept a portrait of Rachel on her walls, and nothing was to give her greater pleasure than to hear that she had equalled—or surpassed—her idol.

PART TWO

THEATRE LIFE

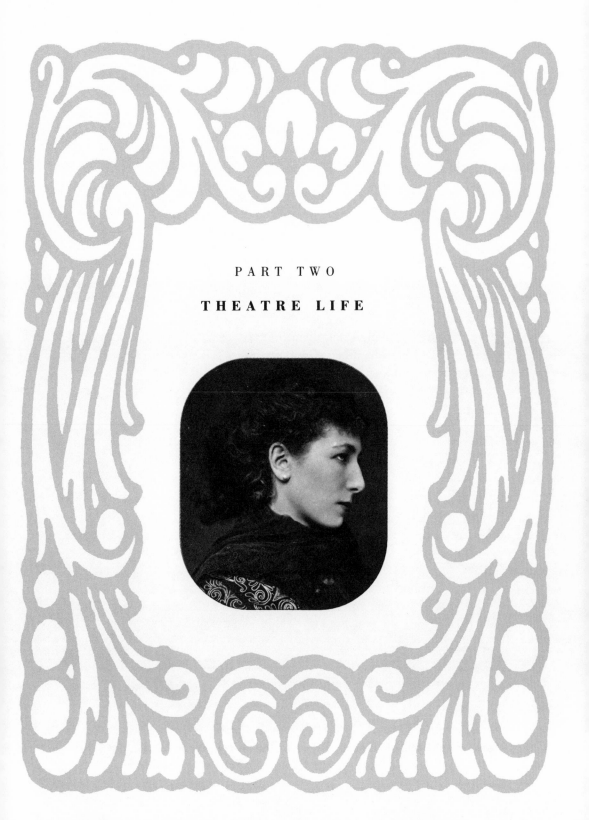

Sarah as Julia Vidal in Adolphe Belot's *Le Drame de la rue de la Paix*, 1868

I N 1 8 5 9 , when Sarah took her entrance examination at the Conservatoire, she was nearing her sixteenth birthday. As might be expected, there was more discussion at home about what she should wear than what she would perform. Unfortunately, it was Youle who decided. The result was ludicrous. Sarah, who seems to have remembered everything she ever wore, recalled her dress with horror.

"My mother," she wrote, "had a black silk dress made for me. Slightly décolletée, it was short enough to show the *broderie anglaise* pantaloons, that came down to my high-button kid shoes. My hair was parted on my forehead, and fell every which way, as no pin or ribbon could hold it in place. To complete the costume, I wore a large straw hat although it was late in the season. Everyone came to inspect my dress, and I was turned round and round, and made to rehearse my bow."

A fortifying cup of jellied consommé, a last, desperate could-that-be-me glance in the mirror, a dispirited "*merde*" from her mother, and Sarah, with the faithful Guérard and Brabender at her sides, was off to try her luck. A crowd was milling about when they arrived at the school. Officious stage mothers, actresses, singers, cocottes, and shopkeepers bristled competitively, fussed with their children's clothes, and whispered last-minute advice. *Huissiers*, those ushers as splendid as Roman sentries in their brass helmets, towered above the throng. Suddenly Monsieur Léautaud, the prompter at the Comédie Française, called out the name of the first contestant. Sarah looked on as, one by one, the aspirants were led away like victims to the guillotine. When her turn came, Monsieur Léautaud asked what she planned to perform.

"A scene from Molière's *L'Ecole des Femmes.*"

And who would give the cues? Sarah had no idea.

Then what was to be done, asked Léautaud. One can't do a scene by oneself.

In that case, she would recite La Fontaine's "Les Deux Pigeons." Léautaud was still muttering his disapproval as he went off to announce her. Convinced that all was lost, Sarah followed him into the examination room.

"And there I was," she remembered, "all alone in that bizarre hall with a platform at one end and a large table in the center. Around it sat a group of men, grumbling and ironic. There was a woman too, very outspoken, who kept exchanging her pince-nez and her lorgnette."

Sarah had barely begun "Two pigeons loved each other tenderly . . ." when one of the judges thundered: "What's this, a nursery? We're not here to listen to fables!" It was Léon Beauvallet, the foremost tragedian of the Comédie Française, who had often played opposite Rachel. Sarah stopped short.

"Go on, go on," urged Jean-Baptiste Provost, who was to be Sarah's first teacher.

"Louder, a little louder," Rachel's teacher, Samson, called out.

"I stopped again," Sarah wrote, "speechless, confused, and so nervous I could have screamed and howled."

"Look here, we're not ogres," Samson assured her. After a whispered consultation with Auber, the director of the Conservatoire, he added: "Just begin again, a little louder this time."

"Oh, no!" sighed Augustine Brohan, the lady with the lorgnette, "if that child begins again, we'll be here all night!" The judges collapsed in laughter, but Sarah plunged on. Halfway through the poem a bell rang. It was the end of her ordeal. She left the stage, overwhelmed by that mixture of exhaustion and resentment that comes with a sense of failure. She was making her disconsolate way through the corridor when Monsieur Auber caught up with her. The composer of fifty operas, *Fra Diavolo* among them, Auber was kindness itself. Too nervous to attend his own premieres, he understood Sarah's anguish only too well. "You have been accepted," he said in answer to her beseeching look. "My only regret is that your lovely voice is not destined for music." In her memoirs Sarah recalled:

I was mad with joy. I thanked no one. I ran out of the door. I imagined I saw the word *accepted* on all the shop windows, and when the carriage that was taking us home stopped for passersby I felt everyone was looking at me in astonishment. I found myself nodding my head as if to say: "Yes, yes, it's true, I've been accepted!"

The convent was forgotten. How proud I was to have succeeded at my first audition, and to have done it all by myself! I kept poking my head out the window of the fiacre, shouting: "Faster, coachman! Faster!"

When I entered the courtyard, I threw off my coat so that I could run to my mother. Suddenly I was nailed to the spot. Mme Guérard, her hands cupped to her mouth, was shouting up to *maman*: "She's been accepted!" I struck her in the back with my fist and wept with rage for I had planned a little scene that would end with the good news. I would pretend to be depressed when they opened the door, downcast and upset. *Maman* would say: "I am not surprised. You are so stupid, you poor thing." Then I would fling my arms around her and shout: "It's not true, it's not true. I've been accepted!"

I was still grumbling when I reached my mother's apartment and found the door wide open. She kissed me when she saw my pouting face and said: "Well, well. Aren't you happy?"

"Yes, but it's Guérard. I'm furious with her. Be sweet, *maman*, and pretend you don't know. Close the door and I'll ring the bell." And so I rang. . . . And *maman* pretended to be astonished. And so did my sisters, and my godfather, and my aunt. When I kissed my mother and said: "I've been accepted," everyone shouted for joy. My gaiety was restored. I had made my effect after all. My career had taken possession of me without my knowing it.

Without her knowing it, Sarah's career might never have taken possession of her at all, for it is more than likely that she would have been rejected had the Duc de Morny not asked Auber to "look out for the little Bernhardt"— a recommendation few would have dared to ignore.

When Bernhardt was in her seventies, she wrote *L'Art du Théâtre: La Voix, Le Geste, La Prononciation*, a book filled with the common sense born of experience. In it we read that voice production, gesture, and diction can be acquired, but that true artistry must be self-sought and self-taught. During her two years at the Conservatoire, Sarah slowly and painfully learned the basic techniques, in acting classes, student productions, and endless discussions with her fellow students at the tearoom around the corner.

But that was not enough for the passionate girl who in moments of monumental ambition felt she must become "the finest, most celebrated, and most envied of actresses. I counted all my qualities on my fingers: grace, charm, distinction, beauty, mystery, and piquancy. . . . and a combative ego that permitted no argument." To this immodest evaluation Sarah could have added instinct, temperament, a beautiful speaking voice, and a knack for imitating those around her with devastating accuracy. Yet her varied gifts were not enough to satisfy her. As the years went on, she was to discover a malleable substance deep within herself, a precious substance that she alone could mold. Sarah was to become both Pygmalion and Galatea, both the creator and the creation.

A zealot at the convent, Sarah became a fanatic at the Conservatoire. In a sense, she exchanged religious belief for the make-believe of the theatre. The girl who rarely opened a book now devoured volumes of poems and plays. Like Miriam Rooth, the heroine of Henry James's novel *The Tragic Muse*, she felt safer in "the representation of life than in life itself." And with Miriam, she could have said: "I like it better than the real thing—one can lose oneself in it."

Sarah was introduced to "representation" by her teachers, all leading actors of the Comédie Française. Accustomed to the affected ways of the demimonde, she was thoroughly at home with their theatrical mannerisms. She loved their mobile features and mocking good nature, their studied laughter and easy camaraderie, their promiscuous kisses and racy physicality. She was amused by their backbiting intrigues and malicious stories, their comic vanity and stylized modesty, their way of drawing out a vowel and spitting out a consonant. Like the Sarah-to-be, they were larger than life, and only the proscenium arch could reduce them to human proportion. The way that actors, like circus folk, closed ranks against their common enemy, the outside world, made her feel she had found a home at last.

Still there was much that the "little rebel," as her teacher Provost called her, would not accept. At the top of her list was the professor of deportment. A relic of the First Empire, Monsieur Elie, with his heavy make-up, curled hair, and lace jabot, seemed hopelessly old-fashioned to the 1860 modernist. Baton in hand, he addressed his class in a refined falsetto: "Now girls, straight backs, heads high, toes pointed—there, that's lovely. One, two, three, walk!" And walk they did. They were taught the walk of nonchalance, of fury, and of terror; the walk of victims, fanatics, saints, and sinners. *L'assiette*, the art of sitting, came next: sitting with dignity or lassitude, sitting that meant, "I'm listening. Speak, sir!" accompanied by mute looks that signified a desire to know, a fear of understanding, a decision to leave, or a wish to stay.

"How many tears it cost me," Sarah wrote, "to sit ironically. Oh! That one! The body thrown back, the scornful half-smile, the glint of laughter, the imperceptible shrug. It took me years to forget what that poor man taught me."

Provost, one of the subtlest actors at the Comédie Française, was one of the finest teachers at the Conservatoire. Unfortunately, he disliked Sarah and found her self-centered and inconsiderate. He was getting on in years and the sight of her, always rushing into class, late and out of breath, annoyed him. When he coached her in Voltaire's *Zaïre*, he did everything but beat her. For hours on end he corrected each uncertain gesture, each forced cry, each false inflection. Sarah wept, but persisted. The lesson over, Provost clapped his broad-brimmed hat on his head, fixed her with a wintry look, and delivered the coup de grace: "*Voilà!* There's a role you must remember never to play."

"If only," a fellow student wrote, "Provost could have seen his pupil thirteen years later, how happy the dear man would have been to see his cruelty so well rewarded, for beneath her admirable gifts one could see the luminous teaching that old *père* Provost provided so unsparingly."

These words were written by Paul Porel, Sarah's friend at the Conservatoire. Porel, who was to become the director of the Odéon Theatre and the husband of that enchanting actress Réjane, was a poor boy, thin as a needle. He earned his way as a bookbinder's apprentice in a dim little shop in the rue Gît-le-Coeur, where he slept on the floor with a volume of Balzac for his pillow and dreamt of the theatre as a golden shrine of poetry. The young acting students were drawn to one another by their love of art and their adolescent contempt for the practicalities of life. Sarah, hounded by the incessant talk of money at home, basked in Porel's idealism. As for Paul, he was able to forget the drudging discomfort of his life in his adoration of her seductive femininity. Although the details of their youthful liaison are lost, it is quite likely that he was her first love.

Years later Jacques Porel, the son of Paul and Réjane, wrote about a photograph Sarah had given his father. "Its tender inscription," he recalled, "certainly leads one to think that there was more than a simple friendship between them. Naturally, my father never mentioned it directly, yet his look when he reminisced about the old days gave him away."

Jacques Porel spoke more openly to the present authors. He described walks along the quais, stolen kisses, passionate confidences.

"Imagine, Jacques," his father had said to him, "you who worshipped Sarah, imagine what that fascinating woman was at sixteen—her verve, her incandescent smile, her energy!"

Sarah had learned about the varied guises of love at home. Now she was about to add to her education at the Conservatoire, where a web of sexual intrigue lurked behind an air of propriety.

In her own memoirs, written in 1898, Marie Colombier swept aside the flimsy curtain of Second Empire decorum:

There was a very special atmosphere at the Conservatoire, an atmosphere that has disappeared in our more practical times. The inevitable pro-miscuity was masked by a certain correctness and a discreet sense of mystery. Now budding actresses get a more or less opulent sum from the men they sleep with. But in those days they were kept by lovers who, by and large, were older, well-established men with important positions at Napoleon III's court. These gentlemen passed themselves off as the girls' guardians in the hope of concealing the true nature of their relations behind a screen of paternal interest. These "protectors"—generals, admirals, of-ficers of the Imperial Household—were more useful to the future actresses than their counterparts of today. With their influence in high places they were able to further the careers of their *protégées*, from their schooldays to their hoped-for entry into the Comédie Française. Furthermore, they took a real interest in the girls' artistic future while providing for their daily needs. It cost them very little as the students still had the unde-manding mentality of *grisettes*, and behaved like promiscuous working girls with their aristocratic mentors. For fifteen *louis* a month, or less, the little ingénues were quite content to bring sunshine into the lives of their aging heroes, men who had earned their medals in the North African campaign or at the Battle of Magenta. And so there were economic advantages as well as sexual gratifications for these half-paternal, half-perverse, lech-erous gentlemen who took on the young girls with such avidity.

Today's young actresses hope to become capitalists thanks to the *so-ciétaires* system at the Comédie Française, which guarantees handsome

pensions. But in those days the Conservatoire sheltered a nestful of twit-
tering, carefree young birds. . . .

M A R I E Colombier failed to mention that her Second Empire birds were kept on at the Conservatoire only if they
showed progress. In fact, the yearly examinations in performances of dramatic and comic scenes were passports to the theatres of Paris.
Prizes were awarded to the most gifted students, and a select audience was
invited. Actors, critics, protectors, and would-be protectors crowded the
school's small theatre in the hope of discovering new talent, future bedmates,
or both. It was one of the sporting events of the season. In July 1861, the
end of her first year, Sarah won a second prize for tragedy and an honorable
mention for comedy. It was a blow to the girl who had had her heart set on
winning a first in both.

The next year brought further disappointment. Provost fell ill two
months before her final test, and Samson took her into his class. Astute
though he was, he misjudged her gifts and insisted she perform two ungrateful
scenes by Casimir Delavigne, a writer of rather stiff historical plays. Calliope
herself could not have breathed life into the playwright's lackluster lines.

Youle too was more a hindrance than a help when she decided to
have her daughter's hair straightened. A seance at the hairdresser's under-
mined Sarah's last vestige of confidence. After circling his victim, the "idiot
Figaro," as Sarah called him, said: "Good God! All the whores in Tangiers
have hair like this." Then, with a flourish of his hot curling iron, he pressed
beef marrow into her hair, accidentally burning her scalp. Sarah's screams
had no effect on the coiffeur, who pinned and pulled, combed and brushed
with fiendish concentration. When at last he gave Sarah a mirror, she could
barely recognize herself and burst into tears. Her hair was plastered down
at the temples, her rather large ears stuck out, and rows of tight sausage
curls lay piled on her head in imitation of an ancient Grecian style.

On reaching the Conservatoire, Sarah ripped the pins out of her hair.

As the greasy strands unravelled about her face, she shook her head in a "mad rage." Her voice worn by sobs, she was barely able to get through her scene from *La Fille du Cid* and fainted when she left the stage. But there was still some fight in her. Half an hour later she played a comic excerpt from *L'Ecole des Vieillards* with delicacy and charm. Still, the girl who had to be first in everything received only a second prize, as did Paul Porel. The first prize went to her friend Marie Lloyd, a ravishing beauty who was to have a rather dim career at the Comédie Française for the next thirty years. As Marie had no relatives in Paris, Sarah invited her to lunch:

> On the way home we made fun of the other students and laughed like idiots. Mother greeted Marie Lloyd with her special blend of charm and indifference. Then my godfather had his say: "Well, you've made a fine mess. Why be so stubborn about the theatre? You're too thin, too small. Your face is nice close up, but ugly from a distance. Besides your voice doesn't carry."
>
> "Your godfather's right," Monsieur Meydieu interrupted. "Get married, my dear. You'll never amount to anything in the theatre."

After lunch, Youle had a little chat with Sarah. She was not to feel defeated, nor was she to worry about the future. A marriage to her Dutch suitor could still be arranged.

She would consider it, Sarah said, but she was hedging. She felt that despite everyone and everything she belonged on the stage. Was it then, perhaps, that she adopted her *devise, quand même* (roughly translatable as "despite all odds"), the motto with which she was to defy the world all her long life?

Her decision to be an actress—*quand même*—was one thing; to find employment, quite another. Had Sarah been a writer or a painter, she could have set to work there and then. But she was a performer and performers cannot display their talents without an audience. Who would engage her? Where could she find a public? The answer, miraculously enough, lay in a note that she found on her bedside table that night. The handwriting was Madame Guérard's:

> While you were asleep, the Duc de Morny sent word to your mother. Camille Doucet has just told him your engagement at the Comédie Fran-

çaise is settled. So don't be unhappy, my dear child. Have confidence in the future.

Two days later Sarah received a message from Edouard Thierry, the director of the Comédie Française: She was to come for her contract. Once again there was the problem of what to wear, and once again the solution was ludicrous. This time it was thought that, as a recognized actress, she should wear one of Rosine's elaborate dresses. To heighten the effect, Rosine lent Sarah her splendid carriage: coachman, footman, and all. When she departed in Rosine's magnificent equipage, she looked every inch the successful young cocotte. Her grandeur was ill-advised. Camille Doucet (Chief of the Theatre Division of the Ministry of Fine Arts) and Léon Beauvallet (in Sarah's opinion "the rudest man in France") were chatting at the stage door when she left, contract in hand.

"Well, well," the actor said, "so you have a carriage."

"It's not hers, it belongs to her aunt," Doucet assured him.

"Glad to hear that," Beauvallet replied, his face a study in doubt. But nothing could dampen Sarah's spirits. She was on her way, she was about to make her debut at the world's greatest theatre, and the great Camille Doucet himself had predicted a brilliant future for her.

A week later, Rosine gave a dinner in Sarah's honor. It was a moment of self-congratulation for Rosine. It was not every cocotte who could surround herself with such dignitaries as the Duc de Morny, Rossini, and Minister of Fine Arts Comte Colonna-Walewski.

When the after-dinner guests arrived, Rosine sang a popular ballad to warm applause. Then glasses were raised to Sarah, and everyone clamored for a poem. While she recited Delavigne's *L'Ame du Purgatoire* (*The Soul of Purgatory*), Rossini slipped onto the piano bench and improvised a musical background. Sarah was radiant. To complete her happiness, Youle kissed her fondly, saying it was the first time her daughter had really moved her, a double-edged compliment Sarah was too excited to resent.

On 11 August 1862, Sarah was to make her first appearance in the title role of Racine's *Iphigénie*, one of three "debuts" in three different roles which, in the tradition of the Comédie Française, she would perform within a short period of time. At the first rehearsal she arrived far before the hour to find herself alone on the vast stage. Unprepared for the gloom, the silence, the crypt-like cold, and the tortuous tangle of ropes, weights, and pulleys above, she felt threatened. The ghostly atmosphere had little to do with the glorious vision of colonnades and painted clouds she remembered from her first visit to the Comédie Française. The actors who began to wander in only added to her disappointment. Could these surly people be the exalted creatures who had moved her to tears? A mistrustful look at the uneasy debutante, a hasty run-through, a few hints to the newcomer, and they were gone. The next day, after another rehearsal and a few cursory suggestions, Sarah was pronounced ready. An *affiche* announcing "The Debuts of Mlle Sarah Bern-hardt" was posted outside the theatre. Sarah studied it with awe. "I have no idea of how long I stood there, fascinated by my own name," she wrote. "It seemed as though every passerby who stopped to read the *affiche* knew who I was. I felt myself blushing to the roots of my hair."

Inexorably, the day of her first debut arrived. As she climbed the dimly lit stairs to her dressing room, she was overcome by a stifling excitement, an agonizing tension. *Le trac*, stage fright, every performer's nightmare, had come to pay its first call.

Sarah, who was always to suffer from stage-fright, was not spared this backstage agony. Nor did the knowledge that the audience was made up of vacationing schoolteachers and non-French-speaking tourists calm her fears. As she examined herself in the dressing-room mirror, her eyes stared back at her. Her face beneath the paint and powder seemed commonplace. The callboy's sudden warning struck her like a blow. There was no escape. It was a momentary relief to find Provost and Samson waiting in the wings. But when they teased her, embraced her, and assured her all would go well, she was doubly frightened. It was they, more than anyone, who would judge her: they who had taught her each gesture, each inflection. As she stood behind the stage set, she listened apprehensively to the actors' muffled voices coming nearer and nearer to her cue. "But the blood rushed to my ears and I could hear nothing," she remembered.

When her cue came, Provost whispered "*merde*" and pushed Sarah onto the stage. Three actors, alert, practiced, inhuman in their profession-alism, waited for her to speak. There was a dangerously long silence. At last Sarah found her voice and spoke her lines, but like a somnambulist she was aware of neither sound nor movement. Only memory and training carried her through. When the curtain came down she fled to her dressing room and tore off her costume. The poor girl had forgotten there were four more acts to come. "I knew there would be serious trouble if I allowed myself to give way to my nerves," she recalled. "I finished the performance. But I can hardly claim that I made an impression."

Sarah finished the performance but not before she heard rowdy laughter when she raised her frail arms in supplication. Some days later Francisque Sarcey, Paris's most powerful critic, had his say:

> Mlle Bernhardt. . . . is a tall attractive young woman with a slender waist and a most pleasing face; the upper part of her face in particular is remarkably beautiful. She carries herself well and pronounces her words with perfect clarity. That is all that can be said for the moment.

The casual reader might have thought these words kind enough, but Sarah wept when she read them and reread them. What was wrong with the lower part of her face? Did the critic mean to encourage or discourage her with his noncommittal "That is all that can be said for the moment"? Sarah's next appearance, in Scribe's *Valérie*, went virtually unnoticed, but her third debut, in Molière's *Les Femmes Savantes*, put Sarcey on the warpath:

> That Mlle Bernhardt is inadequate is unimportant. She is making her debut and it is natural that there are some beginners who do not succeed. But what is sad is that the other actors are not much better than she. And they are permanent members of the company! The only difference between them and their young comrade is that they are more experienced. They are what Mlle Bernhardt may become in twenty years if she remains at the Comédie Française.

Sarcey's wholesale destruction did not endear Sarah to her fellow actors. There had been mutterings about her sharp tongue and her pretentious manner, but to be swept into the same dustbin as the untalented nobody was too much for them. Poor, ambitious Sarah was ignored by the management and not assigned any other roles for four disheartening months.

Things were not much better at home, where her mother's "I-told-you-so's" and brave little smiles did nothing to lighten her spirits. Only her youngest sister seemed to love her. At nine, Régine was an eccentric little girl who rarely uttered a word, unless it was to startle her family with well-chosen obscenities. Sarah loved her and took her everywhere. Nothing could have been better calculated to irritate her fellow actors than the sight of Morny's obstreperous protégée dragging her sister up to her dressing room for company. Such behavior was unheard of at the Comédie Française.

On 15 January 1863, the theatre held its annual birthday celebration in honor of its founder, Molière. It was a solemn rite. The actors of the company were to assemble, then, two by two, step forward to lay palm fronds on the playwright's bust. When Régine heard about the event, she begged to be taken along. Sarah foolishly consented. Hand in hand the sisters watched the druid-like procession. In front of them stood Madame Nathalie. An old battle-ax, with a formidable manner, a formidable bosom, and a purple gown that trailed three feet behind her formidable haunches, she was the terror of the company. As she started forward, palm fronds at the ready, she found that she was unable to move as Régine had planted herself squarely on her train. With a Medea-like howl, Madame Nathalie pushed the child, who fell against a marble pillar. Régine screamed and, her face covered with blood, flung herself into Sarah's arms. "You beast," Sarah cried, throwing herself at Madame Nathalie. Before the stout lady could answer, Sarah slapped her hard on both cheeks. All the while Régine protested that she hadn't done it purposely, that the fat bitch had no right to shove her. The child's supporters beamed their approval, Madame Nathalie's sympathizers shrugged their shoulders in disgust, and the audience became impatient at the delay. Finally, the festivities began with poems declaimed to the glory of Molière and scenes from his plays.

The next day Sarah was called in by Monsieur Thierry. An apology was in order. If Madame Nathalie accepted it, Sarah would have to pay a large fine; if not, he would be forced to ask for her resignation. Monsieur Thierry explained what a privilege it was to be a part of the Comédie Française and the dangers she would expose herself to if she left it. After such outrageous behavior it is hardly surprising that she was not given any roles. The one exception was a single performance in March of Molière's *L'Etourdi* in honor of her teacher, Samson, who was about to retire from the stage.

With nothing to do, Sarah was frustrated, bored, and miserably uncomfortable in a company where everyone disliked her. Since she repeatedly refused to apologize, her contract was terminated. Imprudent, stubborn Sarah, her *amour-propre* intact, was not to return to the Comédie Française for almost ten years.

13. Sarah rides.

14. She shoots (in Brazil).

15. She weeds (in Paris).

16. She bats (in Belle-Ile-en-Mer). Maurice is at left, Sarah at the net.

17. She picnics (in Belle-Ile-en-Mer).

18. She plays.

19. She sculpts.

20. She paints.

21. She decorates.
Maurice's wife Terka is on the
right. Partially obscured by the
chandelier is Clairin's most
famous portrait of Bernhardt.
The studio is her last house,
on the Boulevard Péreire.

22. She muses.

23. She poses.

24. She chats.

25. She models fur.

26. She listens to her voice.

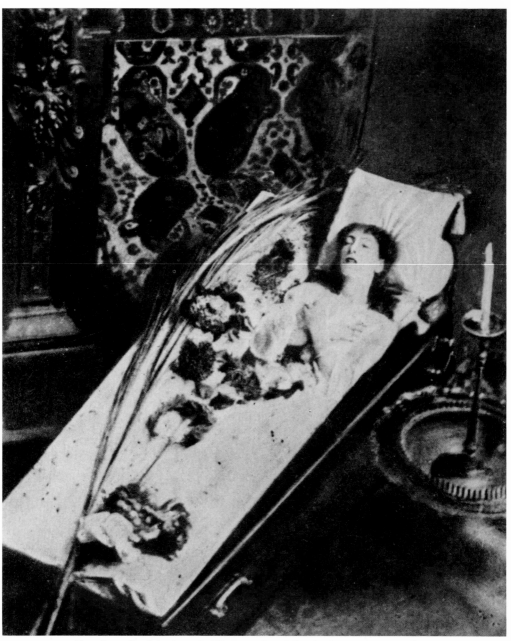

27. She plays dead (at home). Photographs of Sarah sleeping in a coffin were widely sold and brought her enormous notoriety.

S A R A H struck Madame Nathalie and the world struck back. A year earlier she was the girl who got into the Comédie Française through Morny's "pull." Now she was just a troublemaker without sufficient talent to warrant the duke's protection. She had attacked partly to avenge her sister and partly because she felt humiliated by her failure in the eyes of the world. Theatre people washed their hands of her, her mother was tired of supporting her, and her godfather's suggestion that she open a candy shop sickened her.

These were Sarah's hard times as it was in bed, by and large, that she was to earn her keep in the next years. The temptation is to leave her discreetly tucked away, were it not that for the future tragédienne the trials and rewards of *la vie galante* deepened her understanding of the courtesans she was to portray so compellingly.

In the 1860s, Sarah, blond and slender, and Marie Colombier, dark and voluptuous, were girls on the town. Both were as fresh as the new paint and the wide boulevards with which the Baron Haussmann was transforming Paris. For a new Paris was rising—and with it a new way of life. Money and enterprise were changing the face of the city and its spirit as well. Another "modern" era had arrived: confident, cynical, and exuberantly martial.

Sarah, a daughter of the time, was caught up in its pageantry and spendthrift gaiety. Like her mother, she wanted a piece of the pie and the largest piece she could get. The similarity ended there. Youle plied her trade in exchange for luxury and comfort. Sarah thought such aspiration death to the spirit. Her desire was to express herself in poetic drama; her love was the stage—even in failure. Reluctant but intrigued, she drifted into the life of a demimondaine. And with a vengeance, it might be added. Her heart was not in it, however. She was too proud, too impatient to submit to the mighty male egos of the Second Empire, who tended to consider their wives bores and their mistresses whores.

Sarah was an anonymous, easygoing girl after she left the Comédie

Française. When, as a celebrated actress of fifty-four, she wrote *Ma Double Vie*, she chose, understandably, to describe her past with discretion. In that book she alludes briefly to a certain comte de Kératry—generally thought to be her first serious lover—as one of the guests at Rosine's party in her honor. The count, according to Sarah, was "an elegant young hussar," who flirted with her and invited her to recite at his mother's salon. Marie Colombier, however, was to describe their first meeting as having taken place under infinitely less elegant circumstances:

> Returning from the theatre where she had made her debut a few days before, Sarah threw down her hat and gloves and sank into a sofa. She had been disillusioned once too often and was in a ferocious mood. . . . Her artistic pride had been humbled by her ignominious debut. She had appeared with no fanfare. The journalists had hardly bothered to announce the event. She had not gone to see Sarcey beforehand and now, she realized, he was having his revenge.
>
> There lay her chief regret. Since she loved the theatre she should have swallowed her pride and allowed herself to be seduced by one or two of the critics. That would have assured rave reviews and launched her career. And then her mother was tormenting her. Every day, twenty times a day, she sang the same tune: "You've been at the theatre for over a month and you still haven't found a way to make yourself useful!" It was enough to drive her mad!
>
> But no one was courting her. She couldn't very well stop men in the streets by pulling at their coat-sleeves. . . . Aunt Rosine calmly let the storm pass, then said: "My pet, nothing is accomplished by screaming and shouting. You must go after what you want, make the most of your opportunities. Tonight is an opportunity not to be missed. Your mother is getting tickets for the *Variétés*. Come with us. There's always a high class crowd. If you can't pick up someone there, you're hopeless. Trust me." Following her aunt's advice, she went to her room, where she remained for two hours to make herself beautiful. When she emerged she was radiant. Soon the three women were on their way to the *Théâtre des Variétés*.
>
> During the performance, Sarah did not glance at the stage. Instead, she sat in the front of the loge and examined the men in the stalls through her opera glass. Meanwhile, the men below had noticed the strange girl with the beautiful eyes and eccentric coiffure. "*Très chic,*" they muttered approvingly. Those who knew Rosine and Youle were curious to know

who their companion might be. Sarah studied the men carefully, coolly, impassively. Suddenly her eyes fixed themselves on a young man seated directly below. When he returned her look she blushed. At the end of the performance Youle and Rosine left quickly. When they reached the rue Vivienne, Sarah caught up with them, breathlessly claiming that she must have lost them in the crowd. The two women longed to question her, but they remained silent, reassured by her exultant expression. Sarah turned to see if anyone was following her. Rosine, as curious as her niece, glanced back as well. There, close behind them, was the man who had caught Sarah's eye in the theatre. . . . The sisters were like parents watching their child take its first steps and, at the same time, like veterans in the profession watching a protégée make her debut. By now they were in the rue St. Honoré and the stranger was still following them with the air of a casual stroller. The sisters hastily entered Youle's building, giving Sarah time to speak to her admirer. When they reached their landing, the girl caught up with them. For the first time in many months Youle embraced her daughter before going to bed, saying, "You're a good girl," and Aunt Rosine, sincerely moved, took Sarah to her bedroom door. Kissing her tenderly she whispered, "My compliments! You have taste. He's very good. Now you must play your cards well."

Sarah felt she needed advice. "Dearest Aunt," she murmured, "there were two men who noticed me. The young one was very attractive, but the old one seemed richer. He sent his carriage away so that he could follow me and gave me his card. I can see him whenever I wish. I don't know what to do. Which one should I choose?"

The courtesan was moved. "Look, darling," she said: "this is between us—in your place I would give myself to the young one. The important thing is to begin."

With the flair of the expert, Rosine had made the right choice. Emile de Kératry was a handsome, distinguished man of thirty. Launched into society, the young lieutenant was the leader of a group of fashionable men about town. With a glass of champagne in his hand and a gardenia in his buttonhole, he handled women in the cool, elegant style with which he led his men into battle. Certainly his high spirits, his biting wit, and his gift for inventive debauchery made him superior to his companions.

As a jaded man about town he was intrigued by Sarah's bizarre mixture of naïveté and corruption. As for Sarah, though she was very attracted to him, she certainly did not love him, for she was one of those women who are incapable of love. After his passionate embraces, she liked him even less. Vague feelings of disgust and disillusion swept over her. Was *that* what love was about? And she had preferred the young fellow to the rich old man! Her disillusion was sharper than her disgust, a disgust she knew her friends did not share. She felt incomplete, and it shamed her.

When the love-making was over and it was time to leave, Kératry sweetly teased her about her dress and told her she needed prettier clothes. Here she was already the consummate actress. She made the young officer feel he must persuade her to allow him to give her money and to be useful in other ways. When she went home, she threw the money on the table and said to Youle: "I hope you won't bother me anymore."

"Bother you!" cried Youle, who went on to say that she was thinking only of Sarah's good, only trying to set her on the right path. That morning, in fact, she had rented a larger apartment in the boulevard Malesherbes, where Sarah would have her own room with a separate entrance so that she would be completely independent. In that way she would have the advantages of both family life and privacy.

Descriptions of the sexual activities of others are based largely on conjecture and hearsay. Sarah's letters reveal that she was complicated about love-making and habitually postponed rendezvous with lovers who, she insisted, had satisfied her most heated fantasies. Perhaps, and this too is conjecture, the experiences of Lélia, the heroine of George Sand's novel, come close to Sarah's own:

> When I was near him I felt a sort of strange and delirious greed which . . . could not be satisfied by any carnal embraces. I felt my bosom devoured by an inextinguishable fire and his kisses shed no relief. I pressed him in my arms with a superhuman force and fell next to him exhausted, discouraged at having no possible way to convey my passion to him. With me desire was an ardor of the soul that paralyzed the power of the senses before it awakened them. It was a savage fury that seized my brain. . . . My blood froze, impotent and poor before the immense soaring of my will. . . . When he was drowsy, satisfied, and at rest I would lie motionless beside him. He seemed so handsome to me. There was so much force and grandeur on his peaceful brow. . . . Waves of blood mounted to my face. Then unbearable tremblings passed through my limbs. I seemed to experience again the excitation of physical love and the increasing turmoil of desire. I was violently tempted to waken him . . . to ask for his caresses.

But I resisted these deceiving entreaties of my suffering because I well
knew it was not in his power to calm me.

It is likely that George Sand was speaking from experience. If that is so,
Sarah's frustration, like Sand's, was a stimulant that urged her on to countless
affairs. Her liaison with Kératry lasted for several months—until he was
sent to Mexico on military duty.

In March 1863, three weeks after her break with the Comédie Française,
Sarah was hired to play small parts and to understudy the leading ladies at
the Gymnase, Paris's most fashionable theatre. If the engagement was a
distinct step down, it had its advantages. Her premature debut at France's
national theatre had placed her in a false position. Now, out of the limelight,
she was able to say her few lines without being terror-struck, learn the tricks
of her trade from her colleagues, and develop her talents at a proper pace.
Each night Sarah watched the lamplighters begin their evening rounds. One
by one, the stage, the vestibule, the corridors and dressing rooms were
touched with amber light. The ornate chandelier, its gas jets at half flame,
was lowered to reveal row after row of armchairs surrounded by a gilded
crescent of boxes. Cleaning ladies muttered inaudibly as they shuffled in to
unwrap the shrouded chairs and wield their feather dusters in aimless fashion.
Helmeted firemen, spruce and military, took their stations while their chief
kept vigil at the footlights, that line of flame so often the cause of tragic
fires. Up above, huge vats of water hung suspended in case of emergency.
Preparations continued as the noisy stage crew shouted orders, battened
down the flies, and tugged weights and pulleys like sailors tending the rigging
of a ship. The claques seated themselves beneath the chandelier and waited
to cheer the actors who had bought their enthusiasm for the evening. The
orchestra tuned up. The stage manager checked the props. When the bell
ringer shook his bell a hush descended. The actors scurried into the wings
as the orchestra played the last notes of the overture. The curtain parted,
and suddenly actors and audience were joined in the evening's entertainment.

Sarah played seven roles, some delightful, some mediocre, in the
1863–1864 season. The plays she appeared in—allowing for the particular
assumptions and orthodoxies of the day—were much like those of our own
time. Then, as now, interest centered on dramatic or comic views of love
affairs, infidelity, jealousy, domestic problems, intrigue, and crime.

Sarah, who had felt stifled by what she considered the sepulchral righteousness of the Comédie Française, now felt, in her contrary idealism, far above the frivolity of the Gymnase. The future queen of tragedy wished to boil, not to bubble. But bubble she did when she sang such ditties as "*Un baiser? O non! non!*" ("A kiss? Oh, no! no!")

I N   A P R I L   1 8 6 4 ,   Sarah made her last appearance at the Gymnase, in *Un Mari qui Lance sa Femme* (*A Husband Who Launches His Wife*), a comedy by Labiche and Deslandes. The husband may have launched his wife, but the play did nothing to launch Sarah.

"I was neither a success nor a failure," she wrote, "I simply went unnoticed. That night my mother said to me: 'My poor child, you were ridiculous as that silly Russian princess. You made me very unhappy.' I did not say a word but I really wanted to kill myself."

It was not only Youle's criticism that drove Sarah to thoughts of suicide. She was pregnant and, with no visible husband or lover, in a difficult position.

At this point in *Memories of My Life*, as one American edition of *Ma Double Vie* was called, in a chapter aptly named "Castles in Spain," Bernhardt's imagination took flight. Some of what follows may be true, but it is equally possible that most of it is an invention.

"I slept very badly that night," she wrote, "and toward six in the morning I rushed up to Mme Guérard's. I asked her to give me some laudanum, but she refused. When she saw that I really wanted it, the poor, dear woman understood my idea. 'Well, then,' I said, 'swear by your children that you will not tell anyone what I am going to do, and then I will not kill myself.' "

Bernhardt goes on to say that instead of killing herself, she impulsively left for Spain early that morning, taking a maid with her and asking Guérard to deliver two letters: "an affectionate letter to my mother begging her to forgive me" and "a stupid letter to the manager of the Gymnase Theatre that did not explain anything. I finished up with these words: 'Have pity on a poor crazy girl.' "

There are pages of picaresque adventures in Marseilles and Madrid, and a decision to live in Spain forever, cancelled by a telegram saying that Youle is very ill. Upon her return to Paris, there is an emotional reunion with her mother, after which it is agreed that Sarah will move to a flat in the rue Duphot nearby, taking Régine to live with her, and that Jeanne will live with Youle. The only adventure that is passed over in silence is what is probably the most momentous event in her personal life, the birth of her only child, her son Maurice, on 22 December 1864. She never refers to the father in her memoirs, nor is Maurice mentioned until he is four years old. For while at twenty Sarah was hoping to lose her anonymity, by the time she wrote her memoirs she was struggling to maintain some semblance of privacy.

Acting, impersonation, and prevarication are blood relations (the Greek word for actor is, after all, *hypokrites*), and Sarah was gifted at all three. She told many conflicting stories about the romance that led to the birth of her son. In her lighter moments, she liked to say she never could decide whether Maurice's father was Gambetta, Victor Hugo, General Boulanger, or the Duke of Clarence—a rather startling idea, since she knew none of these men at the time of Maurice's birth.

Like all actors, Sarah lived in fear of boring her audience, even an audience of one. And so when her granddaughter, Lysiane Bernhardt, was gathering material for the official "as-told-to" biography, Sarah obliged her with what she claimed was the true story of her life. Yet when Lysiane's husband, the playwright Louis Verneuil, wrote *his* "official" biography, she did not hesitate to regale him with quite another "true story," a diversionary tactic designed to conceal sad truths from Maurice and his children and even sadder truths from herself.* Here, more or less, is the gist of what Sarah told her grandson-in-law:

During Sarah's days at the Gymnase, the company was invited to present a program for Napoleon III and his court. A command performance at the

---

*Verneuil was a very successful popular playwright whose admiration for Sarah was obsessive. He and her granddaughter, Lysiane, were married in 1921. They were divorced shortly after Sarah's death in 1923, which makes one wonder if he was more in love with Sarah than with Lysiane. Verneuil's biography of Bernhardt was published in 1942, Lysiane's in 1945.

Tuileries was a signal opportunity and Sarah was determined to outdo herself. When her turn came she took her place, curtsied in great style, and announced that she would recite a poem by Victor Hugo. It was one of Sarah's more spectacular gaffes. The Emperor had banished the republican poet more than ten years earlier, and here was a little actress from God knows where, confronting him, and in his own palace, with subversive words he did not care to hear.

An arctic chill swept the room. Sarah, thinking, perhaps, that her choice was too gloomy for the imperial audience, began a more cheerful work by the poet in exile. At this, the Emperor rose, solemnly gave his arm to the Empress and made his disapproving way to an adjoining salon, followed by his scandalized guests.

And there was Sarah, alone on the stage, facing rows of empty seats. She was not alone for long. The manager of the Gymnase bounded onto the platform, cursing and threatening to beat her. At that moment a commanding voice barked: "Leave that child alone!" The knight-errant come to the rescue was the blond, handsome, and noblest of Belgian princes, Charles-Joseph-Eugène-Henri-Georges-Lamoral-Prince de Ligne.

Verneuil ends his account on a rapturous note:

> Excited, in love with romance, always moved by anything noble or rare, [Sarah] was immediately deeply interested by the courtly young gentleman's vigorous defense of an unknown, insignificant little actress. . . . The prince, in turn, at this first meeting was visibly attracted by the peculiar beauty and the vibrant nature of the young artist.
>
> At the end of the evening he escorted her to the door of her mother's house. They met the next day, and the day after—every day and every night until the summer. This great love soon grew into a veritable passion which was sincere on both sides, the rarest and most touching reciprocal feeling which ever united two young hearts.

Sarah provided Lysiane with an equally romantic little drama. At the dress rehearsal of *A Husband Who Launches His Wife*, Sarah caught sight of her disapproving mother in a loge with Dumas. Late that night Dumas called on Sarah. There was something dreadfully wrong. It was true that he had encouraged her to be an actress. Perhaps he had been right, perhaps not. But one thing was certain: she had taken a false turn. What she needed was a rest, a change of scene, and time to realize that she was her own worst enemy. In a word, she must get away from Paris. Sarah protested that she could not abandon the play or her mother. Dumas promised to take care of all that. He would write to Monsieur Jean Bruce, a friend in Belgium who would look out for her. A few days later Sarah was in Brussels on her way to a masked ball.

She would never forget that long-ago June night, Sarah told Lysiane. Her *carnet de bal* was quickly filled with noble names. And, most memorable of all, a masked stranger flirted with her. He was disguised as Hamlet, she as Elizabeth of England. With the urgent pressure of his gloved hand on her back, she was led through the maze of waltzing couples, through the open doors and onto the balcony.

He: Madame—or is it Mademoiselle? Would you remove your mask?
She: Why, Monsieur?
He: To give me pleasure.
She: And why should I give you pleasure?
(Hamlet takes Elizabeth in his arms and tries to kiss her. She slaps him.)
She: Ah, Monsieur Hamlet, do not take liberties with me! I am not Ophelia.
(Hamlet catches sight of himself in a mirror, chiding Queen Elizabeth. He roars with laughter.)
He: The Prince of Denmark humbly begs the Queen's pardon. (And, in English) To forgive or not to forgive?
She: (in English, smiling) To forgive!

At the end of the evening the prince presented Sarah with a rose. A note was wrapped around its stem: "This flower, Mademoiselle Bernhardt, is like your character, bristling with cruel thorns. Since I have learned your name but do not know your face, carry this rose tomorrow on the promenade and I shall find you. You owe that much to your melancholy Prince of Denmark."

In the morning, Sarah hired an open fiacre, pinned the rose to her lace fichu, and joined the long line of carriages that made their way up and down the fashionable avenue Louise. In her billowing yellow dress and pretty Paris hat, she looked every inch the languid woman of the world. Soon a handsome young cavalier drew up alongside her carriage. "Madame Elizabeth," he said, as he removed his top hat with an elegant flourish. "Monsieur Hamlet," murmured a blushing Sarah.

And so the great love affair began. A letter written by Monsieur Bruce to Alexandre Dumas seems to support Sarah's tale:

Brussels, June 1863

My dear Dumas, your young friend Mlle Sarah Bernhardt has conquered Brussels. At our ball she captured the heart of the prince de L. . . . It seems they have been meeting. Are you angry with me for offering the girl too much distraction from her troubles or do you congratulate me for giving an actress the means to free herself?

P.S. I have just returned from her hotel. Sarah has not been seen there for a week. It seems she has been travelling with friends. I fear these "friends" merge into one man, and that they have not travelled farther than the avenue de la Toison d'Or. That's what happens when you let a dragonfly loose with a butterfly.

Never at a loss, Sarah provided not only two new versions of her affair— but two denouements as well. Both ran perilously close to Marguerite's renunciation scene in *La Dame aux Camélias*. Sadly enough, her romantic fantasies did nothing to conceal the fact that the prince was not as princely as she had hoped. He neither recognized the child as his son nor offered to support him. Not until *la petite Sarah* became *la grande Sarah* did he try to make amends. Sarah never forgave him—or forgot him. Years later, in letters to other lovers, she was to dwell on her deep love for Ligne: of her "hopes deceived, impotent tears, despair that led to thoughts of suicide."

Marie Colombier confirms Sarah's unhappiness in *The Memoirs of Sarah Barnum*. Marie, who, like her "best friend," savored the Prince de Ligne's good looks and monocled manner, remembered Sarah rushing "all in tears, to the author of her misfortune." The prince was having a house-warming and had failed to invite Sarah. At the sight of her tears, he stiffened. His *petite amie* was about to ruin his evening. But nothing could shake the worldly composure he had inherited along with his titled wealth. At the word "seduction" he laughed discreetly. But his laughter turned to disbelief when Sarah told him she was pregnant with his child.

"My dear girl," he said, "as the actress Augustine Brohan so wittily observed, you must realize that if you sit on a pile of thorns, you can never know which one has pricked you." Then he explained that he could not neglect his guests any longer, kissed her hand, and saw her to the door.

Ligne withheld love and money, but he gave Sarah an infinitely more precious gift: a child who would elicit a devotion she did not know she was capable of. But Sarah was a restless madonna. Only twenty when her son, Maurice, was born, the tenderness she felt for him, her anxiety about each of his sniffles and tears could not fulfill the needs of a woman with her infinite energy. With no offers of work in the theatre, it was not long before she turned to other aspects of what she called her "Moi."

"I know I had very little talent but I was determined to have a go at everything," she wrote. Among Sarah's "everythings" was a passionate interest in painting and sculpture, an interest which may well have been born in the studio of Félix Nadar, for art was in the air of that great photographer's rooms. Everyone sat for him: Verdi, Berlioz, and Rossini; Baudelaire, George Sand, and Flaubert; Delacroix and Courbet; the Goncourt brothers, the Russian anarchist Mikhail Bakunin, and the dying Rachel.

These luminaries were famous when Nadar photographed them. Sarah, on the other hand, posed for him when she was virtually unknown. His first studies of her could be called *Young Woman on the Threshold of Life*. Nadar shows her with the skill of a master portraitist. It is clear that Sarah moved him and would be able to move audiences as well. These photographs are alive with what performers call "presence." Draped in Titian-like folds of velvet, Sarah reveals a talent for characterization. In one portrait, she plays a virgin dreamer, ardent and melancholy. In another, she gazes seductively at the camera, sybilline, sensual, and eager for the pleasures of the flesh. In later years Nadar's son Paul would take literally hundreds of pictures of Sarah.

To be an *habitué chez Nadar* was an education in itself. All was flamboyant, noisy, and new. The conversation was new, the paintings were new, and photography was new. Nadar's studio was new, the boulevard des Capucines where it stood was new, even his name—he was born Tourna-chon—was new.

A giant of a man, Nadar was a study in red: his hair, his mustache, the flowing robe he worked in, the walls of his atelier and the façade of his studio building were all ablaze with his favorite color.

Nadar's studio was a meeting place for *le Tout-Paris artistique*. Dumas rubbed shoulders with Offenbach, Sardou with Doré. While Nadar took picture after picture, his friends practiced fencing in a corner of the huge atelier. Others drank, gossiped, argued about art and politics, discussed their love affairs and their host's balloon ascensions.

It was probably in this bohemian atmosphere that Sarah posed, nude behind a fan. What enticement lay in that slender yet voluptuous body with its small, high breasts and a delicate waist that melted, like a subtle "S," into narrow hips! Despite her height—she was just over five feet tall—her slim figure and short hair suggest a girl of this century rather than a belle of the Second Empire. Sarah's willingness to be photographed nude would seem to indicate that she was in need of money and not above displaying her body to get it. Her career was at a standstill. Between April 1864 and August 1866, Sarah appeared in only one production, a *spectacle*, or *féerie*, at the Théâtre Porte Saint-Martin called *La Biche aux Bois* ("The Doe in the Wood").

The poet Robert de Montesquiou—one of Proust's models for the Baron de Charlus—remembered the sight of his future friend "asleep on one of those strips of grass that the primitive machinery of those days moved back and forth. She had slightly wavy reddish hair, a slender grace and the profile of a lamb. Amidst the gay glitter of the show, moments of sadness overcame her. It was in those moments that she moved me most."

If Bernhardt's short engagement in this popular "spectacular" was a step back, she enjoyed it immensely. Like most serious actors, she relished the innocent vulgarity and the consummate finesse of music-hall performers. Nostalgic about those popular stars, already forgotten when she wrote her memoirs, Sarah spoke affectionately of Madame Ugalde, who coached her in their duets. "Yes," she wrote, "I was going to sing with a real singer, the leading artiste of the Opéra-Comique, who encouraged me and said my voice was pretty even though I always sang out of tune." For Maraquita, the dancer of the moment, she had fond praise: "Oh, what charm she had, that delicious Maraquita, with her high-spirited dances and her true distinction."

IT W A S amusing, even enlightening, to play *La Biche aux Bois*, but it did not begin to pay Sarah's bills. The soul of impracticality, she ignored them. Thrift was beneath her and debt only a springboard to further extravagance. Her clothes—she was far beyond Rosine's hand-me-downs—were costly; Maurice, with or without his father, was indulged like the little prince he might have been; and irritating though it was, the nurse, maid, and cook expected to be paid regularly. There was no choice but to play her mother's game. And so, with one eye on the lookout for possible engagements, Sarah, like many of her actress friends, became more and more dependent on lovers. For the most part, she thought it great fun to open her white satin salon to aristocrats, ambassadors, bankers, and—Sarah had learned her lesson—theatre critics.

"What's odd," she confided to Marie Colombier, "is how well they get along together. They never quarrel and seem to adore one another. I sometimes think that if I were to disappear, my menagerie would continue to congregate in my apartment with the greatest pleasure."

Sarah underestimated herself. She was a beauty, an original whose vitality galvanized those who surrounded her. Her erratic behavior delighted them. They were highly amused when she hid from her debtors in the house she rented in Auteuil. They made room for her in their beds when it was too late for her to go back to her rural hideaway after an evening's pleasures. When the servants made off with her furniture because she failed to pay them, her lovers replenished her rooms with chairs and tables, linen and silver. One generous, and presumably prudent, gentleman even supplied her with a handsome new bidet.

Sarah was, in fact, enjoying more success as a courtesan than she had as a member of the Comédie Française. At twenty, she had not had full opportunity to show off her personal gifts. Perhaps she had not believed in them. Her theatrical failures and Youle's belittling presence had done little to bolster her confidence. Now, under her own roof, reassured by her smiling "menagerie," she made a startling leap from adolescence to womanhood. That she had no stage to perform on did not prevent the born actress from acting. Indeed, it took a certain dramatic skill to simulate passion and pocket her lovers' money with nonchalant ease. Moreover, it was an opportunity to study herself; she staged her entrances and exits, her laughter and tears, her sinuous gestures with a vigilant self-love that made her as irresistible to herself as she was to her coterie.

Fifteen years later the English critic Tom Taylor was to recall the results of the discipline she had imposed on herself during her courtesan years: "the wooing music of her sweet and silvery voice, the winning, winding caresses of her lithe arms and slender figure, all the vocabulary of a loving woman's self-surrendering abandon. . . ."

Such charms are not taught at dramatic academies or learned in the privacy of the study. To heighten reality is the actor's task, to mine the vein of experience his obligation. And so, subtly but surely, Sarah's frivolous, promiscuous years contributed to the fascination of her stage presence and enriched her artistry.

Like Henry James's Miriam Rooth, she could have said of the "base, bad world: Make it pay, without mercy, knock it silly, squeeze it dry. That's what it's meant for—to pay for art." Sarah, like Miriam (surely James had Bernhardt in mind when he wrote *The Tragic Muse*), never lost sight of her goal.

She had been "at liberty" for more than two years when in 1866 she wrote to Camille Doucet for an appointment. He had helped her get into the Comédie Française; perhaps he would help her once again. Doucet sent for her the next day. After a scathing lecture, condemning her uncontrollable temper, her indiscreet life, and her unpolitic behavior, he offered to recommend her to Félix Duquesnel, the associate director of the Théâtre de l'Odéon, France's second national theatre. There was one condition, he said sternly; she must promise to behave. Sarah promised and wept, but she was smiling through her tears. She knew her clever Aunt Rosine had invited Doucet to dine later in the week and that he would surely prefer to bring good rather than bad news to the family table.

Duquesnel, one of Paris's master directors, never forgot his first meeting with Sarah. He had sent her a letter, but received no reply when, as he wrote:

One day, my chambermaid entered my room in a panic and said, "Monsieur, Monsieur, there is a Chinese lady here who insists on seeing you!" Rather intrigued, as I had no relations in the Middle Kingdom, I motioned her to show in the "Chinese lady." Then, before my eyes, appeared the most ideal charmer one could dream of, Sarah Bernhardt in all the brilliant, the indescribable splendor of her youth. She was more than pretty, much more dangerous than that! . . . She was dressed in a tunic of light-colored crêpe de chine with iridescent embroidery, of a Chinese cut that left her bare arms and shoulders lightly veiled with lace. She sported a small plumed fan at her waist. On her head sat a coolie hat of finely woven straw hung all round with bells that trembled at her slightest movement.

Our interview was short as we understood each other instantly. I felt that I was face to face with a marvellously gifted creature of rare intelligence and limitless will-power. Artistry emanated from her entire being. All she needed was to be set on the right path, to be exposed to the public. What can I say about her voice? Pure as crystal, it went straight to the heart like celestial music. I was conquered, body and soul. . . .

Sarah too was conquered. She could not imagine that anyone so young, so elegant, so charming and cheerful could be a director. At the end of the interview, Duquesnel asked her to come back at two that afternoon to meet his superior, Charles de Chilly. Sarah dreaded the encounter. She had auditioned for Chilly once before, and he had not liked her looks, her voice, or her reputation. Nonetheless, she who was always late arrived on the minute, only to be kept waiting for more than an hour. Like most unpunctual people, Sarah thought it unforgivably rude of others to keep her waiting.

"I began to gnash my teeth," she remembered, "and only my promise to Doucet prevented me from walking out." At last Duquesnel appeared. Now, he said with a conspiratorial grin, she would meet the other ogre. Five minutes later Chilly, a testy ex-actor, rushed into the room, studied Sarah from head to toe, and, without a word, presented her with a contract. Then he pointed an accusing finger at Duquesnel and barked: "You know it's he who's responsible.* Had I been alone in this, I would never have given you a contract." Never at a loss for words, Sarah snapped: "Monsieur de Chilly, had you been alone in this, I would never have signed it." There was good

*As associate director, Duquesnel was allowed to engage two actors without Chilly's approval and was guaranteed full directorship in the event of his resignation or death.

reason for her outburst. The contract was valid for one month, to be extended only on condition that she proved satisfactory. Sarah swallowed her pride and signed the humiliating document. At least she was back in the theatre.

On 15 August 1866, the Odéon presented a gala evening to honor the emperor's birthday. Sarah played Aricie in *Phèdre* and Silvia in Marivaux's delightful *Le Jeu de l'Amour et du Hasard.* Her Aricie went well enough, but the rococo Marivaux was out of her line. To add to her troubles, her white satin costume, covered with red and blue ribbons and bows, did not suit her. Chilly could hardly wait to complain to Duquesnel. That so-called actress of his was awful, he told Sarah's admirer. Her diction was bad and her voice even worse. As for that tricolor dress, she looked as though she were about to burst into the Marseillaise! Box-office receipts were bad enough without her. The girl must go.

Duquesnel had faith in Sarah and offered to pay part of her salary out of his own pocket if Chilly would agree to keep her on. The arrangement, it was understood, must be kept secret. But there are few, if any, secrets in the theatre. Before long, the entire company knew that Duquesnel was sleeping with his protégée. And enjoying it, as he said, "body and soul."

On 14 January 1867, Sarah made her official debut at the Odéon as Armande in Molière's *Les Femmes Savantes.* Less than a century had passed since Marie-Antoinette had honored the theatre with her presence. At that time it was known as the Théâtre Français de l'Odéon. But France, ever the quick-change artist, was to rename it with each successive government. With the adoption of the Declaration of the Rights of Man in 1789 it was decided that Théâtre de la Nation was more suitable. As revolutionary fervor mounted, it was changed to Théâtre de l'Egalité. All things having proved *un*equal, under Napoleon I, it was christened Théâtre de l'Impératrice. As the seesaw of power continued, workmen replaced the gold letters on the façade. With Napoleon in exile, the theatre was dubbed Théâtre Royal. On his return for the One Hundred Days, it reverted to Théâtre de l' Impératrice, only to go back to the Royal when the monarchy was restored. Finally, it became the Théâtre de l'Odéon, a name the neoclassic building suggested in the first place and the name it bears to this day.

In Sarah's time, the Odéon was a Left Bank institution, a center for artists, intellectuals, and students from the Sorbonne, all in the market for novelty spiked with anti-imperialist sentiment. Victor Hugo, grown even grander in exile, was their god; George Sand, their presiding genius.

Oh, the Théâtre de l'Odéon! [Sarah wrote]. It was the theatre I loved more than any other. I left it with regret. We all adored one another, and everyone was happy. It was quite like a continuation of schooldays. The audience was young, Duquesnel was gallant, witty, and bursting with enthusiasm. Often a group of us would play tennis in the Luxembourg Gardens during rehearsals of scenes in which we did not appear.

I would look back at my few months at the Comédie Française where I was surrounded by those stilted, jealous gossips. Or my time at the Gymnase where there was nothing but small talk about hats, dresses, and other nonsense that bore no relation to art. At the Odéon I was content. We thought of nothing but our plays. We rehearsed morning, noon, and night. How I loved that!

I lived in a small pavilion in the Villa Montmorency enclave at Auteuil. To get to the theatre I drove myself along the quais at breakneck speed in a small carriage pulled by two spirited ponies my Aunt Rosine had given me. And despite the brilliant, sunny July days, despite the gaiety of the noisy streets, just to climb the rickety stairs to my dressing room filled me with joy. I shouted *bonjour* to all and sundry. Then I flung my hat and gloves aside and leapt onto the stage, thrilled to be in its boundless shadows at last. A few dim worklights here and there picked out a tree, a tower or a bench. The actors could barely see each other. For me nothing was more invigorating than that germ-laden atmosphere, more cheerful than that gloom, more luminous than that darkness. I wanted to spend my life there for it was there that I felt most alive.

Soon after her debut Sarah received an encouraging notice from Sarcey, who spoke of her charm and the fine future that lay ahead if she were willing to apply herself. Sarah was more than willing. All she needed was an indulgent smile from that capricious goddess of the theatre, Lady Luck. That summer she appeared in the person of George Sand, who had first noticed Sarah in Racine's *Athalie* as restaged by Duquesnel.

Sarah's protector, always on the lookout for new ways to do the classics, had added Mendelssohn's incidental music to *Athalie* as a way of intensifying the drama. Acting students from the Conservatoire were to declaim the spoken choruses. It was a splendid idea, doomed to failure. At the rehearsals, the students, bewildered by the complicated musical cues, floundered about and had to be dismissed. Duquesnel solved the problem. Sarah was both musical and a quick study. Why not use her as a one-woman chorus? Thanks to the years of piano lessons Youle had forced on her, Sarah sailed through with no difficulty. Even the dreaded Chilly was impressed when she memorized her lines overnight. And more impressed when the purity of her diction and her simplicity of manner won bravos on opening night.

Her success brought her an insignificant role in George Sand's *Le Marquis de Villemer*, a novel the author had dramatized with considerable help from Alexandre Dumas *fils*. The play had roused the public to paroxysms of anticlerical protest at its first performance three years earlier. Huge crowds had milled about the Place de l'Odéon, waving their hats and shouting: "Down with the Church! Long live George Sand!" Inside the theatre the audience had been caught up in the kind of violent demonstration Parisians indulge in from time to time. Exhilarated by their own bravado, they hissed and howled, whistled, stamped, and threatened one another with bodily harm. The emperor, who would be driven from his throne four years later, applauded apprehensively. George Sand's son reported that Flaubert "wept like a woman." In retrospect, the scandal is puzzling. *Le Marquis de Villemer* is now as faded as the ink in which it was written, and its hostile references to the Church are barely noticeable. It would not be the last time that social or political content would camouflage indifferent literary quality.

The 1867 revival was not particularly eventful, but it was a fine step up for Sarah, who was overjoyed to find that George Sand had taken to her. Here was a model to emulate; a courageous woman, a magnificent ego, who, with what Henry James called her "monstrous vitality," had challenged the morality of her day yet managed to win a sanctified place in French hearts.

A gentle, charming creature [Sarah wrote], Madame George Sand was extremely shy. She spoke little and smoked incessantly. Her large eyes were full of dreams. Her mouth, though somewhat coarse and heavy, showed great kindness. She had probably been of average height, yet she seemed to have shrunk a little. I looked up to her with romantic tenderness. Had she herself not been the heroine of a beautiful love story?* I used to sit close to her and hold her hand as long as I dared. What enchantment, what sweetness there was in her voice!

*Bernhardt's reference is to George Sand's liaison with Alfred de Musset.

A month after her appearance in *Le Marquis de Villemer*, Sarah played Mariette in *François le Champi*, another George Sand dramatization of one of her novels. It was a shrewd bit of casting. Mariette, as the author described her, is "a pretty young woman, rosy as the dawn . . . lively as a cricket . . . irresponsible, short-tempered and susceptible to compliments." Sarah acted the role with the proper pathos and charm. But her real talent lay elsewhere.

That year the Comédie Française revived Victor Hugo's *Hernani* with resounding success. Eager to give further support to the republican poet, the Odéon asked for permission to present his *Ruy Blas*. The answer was an imperial "No." In its place, Duquesnel decided to mount *Kean*, Dumas' superb portrait of the great English actor and one of the great plays of the nineteenth century. One can imagine what satisfaction it gave the aging author to know that his protégée, now all of twenty-three, would play the seductive Anna Damby to Pierre Berton's Kean and how amused he must have been to find that his admirable leading man was head over heels in love with his leading lady.

If Hugo was the soul of Paris, Dumas was its heart. His name alone brought smiles to Parisian faces. For like his writing, the swaggering mulatto was absurdly, contagiously alive. Paris would not have been Paris without his presence at literary gatherings and state balls, or backstage, arranging assignations with pretty young actresses. Despite their affection for him, the anti-imperialist audience at the February 1868 revival, disappointed by the substitution of *Kean* for *Ruy Blas*, was geared for a fight. The moment Dumas entered his box, Sarah recalled, the students began to howl and stamp their feet in unison. "We want *Ruy Blas!*" they shouted again and again. "Fascinated, my nerves on edge, I watched them through a hole in the curtain. There was the great Dumas, pale with rage, shouting, cursing, and shaking his fist, a useless demonstration which lasted an hour." When finally the curtain rose, a mindless torrent, a crescendo of ear-shattering catcalls and stamping feet stopped the actors in their tracks. And when Sarah entered, outlandishly dressed as an Englishwoman of the 1820s, the tumult turned to wild guffaws. Momentarily terror-stricken, she clung to the door through which she had entered. At that moment, those she called "my dear friends, the students" began their counterattack.

As young and fiery as the students themselves, Sarah strode down to the footlights. "You want to defend the cause of justice?" she shouted above the din. "Do you think you are encouraging justice by holding Alexandre

Dumas responsible for Victor Hugo's exile?" Silence fell. With a radiant Joan of Arc smile, Sarah stepped back into character. As the play went on, jeers turned into cheers. At the final curtain the noisy zealots, recognizing Sarah as one of their own, greeted her with fraternal enthusiasm. Backstage Chilly was all smiles. Duquesnel had been right after all. The girl had quality and deserved not only a pat on the back but a raise in salary.

Some days later Sarah opened *L'Opinion Nationale* to read: "Mlle Bernhardt appeared in an eccentric costume that made the storm even wilder, but her warm voice, her astonishing voice, moved the public. Like a little Orpheus she had tamed it." Sarah was on her way at last. At the end of the season Sarah played three other roles, including Cordelia in *King Lear*. Théophile Gautier wrote of her grace and the beauty of her death scene. And the audience took *la petite Sarah* to their hearts. All that was needed was a role which would give full scope to her gifts.

IN   J A N U A R Y   1 8 6 9,   Agar, a voluptuous beauty who was the Odéon's leading tragedienne, asked Sarah to read *Le Passant*, a one-act play by a little-known young poet named François Coppée. Set in a Renaissance Florentine garden, it tells the story of an ecstatic encounter between Silvia, an aging courtesan, and a young troubador called Zanetto. Coppée, timid, pocket-sized, and panting with love for the statuesque Agar, had created, in Silvia, the perfect role for his mistress, who told him that one of her young comrades, the slender, charming Bernhardt, was born to play Zanetto. Their only problem was to convince Chilly to produce the lyric duologue. Duquesnel remembered Agar bursting into the director's office. "Brandishing a sheaf of papers, she cried, 'Monsieur de Chilly, Monsieur de Chilly, I've discovered a masterpiece!'

" 'In verse?' Chilly asked suspiciously. 'In admirable verse,' the actress replied in sonorous tones. 'All verse is admirable,' Chilly sniffed." It took a good deal of flirtatious wheedling to persuade the director to read the manuscript, but once he had, skepticism turned to enthusiasm and he accepted the play for one or two performances. The décor would be a hand-me-down from another production, Sarah would play the ardent minstrel boy, and Jules Massenet would compose a serenade for her entrance.*

Written in what might be called hand-tinted verse, *Le Passant* is all high-flown romance and renunciation. The troubador wanders into a moonlit garden, declares his love to the world-weary courtesan, and, the next morning, goes on his way as his lady sighs: "What a gift is love that gives me back my tears!"

Four days after the premiere, Sarah opened *L'Opinion Nationale* to read:

> *Le Passant* enchanted the public, overcome with surprise and admiration. The short play appears to be a masterpiece—tender, poetic, and graceful. Perhaps it twitters too much of azure skies and green fields, but the poetry is exquisitely elegant.
>
> Mlle Bernhardt, the Zanetto, looked like Dubois's sculpture, *The Florentine Minstrel* [Sarah's costume was, in fact, copied from that popular statue], and spoke her delicious lines with delicacy and charm. If she was a little precious here and there, it was a preciousness that added charm to her characterization. The public, ravished by her performance, called her back again and again. A triumph!

The article was signed by Francisque Sarcey, Bernhardt's increasingly enthusiastic admirer. Like many a critic, then as now, he had mistaken tinsel for gold. With the passage of time, *Le Passant* has lost its luster. Still, at twenty-four Sarah had arrived. Photographs of her as Zanetto suggest the quality of her achievement. The pictures speak of her poetic intensity, her instinct for apposite gesture, and, above all, her passionate identification with the character she portrays. She created a romantic icon for her time, a tender symbol of young love which even cynical Paris took to its heart.

---

*In Coppée's charming memoirs, *Souvenir d'un Parisien*, he tells how for this serenade, "*Mignonne, voici l'Avril*," the conductor, Annecy, composed a song for Sarah which, "though not as good as the one Massenet later wrote, was very agreeable; and, as in those days every theatre still had a string and woodwind ensemble to play during the entr'actes, Chilly decided to have them provide a discreet accompaniment to my verses now and then. For this purpose, old Annecy made tactful selections from the graceful score of *Giselle*." Years later, Sarah told Reynaldo Hahn that she preferred to sing Annecy's serenade, as Massenet's was full of trills that she found very difficult.

Bernhardt performed *Le Passant* one hundred and forty times with Agar and, when that lady was unavailable, with Marie Colombier. It was her first taste of fame. Manuscripts, love poems "too long to read," flowers, gifts, proposals—decent and indecent—flooded her dressing room. Until *Le Passant*, Bernhardt had been a mere mortal; now she became the students' idol and the poets' muse. "A secret instinct moves her," Théodore de Banville wrote. "She recites verse the way nightingales sing, the way the wind sighs, the way brooks murmur, the way Lamartine wrote in days gone by."

To crown their success Agar and Bernhardt gave a command performance at the Tuileries. The honor seemed all the sweeter when Sarah recalled Napoleon III's wrath at her recital of Victor Hugo's poems. This time the emperor was all smiles, particularly when he caught her unawares backstage, perfecting her curtsy and intoning *"Sire, Sire"* over and over again in an attempt to find the proper court inflection. Sarah, in turn, was amused by the sight of the empress, her dignity diminished by the loss of a shoe, hobbling out on the arm of an impassive courtier.

PART THREE

LOVE AND WAR

Sarah in the late 1860s

I T W A S during this period that Bernhardt, who was to be the chief inspiration for the actress Berma in Proust's *Remembrance of Things Past*, met Charles Haas, Proust's model for Charles Swann. From a Proustian view, they were characters lost in time, in search of a novelist yet unborn, for they met two years before Proust's birth and forty years before he began to weave them into his tapestry of Parisian life. Bernhardt is remembered for her splendid achievements; "Haas," as Proust was to write, "despite the fact that he produced nothing, will be remembered because someone he considered a young idiot made him the hero of one of his books." Yet at the time of their meeting Haas was the catch and Sarah the lucky girl who caught him.

"Monsieur Second Empire," as Charles Haas's friends affectionately called him, was a leading light of Parisian society. One of the few Jewish members of the Jockey Club, he was an intimate friend of the Prince of Wales and of the painters Tissot and Degas and a favorite with the ladies and gentlemen of the faubourg Saint Germain. A man of immense distinction, Haas had the best tailor in a well-tailored town. But it was not only his perfect frock coat and the fresh gardenia in his buttonhole that attracted Sarah; it was his reputation as a ladies' man, and his willingness, rare in Second Empire roués, to share his cultivated views on art and life with a mere actress.

In Sarah's letters to Haas, we see her in her mid-twenties, girlish, vulnerable, and seductively vulgar, playing a role she thought might satisfy her new lover's ripe urbanity and his taste for low life. Her instinct was sound. In his eyes, she belonged to the world of loose women with whom gentlemen condescended to fornicate when not occupied with higher social duties.

In one of her first letters to Haas, Sarah made a pretty drawing of a
rumpled four-poster bed, beneath which she scribbled "Come! Come!!
Come!!!" The crescendo of exclamation points suggests that he had lived up
to his reputation as a lady-killer. Another note, equally suggestive in its
punctuation, reads: "I'm absolutely dying to——see you. I have a thousand
lovers but only one who is the real thing." Such unbuttoned messages—so
unlike the aloof tone of the ladies of the faubourg—were not enough to keep
Haas faithful to Sarah, as one can see by the letters that follow:

Mon Charles adoré,
I cannot retract my words. I love you. I know perfectly well that you don't
return my love but please behave as though you did. Dear friend, come
to me at three o'clock. It would give me so much pleasure. Who knows?
perhaps I missed a *good deal* by not showing up last night!!! Do you like
my way of putting it? Come, and give me your lips.

Thank you for your letters, my dear love. Above all, thank you for your
visits. No, really, I'm doubled up with laughter! Come double up with me
in. . . . laughter, of course. I send twice the kisses you sent me. What
an avalanche! Please send a message, a less ethereal one this time. . . .

Sarah's frivolity turned to gloom when she discovered through their mutual
friend, the publisher Arthur Meyer, that she was not Haas's only mistress.

. . . It's all the same to me but it does make me a little sad. I know I'm
being ridiculous but this is hardly the moment to try to make me laugh.
I'm ill, and my lungs are acting up again. Come back as soon as possible,
dear Charles. I long to see you. I have always clung to my childish vision
of the ideal man despite everything. I thought I would never find him.
Then, by chance, I met someone with all the physical and moral qualities
I cherish. I risked all to add this rare flower to my bouquet, as I do not
wish to die before my dream is fulfilled. You see I live for love, with
fantasy as my guide. It explains my nervous melancholia. I had always
hoped to find my direct complement, but alas when I did, he proved to
be too devious. That is why I reached out to you, Charles, that is why I
gave myself to you. That is why I love you.
My hand, all my being goes out to you. . . .

The ideal man Sarah refers to as the source of her disillusion is, of course, the Prince de Ligne, who had left her with a wound that would not heal. How could it, when her son, Maurice, looking more like his father every day, was a constant reminder of her lost love? When the debonair Haas decided the time had come to part from his little actress friend, he tried to make the break as cheerful as possible, but Sarah took it hard:

> All this is heavy drama for someone as light-hearted as you. If it gives you a good laugh so much the better. It has only brought me tears. Farewell, my dear Charles. I adore you. If you cannot return my love it is not your fault. Nor is it mine. . . .

At the end of their affair, Haas discreetly paid her off.

"I accept," Sarah wrote, "but only if it's a loan. Thank you, dear friend, thank you."

They were to remain friends until Haas's death in 1902. As though to mark the end of their affair, one evening when Haas and Arthur Meyer were dining with Sarah in her apartment at 16 rue Auber, a fire broke out, ruining the apartment and everything in it. No one was hurt, but Sarah, who was not insured, was left homeless and penniless.

There was a surge of sympathy when the accident was reported in the newspapers. Letters and poems of consolation arrived. One such effusion, addressed to "Le Passant," suggested that a free spirit like hers needed neither possessions nor ornaments: "Your bracelets? Your naked arms, like those of Venus, will gleam without them! Your diamonds? Your luminous eyes will sparkle without them! . . ."

Sarah was not moved by these unworldly sentiments. Nor was Duquesnel, who helped her recoup her losses by arranging a gala Bernhardt benefit at the Odéon. To everyone's surprise, the internationally famous opera star Adelina Patti was among the artists who contributed their services—a surprise since the great diva was not given to warbling for the benefit of anyone but herself. Who had bagged La Patti was the question around town. The answer was: Sarah herself. The young coloratura had recently married the Marquis de Caux, a charter member of Bernhardt's menagerie. Not above a little blackmail, Sarah had promised to be discreet if he could persuade his bride to donate her trills and roulades. "I made them both 'sing,' " Sarah gleefully confided to Marie Colombier.

Patti enchanted the public, which demanded two encores of Rossini's *"Una voce poco fa."* "Feverish with the love of art," as Sarah put it, the students stood on their seats and created such a shouting, stamping, Left Bank rumpus that the terrified singer did not know whether to take a bow or run for cover. When she left the theatre, she was escorted by a group of fervent young music lovers whose cries of "Vive la Patti!" may have compensated her for raising her voice gratis. The proceeds were impressive, and Sarah, who had been forced to take refuge at her mother's, was able to rent a small apartment in the rue de l'Arcade, then soon afterward move to a larger apartment at 4 rue de Rome, where she would remain for the next five years. A phoenix risen from the ashes, she was more than ever in the public eye.

In 1870, Sarah was given the leading role in *L'Autre*, a new play written and directed by George Sand. As it was the plum of the season, she felt close to the great lady and did not hesitate to confide in her as they strolled along the gravelled paths of the Luxembourg Gardens. That her confidences about her life, loves, and ambitions were falling on somewhat callous ears did not occur to her.

Entries in the journal the author kept while she was directing *L'Autre* show Sarah's "gentle, charming creature" in a rather cantankerous mood.

29 Jan. At the rehearsal [Pierre] Berton made quite a scene with Sarah. Will she be sulky tomorrow?

2 Feb. I scold Sarah.

3 Feb. They are all coming along nicely except Sarah. A good girl, but decidedly stupid.

5 Feb. In many respects Sarah is stupid, but she has a charming nature.

9 Feb. Sarah and Berton absent. Jeanne [Bernhardt] had a miscarriage.

10 Feb. Mlle Sarah keeps us waiting, really doesn't give a damn about her sister, hasn't worked, and interprets her role like the great tart she is.

10 Feb. It's Sarah, the tart, who doesn't get the point of her role. How stupid these creatures of the theatre are!

14 Feb. I'm afraid Mlle Sarah is dotty but everyone says she'll be fine.

20 Feb. All the acting has improved, especially Sarah's. She was jolted

by my reproaches. At last she has identified with the young, honest, and interesting character.

26 Feb. The chief success is Pierre. Sarah too.

One might think the champion of the underprivileged would have been above the general contempt for actors prevalent at the time. Certainly her "stupid creatures of the theatre" are not more stupid than other people. On the contrary, they have an instinctive intelligence, a wit and a gift for observation that is their own. One would imagine that her long years as a playwright would have accustomed the author of *Consuelo* to the searchings and flounderings that go into the creation of a role, just as one would think she might have understood Sarah's concern about her sister's miscarriage. It was perhaps this lack of sensitivity that enabled George Sand to make love to the handsome Italian doctor in the legendary Venetian hotel room while his patient, her young lover Alfred de Musset, looked on from his sickbed. As for Sand's name-calling, she had reached the age of celibacy and chose to forget the greedy promiscuity of her earlier years. It is clear that she was repelled by the idea of accepting money in return for love when she refers to Sarah as a tart. Yet in her much-vaunted search for sexual satisfaction, the suffering she inflicted on her lovers was surely more costly than a mere exchange of currency.

Sarah knew nothing about her friend's unpublished journal, but she was fully aware of her own success in *L'Autre* when Théophile Gautier, less grudging in his praise than George Sand, said it was her finest creation. "Young and charming," he wrote, "Bernhardt has that quality, chaste and audacious, of a real girl who knows nothing, fears nothing, and reproaches herself with nothing. There is a note of tenderness both moving and sympathetic in her performance."

The curtain came down on Sarah's burgeoning career when on 19 July 1870 Napoleon III declared war on Prussia. The emperor's decision was suicidal. He had until then carefully avoided a war with Prussia. Now, it appeared, he had swallowed his own propaganda and was determined to prove that France was not only the most civilized of nations, but the mightiest as well. He might have hesitated had he done his homework, for while he boasted about *la gloire*, Prussia was hard at work making powerful weapons of war.

Paris had seen evidence of Prussia's power at the Great Exposition three years earlier. Herr Krupp had displayed a new fifty-ton gun and a steel cannon (until then cannons had been cast in bronze) which he presented to the emperor. The ladies of the court were enchanted. Napoleon III, on the other hand, was more taken with the novel substance called aluminum and ordered an imperial dinner service made of the amazingly light metal. The exhibition was dashingly up to date. The Americans introduced Edison's astonishing electric light bulb as well as modern medical kits and a new kind of chair on rockers. The English sent railroad trains. Nadar flew visitors over the exhibition grounds in a double-decker balloon, while *bateaux mouches*, the last word in sight-seeing boats, chugged up and down the Seine.

"Art elbowed Industry," Gautier reported, "with white statues next to black machines." Music played its part as well. Gounod's *Romeo et Juliette* was given for the first time, and Offenbach presented *La Grande Duchesse de Gérolstein*, an operetta about blundering Teutonic stupidity that had Bismarck rolling in the aisles. Alas, the French, who prided themselves on their subtlety, did not understand the Iron Chancellor's laughter until they were defeated by the Prussian army.

The pleasures of life are quick to disappear in a city threatened by war. Theatres closed their doors as actors were called to arms. Sarah, concerned for her family, managed with great difficulty to find places for them on a train bound for Le Havre and safety. As she stood on the platform of the Gare Saint Lazare, she was overcome by regret. Her first impulse had been to leave with them: Maurice had never been far from her side. As for Youle, Jeanne, and Régine, it was one thing to feel ambivalent about them, another to watch them wave their sad adieus from the overcrowded wartime train. Yet just as she could not imagine leaving the stage during a performance, so she could not bring herself to leave Paris at a moment of such high drama. And so in the vague hope that she could be useful in some way, she went back to her empty apartment in the rue de Rome.

Sarah was not at a loss for long. The actresses of the Comédie Française had converted part of their theatre into a convalescent hospital for the wounded. Why not do the same with the Odéon? All that was needed was permission from the prefect of police. Sarah felt apprehensive when, a few days later, she entered police headquarters in the Tuileries. But the moment she was ushered into the prefect's office she knew that all was well, that love's labors had not been lost, for he was none other than the Comte de

Kératry, her handsome lover of long ago. Breathlessly, Sarah plunged in: she would need bread, milk, meat, vegetables, sugar, potatoes, eggs, coffee—and a permit to open a convalescent hospital. Full of fond memories, Kératry assured her she would be supplied "above and beyond her wishes." But too much was never enough for Sarah. She caught sight of his luxurious fur-lined coat and wanted it for one of her soldiers. Kératry laughed uproariously and gave it to her. As he emptied the pockets, he asked if she would allow him to keep his silk scarf. With mock resignation, she agreed.

Encouraged by her success, Sarah went scavenging for more. Donations poured in. The Rothschilds sent casks of wine and brandy. Her onetime neighbor Félix Potin delivered rice, lentils, and sardines, while the great chocolate manufacturers, the Meniers, provided chocolate. An old school friend supplied quantities of salted butter. And her grandmother's sister Betzy sent "three hundred magnificent nightshirts" all the way from Holland. Soon the Odéon was bustling with activity. Sarah's cook was installed at an immense coal stove. Cook's husband was commandeered to run the cumbersome horse-drawn ambulance. And Sarah, Guérard, and Marie Colombier, splendid in their voluminous nurses' uniforms, were ready for action. There was only one problem: the wounded failed to appear.

"Sarah was forced to sit in idleness," Marie recalled. "The artiste paced the balcony looking out, like Sister Anne, to see if anyone was coming. Oh, how she would have blessed the sight of a Red Cross ambulance with a nice, lame, interesting soldier, one of those that one bandages, that one operates on with shiny instruments. For two pins she would have taken her revolver and shot someone, just to have a real patient. But let me hasten to add that when the wounded finally did arrive, the actress took care of them with tender solicitude and absolute devotion."

This was high praise from Sarah's ironic second-in-command. Sadly enough, when at last the casualties were brought in, they arrived in horrifying numbers. Beds were set up in the auditorium, the dressing rooms, the bar, and the foyer. Even the stage was filled with the mutilated and the dying. Until then Sarah had thought of the war as martial allegory, exciting but remote. Now it became an ugly reality. A few months earlier, thousands of foot soldiers and cavalry, proud of their colorful uniforms, had paraded through the boulevards, shouting *"À Berlin! À Berlin!"* with naïve optimism. Now the thunder of Krupp's cannons could be heard as the Prussians encircled the French capital in a deadly embrace.

Ah! The injustice of war! [Sarah wrote]. Will that dreamed-of moment never come when war is no longer possible? When a monarch who calls for war will be dethroned and imprisoned as an evil-doer? Will the time never come when an international group, composed of the wise men of each country, meets to discuss the rights of man with respect? So many men think as I do! So many women speak as I do! Yet nothing is done. . . .

N O   O N E   was prepared for the arctic blasts that swept through Paris in January 1871. Fuel was so scarce that the scaffolding of half-completed buildings, the shutters of houses, the benches of the Luxembourg Gardens, even the props and the seats of the Odéon were chopped up for firewood. Frostbitten women and children huddled together in the entryway of the theatre. Street lamps, those sentinels of the night, stood unlit for months. Famine threatened. Cattle, which had been herded into the public squares, were slaughtered and eaten. Dogs and cats were no longer seen on the streets, and Castor and Pollux, two baby elephants that had been the joy of Parisian children, disappeared from the zoo at the Jardin des Plantes.

One fashionable butcher hung wolf meat in his shop window. Another offered, "at a special price," two race horses which had been presented to Napoleon III by the tsar. Kangaroo was served at Brébant's, the hangout of the literati, and Victor Hugo, back from exile, was sent gifts of bear and antelope. As might be expected, a black market sprang up, and the well-fed pooh-poohed the complaints of the hungry. But the French were still capable of laughter, as a menu concocted by some die-hard wit would indicate: Horse Consommé with Millet; Skewered Dogs' Kidneys, *maître d'hôtel*; Saddle of Cat, *sauce mayonnaise*; Begonias *au jus*; and Plum Pudding with Rum and Horse Marrow.

As the Germans drew close, they began to bombard the Left Bank night and day. The result was chaos. Twenty thousand residents fled their homes with their belongings on their backs. Yet, like Londoners during the blitz, Parisians were fascinated by the spectacle of war.* Crowds gathered in the Place de la Concorde to watch the bombs fall on Saint-Cloud. A mother was heard to say to her child: "This is the last bombardment I'll take you to, unless you stop your fidgeting." The painter Auguste Renoir remembered an absent-minded friend asking who was firing when a shell exploded near his house.

Many did not escape so easily. One day Sarah sent a young boy to a nearby pharmacy for medical supplies. As she leaned out the window to hurry him on, he turned to give her a reassuring smile. At that instant he was killed by a bomb.

> Oh what horror [she wrote], what awful horror! The poor child's intestines had spilled onto the ground, his chest and his chubby red face had been flayed. No eyes, no nose, no mouth, nothing, nothing! Only a lock of bloody hair at the end of a shapeless mass a yard from where his lifeless body lay. It was as though a tiger had mauled the poor corpse with rage and refinement.

When the Odéon district itself was bombarded, Sarah was forced to move her patients to the cavernous basement below. It was useless. The frozen pipes had burst, rank sewage lay inches deep, and hungry rats scurried about the beds trying to gnaw at the invalids' flesh. There was nothing to do but close the theatre and send the most serious cases to the Val-de-Grâce military hospital. Sarah rented an empty apartment for the others and, with Guérard's help, nursed them back to health. By this time Marie Colombier had defected, saying that for Sarah war work was just a way to draw attention to herself. Marie's complaints notwithstanding, Sarah was heroic. Although she was far from well, and miserable with no news of her family, she found the strength to participate in war-effort benefit performances, to spend sleepless nights with the wounded, and to comfort the dying on the frozen battlefields. If, as Marie said, she was playing a role, she played it with a single-mindedness that won the hearts of her countrymen and gave her a new and lasting self-respect.

*One newspaper advertisement read: "Notice for the benefit of English gentlemen wishing to attend the Siege of Paris: Comfortable apartments, completely shell-proof. Rooms in basement for impressionable persons." And as one of the English gentlemen observed: "Everyone enjoyed it hugely."

Toward the end of the siege, Sarah received word from her mother through the American ambassador. All was well. Youle had taken the entire family from Le Havre to Bad Homburg, a spa near Frankfurt. They were safe and sound, and Sarah was not to worry. Sarah was more than worried; she was appalled. Her enemies had always claimed she was German. Now after months of service to her country, her own mother had managed to add fuel to the xenophobic flame. In desperation, Sarah left for Germany soon after the armistice was signed. Eleven days later, after harrowing trips by coal train, garbage wagon, and peasant cart, she collected her family and, with "Maurice tight in her arms," took them all back to France.

There were new horrors to face at home. The French, humiliated and embittered by the defeat at Sedan, had turned on one another in a bloody civil war. The oppressive regime of Louis-Napoleon's *notables* crumbled; in Paris workers, artisans, and disaffected riffraff embarked on the world's first experiment in communism. The Commune did not last long. Within twelve months, brutal and efficient repression by the French army laid the foundations of the Third Republic. Sarah had never given a thought to social issues. A child of the Second Empire, she had taken its display of wealth and its indifference to poverty as a matter of course. Hers was a narrow existence. Work in the theatre followed by gay supper parties hardly led to an interest in the inhumanly long hours and the miserable living conditions of the working class.

If the Franco-Prussian War was chauvinistic, xenophobic melodrama, the Commune was drama of a more complicated, fratricidal sort. With Napoleon III a prisoner in Germany, Sarah watched his political enemies, muzzled for almost twenty years, tearing at each other's throats. Once again *Liberté, Egalité,* and *Fraternité* were dangled before a hopeful people; once again they proved to be a mirage. Sarah was both intrigued and revolted by the brutal, self-seeking machinations that masqueraded as love of *la patrie.* Yet she felt the Commune was an awakening of sorts, a "life after death." For her, "life after death" meant being in the thick of things, and soon such powerful political figures as Léon Gambetta, Henri de Rochefort, Emile de Girardin, and Paul de Rémusat were among her friends. "Each of them interested me, even the wildest, the most extreme," she wrote. (And each of them was to play a role in the founding of the Third Republic.) During this time, one hundred thousand people left Paris. When one considers what Clemenceau described as "the pathological blood-lust that possessed Parisians under the Commune," the exodus is readily understood. Paris, which had been ravaged by the Prussians, was about to be destroyed by the Parisians themselves. During the negotiations of the peace treaty between France and Prussia, the French National Army reassembled its forces at Versailles and laid siege to Paris while the victorious Germans looked on from the surrounding countryside.

Sarah herself took refuge in nearby Saint-Germain-en-Laye, where she joined hundreds of incongruously well-dressed Parisians to watch, unbelieving, as their beloved city went up in flames. At her side was her latest admirer, Captain Arthur O'Connor, an aristocratic Irishman attached to the French National Army. O'Connor, it was said, had been plucked by Sarah from the bed of her sixteen-year-old sister, Régine. Be that as it may, it was a sad truth that Sarah's troubled youngest sister had become a prostitute and, sadder still, a prostitute with only two and a half years to live.

While Paris burned, Sarah and O'Connor made love and went riding in the forest of Versailles. Their excursions were not without danger as the woods were alive with armed rebels. One evening a Communard tried to shoot O'Connor. The bullet strayed, Sarah's horse reared, and she was thrown to the ground. She was about to remount when O'Connor turned on his assailant and shot him. Before he could deliver the *coup de grâce*, Sarah stepped in, and begged him to let the fellow live.

"I could scarcely recognize my friend," she wrote. This handsome, very proper man—a bit of a snob, but charming—had turned into a brute." Their friendship continued, but Sarah, haunted by the scene, said she was always to see a killer behind O'Connor's smiling face. The captain was not Sarah's only lover. In classic courtesan tradition, she had two. One, her *amant de coeur*, had a hold on her heart and access to her bed when it was not otherwise occupied. The other provided her with an allowance and had first claim on her time. O'Connor was her *amant de coeur*, Jacques Stern, a rich banker, her source of income. The situation called for discretion and manipulation. Sarah had little talent for either. Indeed, as soon as she became financially independent she tended to give herself to attractive young artists rather than sell herself to affluent old men. But in 1871 she was still the maladroit cocotte, as Marie Colombier hastened to point out:

O'Connor had fallen in love with Sarah. There were jealous scenes as he could not bear Stern and found the situation humiliating. To be the lover of a woman kept by another man was, he felt, unworthy of his rank. One day, having won fifty thousand francs at his club, he rushed to Sarah's. "My angel," he cried, waving his wallet, "here's a pretty collection of francs. Now do me a favor. Show your banker the door and allow me to make love to you whenever I choose." Sarah did not say Yes or No. But she plotted her next move. The next time Stern was in her boudoir she had the chambermaid interrupt them to say that there was a man at the door demanding instant payment on an overdue bill.

"Darling, give me ten thousand francs to settle this stupid matter," Sarah cooed. The financier turned a deaf ear to her request. She knew he wasn't stingy, he said, but, as he had just paid her three months in advance, he really couldn't be expected to do more. . . . "So that's how it is!" Sarah said. "You don't seem to realize that it's purely out of love that I come to you for money. O'Connor offered me fifty thousand francs to leave you. What a fool I am! I had only to say the word."

"Really, my dear," Stern replied, stroking his sideburns; "and I thought you were an intelligent woman. What! O'Connor offers you fifty thousand, and you hesitate! Take it. I'll be your *amant de coeur*."

And so O'Connor gave her the fifty thousand francs, became her official lover, and was able to hold his head up without blushing. As for Stern, he philosophically rubbed his hands, feeling that he had made a splendid deal. As things worked out, every Sunday Sarah lunched with him and found twenty-five thousand francs under her serviette. In that way he paid only half her former monthly allowance. When O'Connor rejoined his regiment, Sarah tried to get Stern back on the old terms, but he refused. Finally he broke with her completely. Ten years later he would marry Sophie Croizette, Sarah's childhood friend, and future rival at the Comédie Française.

In the last week of May 1871, the French army killed what has variously been estimated as between twenty and thirty-six thousand Parisians and the Commune was at an end. It was then that the history of the Third Republic may be said to have begun. Fortunately, Sarah's apartment had been spared, but the Paris she had known was gone forever. The Communards had set fire to the Palais de Justice, the palace of the Tuileries, and the magnificent Hôtel de Ville along with many theatres and churches. Entire streets had disappeared. Piles of stones, plaster, and broken glass spoke of the millions of francs of damage from the six weeks of fighting between the French army and the Communards. All that remained, it seemed, was gloom and an inescapable stench, an acrid reminder of France's shame.

Bitterly disillusioned, Sarah sprayed her rooms with perfume, drew the curtains, and waited for life to begin again. One day, Monsieur de Chilly called on her to say that the Odéon was being restored and a new play was under consideration. She, of course, would play the lead. Stretched out on her chaise longue, the actress breathed a weary "No." Chilly rose to leave, but he knew what he was about. At the door, he muttered the name of a rival actress he would be forced to take instead. He had touched a nerve. "Oh Chilly, darling Chilly," Sarah cried, jumping to her feet. "When do we start?" She was back in harness, eager to rehearse for an October opening. The play which lured her back into the theatre was André Theuriet's *Jeanne-Marie*, an Enoch Arden-like tale of a Breton girl who marries under the mistaken impression that her fiancé has died at sea.* Bernhardt and Paul Porel, who played the fiancé, moved the audience to tears. It was a touching moment for actors and public alike, as everyone knew that she had nursed his wounds in this same theatre only a few months before. Ten days later, Sarah appeared in Coppée's *Fais ce que Dois* (*Do What You Must*), a patriotic curtain raiser of little consequence. It marked the Odéon debut of her sister Jeanne, who had been performing and sleeping around town since the age of seventeen. Sarah, who remembered her own early failures, was optimistic. Her beautiful sister, she promised Chilly, would work hard and cover herself with glory. Her prediction was sadly inaccurate as Jeanne was a mediocre actress, addicted to drugs. Sarah, however, was able to arrange a three-year contract for Marie Colombier with far more gratifying results, as Marie was talented and, unlike Jeanne, she amused Sarah.

A letter Sarah had sent her after a tour of German spas in *Le Passant* gives the tone of their camaraderie:

Paris, August 1869

. . . I'm bored to death, do you understand, to death! I love you, darling Marie, I really do. I'm working hard, but I'm terribly tired because of a nasty cold I caught on the train. My purse is getting empty, and I see the day when I won't have a sou. But we've been through that before.

My son returned from his trip yesterday morning. What a magnificent

---

*Many years later, Sarah was to play this role in a private performance for Queen Victoria in Nice.

beauty he is! You'll see! There's not a soul here. Nothing but monsters, and not even gilded ones at that. Imagine big, leaden butterflies fluttering around your frail *demoiselle* Sarah. It's really not worth the effort to net them unless some of their gold dust sticks to one's fingers. Am I being Jewish enough?

A thousand kisses and hugs

There was a big change in Sarah from the free-and-easy prewar girl who wrote that letter and the woman who had seen the horrors of war and worked tirelessly to help those who were its victims. She was not exaggerating when she told Chilly that she was exhausted. It was no easy matter for her to return to her former brilliance, and, quite understandably, the same could be said of the Odéon theatre itself.

In November 1871, it presented her in *La Baronne*, the story of a woman driven mad when unjustly confined in an asylum who regains her sanity, kills the enemy who sent her to the asylum, then successfully feigns madness to avoid punishment. Even the melodrama-loving audience found the plot ridiculous, and the play was quickly forgotten.

Hopes were higher when in January 1872 Sarah was cast in the title role of *Mademoiselle Aïssé*, a play in verse by Louis Bouilhet, directed and designed by Gustave Flaubert. Bouilhet, whose earlier plays enjoyed a certain success, had died two years earlier and Flaubert, his devoted friend, was determined to reaffirm his talent to an uncaring world. Sarah, Marie Colombier, and Paul Porel applauded and wept when the gruff Flaubert, visibly moved, read Bouilhet's lines to them. But hard work—Flaubert even had the seductive Marie Colombier in for private lessons—did not bring the piece to life. The audience was not amused by a play that bore too many startling resemblances to Dumas' *La Dame aux Camélias*. *Le Figaro* found Sarah's performance as the heroine "dignified and sensitive on the whole," but complained that her lack of physical strength often limited her voice to a dull lugubrious sound and warned her to guard against the resultant monotony. Colombier, however, was considered perfectly suited to the role of a debauched *intrigante*. With another failure on its hands, the Odéon, and Bernhardt, were desperately in need of a hit, and a distinguished hit at that. Victor Hugo was to supply it in spectacular measure.

A F T E R twenty years of exile, Victor Hugo, like a grizzled hero out of Homer, had returned to his country triumphant. Few personalities in literary history have moved their compatriots as he did. A symbol of the republic, through his poetry he gave renewed hope to a defeated people in a downtrodden land.

> *Laissez entrer en vous, après nos deuils funèbres,*
> *L'aube, fille des nuits; l'amour, fils des douleurs.*

> Let in the dawn, after our times of weeping,
> Dawn that is daughter of night, love that is misery's heir.

When Sarah was told that the writer had chosen her to play Doña Maria de Neubourg, the unhappy Queen of Spain in his *Ruy Blas*, she was filled with pride—and misgivings, pride because she had read Hugo's works "with passion," misgivings because her "imbecile court" had convinced her that his politics were odious. And so she felt uneasy when she learned that he expected her to come to him for the first reading instead of meeting on the neutral ground of the theatre:

> When I told my five o'clock court about this, they were outraged. "What! Go to that man who was an outlaw only yesterday, to that nobody who dares ask our idol, our queen of hearts, our magician of magicians, to be at his beck and call. Write him this,—write him that—"

They were helping her to compose impertinent replies when Maréchal Canrobert interrupted. "Show the respect due to genius," he said, "but excuse yourself on the grounds of illness."

Sarah followed Canrobert's advice. "Monsieur," she wrote, "the Queen has taken a chill and her Lady in Waiting forbids her to go out. You, better than anyone, know the etiquette of the Spanish court. Pity your Queen, Monsieur."

The poet, amused to hear echoes of *Ruy Blas* in Sarah's words, answered in the same vein.

> I am your servant, Madame.
> Victor Hugo.

When finally they met, Sarah found it difficult to believe she had allowed herself to be swayed by her menagerie. Here was a fine and gallant gentleman, rumpled perhaps, but with a lordly manner that put her Jockey Club friends to shame. Yet observant actress that she was, she saw him clearly: she found his paunch too big, his nose too common, his lips too heavy, and his glance too lecherous. Such minor drawbacks did not prevent her from flirting, however. While Hugo coached one of the actors, Sarah hoisted herself up onto a table and began to swing her legs. It was the kind of behavior that maddened George Sand during the rehearsals of *L'Autre*. But Victor Hugo was not George Sand. At the sight of Sarah's pretty ankles he rose from his seat in the orchestra and improvised:

> *Une reine d'Espagne, honnête et respectable,*
> *Ne devrait pas ainsi s'asseoir sur une table.*

> A queen of Spain, virtuous and able,
> Must never sit that way upon a table.

Sarah longed to reply, but for once she was speechless.

A momentous event in the history of the French theatre occurred on 19 February 1872: the long-awaited revival of *Ruy Blas*. A brilliant audience welcomed Hugo ecstatically, and Sarah glimmered and shone, as a star should. The very unexpectedness of her appearance dazzled the public. Could this regal creature be the actress they knew, *la petite Sarah*? Hugo's stage directions describe her entrance, dramatically placed just before the fall of the first-act curtain: "The Queen, magnificently dressed, enters under a canopy of scarlet velvet born aloft by four courtiers. She is surrounded by ladies of the court and attendant pages." Impressive though that was, it was the vision of Sarah in the second act that captivated the public. In shimmering white brocade shot with silver thread, an exquisite silver crown on her aristocratic head, she was a matchless work of art. Her performance was a triumph. The grace of her gestures, the beauty of her voice, and her superb declamation of Hugo's verse were considered beyond praise. Théodore de Banville would write of her Doña Sol: "to the end of time the image of Sarah Bernhardt will be evoked whenever Ruy Blas shall say: 'Elle avait un petit diadème en dentelle d'argent.' " ("She wore a little crown of silver filigree.")

Sarcey, who ten years earlier had doubted Sarah's talent, spoke rapturously of her plaintive, melancholy dignity, her noble, harmonious gestures, her poetic grace. For him, her most glorious gift lay in the myriad inflections of her beautiful voice. "Her delivery," he wrote in Le Temps, "is so true in rhythm, so clear in utterance that not a single syllable is lost, even when the words float from her lips like a whispered caress. And how she follows the curve of every speech, allowing it to unfold with never a break, projecting the fluid harmony of its lines! And with what discerning delicacy of intonation she emphasizes certain words, words she invests with extraordinary value!"

About a later performance, he was to write: "With uncanny intuition, Sarah Bernhardt supplied the melody. She sang, yes, she chanted the lines with her melodious voice, lines wafted like the sighs the wind draws from an Aeolian harp."

If Sarcey's words suggest that he was thinking in terms of music, that was his intention. He wrote that Hugo's plays are dotted with arias and duets which beg to be set to music: that the plot is the libretto, the poetry, the musical score.*

When the curtain came down on Bernhardt's first performance of Ruy Blas, friends and strangers alike rushed backstage to gape, to touch, to coo over the new phenomenon. Suddenly everyone fell silent. The waves of admirers parted to make way for Victor Hugo who, accompanied by Emile de Girardin, had come to pay his respects:

All the stupid thoughts I'd had about this immense genius passed through my mind. I recalled our first meeting, when, affecting a lofty manner, I

---

*Several of Hugo's plays have, in fact, been turned into operas. Some, like Marchetti's Ruy Blas, are quite forgotten, but others are now performed more often than the plays that inspired them. Two are based on plays Bernhardt was closely associated with: Verdi's Ernani (Hernani) and Ponchielli's La Gioconda (Angelo, Tyran de Padoue). Verdi's Rigoletto (Le Roi s'Amuse) is, of course, the most frequently performed of all.

was barely polite to this kind, indulgent man. At that moment, when my life was taking wing, I longed to beg his forgiveness and speak of my devout gratitude. But before I could utter a word, he knelt at my feet and, pressing my two hands to his lips, murmured: *"Merci, merci."* Thus it was he who thanked me: he, the great Victor Hugo, whose soul was so beautiful, whose universal genius filled the world. How small I felt, how ashamed, how happy! . . . He was so handsome that night, with his broad forehead that seemed to catch the light, his thatch of silvery hair, like new-mown hay in the moonlight, his laughing, luminous eyes. Not daring to fling myself into Victor Hugo's arms, I fell into the arms of Girardin, the trusted friend of my first steps.*

Sarah was to overcome her timidity about flinging herself into the arms of Victor Hugo, or so entries in his journal beginning the day after the opening of *Ruy Blas* would lead us to believe:

> 20 February 1872: House full. Saw and congratulated Sarah Bernhardt. Kiss on the mouth.
> 24 February: M. Gustave Flaubert came to see me with Sarah Bernhardt.
> 28 March: Went to the Odéon. Saw Mlle Bernhardt in her dressing room. She was changing.

On 10 June, Victor Hugo gave a dinner to celebrate the hundredth performance of *Ruy Blas*. Once again Sarah was able to overcome her shyness. "Come!" she sang out. "Give all the ladies a kiss. Start with me!" The virile seventy-year-old poet was more than willing to make the rounds. "And end with me!" Sarah shouted above the din. The boisterous party ended on a tragic note. Chilly suffered a stroke during the congratulatory speeches. Three days later he was dead, and Duquesnel became the sole director of the Odéon.

Some years later, a friend saw an agitated Sarah leave Victor Hugo's house. "What's wrong," he asked. "I've never seen you with that expression on your face."

---

*Often called the founder of the modern newspaper, the publisher-journalist Emile de Girardin was one of Sarah's first lovers as well. It was he, along with the Comte de Kératry, who had helped smooth the way for her to convert the Odéon into a convalescent hospital. An impressive bronze bust Sarah made of him was exhibited at the 1878 Salon.

"I've just received the Poet's kiss" was her reply, for their sporadic affair spanned several years.

Hugo's gallantry was not Sarah's only reward. Long before the ill-fated dinner party, she had been invited to rejoin the Comédie Française. Nothing could have given her more satisfaction. The salary was higher, the prestige greater, and the fact that France's most important theatre had, in effect, apologized for dismissing her ten years earlier was balm to her pride. The only obstacle in her way was her contract with the Odéon, which had another year to run. But ethical behavior was not Sarah's forte. She signed a contract with the Comédie Française without bothering to get a release from the Odéon and played out the spring season in a hostile atmosphere. Her double-dealing cost her six thousand francs in fines, angry scenes, and a break with Duquesnel. It was not the first time she had made trouble for her devoted friend. One evening during the entr'acte, her maid had found her stretched out on her dressing-room floor in an attitude of death, a beatific expression on her face. The cast crowded in, sobbing and crossing themselves in horror. A shattered Duquesnel stepped before the curtain to announce the dreadful news, when suddenly shrieks of laughter were heard. Sarah had risen from the dead. Duquesnel, not at all amused by her little joke, dismissed her from the company, only to take her back again when he realized he had cut off his nose to spite his face. But this time his star, his favorite actress, his discovery, his protégée had gone too far.

"He was hurt and I was a little ashamed of myself," Sarah admitted. "This man had always been kindness itself. It was he, despite Chilly and other enemies, who opened the door to my future."

I T WAS a different Sarah who returned to the Comédie Française after a ten-year absence. At seventeen she had been an unknown girl, plagued by uncontrollable stage fright. Now, at twenty-eight, she was an accomplished actress who fascinated theatre-goers with her insinuating charm and arrogant chic. As might be expected, many actors of the Comédie Française did not share the general enthusiasm. It had, in fact, taken a good deal of drum beating from Sarcey, Girardin, and other powers of the press to convince them that Bernhardt belonged in their company. Certainly they took it hard when they read Théodore de Banville's: "Sarah Bernhardt's engagement at the Théâtre Français is a revolution. Poetry has entered the domain of dramatic art. Or, if you like, the wolf has entered the sheep-fold."

Although the company was hostile to Sarah, it was in need of young blood and a thorough shaking up. Familiar accomplishment and overfamiliar faces had lowered the temperature of the house. A state-supported institution, it was meant to present classic and contemporary works of high literary quality and did not have to earn its way. As a result, it often played to half-empty houses.

What was lacking was a new approach and a new Rachel to stoke the flames and set the box office on fire. Emile Perrin, who had been appointed the director in 1871, was a sound judge of such matters. A painter and art critic, Perrin had been in charge, first of the Opéra-Comique, then of the Opéra, where he set Parisians on their ears with lavish first productions of Verdi's *Don Carlos* and Meyerbeer's *L'Africaine*. It was an even greater challenge to be the head of what was variously called the Comédie Française, the Théâtre Français, and the House of Molière. By whatever name, it was one of France's most civilized institutions. The French had been the leaders of European theatre since the days of Louis XIV. Just as French was accepted as the international language, French plays were given wherever dramatic art existed, and French actors were considered the best in the world. It was Perrin's responsibility to maintain this superior position.

To excel, art must renew itself. Molière, who said there was no rule but to please the public, had brought new life to the theatre. But over the years the frolicsome spirit of France's greatest comic playwright had given way to something close to solemnity. Sarcey, tenacious as a terrier in his admiration for the venerable establishment, said it was like "a great family house, rich and grave." A committee of complacent older actors sat in judgment, ready to frown on new plays and new recruits. It was they who had the power to promote *pensionnaires*, regular members of the company, to *sociétaires*, those who, in addition to their salaries, were entitled to a life share in the theatre's profits. To be sure, there was charm in the consecrated atmosphere and age-old traditions of the House of Molière, even if the dome was grimy, the seats narrow, and the walls sorely in need of paint. But far more important than charm was the dazzling perfection of ensemble acting by a homogeneous group of performers almost all of whom had been schooled at the Conservatoire.

Perrin, who understood the danger of inherited glory in state establishments, knew that an artistic house cleaning was in order. While he moved slowly, he moved with intelligence. Anachronistic costumes gave way to historically accurate ones. Authentic sets and furnishings were introduced. Even acting, that thorniest of subjects, was re-examined. The older *sociétaires*, incomparable *diseurs* though they were, recited in a pompous style that smacked of other, more formal days. Realism was in the air, and Perrin planned to meet it by engaging young, "modern" performers whose style was attuned to the new, postwar decade.

Sarah made her re-entry into the Comédie Française on 6 November 1872 as Gabrielle in Dumas *père's Mademoiselle de Belle-Isle*. Whether she was haunted by her disastrous debut ten years earlier, or afraid she could not live up to the publicity that preceded her re-engagement, she fell below her usual standard. It was only toward the end of the evening, Sarcey reported, that Bernhardt, "aroused by her cold reception, found herself. Here indeed was our Sarah, the Sarah of *Ruy Blas* whom we admired so much at the Odéon." Later performances saw the actress in excellent form. Sarcey, who had urged Perrin to present Bernhardt first in classical tragedy, felt fully justified when he saw her as Junie in *Britannicus*, her next role.

"Dressed in magnificent taste," he wrote in *Le Temps*, "she has an indescribable charm, and recites verse with a Racinian grace and purity. Victory is hers today. From now on, no one can complain of her admission to the Comédie Française. She belongs to the house."

Victory was not hers alone. That same performance marked the impressive third of the three traditional debuts of a superb-looking young actor named Jean Mounet-Sully, who was to be her troubled and troubling lover for the next two years. A country boy from Bergerac, he had lived his first twenty-six years in an atmosphere of pious Calvinism. But life in a small town in southwest France was too stifling for an artistic young man who, even while he prepared for the ministry, dreamt of becoming a painter, a composer, or a tragedian declaiming heroic verse to a worshipful audience. After a stormy struggle with his conscience, Mounet left the family vineyard to take his chances at the Paris Conservatoire.

A passage from his memoirs, *Souvenirs d'un Tragédien*, gives the flavor of his old-fashioned upbringing:

The prejudice against actors was still amazingly strong everywhere, but especially in the provinces. After much insistence I received permission to leave home. The day I left, my dear mother kissed me and said: "Your father left us a small fortune and a spotless name. Do not bring shame to either."

"*Maman*," I replied, "I swear to you that one day I shall be a millionaire, decorated with the Legion of Honor." Those were tremendous words, and I felt I was promising more than was reasonable. But I had Faith! . . . Then I asked for her blessing and her consent. "I cannot approve of your decision to be an actor," she said, "but my blessing will follow you wherever you go." The sainted woman! The memory of her is surely the most precious treasure of my life.

In 1867 Mounet entered the Conservatoire and found work at various theatres around town as gifted students sometimes did. The following year, he auditioned for Chilly, who engaged him to play small roles at the Odéon, among them Cornwall in *King Lear*. On 6 April 1868 the inexperienced student actor made his debut, surrounded by a brilliant cast: Beauvallet as Lear, the great Taillade as the Fool, Agar as Goneril, and Bernhardt as Cordelia.

In those years, Mounet recalled, "Sarah Bernhardt was already being talked about, on her way to becoming famous. I admired her passionately. She didn't know me, never even noticed me. I was nothing. She passed before me like a distant star." Indeed, by then Sarah was riding high and paid no attention to the raw young man, unless it was to make fun of his bumbling ways. During a performance they were to laugh about later, he moaned an "Ah!" so titanic that the audience began to snicker. Blind with shame—Mounet was never given to the small emotion—he lunged toward the exit only to crash into the door. Needless to say, the set shook—as did the laughing public. When at last he managed to get off the stage, he burst into tears. Duquesnel tried to comfort him, but he would not be consoled. He was finished, he would never amount to anything, he sobbed, beating his great fists against the wall.

Mounet was a very discouraged actor when he was taken into the army at the beginning of the Franco-Prussian conflict and even more downhearted when, at the war's end, he tried to pick up the pieces of his career. Duquesnel offered to take him back into the Odéon, but at such an insultingly low salary that he refused. Tired of drifting from theatre to theatre, he decided to go back to his mother and the vintners' life. His bags were packed and he was about to leave for the train when he learned that Perrin wanted him to read for the part of Oreste in Racine's *Andromaque*. That evening he wrote an ecstatic letter to his mother. He would not only play Oreste, but, miracle of miracles, he had been given a three-year contract, unheard of for a beginner.

His superb talent was to make him the most illustrious tragedian of the Comédie Française for over forty years. With his leonine head, tangled chestnut mane, chiseled features, and gladiator's body, he was the baroque ideal of the Racine hero. His passionate gestures were flamboyant in their outsized grandeur. As for his powerful voice, the irrepressible Sacha Guitry was to say that when Mounet spoke in an intimate tête-à-tête, he sounded as though he were shouting across a river.

"I can see myself at the time," Mounet wrote, "drunk with enthusiasm, rehearsing *Oreste* in the streets. I remember taking advantage of the noisy traffic to shout at the top of my lungs: 'Oh gods, what rivers of blood flow around me!' I would never have dared raise my voice like that at home for fear of terrifying the neighbors. My hair was so theatrically long that people turned to stare at me in the streets." It was not only startled pedestrians who could not believe their eyes. One day Sarah stopped him in the wings of the theatre.

"Is that you, Mounet?" she asked.

"It is!" he thundered.

"But what's happened to you? You've become so handsome."

"So I've been told," the actor confessed.

"But I must be going mad," Sarah said, "you weren't this good-looking at the Odéon, were you?"

"I believe I was."

"Nonsense, I would have noticed it," Sarah insisted, adding, "Are you on tonight?"

"Yes."

"Then I'll come to see you from the front of the house." That night, after the performance, Sarah was granted what many women in the audience had yearned for. Nor would they have been disappointed, for Mounet, who at sixty was to say that he had always thought "that thing down there was a rigid bone," was as passionate in bed as he was onstage.

So began an affair which was to lock two towering egos together, as much in combat as in love. It is rare for the exceptionally gifted to surrender their hearts to one another, as their hearts are often preoccupied by the steady beat of self-love. Certainly the odds were against Bernhardt and Mounet-Sully. A Parisian, born and bred, Sarah was more than experienced in the ways of the world. Her numerous liaisons had taught her to deal with men much as they dealt with her. To meet callousness with worldliness was a game she had mastered long ago. Beyond that, her growing fame had given *le Tout-Paris* a new respect for her. Now it was not only Left Bank students who swarmed across the Seine to dream at her shrine. Artists and society people felt they were not in the swim unless they could drop her name. Had not Victor Hugo himself knelt at her feet? In a word, she had arrived. Caricatures of Bernhardt appeared everywhere. Women copied her mannerisms, and her admirers took pleasure in repeating—and embellishing— the gossip that surrounded her. Still, to have an affair with a spoiled mother's boy from the provinces was outside Sarah's experience. His belief in the pure and the good, both in life and in art, seemed refreshing after the blasé Lignes and Haases she had known.

On the other hand, Bergerac and the prudish advice of his God-fearing mother had hardly prepared Mounet for the casual promiscuity of women like Sarah. He did not understand the protocol that went with having an actress from the demimonde for a mistress. It never occurred to him that Sarah would think of him as her *amant de coeur*. Where would he have learned the lies and intrigues that were part and parcel of such affairs? His was a simpler world, where mothers were sacred, wives were submissive, and sweethearts were faithful.

To give a woman the gift of his body was a release, an explosive proof of manliness, but to respect a woman who gave herself freely was unthinkable. His hope, he was later to reveal, was to raise Sarah from the mire of sin and lead her, good Calvinist that he was, onto the path of righteousness.

Sarah had been to quite another school. She did not consider herself a fallen woman, but a woman who had risen in the world. She belonged to no one and thought herself free. To take on a handsome young actor with the pitiful salary of six thousand francs a year was a carnal diversion, a luxury she felt she could afford. Certainly she had no thought of dismissing the menagerie who paid her bills and kept her in the clothes and jewels she loved. After all, it was she who had received recognition and Mounet who hoped to achieve it; she who was the seducer and he the victim of her charms. To add to her amusement, she found him a pleasant change from the journalists and jaded clubmen who formed her court. Vanity and ambition played their part of course. Their joint success in *Britannicus* led to dreams of a glorious partnership, dreams that became reality when the audience came to see that Mounet's heroic stage presence was in telling contrast to her fragile femininity, his fiery declamation the ideal foil for her lyric outpourings. And, for Sarah, there was the double satisfaction of being seen on the arm of the handsomest man around and of having won him away from his mistress, Maria Favart. Considerably older than Bernhardt, Favart was a distinguished leading actress of the company who "owned" many roles Sarah coveted. If Bernhardt and Mounet-Sully were to become recognized as *the* romantic couple of the Comédie Française, Sarah might succeed in replacing the older actress in the theatre as she had in life. It was not a pretty thought, but then backstage is not a very pretty place. In no time, the Bernhardt-Mounet affair was the talk of Paris, as few things are more titillating to theatre-goers than to know that the lovers they admire onstage are offstage lovers as well. Together, Sarah and Jean created theatre magic. Perrin, canny manager that he was, cast them in the same play as often as he could.

 N   N O V E M B E R   1 8 7 2 , during rehearsals of *Britannicus*, Bernhardt and Mounet-Sully began to write to one another, in the high-flown and highly charged style of the period. It would seem that Sarah meant more to Jean than he meant to her, as she allowed most of his letters to disappear, while he numbered, dated, and saved almost a hundred of hers. Their correspondence provides a vivid picture of an acting couple in the throes of what might be called love.

It would be misguided optimism to look for the "real" Sarah in her seemingly candid messages; she was far too chameleon, too much the role player for that. In her letters to Haas, the sophisticated man about town, she had posed as his inferior, eager to please, but now, as an established actress, she felt superior to Mounet and assumed quite another role, one attuned to the weaknesses of a provincial romantic gullible enough to believe in true love. After reading a few of her first frivolous notes, it is both touching and ironic to see Sarah, the irrepressible troublemaker, give surprisingly hardheaded advice to her equally difficult lover:

> 9 January 1873
>
> This is not a love letter, my dear friend, but a sensible letter. I've just seen our director [Perrin] who spoke to me about your incredible stubbornness and the trouble it makes for everyone. . . . I beg you in the name of Art, in the name of the deep love I feel for you, try to control yourself. It was said you were to be made a *sociétaire* next week. I can confirm this. But now the numerous enemies your talent has created are gaining the upper hand, and all because of your contrary nature. Several of your friends, aware of my infinite affection for you, have taken me aside to tell me that you frighten them by your determination to contradict, no matter what the circumstances, and that they dread the violent arguments you inevitably begin whenever there is a discussion.
>
> And so my dearest, I beg you, I implore you, give up the idea that everyone is against you. . . . Restrain yourself a little, just a little!

As Bernhardt was to learn, Mounet's resistance to advice was as monumental as his resistance to direction. Everything had to be explained, made real for him. In *Britannicus*, when he was meant to hold a snake, he insisted that it be a live one, not a prop. Told to exit right, he exited left. Told to shout, he whispered; told to whisper, he shouted.

Mounet's need for explanation went far beyond the theatre. Soon after they became lovers, he received one of the many apologetic letters in which Sarah explained why she was forced to cancel a midnight rendezvous:

> January 1873
>
> Don't frown, my beloved, and don't be too angry with me. I've brought my little boy to Paris for a month as he has a high fever. Tonight I feel quite uneasy about him and shall stay with him until the doctor comes in the morning. I hope it is nothing, but I am, above all, a mother.
>
> You realize that I am telling you the truth, my friend, for you know

that in this world there are excuses one would never dare to tempt fate
with, not even to conceal a caprice. And so, my beloved, don't be angry,
but let me tell you that I love you madly, that I love you with all my soul,
that my heart is yours, and that I am almost happy; that I shall perhaps
begin to love Life now that I love Love, or rather that I know what Love
is! Have I told you of my feverish past loves and of my hopes deceived?
And of my never-ending search for love, always followed by nothingness,
by emptiness? And of my tears of rage, my impotent cries, the despair
which led me to suicide? If I have not told you all this, I tell it now in
all sincerity, my dear lord and master, for it is thanks to you that I no
longer weep, that I am filled with hope. To you, above all, I owe my
knowledge of love, not the love I inspire in others, but that love which I
feel, which is mine to give. I am so happy to love at last, and to love you!
. . . Lean on my heart, warm my sadness and my skepticism with your
ardent soul. Open your being and let me enter it so that I am yours
completely, and take, with this kiss made of memories and hopes, all that
is poetic and good in a woman's heart. I love you with all my soul; I cradle
your head in my arms, and press my lips to yours. I murmur all the words
of love.

Despite her protestations of love, Sarah's letter contained the seeds of Mounet's unhappiness. With his relentless need to analyze, he might well have
wondered why she was "*almost* happy," why she would not dare to tempt
fate, "even to conceal a caprice." Which of her dubious caprices was the
question.* But it was the mention of her former liaisons which threw Mounet
off balance. Intentional or unintentional, flirtatious or cruel, Sarah's words
opened the floodgates of his jealousy. From then on, he was haunted by her
former lovers, phantoms he could neither confront nor forget. If her past life
was filled with "feverish loves," why would her present life be any different?
He was obsessed by a tortuous desire to know what lay behind her every
move, her every word. Flattered but frightened, Sarah called him "lord and
master" and pleaded with him to be calm. Even her playful "As soon as
you're ready, whistle, and I'll come to your dressing room" was followed by
an anxious "Don't be angry, and don't leave this note lying about."
    As the weeks went by, Sarah responded less and less to Mounet's

---

*In his novel *La Dame aux Camélias*, from which his play was drawn, Dumas *fils* states that
"courtesans use 'caprice' as a code word for the noncommercial affairs in which they indulge
from time to time as a relief, and a consolation."

whistle. Yet it intrigued her, half enamored as she was, to keep him dangling
and, when she felt her power slip, to send him passionate letters and allow
him to make love to her. As a result, Jean found it difficult to distinguish
her truth from lies, her love from play acting. What was he to make of her
endless excuses? She was tired, she had business to attend to, she had to
consult Maurice's doctor, to entertain the boy's friends, to study. When all
else failed, she fell back on the eternal "too sick to make love." And perhaps
she was. From the beginning, Sarah had never hesitated to put Mounet off,
with illness as her excuse:

February 1873

I am not well, my friend Jean, not well at all. I do not dare to bring this
sick little being to see you. So I send you only my heart, my soul, and
my kisses full of love and tenderness. Do you know, my sweet lord and
master, that I never stop thinking of you, that I dream only of you, that
my one, my unique wish is to belong to you without ever giving you cause
to frown; to be your mistress, your possession, your very own? Do you
know that everything that reminds me of you makes my heart leap? Finally,
do you know that I love you passionately with all the power of my soul,
with all the regrets and tears of my unhappy past?

I should like to take up again my life, my kisses, all those idiotic
sensations; I should like my spirit to be as virginal as my heart was when
I fell in love with you. Last but not least, know that I love you. It's true;
it's as great as love itself. My lips greet your lips, and now listen to what
they have to say, those naughty little chatterboxes!

Sarah's lips were not the only little chatterboxes in Paris. The actors of the
Comédie Française were amused to see her play the game of infidelity with
her jealous lover, to blame her, and to make fun of him. An incident at the
theatre added to the general hilarity. After a matinée, Mounet noticed Sarcey
pacing up and down backstage. What was he waiting for, the actor asked
suspiciously. To take Sarah to dinner, Sarcey explained. Mounet, certain
that the rapacious little critic expected an after-dinner treat, threw caution—
and favorable reviews—to the winds. Sarcey was a son of a bitch, he shouted,
and challenged him to a duel. He was not in the habit of fighting with
children, the journalist said, as he took Sarah by the arm and marched her
off to their suspect rendezvous.

Mounet's jealous outbursts were not confined to the theatre. In a fiacre one night, on the way to his apartment, he and Sarah quarreled bitterly.

Marie Colombier was pleased to tell the story:

At the end of his tether, drunk with fury, unaware of what he was doing, Mounet, to prevent himself from strangling Sarah, broke the windows and kicked in the front of the cab. The coachman cursed and stopped the carriage. When a crowd gathered, Sarah slipped out and quietly disappeared. Mounet was taken to the police, where he had to pay a fine. Then, ashamed of himself, and disgusted with his mistress, he went home, only to find her sound asleep in his bed.

It was enough to dampen any man's ardor, except, it seems, Mounet's. All the same, he could not have been pleased by the following letters, written when Sarah was trying to juggle tense rehearsals on the stage of the Comédie Française with the nerve-wracking offstage dramas she played with her demanding lover. She was, in fact, exhausted.

February 1873

Oh, don't be angry, I beg you, Jean my beloved. I must absolutely be good. If you want to be kind, come to kiss me. But after that you must go home to sleep. . . . A secret: I'm sick at heart that I made you unhappy yesterday. I regret it infinitely and love you all the more for it. I won't be naughty again. No, never, I swear it. Don't laugh, I love you. I wish it were tomorrow night, as I really have recovered. I breathe in your kisses and give all of myself to you.

Jean was not Sarah's only problem, however. In the spring of 1873 Perrin was to undermine Sarah's confidence by casting her as the worldly Italian Princess Falconieri in Octave Feuillet's *Dalila*, a role she felt would show her in a bad light. Feuillet, a gifted writer, was admired for perfumed plays that dealt with highborn sinners and the misadventures fate has in store for them. Perrin, aware of Sarah's double-dealings with Mounet, thought her ideally suited to the part of a femme fatale who deceives her lovers. Oddly enough, Sarah believed that such deviousness was foreign to her nature and asked to play the virtuous heroine. But that sympathetic role had been promised to the brilliant and beautiful Sophie Croizette, Perrin's mistress.

A tall, fetching blonde and the darling of the company, La Croizette was all that Sarah was not: a model of good health, good nature, and good behavior. To complete the picture, Sarah had been close to her rival since childhood and was very fond of her.

Success depends, in part, on fear of failure. But neither fear nor the horsehair Sarah stuffed down her bodice to round out her figure succeeded in bolstering her confidence. Her nerves on edge, convinced that Perrin had miscast her deliberately, she reached out to her "lord and master":

March 1873

My beloved Jean: I collapsed at the rehearsal, overcome by fits of coughing and spitting blood, and had to be carried to my carriage by Messrs Perrin and Feuillet. I am in bed. I beg you my adored one, come to see me. It would give me so much pleasure. . . . Please forgive me for all the trouble I've caused you. . . . You must overlook a great deal. . . .

There can be little doubt that Sarah's seizure was brought on by the complicated pressures of her love affair, exacerbated by the feeling that she was working in a hostile atmosphere. In her four months at the Comédie Française, in addition to her success in *Britannicus*, she had appeared, to mixed reviews, in *Mademoiselle de Belle-Isle*, Beaumarchais's *Le Mariage de Figaro*, and Jules Sandeau's *Mademoiselle de la Seiglière*. And now, just as she feared, her Princess Falconieri was a failure. Deeply troubled, she clung to Jean, yet never failed to find new ways to torment him:

I did not play *Le Passant* until half past midnight and got home at 1:30. I could not have come to you until two in the morning and that would have killed me. I was very upset when I got home as there was no way to let you know, and I was absolutely sure that you were accusing me of a thousand vile things. That is bad, very bad, my beloved. But I cannot be angry with you. . . . For me, to love is to love you, and I want to love you for a long time—as "forever" is an irony. Send me a word of encouragement for tonight's performance. Send me a kiss, or better still bring it to me in my dressing room. . . . I shall hang on your neck, my adored one, until my kisses bruise your mouth.

Sarah's words brought cold comfort. To say she knew he suspected her of "vile things" was to feed his suspicions, not to allay them. As for her cynical "to love . . . forever is an irony," it could hardly bring cheer to a man who hoped to marry her. All through the spring, Sarah sent Jean letters designed to bind him, to inflame his jealousy and torture him with the thought that he might lose her: she was sick, she was dying, she loved him passionately; she was too exhausted to come to him; she would see him the next night; fever had laid her low; her son, the only person who really loved her, was ill. She wished all their troubles would disappear so that she could be what he wanted her to be; if the slightest suspicion crossed his mind, he could drop in to see her at any hour of the day or night to check on her whereabouts.

A letter dated 2 April 1873 leads one to believe she had left him for someone else.

Oh, weep no longer, Jean, I beg you. . . . I do not know why, but your tears follow me, burn me. I am very unhappy. . . . My sweet friend, my adored lover, my dear love, I shall come back. Wait for me!!!

Yes. Indeed, why do I hesitate when happiness holds out its arms to me? And then, when you no longer love me, the tomb is so near, is it not, and it is so easy to sing one's swan song. Must it be that because your path was crossed by a creature to whom you gave your love, to whom you revealed the life-giving mystery—must it be that your beautiful, loyal soul should suffer agonies? No! A thousand times No!

I shall come to you tomorrow. I would have come tonight, but I ache in all my being, and my tears have reddened my eyes, while your tears make my heart pound.

Sleep! Love me! Love me, and hear my cry of sorrow, of regret, of passion. . . .

Jean immediately dashed off an ecstatic reply:

. . . Just as I was about to cry out: My God, what is to become of me?"— my habitual cry, alas, since I *no longer* expect you to appear—I found your dear note on my night table. Oh, how happy I am, my Sarah—how happy and proud of the generous impulse you followed in writing to me! . . . If you knew how right you were to obey your heart and let yourself come to these two arms, so obstinately held out to you. Ah! How far away seem my tears, my fears, my anguish! Each painful memory is effaced by the present, lit up by the sunshine of the future.

This afternoon you told me that you are afraid of my jealousy, afraid I

will recall the past. But the past does not exist unless it has an echo in
the present. Now after the sincere cry of passion that you were unable to
hold back, that overwhelmed your entire being, and that reached me, warm
and luminous—I believe! I am confident and filled with hope!! Oh, Sarah!
Sarah! My Sarah! You love me at last! It's true! It's really true! No, never
again will I torment you with my jealousy. That would be truly insulting
to the woman whom I so loved. . . . the woman I despaired of ever meeting
except in my dreams, that woman whom I believed to be a chimera of my
unhealthy imagination, and who was imprisoned in your frail body, that
woman who has no past, (Do you hear me?) I know her at last. She exists.
I saw her for a moment today, and I shall see her tomorrow, and forever!
Oh, joy! She has your features; she is *you!* I *see* you now, I *know* you, I
possess you. You are *we!!* So fear nothing, you shall be happy. I shall
place an aigrette on your brow, and cover your arms with lace made of
kisses, since my naughty girl cannot do without luxury!!! Dear lover, dear
wife, dear beloved mistress, you too must have faith, confidence and hope.
The future belongs to people of good will!! And we are young and strong,
and we love one another!!

Mounet was soon to realize that despite Sarah's cries of ecstasy in response
to his love-making, she was still the elusive creature she had always been.
In the naïve hope that marriage guaranteed fidelity, he proposed, not once
but several times. Sarah refused him each time, unable to see herself as a
permanent victim of his jealousy or as his faithful, loving wife.

      Weeks went by in frigid silence. When the ice broke, it revealed
darker, more turbulent waters:

Saturday morning, 26 July 1873

My dear Sarah: Don't worry, I shall not try to defend myself. There will
be no recriminations. What is done is done. I don't expect you to forget,
but I ask you to forgive whatever suffering I have caused you, in consideration of my love and my own suffering. You say I struck you, my beloved,
my adored one. I have no memory of it. But I still see the dark bruises
on your arms, made by my hands. And your eyes, swollen and red from
the tears of that night, haunt me like a bad dream. I behaved brutally,
and fear I had no reason to. I tell myself that quite possibly I was deceived
by appearances, and that your unhappiness . . . so violent, was caused
only by the injustice of my accusations. But I *did* throw myself at your

feet, I *did* beg you to pardon me with all my heart. Yet throughout that long night you remained as cold as ice, deaf to my supplications and blind to my tears.

How is it possible? Tell me! If you were sincere two days ago, when you found words to convince me of your love, to make me wildly drunk with a joy that, for a moment, made me believe in the possibility of a *future*, how, why, did you suddenly tell me yesterday that you had ceased loving me a month ago? A month ago! What does that mean? What happened a month ago? I wrack my brain—and find nothing!

Ah, those bruises! The marks on your arms will heal and be forgotten in a few hours, but how can the frightful wounds left by your words ever heal? When were you lying? Was it beforehand? Was it afterward? And why this lie? You accused me of egotism and meanness—I who love you for *yourself alone*, as you well know! . . . Sarah! Sarah! I wanted to tell you of my projects, my plans for our future. For I had many plans, and such beautiful ones! . . .

I am afraid I was unjust last night. Forgive me. Above all, it is those words I wanted to say to you for I realize, yes, I realize that perhaps I was in the wrong, and it's important to me that you know this to be so. . . . Were you not weeping because I accused you at the very moment you hoped to make our dream come true by giving me that final proof of love I had waited for so long, and which I asked of you even more for your sake than for mine? If only you would answer Yes! Don't be angry with me any longer. It would be unfair. . . . All that matters is that you should know that I would be more miserable than I can possibly say if you were to continue to live in fear of your very repentant supplicant,

The next day Sarah replied:

Sunday morning, 27 July 1873

Yes, Jean, you were brutal, unjust, and you have gone too far. I felt that your despotism destroyed my dreams of the future forever, for I, too, had dreams. . . . You must not reproach me for the few lies I told you, lies that only prove my affection. I told the truth, Jean. In this past month I have been blocked so many times by that uncontrollable jealousy which makes you trample underfoot all rules of decent behavior, at every turn, no matter where we happen to be. Last night you made me suffer all the anguish of regret. I wept with sorrow, real sorrow, as I saw my heart's dream, my cherished plans for the future collapse under your brutal hands. The last time you made such terrible scenes it seemed that you were trying very hard to shatter my castles in the air. But they remained standing, supported by my love. But Jean, this last, sad night they came tumbling down, and the debris is drowned by my tears. Let my sweet dreams sleep; I have no desire to wake them.

No, I did not lie to you two days ago. For once again my heart had found in your heart the echo of my sadness; my eyes met your kind eyes all luminous with tears. I was moved and I *did* love you then. I don't want to make you unnecessarily sad, but you see, my heart is bruised, and I do not know whether it can be healed. I felt you degraded my dignity as a woman when, as I had asked my friends to wait while I undressed, you imposed yourself, despite everything, and entered my dressing room while they waited at the door. It was as though you were saying: "But I know her, she's my mistress; I see her like this, naked, every day." . . . I had to submit to your violence in order to avoid a scandal. In fact, you've tortured me with weapons that I myself put in your hands. You used my affection and my love like a flag carried into battle.

Ah! You have hurt me very much, Jean, but I forgive you since that seems to be your wish. Still, to forgive is not to forget. Give my heart some time to reflect, and we'll see what can be made of the scraps that remain of our love. Don't be unhappy. In a few days Art will bring us together once again. Let us not force our love. I give you my brow which you brutalized in such a cowardly way. Perhaps your kisses will revive my love. I doubt it.

IT W A S in these days of turmoil, when Mounet was brutalizing Sarah and tormenting her with his impassioned letters, that the Comédie Française called on her to demonstrate her gifts as a comedienne in *Chez l'Avocat*, Paul Ferrier's witty free-verse sketch. It was a severe test as she was cast opposite her old friend, Constant

Coquelin, who was to become France's great comedian. Under the circumstances, it is not surprising that some of her reviews were quite bad.

One of Mounet's more endearing qualities was his devotion to Sarah's artistry. He was as sensitive to criticism of her as he was to criticism of himself. And so she was touched, *quand même*, when he sprang to her defense, in the following letter:

(end of) July, 1873

I promised myself never to write you again. The haughty, glacial manner in which you recalled all the wrongs that my only too violent love may have inflicted upon you filled my heart with sadness . . . for now I can have no doubt that you no longer love me, if in fact you ever did. So it is not to speak of *us*, my ever-beloved that I write, but confronted by the attitude of several newspapers in regard to your latest role, I cannot help crying out across the ocean of ice that separates us: "Fear nothing!" You are on the true path. . . . Don't be discouraged. You have achieved a veritable tour de force. . . . If it ever occurs to the critics to see you again in that small role which you transformed into the poetic epitome of womanhood (I am quite serious!) you will be avenged. . . . For they will be forced to eat their words, or else to live forever with an uneasy conscience, the worst thing that can happen—especially to a drama critic.

On that note, dear angel, I kiss—as platonically as possible—the tips of your pretty pink claws. . . .

If Mounet's love was blind, his loyalty was clear-sighted. Bernhardt was not limited to tragedy: she was radiant in comedy as well. Her public adored her in *Chez l'Avocat*, and although some critics, accustomed to think of Sarah as a tragedienne, could not accept her as a lyric comedienne, others found that Bernhardt and Coquelin, playing a squabbling pair with extraordinary charm and verve, made an incomparable comic duo.

Any doubts about Sarah's talents were dispelled when, on 22 August, she had an "immense success" in the title role of Racine's *Andromaque*. Mounet, too, was admired, not least by Sarah, who was to pay tribute to him in her memoirs: "I shall never forget that first performance in which Mounet-Sully received a frenzied ovation. Ah! How beautiful he was in the role of Oreste! His entrance, his rages, his madness; the sculptural beauty of his body and the way he moved; how wonderful it all was!"

A month later, in the secondary role of Aricie in *Phèdre*, hers, she modestly admitted, was the real success of the evening.

Bernhardt, like Mounet-Sully, was well aware that they were beginning to be talked about as the leading acting team of the Comédie Française. In fact, the end of 1873 marked the consecration of Sarah as a classic tragedienne. Spurred on by her success, she took no vacation and continued to play Aricie and Andromaque during the summer. In spite of their joint triumphs, their liaison, Sarah realized, was a failure. Five days after her first performance as Aricie, a role she acted, according to Mounet, with "unforgettable beauty, rhythm, and restraint," she wrote to him:

> 22 September 1873
>
> . . . Our happiness depends on our separation. I could never bear such tyranny, such despotic fidelity. Therefore let friendship unite us. I have never known love except from you, and through you. I shall stop up my heart while it is still burning. . . . Let Art rejoice in its triumph. For its sake we shall remain lovers on the stage. Do you agree? Our poor summer of flowers is over. Autumn leaves already scatter sadness. Farewell, then, to love. You have known how to give it birth, but not how to let it die.

A few hours later, Sarah received Mounet's reply:

> I understand nothing, nothing, nothing, my friend, my lover, my mistress. I understand nothing except that the beating of my heart has never been so painful. For two days I've waited for you, with the same anguish in my soul, the same tears in my eyes, and just so shall I wait for you . . . until you come back to me, or until I die.
>
> P.S. Until tomorrow then, at lunch. If you prefer, we will not talk about ourselves, but at least my eyes will look into yours.

Early in October, Sarah did go back to Jean, only to prolong the tortuous drama created by her teasing manipulation, her ability to inflict pain or give pleasure at will. Although she was "in love with love" and, in her way, in love with Jean, she could not resist the game of advance and retreat. One leitmotif found in her letters harked back to the Prince de Ligne's callous treatment of her. What she perhaps did not recognize in herself was her wish to make other men pay for her past unhappiness.

In the autumn, Sarah's youngest sister, Régine, was to become another victim of her unconscious mixture of affection and cruelty. In a note to Mounet Sarah found a new excuse to break a rendezvous:

> A telegram from Régine announces her arrival at five this morning. She has no home but mine, so I am forced to stay here to receive her. . . . At least I can do something for my family.

To protect Régine from Youle, Sarah had taken her in when she moved to the entresol apartment in the rue de Rome. But her kindness, it appears, was not a cure for early neglect. Tragically enough, her plump little baby sister was now an emaciated whore of eighteen, in the last stages of tuberculosis.

A sinister passage in *My Double Life* gives Bernhardt's account of her unfortunate sister's last days:

> My apartment in the rue de Rome was small, my bedroom minuscule. A large bamboo bed took up all the space. The coffin in which I often installed myself to study my roles was in front of the window. Thus, when Régine came to stay with me, I found it perfectly natural to sleep in the small, white satin bed which was meant to be my last resting place, and put her in the large bed under masses of lace. She, too, found it quite natural since I didn't want to leave her at night, and it was impossible to get another bed into that small room. Besides, she was used to my coffin.
>
> One day my manicurist . . . came in to do my nails. My sister asked her to enter the room quietly as I was still asleep. The woman looked around, thinking I had fallen asleep in an armchair; but seeing me in a coffin, she fled, shrieking like a madwoman. From that moment, all Paris knew that I slept in a coffin, and ill-natured gossip with its slanderous wings took flight in all directions.

It was not gossip alone that spread the news. To capitalize on the situation, Bernhardt had Melandri, one of Paris's leading photographers, take pictures of her in her flower-laden bier, all in white, her arms crossed, her eyes closed in what appeared to be eternal rest. Soon the photographs were available in the shops. They made a good deal of money for Melandri, who sold them in postcard form, and for Sarah, to whom he paid a handsome fee. In fact, they are still available in Paris. (It was quite customary for theatrical celebrities, even such dignitaries as Ibsen, to add to their earnings through the sale of photographs.)

Where the coffin came from is difficult to determine. Sarah said she bought it to accustom herself to the idea of death. One unlikely story has it that her mother gave it to her. Even more unlikely is Marie Colombier's claim that it was a gift from a lover, a necrophiliac Romeo who enjoyed fornicating in it. Incredible as that may seem, the coffin was tangible evidence of Sarah's morbid nature, like the skull on her desk, a gift from Victor Hugo, suitably inscribed with a gloomy quatrain, and the anatomical skeleton in her studio, cheerfully referred to as Lazarus. Along with many artists of her time, Sarah was fascinated by the mystery of death and the glamour of debauchery. Like Baudelaire, who spoke for many of her generation, she longed "to plunge to the depths of the abyss, be it Heaven or Hell/To the depths of the unknown to discover the new." *(Plonger au fond du gouffre, Enfer ou Ciel, qu'importe?/Au fond de l'inconnu pour trouver du nouveau.)*

Had Régine not been close to death, there would have been a certain romanticism in Sarah's love of the macabre:

26 November 1873

My dear Jean

I am suffering. . . . Often I suffer from nerves, but No, No, it is my soul that is stricken, my heart, the essence of my being. Everything is against me. Everything cries out to me: "Pain! Weariness! Bitterness!"

Forgive me, and receive this kiss—made of my tears, the sad dew of frightful storms—as the most loving of kisses from one who loves to love you, and who is yours.

And a few days later:

I have not written because I am worn out. For four nights I have struggled with Death over her poor little body. I am victorious for the moment, but shall I be for long? My eyes, reddened by tears, offer themselves to your kisses, and my friendship embraces your love. . . . Good-night, Jean.

Sleep, and do not make yourself unhappy over that anxious, strange, and morbid being named Sarah Bernhardt.

The three words Sarah chose to define herself, "anxious, strange, and morbid," could not have been more accurate, for she did not seem to realize that the presence of a coffin would aggravate the dying girl's anguish. It was almost as if Sarah—always convinced that she herself would die young of tuberculosis—was competing with her sister and, even in her concern, was trying to upstage her. Marie Colombier felt the least Sarah could have done was to move the hateful box to another room. "The poor consumptive [she wrote] suffered martyrdom every time she looked at it. Horrible nightmares haunted her rare moments of sleep. When she was alone she was terrified, and just as terrified at the sight of her sister climbing into the coffin. At last the doctor was forced to tell Sarah to remove the sinister reminder of death."

10 December 1873

This long, painful agony is an irony of fate. The struggle with death an injustice. Her eighteen years cry out for mercy. Jean, I send you my most sorrowful smile. It must be this way for your peace of mind and for our Art. I love you very much, but I am no longer in love with you. . . .

On 16 December 1873, Mounet received a photograph of Régine, enclosed in a sheet of black-edged mourning note paper with the words "She died this morning."

"The funeral was superb," Marie reported, "and Phèdre was drowned in tears. Old Perrin, seeing her cry so hard that her veil was in danger of going limp, said: 'Decidedly, she is magnificent.' Never had a member of his company reached such heights of pathos as Sarah did when she stood at the gates of the Père-Lachaise cemetery receiving the condolences of le Tout-Paris. As one journalist remarked: 'It's not a funeral, it's a première.' "

For Sarah to do a star turn in her grief was as predictable as it was for her friends to make fun of her. It was not just her tears they found ludicrous. Months before, she had threatened to leave the stage forever to devote her life to sculpture and painting. Another exaggeration, they thought, another madness. But they underestimated her. She had, in fact, taken a studio, found a teacher, and was working at her sculpture "with frantic enthusiasm." The results were impressive. For twenty-three years, from 1874 to 1896, Bernhardt's works were exhibited at the official Salon, where they fetched prices high enough to exasperate professional artists and irritate her fellow actors.

Sarah's sunlit atelier in Montmartre was more than a place of work, it was a refuge from the internecine rivalries at the Comédie Française, where, realistically enough, she felt she had more enemies than friends. In her studio, high above the city, she surrounded herself with artists and writers, friends she could trust. Among them was Alphonse Daudet. His interest in Bernhardt went beyond admiration for her acting. He observed her with a novelist's eye—in her studio, at his own dinner table, and in the salon of the publisher Charpentier, where literary and artistic Paris met each week. In 1876 he would publish a *roman-à-clef* called *Le Nabab* (*The Nabob*). An instant success, the book was transparently—some thought too transparently—about Sarah (as Felicia Ruys) and the Duc de Morny (as the Duc de Mora). Daudet had been Morny's secretary in his youth and took the opportunity of repaying him for past unkindness. Bernhardt, thinly disguised as a sculptress, is depicted as a sensitive, if tempestuous woman, consumed by her art and impatient with life. With a novelist's license, Daudet transports Morny from Youle's and Rosine's arms to Sarah's. There were, of course, those aficionados of theatrical gossip who were convinced that the Duc de Morny had enjoyed the favors of all three. In any event, *The Nabob* was to add a piquant spice to Sarah's presence on stage for those more interested in the actress's life than in her art.

Despite her friends' jokes, Sarah was not all histrionics. On the contrary, Régine's death left her so shattered that her doctor ordered her to go to the south of France to recover, but being Sarah she decided to go to Brittany instead. With her went her new lover, the charming, handsome artist Gustave Doré.

In January 1874, Sarah realized she must not go back to playing temptress to Mounet's victim. To reject him was difficult, but then so was lying to him. And so she told him the truth, or at least as much of it as she was able to deal with.

She was worth more as a friend than a mistress, she wrote. Could he accept this with courage? Would he allow his affection to serve as the guardian of her life—a life "so chaotic, so restless, so sick"?

Two weeks later, Sarah, unable to cope with Mounet's displays of anger in response to her letter, wrote him another, startlingly explicit letter about her own sexual problems:

As far as I know, I have done nothing to justify such behavior. I've told you distinctly that I do not love you any longer. I shook your hand and asked you to accept friendship in place of love. Why do you reproach me? Surely not for lack of frankness. I have been loyal; I have never deceived you; I have been yours completely. It is your fault that you have not known how to hold on to what is yours.

Besides, dear Jean, you must realize that I am not made for happiness. It is not my fault that I am constantly in search of new sensations, new emotions. That is how I shall be until my life is worn away. I am just as unsatisfied the morning after, as I am the night before. My heart demands more excitement than anyone can give it. My frail body is exhausted by the act of love. Never is it the love I dream of.

At this moment I am in a state of complete prostration. My life seems to have stopped. I feel neither joy nor sorrow. I wish you could forget me. What can I do? You must not be angry with me. I'm an incomplete person, but a good one at heart. If I could prevent your suffering I would do so!!! But you *demand* my love, and it is you who have killed it!

I beg you, Jean, let us be friends.

Sarah's old refrain, "I have never deceived you; I have been yours completely," could only have rekindled Mounet's resentment. But to be told that he was incapable of satisfying her sexually, to realize she had been false, had "deceived" him even while she moaned in pretended ecstasy, was too much for the great lover's masculine pride. It might be thought that rancor, jealousy, and violence would be enough to bury love beneath their collective weight. But Mounet's obsessive passion was proof against reason. It would be six months before he was able to free himself from the clutches of what he called her "pretty pink claws."

WH E N all was at an end, Mounet, more fastidious in life than in love, collected Sarah's letters and the pencilled drafts of his replies, bound them with a ribbon, and put them away in a handsome silver casket decorated with her motto, *quand même*. Sarah, on the other hand, tried to banish him from her mind—if not from her life. That, it turned out, was not easy. Before their affair was over, they had become on the stage what they had never been in life: an ideal image of romantic love. For if Sarah had to simulate ecstasy in the bedroom, she had no need to do so in the theatre. There she could seduce the public, her "beloved monster"; there she could satisfy and be satisfied, assume the many facets of her complex nature, and be praised, not blamed. At that point in her life, perhaps acting, with its concentrated intensity, its climaxes of applause followed by an afterglow of contentment, gave her more pleasure than her frustrating quest for sexual fulfillment.

In *Cousin Pons*, Balzac said one lives only for the satisfactions one obtains by oneself. Sarah shared this view. But unlike the novelist, the actress was unable to obtain the satisfactions of creative work whenever the spirit moved her. On the contrary, she usually performed twice a week, thought to be sufficient in a company that prided itself on the hundred plays it kept in its repertory and the large number of first-rate actors it employed. Alas, it did not suit Sarah to be at the beck and call of others. She was meant to be a diva, a star who would shine every night, choose her roles and her supporting actors, and be the center of her universe. Instead, whenever she asked Perrin for a specific role he told her he had promised it to someone else. Neurasthenic, ambitious Sarah spent many nights weeping. Her fainting spells and bouts of vomiting blood became more frequent. Her friends were seriously concerned. It was then that she shut herself up in her studio in Montmartre. As she felt the Comédie Française gave her no opportunity to be creative, she decided to concentrate on her sculpture. At eight every morning she had her horse brought round and went riding. By ten she was hard at work in her atelier at 11 boulevard de Clichy.

At last, after pressure from the press and the Ministry of Fine Arts, Perrin gave her the second lead in Octave Feuillet's new play, *Le Sphinx*. It was to be the event of the season. To no one's surprise, Perrin had assigned the title role to his favorite, the talented Sophie Croizette. Despite their rivalry, which divided the public into two warring factions, the rehearsals began harmoniously enough. Dressed in the height of fashion, or rather in her own conception of fashion, Sarah looked like the original she was. Fresh flowers in her hands, she wore a severe black velvet dress, relieved only by a white ruff at her throat. She worked seriously—no detail escaped her attention—but when a pause was called she became quite another woman.

Feuillet remembered her "breaking into a ballet step, hopping about, sitting at the piano to accompany herself in a bizarre Negro-tune which she sang in a very pretty voice. Then she marched about, took great strides like a circus clown, munched the chocolates she kept in her reticule, and restored the carmine of her lips with a rabbit's-foot brush. There was nothing more winning than the sight of Sarah and Croizette, followed by their mothers, leaving the theatre like two startled goddesses. Noses in the air, straw hats set on the backs of their enormous blond wigs, swinging their parasols, talking and laughing at the top of their voices, they would go to Chibouste's patisserie and stuff themselves with cakes."

All went well until the first dress rehearsal. Act III of *Le Sphinx* is set in a forest glade. At stage center Croizette is discovered in the arms of the handsome actor who plays Sarah's husband. A shaft of moonlight catches them in a kiss so daring it receives a burst of applause. Sarah enters across a small footbridge and sees the faithless couple. She is in a ball gown, an evening cloak dangling from her finger tips. Bathed in moonlight, she stops in a pose so irresistibly poignant that everyone applauds again. Everyone except Perrin, who jumps to his feet, shouting: "One moon is enough. Turn it off for Mademoiselle Bernhardt!" But, as Sarah wrote, she would have none of that: "I strode to the front of the stage. 'Excuse me, Monsieur Perrin,' I cried out, 'you have no right to take my moon away. The stage directions read: 'Berthe advances, pale in the moonlight, convulsed with emotion.' I *am* pale, I *am* convulsed, *I want my moon!*' "

Perrin insisted that since Croizette had the principal role she must have the only spotlight. "Then give Croizette a brilliant spotlight and me a less brilliant one," said Sarah.

Perrin refused to budge, as did Sarah, who threatened to leave the cast unless she had her way. Two days went by. Sarah stubbornly remained at home while Perrin tried another actress. At last Feuillet called on her. Everything was settled, he said, kissing her hands. Each of you will have your moon.

The première of *The Sphinx* was a triumph for both Bernhardt and Croizette. The publicity generated by the battles between the "Croizettistes" and the "Bernhardtistes" helped make the play such a popular success that it was given three performances a week, unheard of at the Comédie Française, where the bill was usually changed each day as a matter of course.

Croizette created a sensation when in her suicide scene she swallowed a phial of poison and, helped by special lights and make-up, turned a sinister green, terrorizing the audience with what looked like a severe case of lockjaw and delirium tremens combined. For weeks the newspapers printed heated articles, many from doctors, who argued the authenticity—or ridiculous exaggeration—of Croizette's hideously prolonged death throes. To offset her rival's melodramatics, Sarah played with a quiet power that won the applause of the connoisseurs, Sarcey among them. "In the last act," he wrote, "as the betrayed but forgiving wife Bernhardt displayed a passionate intensity so vehement yet so dignified that it brought forth shouts of admiration. And when she said: 'Do you want to know if I have your letters?' the words came from her trembling lips as sharp and cutting as arrows whistling through the air."

Bernhardt's intensity in reciting these lines may have been inspired by the harrowing letters she was receiving from Mounet at the time, letters that she kept despite their insulting, disagreeable contents. In any case, her naturally high spirits were constantly dragged down by Mounet's insistent demands. As Benjamin Constant wrote: "It is a fearful misfortune not to be loved when you love; but it is a far greater misfortune to be loved passionately when you love no longer."

Sarah loved no longer, if, as Mounet said, she ever had.

In *My Double Life*, Bernhardt speaks of herself as a consumptive who spat blood, fainted frequently, and suffered agonizing bouts of exhaustion. There were those who did not believe her and called her a hysterical hypochondriac. Perhaps they had a point since she was to work hard and live hard until her dying day.

In the exceptionally hot summer of 1874, when Sarah and Jean's painful love affair was exacting a terrible toll from them both, Perrin cast them together in a revival of Voltaire's *Zaïre*—out of the repertory for twenty years. Sarah asked for a month's leave on grounds of illness, but Perrin, who did not trust her, refused, and scheduled rehearsals all through June and July for the August première. Enraged by "the obstinacy of this intellectual bourgeois," she swore she would play on to the death.

A story she tells in *My Double Life* leads one to suspect—as Perrin did—that perhaps she used illness (self-induced, if necessary) as a pretext in order to have her own way. As a child, she recalled, her mother insisted she breakfast on *panade*, a gruel made of bread and butter boiled to a pulp. When the maid revealed that Sarah never touched the hated *panade*, Youle forced her to eat a bowlful in her presence. The moment her mother was out of sight, Sarah swallowed the contents of a large inkwell. Not unexpectedly, she was rewarded by horrible stomach cramps and ran to her mother, screaming: "You've killed me!" Youle, who knew nothing of the ink her wayward daughter had drunk, clutched at her heart and fainted. "Never again was I forced to eat anything I did not like," Sarah wrote, "and after so many years had passed, I had the same spiteful, childish feelings: 'I don't care, I said to myself, I'll rehearse till I fall unconscious; I'll vomit blood; Perhaps I'll die! And it will serve Perrin right! He'll be furious!' Yes, those were my thoughts. At times, I'm as stupid as that. Why? I can't explain it, I can only say that's how it is."

In spite of the heat and their complicated relations, Sarah and Mounet worked well together. Each coached and encouraged the other; each found inspiration in the other's gifts.

On the morning of the première, Jean received one of Sarah's notes:

6 August 1874

My dear Mounet,
You will be superb tonight, I promise you. I implore you to omit that gasp I complained about yesterday. I spent the night working on the scene you spoke of. I shall do everything I can to convey the feeling of terror through my lines. I swear to you that I'll do it with the greatest good will; all I want is to please you.

And till tonight—*courage!*

Determined though she was to drop dead onstage, Sarah did not die. On the contrary, she felt more alive than ever, especially when Sarcey urged the public to see what Bernhardt and Mounet could do with Voltaire. "What grace, what noble attitudes!" he wrote. "It was ravishing. It will be a long time before we see two artists play *Zaïre* with such perfect sympathy, two artists who bring such youth, such fire, such—dare I say it—genius to their roles."

The opening night of *Zaïre*, Sarah felt, marked a turning point in her life:

> I learned that my vital forces were at the service of my brain. . . . And I found, that, having given my all, and more, I was in perfect equilibrium. . . . Until then I had heard, and read in the newspapers, that my voice was pretty but weak, that my gestures were graceful but undefined, . . . that I lacked authority. . . . But now I received proof that I could count on my physical strength, for I began *Zaïre* in such a weak state that one might think I would never get through the first act without fainting. . . . Besides the role required two or three cries that could easily have provoked the vomiting of blood which frequently troubled me at that time. . . . I uttered those cries with real rage and suffering, hoping to break something in my idiotic desire to spite Perrin. Thus my underhanded little scheme turned to my advantage. Unable to die at will, I faced about, and resolved to be strong, dependable, lively, and active—to the great annoyance of those of my colleagues . . . who began to hate me once they were assured I might live for a long while.

Sarah's miraculous recovery leads one to think that she had either exaggerated her condition or that success is a wonderful cure for neurasthenia, if not for tuberculosis. For success it was. Thirty performances were given, the longest run Voltaire's play had ever enjoyed. It is true, however, that after one week Bernhardt was too sick to go on and Perrin was forced to interrupt the play's run until she recovered.

The dream that Sarah and Jean each had cherished, that of becoming the great acting team of France, was now recognized by most critics as a reality. How disappointing for both actors to realize that their dream had turned into a nightmare, that the "perfect sympathy" they displayed in their acting had never existed in their lives. Naturally, each blamed the other, as the following letter from Mounet to Sarah illustrates:

Sunday, one o'clock in the morning

You will not come. I am very sure of that now, and after all is said and
done, you are doing the right thing. . . . Yes, it is true; I have made a
woman weep [Mounet refers, once again, to Maria Favart], a woman who
loved me and who was better and more beautiful than you, just because
you succeeded in taking possession of my heart. But I was honest with
her, and I almost forced her to feel sorry for me, because I was conscious
of the dangers I risked with this mad idea that I loved you. . . . Long ago
I ceased to believe in your love, so often affirmed, so rarely proved. What
still bound me was my desperate need to believe that you had some true
feelings. But that is over. You have been judged. You are no longer
dangerous. Recently you made an infamous proposal, and I said to myself:
"She dares to suggest that because she is certain that I would not accept.
She no longer loves me. It's a subterfuge to make it seem that the idea of
a definitive separation comes from me. . . ." But now I should not be
astonished to find that I have been made a fool of once more. When one
is totally lacking in sensitivity, when one is capable of writing—with no
signature, to be sure—what you wrote this evening, one would have to
delude oneself into thinking that others could share such feelings. Good-
bye then, and really good-bye this time, my poor girl. Pray God that
indifference comes to me quickly as contempt is a dreadful thing for my
weak nature.

We shall never know what Sarah suggested in her unsigned letter—*ménage
à trois?* mutual promiscuity? sexual perversion?—but whatever it was, Mounet found it unspeakable. Her "infamous proposal" gave him the strength
to bring down the curtain on his unhappy attachment. The Calvinist who
had hoped to cleanse Sarah of her sins was free at last, his dignity restored,
or so he thought:

8 November 1874

My poor Sarah,

You have caused me great suffering, but I have loved you so! I forgive
you for having deceived me because I sense that you are unhappy. I ask
only one thing of you, that is to think that perhaps I was sometimes
maladroit, but at least all my efforts were intended to make you a better
person, to make you worthy of yourself. You did not want that. Perhaps
it was beyond you. Be that as it may, I pardon you, and I pity *us*.

10 November 1874

I thank you with all my heart, Jean. I thank you for your happy inspiration, and I thank you for your forgiveness. What you have done is kind, it is good.

I shall always be infinitely grateful to you.

Eight months later, Mounet would send Sarah a postscript to their correspondence. By then hate, like a cancerous twin to love, was gnawing at him:

9 July 1875

. . . You would give me great pleasure by returning the photograph you took from my album *against my wishes*. I treasure it as though it were a holy relic, as my brother carried it over his heart as a protection from Prussian bullets during the war. I should find it most disagreeable to leave it in your hands . . . For me it is a sacred object, and you do not believe in things sacred. You deny their existence, and I am horrified by sacrilege. Therefore send it back to me. . . .

I no longer have any rights over you except one which I intend to use: that is to break all ties that connect us to the past. . . . I have suffered a great deal because of you, but I shall suffer no longer. I shall consider you dead until the day that prostitute's body which resembles yours dies. Perhaps that day the pale ghost of our past love will return to weep in my arms. But until then not only do I no longer love you, but I regret having ever loved you! So you see you have no right to that photograph, or even to my letters, and you must send everything back to me.

Come now, have the courage to accept the consequences of your evil fantasies, and try to behave as a gentleman would, since *nothing* could ever convince you to behave like a lady.

At the end of 1874, Bernhardt was asked to do battle with a powerful antagonist—the ever-present ghost of Rachel. A few days before the "Racine's Birthday" performance of *Phèdre*, Perrin asked her to undertake the title role. The very suggestion made Sarah think she would "die of fright." If the play was pure tragedy, the situation had its comic ironies. Maria Favart, the aging actress from whom Sarah had stolen Mounet, had turned down the part, never dreaming that Perrin would then offer it to her thirty-year-old rival. Mounet, who a few months earlier had found Sarah's "infamous proposal" disgustingly perverse, would now play Hippolyte, the unwitting target of her incestuous desires. Bernhardt may have been irresponsible in love, but she was responsibility itself when it came to her work. With only a few days to prepare the monumental role, she turned to one of her old teachers, François Regnier, for advice. She must not be afraid, he told her. He saw very well what she could make of the role. The chief concern was not to force her voice, to project pathos rather than fury. That, he said, would be better for everyone, even Racine.

Sarah, like all good Conservatoire pupils—and many members of the audience, for that matter—knew a good deal of *Phèdre* from memory. Yet it was a tremendous undertaking to bring the most difficult woman's role in French drama to concert pitch in so short a time. But then Sarah *was* tremendous and arrived letter-perfect for her opening night. As she sat in her dressing room, waiting for the play to begin, an excitable actor rushed in to tell her the house was packed to the rafters, that two hundred people had been turned away. Suddenly she felt the full weight of her task and began to sob. Perrin tried to calm her, but words were useless. Then, with the instinct of a theatre man he took her powder puff and powdered her face with such hilarious abandon that she broke into grateful laughter. At that point, an actor who had a small part in the play walked in to show her how silly his putty nose looked.

"This apparition restored all my gaiety," Sarah remembered, "and from then on I was in full possession of my faculties." Such backstage horseplay is touching in that it enabled Sarah to get onto the stage. She was not, however, in "full possession of her faculties." Stage fright had taken possession of her, as it often did at the first performance of an important role. Her nervousness would always manifest itself in the same way: she would pitch her voice too high, speak too quickly, and overemphasize her d's and t's, and that, unfortunately, is what she did throughout the first act. Worst of all, although she was aware of these faults she was unable to correct them. But one of Bernhardt's greatest strengths lay in her determination— whenever she sensed an audience's disappointment or hostility—to rise to the occasion, to conquer her public *"quand même."* On this night, from the second act on she was superb.

Although in the opinion of the gray-beards in the audience the play still belonged to Rachel, for Sarah (from the second act on) it was a brilliant beginning. She was extremely expressive in what she brought to Racine's lines, lines she was to ponder over, polish, and make her own in the years to come. But on 21 December 1874, Sarah could not know what glories the future would bring. Study, time, repeated performances, and maturity would enable her to convince even some of those who had heard the bronze-voiced Rachel that Sarah's "voice of gold" was able to produce equally beautiful poetry, that Phèdre was Bernhardt's greatest role, and that Bernhardt was its greatest living interpreter. For many of those who found them both sublime, Rachel had the monumental power of a goddess, Sarah the tragic fragility of a woman.

The German poet Heinrich Heine thought Rachel more intelligent than Bernhardt. The English critic George Henry Lewes, George Eliot's consort, compared their delivery of a single line, *"C'est toi qui l'as nommé"* ("It is you who have named him"), and found Sarah finer when, "with a deep shudder of horror," she averted her face from the *intrigante*, Oenone, whereas Rachel had merely looked at her reproachfully. The "single line" is addressed to Oenone, who has revealed that it is Hippolyte, Phèdre's stepson, whom she had tried incestuously to seduce.

In 1908, Bloomsbury's Lytton Strachey saw Sarah as Phèdre. In a passage as impassioned as Charlotte Brontë's description of Rachel in the same role, he wrote:

> To hear the words of Phèdre spoken from the mouth of Bernhardt, to watch, in the culminating horror of crime and of remorse, of jealousy, of rage, of desire, and of despair, all the dark forces of destiny crowd down upon that great spirit, when the heavens and the earth reject her, and Hell opens, and the terrific urn of Minos thunders and crashes to the ground— that indeed is to come close to immortality, to plunge shuddering through infinite abysses, and to look, if only for a moment, upon eternal light.

Quite possibly Sarah never read Strachey's glowing words, but by then she needed neither reassurance nor praise. She had long since proved what powers she possessed when, in Phèdre's Grecian robes, she sang out the rolling lines of Racine's awesome drama of love and death.

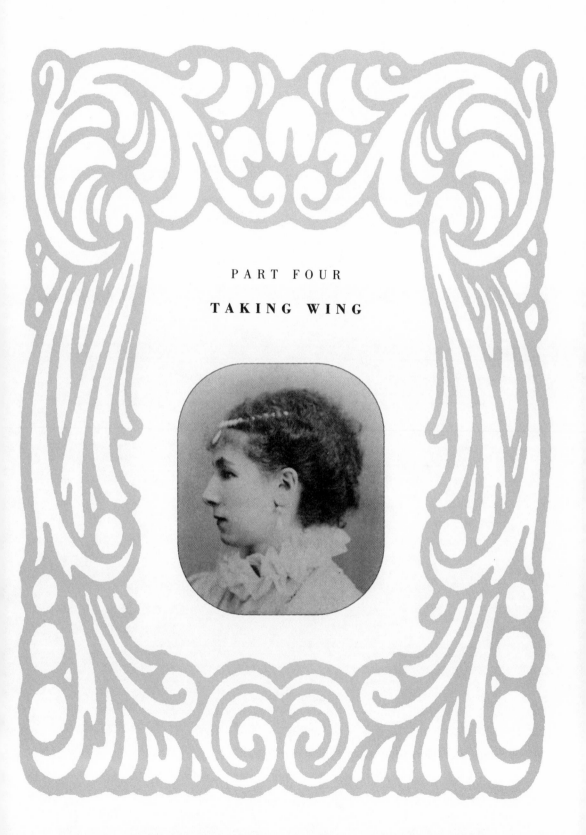

PART FOUR

TAKING WING

Sarah as Doña Sol in Victor Hugo's *Hernani*, 1877

O N 14 FEBRUARY 1875, Bernhardt became a *sociétaire* of the Comédie Française. The next day she created the title role in *La Fille de Roland*, Henri de Bornier's fanciful sequel to the medieval *chanson The Song of Roland*. The play provided her with a short monologue, a description of an offstage duel in which her fiancé vanquishes his Saracen foe. Her stirring delivery of some twenty lines evoked memories of the Franco-Prussian War and brought the audience to its feet. Only a few years had gone by since France's defeat, and the French were, as Henry James put it, "in a mood of almost morbid patriotism." Sarah, costumed to look like a figure on the façade of a Romanesque cathedral, made a profound and lasting impression. It was the first of the many times she would be considered a symbol of her country. Yet official recognition, twelve well-spaced performances of *Phèdre*, rehearsals, fittings, lovers, social and family duties were not enough nourishment for a woman of her appetite. And so she turned more and more to sculpture and the studio life. Her teacher until then had been Mathieu-Meusnier, a reputable artist she met when he presented her with a bronze likeness of herself as Le Passant. Now she found a far more interesting master in Gustave Doré. They had met three years before when he saw her at the Comédie Française and, struck by the beauty of her performance, sent her one of his biblical drawings. The gift led to an invitation to Sarah's dressing room and, as she found love-making the quickest road to friendship, to her bed. It took very little time for Paris to learn about their liaison and the romantic trip they made to the wild shores of Brittany, an escapade, incidentally, that inflamed Mounet's jealousy.

Doré must have come as a welcome change from the long-suffering

Mounet. The actor had expected to reform her; the artist, who had affairs with such eminently unreformed divas as Adelina Patti, the Swedish soprano Christine Nilsson, and Hortense Schneider, the queen of operetta, expected nothing but pleasure. Mounet had offered the domestic security of his small roof-top apartment and the cloistered life of the theatre; Doré offered the stimulation of high bohemia and the limitless horizons of artistic freedom. Even his studio was to her taste, with its vast murals of forests, ruins, and deserted lakes, and its *trompe l'oeil* views of the Rhine.

Doré, at forty, was rich and handsome: a celebrated artist who wore the *Légion d'honneur*, was welcome at the English court, held a lively musical salon, and hobnobbed with the literary and artistic lions of the day. In a word, a man after Sarah's heart. Not that he was universally admired. The Goncourts, who observed him frequently, found him coarse, boring, and pretentious, "a peasant suffering from attacks of cloudy mysticism." It was only after his death that Edmond de Goncourt could bring himself to say, in a grudging epitaph of sorts, that he was a "loyal chap"—faint praise for so prodigious an artist. Perhaps Doré was too earthy, too Alsatian for the fastidious Goncourts, who wrote novels about "real life" but found it repellent when they met it face to face. Certainly they were put off by his uninhibited drinking and dancing and his flamboyant displays of athletic prowess. Indeed, the sight of Doré walking on his hands at a costume ball horrified them. Vincent Van Gogh, who was especially fond of Doré's engravings of scenes from London life, admired him for saying that he "worked like an ox." And Gustave Courbet modestly announced: "There is nobody but he and I. He has blood in his veins."

Sarah, of course, felt no man could have too much blood in his veins to suit her. Nor could she resist Doré's macabre fantasies, the torture and death in the desolate landscapes that filled his books and canvasses.

The letters Sarah sent Doré were, alas, all too reminiscent of those she had written to Mounet. She had changed lovers, but not her approach: he was her adored one, her beloved, a great artist who possessed her, body and soul. She was his, more and more profoundly his. He must know she did not say such things lightly. That, she insisted, was the truth. Having advanced, Sarah retreated. She could not keep their rendezvous for Monday, but would be his on Friday, Saturday, and Sunday. How, she asked in another letter, could she have forgotten last night's promise to meet him? How could it have slipped her mind? Then, reverting to old formulas, she would cancel a rendezvous on the grounds of Maurice's illness or her own.

Doré accepted her excuses with a calm Mounet might well have envied. But then Mounet had loved her with melodramatic intensity and a jealousy akin to madness, while Doré loved her the way one loves a pet: grateful for its affection, but wary of its teeth and claws. Still, they shared many happy moments when she did not hold back or when they worked side by side: Bernhardt, absorbed in the artist's instruction; Doré, touched by her eagerness to excel.

After a time, it occurred to her that Gustave might be put to further use. Their friend Charles Garnier, the architect responsible for Paris's sumptuous new opera house, was now drawing up plans for a casino in Monte Carlo: a theatre with gambling rooms attached. If she could persuade Doré to make a sculpture for the façade, Garnier told her, he would commission her to make a companion piece. Sarah hastened to her desk and wrote to Doré, distorting the facts somewhat to suit her purpose:

> My friend, I've been charged with a diplomatic mission. I'll be blunt and go right to the point. Here it is: Garnier is building a large theatre in Monaco. There are to be a pair of sculptural groups on the façade. He has asked me to do one, and told me he has great hopes that you will do the other, but he is afraid you might turn him down. Could it be true, dear friend, that you would not want me as a partner? It would make me proud! Send an answer quickly to your friend who loves you with all her heart! Say at once whether Garnier dare approach you without the risk of being refused by Your Highness!

Doré was understandably reluctant to agree to these conditions. He was ambitious for his sculpture, having taken it up fairly recently, and tempted by Garnier's offer, but he had no desire to associate his work with that of an amateur. Bernhardt, though a novice at sculpture, was a past master of intrigue. Without consulting Doré, she forced his hand by hinting to the press that they had both agreed to decorate the casino. When her "adored one" read what was news to him, he accused her of double-dealing. Once again Sarah rushed to her desk, this time in the hope of covering her tracks.

> My beloved Master,
> You know perfectly well that the newspapers invent stories, and always get everything wrong. It's all lies. . . . I would never do anything without letting you know beforehand. I love you very much.

When Doré finally accepted, Sarah, elated by her adroit manipulation of art, love, and business, decorated one of her engraved calling cards with the following message and sent it on to him:

> You have made two people happy, Garnier and
> SARAH BERNHARDT
> who sends you a kiss.
> S.B.
> Garnier will come to see you, I think,
> tomorrow or the day after.

Sarah invited Marie Colombier to Monte Carlo for the inauguration of the casino. Ever on the alert, Marie did not fail to notice that "on the train going down Sarah devoured sausage after sausage, so that when a group of admirers invited her to dine, she declined with the ethereal air of a fasting nun." Sarah had no need to put on airs, however, when she saw her sculpture in a niche of its own. Indeed, Bernhardt's *Le Chant*, a winged figure strumming a lyre, with a graceful child at its feet, compared favorably to Doré's *La Danse*. Encouraged by her success, Sarah set to work on *Après la Tempête* (*After the Storm*), a life-size statue of a Breton peasant grieving over her drowned grandson. It moved the public and won an honorable mention at the 1876 Salon. Some visitors did not believe Sarah had made the statue herself. Others felt she should never have made it at all. Rodin, for one, called it "old-fashioned garbage" and thought its admirers a bunch of idiots. Doré, on the other hand, was proud of Sarah's progress and remained her friend until he died seven years later.

It will hardly come as a surprise that Sarah was not devoted to Doré to the exclusion of all others. After one of her visits to Victor Hugo, he noted in his journal of 2 November 1875: "There will be no child." André Malraux in his biography of Hugo quotes a cryptic letter in the Malraux family archives, a letter Sarah wrote that same year to her physician, Dr. de Lambert: "As to England, the trip is put off. . . . The real reason is fear that there might be trouble in connection with Victor Hugo. I am ill and my nerves are on edge . . . the egotistic stupidity of the human race exasperates me. I shall make another effort tomorrow."

Malraux wonders if Sarah hoped to have a child by the great poet, then in his seventies. But it is also quite possible that "another effort tomorrow" refers to an attempt at abortion.

Bernhardt's scandalous life and her immense success fascinated everyone. Still in her early thirties, she was on her way to becoming a legend and a fetish. Visitors from abroad went to see her act with the same curiosity that led them to see the Mona Lisa's smile. Tchaikovsky spoke of her "brilliant performance as Andromaque." William James, the American philosopher-psychologist, as charmed as his brother Henry was by Bernhardt, wrote that hers was "the finest piece of acting I've ever seen—as if etched with the point of a needle—and altogether she is the most race-horsey, high-mettled human being I've ever seen—physically she is a perfect skeleton."

Journalists telegraphed news of her to foreign countries. Novelists, as we know, modelled their heroines after her, and painters exhibited portraits of her. The public, stimulated by a figure they could both idolize and belittle, followed her every move with the avidity usually reserved for political figures and the excessively rich. Her celebrity changed Sarah's view of herself and the attitude of those around her. Her rages were now considered magisterial, her arrogance regal, her promiscuity the divine right of queens. In a word, Sarah had grown larger than life. Of course, her love of publicity was considered vulgar, and no doubt it was, but then vulgarity has many faces. How much more vulgar Bernhardt was than the boastful Dumas, the flamboyant Gautier, or the trousered, cigar-smoking George Sand is open to question. Certainly it excited Sarah, as it did them, to be the center of attention. Yet, to give the devil his due, when the history of publicity is written, Bernhardt must be placed high on the list of its pioneers.

If it is the rule for theatrical celebrities to have devoted followers at their beck and call, it was the one rule Sarah never broke. In classic style she chose two friends, neither of whom had her phenomenal talent nor her phenomenal success. Both very gifted painters, Louise Abbéma and Georges Clairin were always to be at the heart of Sarah's inner circle, a place left vacant when her mother died in May 1876. Not that she had been close to Youle, but rather that her mother was one of the few people with whom she could be herself. Now, she indulged in that rarest of domestic luxuries, a family of her own choosing.

Louise Abbéma, the daughter of a rich, distinguished family, was fourteen years younger than Sarah. A pupil of Carolus Duran, she first attracted attention when, still in her teens, she painted a delightful picture of her family enjoying a day by the sea. Two years later, Sarah posed for her in a stylishly trailing gown. The result was shown at the 1876 Salon along with Clairin's superb oil portrait of Sarah and Sarah's own *Après la Tempête*.

Of course, the growing intimacy between Louise and Sarah did not go unobserved, for Abbéma was a mannish young woman who sported a shirt and tie, wore her hair short, and flaunted her passionate attachment to Sarah. It is not known whether Sarah returned this love or, indeed, whether she had a penchant for women, although it is generally assumed that she did, for with all her seductive femininity, Sarah liked to play the man, offstage and on. Melandri, who had photographed her in her coffin, was now selling picture postcards of her in the white silk shirt and trousers she had designed herself for her role as a serious sculptor. Bernhardt had portrayed ardent, adolescent boys in *Le Passant* and *Le Mariage de Figaro* and would continue on her manly path as Musset's Lorenzaccio, Shakespeare's Hamlet, Maeterlinck's Pelléas, and Rostand's L'Aiglon. Such *romans-à-clef* as Félicien Champsaur's *Dinah Samuel* and Jean Lorrain's *Le Tréteau* would have us believe that she turned to women from time to time. Perhaps it was one of the "new sensations" she had told Mounet she was always in search of. In any event, whatever the favors she granted Louise Abbéma, they were potent enough to keep the painter happily in thrall for almost fifty years.

The stars were in equally happy conjunction when Sarah met Georges Clairin. His was a salubrious presence; he was warm, cultivated, amusing, and, when Sarah misbehaved, critical in the way loving brothers are critical. They began as lovers, and, as was often the case with Sarah, ended up as fast friends. Little is known about the life of Clairin, yet it is through his many portraits of Sarah that we know a good deal about her: how she looked at home, how she looked in her various roles, and, in the many drawings he made for her memoirs, how she looked throughout her eventful career. Clairin painted charming scenes of North Africa, designed the décors for the first production of Bizet's *Carmen*, and decorated ceilings at the Paris Opéra and the casino in Monte Carlo. The day he completed the best-known of his many portraits of Sarah was the day he achieved mastery of a higher sort. The painting gives us Sarah seated on an iridescent, luxuriously cushioned divan, a plumed fan in her hand. She is dressed in a clinging white satin *robe d' intérieur* with white feathers everywhere, at her throat and wrists and at the hem of the opulent train that swirls down to the elegant wolfhound at her feet. She wears black slippers and surprisingly bright blue stockings that echo the blue of her eyes. There is no hint of the great lady in her undulant attitude or her inscrutable smile. Indeed, no lady of the faubourg would have allowed herself to be pictured in such intimate attire or in so inviting a position. But Sarah, beyond such propriety, plays a Parisian sphinx with more secrets from the world than the world considered proper.

Le Tout-Paris crowded around the painting when it was exhibited at the Salon, enthralled by the vision that gazed out at them with such urbane suggestiveness. Once again Bernhardt's name was on everyone's lips, this time as the actress who had succeeded in having her sculpture accepted by the Salon, no mean feat for an amateur, and whose features graced the walls of the exhibition rooms in portraits by a young man and an even younger woman, both of whom were said to be in love with her.

W H E N Henry James was in his early thirties, he lived for a time in Paris and sent his impressions of Parisian life to the New York *Tribune* in a series of "letters" which were later published in a volume called *Parisian Sketches*. In his review of the Paris Salon, dated 6 May 1876, he was far from enthusiastic about Bernhardt's work or the portraits she inspired:

A work which has at the least its share of gazers is a huge representation, by M. Clairin, of Mlle. Sarah Bernhardt, the bright particular star of the Comédie Française. Considering the very small space which this young lady takes up in nature—her thinness is quite phenomenal—she occupies a very large one at the Salon. M. Clairin's portrait is vast and superficially brilliant, but really, I think, not above mediocrity. There is a remarkable white satin wrapper, in which the actress, who is lolling on a sort of oriental divan, is twisted and entangled with something of her peculiar snake-like grace, and which shines from afar; and there are draperies and plants and rugs, and a great deerhound. The only thing wanting is Mlle. Bernhardt herself. She is wanting even more in her second portrait, by Mlle. Louise Abbéma, in which she is standing, in a black walking dress; and in this almost equally large work there are no accessories, good or bad, to make up for the deficiency. . . . Not to be utterly incomplete I must say that Mlle. Sarah Bernhardt, the actress, has a huge group of an old peasant woman holding in her lap, in a frenzied posture, the body of her drowned grandson. The thing is extremely amateurish, but it is surprisingly good for a young lady whom the public knows to draw upon her artistic ingenuity for so many other purposes.

If James felt Clairin failed to capture Sarah, he would, perhaps, have preferred her portrait by Philippe Parrot, painted the year before. In this canvas we find no hothouse atmosphere, no "deerhound" to complete the serpentine curve of her dress, no pretty foot clad in blue to admire. Sarah by Parrot is an inward-looking creature, a young woman uncertain of her future; Sarah by Clairin, a confident adventuress, ready to lead the world by the nose; and both are true portraits of the thirty-two-year-old actress.

Except for her mother's death, 1876 was a banner year for Sarah. To begin with, her reputation as a *femme fatale* was enhanced when two diplomats challenged two journalists to duels to defend what might be called her honor. This foolishness was the result of a malicious article in an obscure scandal sheet. After one encounter, the writer of the piece was wounded seriously enough to take to his bed. Afterward, the other, the offender, although he had won the duel, offered to apologize. "Madame," he wrote, "I throw myself at your feet and humbly beg your pardon," to which Sarah replied: "Pardon granted, but please don't remain at my feet."

While swords clashed in the Bois de Boulogne, Sarah was rehearsing *L'Etrangère* (*The Foreigner*), a dramatic comedy by Alexandre Dumas *fils*. The announcement of the play created great excitement as it was the first time the popular playwright had written for the Comédie Française. A brilliant young cast, Bernhardt, Croizette, Coquelin, and Mounet-Sully, was assembled. The plot was appealing with its conflict of love and social ambition between the poor and pure of heart on one hand and the rich, venal and jaded on the other. Beyond such inducements the very name Dumas spelled entertainment. At fifty-two, he knew every trick of the trade except, perhaps, the secret of how to write masterpieces. For a quarter of a century the canny professional had fed the public spicy dialogue and shocking situations combined with moral judgments, a formula that both titillated his admirers and made them feel virtuous. The new play followed Dumas' usual neat path but startled the audience with its portrayal of Mrs. Clarkson, the pivotal character, played by Sarah. Again Perrin tried to do her in by giving the more sympathetic and believable role, the duchesse de Septmonts, to Sophie Croizette. And again Sarah stormed and threatened to leave. Strangely enough, Sarah and Sophie each coveted the other's role.

Croizette, in a quandary, wrote Dumas: "My heart is heavy because I am about to start into the unknown. For me the unknown is the duchess. But what if I run off the rails? Oh, Heavens above!" On the opening night, it was evident that Croizette had reason to think the role did not suit her and Bernhardt had been justified in fighting for it. Both Alphonse Daudet and Henry James sided with Sarah.

"If Mademoiselle Bernhardt had played the duchesse de Septmonts," Daudet wrote, "she would have been more effective than Croizette and would have rectified the coarser aspects of the part with her poetic charm."

James at his trenchant, puritan best reviewed *L'Etrangère* for the readers of the New York *Tribune*:

. . . The story is both extremely improbable and profoundly disagreeable. Disagreeable above all, for there is not a person in the play who is not, in one way or another, misbehaving grossly. Everyone is in the wrong, and the author most of all. And then his drama is saturated with that aroma of bad company and loose living which is the distinctive sign of M. Dumas' muse. . . . The Foreigner who gives its title to the piece, and who is played by that very interesting actress, Mme. Sarah Bernhardt, is a daughter of our own democracy, Mrs. Clarkson by name. She explains . . . by a mortal harangue—the longest, by the watch, I have ever listened to— that she is the daughter of a mulatto slave girl and a Carolinian planter. As she expresses it herself, "My mother was pretty: he remarked her; I was born of the remark. . . ." Mrs. Clarkson . . . is the least successful figure that the author has ever drawn. Why she should be an American, why she should have Negro blood, why she should be the implacable demon that she is represented, why she should deliver the melodramatic and interminable tirade I have mentioned, why she should come in, why

she should go out, why, in short, she should exist—all this is the perfection
of mystery. . . . She is, on Dumas' part, an incredible error of taste. It
must be confessed, however, that her entrance into the play has a masterly
effectiveness.

One has only to glance at a photograph of Bernhardt as Mrs. Clarkson to
understand why James was taken with her entrance. Apart from her brooding
intensity, Sarah, in a magnificent black and yellow dress, a pool of which
lies luxuriantly at her feet, is theatrical elegance itself. In an article James
wrote for an American magazine, *The Galaxy*, he compares Sarah and Croizette. And good copy it made, for their rivalry had become a *cause célèbre*.

These young ladies are children of . . . [an] eminently contemporary type,
according to which an actress undertakes not to interest but to fascinate.
It would be needless to speak of Mlle. Croizette; for although she has very
great attractions, I think she may (by the cold impartiality of science) be
classified as a secondary, a less inspired, and (to use the great word of
the day) a more "brutal" Sarah Bernhardt. (Mademoiselle Croizette's "bru-
tality" is her great card.) As for Mademoiselle Sarah Bernhardt, she is
simply, at present, in Paris, one of the great figures of the day. It would
be hard to imagine a more brilliant embodiment of feminine success; she
deserves a chapter for herself.

From these words, it can be seen why Sarah felt the Comédie Française did
not appreciate her. Apart from the classic and romantic roles in which she
uniquely shone, she was constantly miscast or ignored. Yet there came a
moment when she deliberately set out to prove that even when she played
"against type" she could steal the show. Several months after *L'Etrangère*,
Perrin, more gifted at staging plays than at evaluating them, produced *Rome
Vaincue*, a verse drama by Alexandre Parodi. The author is aptly named.
Rome Vanquished is like a parody in its pretentious reworking of an ancient
legend. Like many a weak play, it offered unusual opportunities to its
interpreters. Sarah, by now, had acted a sufficient number of inferior roles
to be a judge of their relative value. And so, to everyone's surprise, she
asked, not for the part of the vestal virgin but for the role of her grandmother,
a blind octogenarian, who (to give the tone of the play) stabs her granddaughter in the heart to save her from being buried alive for the blasphemous

crime of losing her virginity. There is a feeling, common to theatre-goers, that one of the tests of a great actor is the ability to render himself unrecognizable in face, voice, and character. Sarah not only passed this test, she surpassed herself. The effect was so powerful that her more knowing admirers made a point of arriving nightly toward ten o'clock, in time—in James's words—to watch Sarah "come out very strong." It was not Jamesian irony. "Mlle. Sarah Bernhardt," he wrote in *The Nation*, "plays, not as might be expected, the guilty vestal but the heroic ancestress. The manner in which she renders the part is one more proof of her extraordinary intelligence and versatility; it is in the highest degree picturesque. She muffles her youth and beauty in long veils and grey tresses until she looks like a perfect *Mater Dolorosa*, a Madonna of a *pietà*. How it is that, to simulate blindness, she contrives for half an hour at a time to show only the whites of her eyes, is her own affair. Her narration of the accident by which she lost her eyesight provokes immense applause by its terrible tranquillity. . . ."

James's praise was reticent compared to the euphoria Sarah elicited from Sarcey. Three days after the opening, the critic who could make or break a French actor with the point of his pen wrote that Sarah was "a force of nature, a fiery soul, a marvellous intelligence. . . . This woman performs with her heart and her entrails. She is a marvel, an incomparable artist, a magnificent creature of the highest order. In a word she is an actress of genius."

By this time Sarah had left her apartment in the rue de Rome and installed herself in her own house at the corner of the rue Fortuny and the avenue de Villiers. It was a grand gesture and a costly one, so costly that many wondered where the money came from. Sarah claimed she had inherited a large sum from a great-aunt, but very few believed her. In her free-and-easy way, she spared no expense and ran up huge debts. All the same, her grandiose establishment was a sign of success and brought her happiness. Indeed, few things had given her more pleasure than watching the building rise from the plains of the newly fashionable Monceau district. Up on the shaky scaffolding or the dizzying heights of the unfinished roof, she would laugh at the horrified warnings of her friends below, joke with the workmen, and discuss plans with her architect. When the house was completed, Sarah thought it "ravishing." It was in fact one of those follies much in vogue at the time, with hints of Renaissance fortifications here and fairy-tale castles there. Decorating the interior presented no problems. With great enthusiasm, Doré, Clairin, Abbéma, Parrot, and other painter friends clambered up ladders and lay on scaffolds to cover the walls with allegorical murals. The most amusing of these was Clairin's vision of Sarah as Aurora, goddess of the dawn, ensconced on the ceiling above her bed, surrounded by a host of her familiars disguised as mythological creatures. The situation was ripe for a house party, and a nonstop house party it became with Sarah in her sculptor's costume presiding over long, hilarious meals in the half-finished dining room. Willy-nilly, she was constructing not only a new home, but a new way of life. From then on, the Jockey Club behind her, she would be an artist among artists, the queen of an extravagant bohemia.

Doré captured the Sarah of the late 1870s in a water color he made about this time. While it is regrettable that she never sat for Manet—as Marie Colombier did—or for one of the great Impressionist masters, it is doubtful that anyone would have given us a more loving picture of Bernhardt on the eve of her international fame. For in Doré's portrait we have the tender, frail, poetic aspect of a creature who was soon to conquer the world.

N 2 1   N O V E M B E R   1 8 7 7   the Comédie Française presented a brilliant revival of Victor Hugo's *Hernani* with Mounet-Sully in the title role and Sarah as Doña Sol. The next day a gift arrived at Sarah's door along with the following note:

> Madame: You were great, and you were charming; you moved me—me the old warrior, and at a certain moment when the public cheered, enchanted and overcome by emotion, I wept. The tear which you drew from me belongs to you. I place it at your feet.

The poet's "tear" was a pear-shaped diamond suspended from a delicate chain bracelet. Needless to say Sarah was overwhelmed by the gift and its message.

The play's first performance in 1830 had provoked one of the finest battles in theatrical history. Long-haired students and suspicious-looking intellectuals, led by the young Théophile Gautier in a rose-pink doublet and pale green trousers, trooped into the Comédie Française to strike terror into bourgeois hearts with their cries of "Down with the bald heads!" Much had changed since then. Hugo's colloquialisms, which had shocked the classicists, were now considered high art. The then young adherents of the new Romanticism—Gautier, Dumas *père*, Sainte-Beuve, and Gérard de Nerval— were gone. Only Hugo was alive to remember the glorious struggle. The once inflammatory *Hernani* had become a harmless classic, for despite its bombast and its improbable plot, the sweep and tenderness of its poetry stirred the imaginative and had them sighing for history's chivalrous past.

Few were more sensitive to the poet's sonorous genius than Sarah. Ever vigilant about her work, she visited him time and again to seek out his views on Doña Sol and to polish each phrase of his verse. The first hearing of *Hernani* had created a riot; the 1877 revival was received with almost religious respect.

Alphonse Daudet, in a moving account, was amazed to see "the always blasé, critical first-night audience—so accepting of the uniform mediocrity and banal adventures of modern comedy—succumb to the beauty of Hugo's poetry." Daudet had nothing but praise for Sarah. "Never has she been so touching," he wrote. "Never has she displayed with such marvellous artistry her rare gift for feeling profoundly, and expressing her feelings with so personal a touch. Those verses which everyone knows, which the entire hall murmured in anticipation, suddenly took on, through the harmony of her diction, a thrilling, unexpected beauty. . . . The verses are admirable; and what charm the actress adds to them. We feared her pure crystal voice . . . would not have sufficient strength for the final explosive scene. But we underestimated the artistic resources of the actress, who, in her very frailty, found heart-rending cries ideally suited to the sinister drama. . . . How well she listens and reacts with emotion as the action quickens."

From Daudet's words it is evident that Sarah had reached the zenith of her youthful powers. Like Hugo, she felt that *"Les mots sont les passants mystérieux de l'ame"* ("Words are the mysterious messengers of the soul"). Seamless and songful, her readings brought their full measure of beauty to the public. Eight years earlier, as Coppée's Florentine troubadour, she had infused the role with such poetic sensibility that she was fondly referred to as "Le Passant." Now she put her stamp on Hugo's heroine so indelibly that she was called "Doña Sol."

In addition to the record-shattering hundred and sixteen performances of *Hernani*, Sarah appeared in Molière's *Amphitryon* and Racine's *Mithridate*. As if that were not enough to fill her time, she sculpted, painted large canvasses, entertained an ever-growing number of friends, and managed to get into a delightful scrape. Ballooning had captured the popular imagination. In his novel *De la Terre à la Lune* (*From the Earth to the Moon*), Jules Verne hoisted Nadar, under the anagram Ardan, into the skies. Victor Hugo, too, paid tribute to the new aeronauts:

> *Audace humaine! effort du captif! sainte rage!*
> *Effraction enfin, plus forte que la cage!*
> *Que faut-il à cet être, atome au large front,*
> *Pour vaincre ce qui n'a ni fin, ni bord, ni fond,*
> *Pour dompter le vent, trombe, et l'écume, avalanche?*
> *Dans le ciel une toile et sur la mer une planche!*

> Human daring! the struggle of the captive! holy rage!
> At last, eruption stronger than the cage!
> What needs that creature, atom of generous brow,
> To vanquish that which has no end, no edge, no base,
> To tame the wind, tornado, ocean's foam, avalanche?
> In the sky a canvas, and on the sea a plank!

Hugo's lines might well have been a tribute to Léon Gambetta, who became a national hero when he ballooned over the heads of the Prussian troops during the Siege of Paris. An intimate, some said a lover of Sarah's, the republican leader had volunteered to deliver documents to army headquarters in Tours in the hope of getting military aid for the beleaguered city. A huge crowd gathered near where the Sacré-Coeur now stands to watch as Gambetta, romantically pale in his fur-lined cloak, climbed into the fragile wicker "gondola," glanced uneasily at the aircraft filled with inflammable gas, and gave the signal for take-off. A ground crew pulled and guided the vessel into the air, while Gambetta unfurled a tricolor flag to cries of "Vive la France! Vive la République!" Then after a sickening series of jerks and spins, the aircraft began its ascent. Moments later, the flying ship, silent and majestic, was headed for Tours.

A favored pet of Sarah's menagerie, Gambetta, not noted for his reserve, regaled his friends with accounts of his adventure. Such dangerous exploits, he felt, were not for women. Sarah, who thought courage knew no gender, did not agree.

During the 1878 Paris Exposition, she was to prove her point by making daily ascents in a captive balloon stationed in the Tuileries gardens and manned by Henry Giffard, inventor of the first dirigible. But to be anchored safely to the ground was not what Sarah had in mind. One day she asked Giffard if he could arrange a free flight. A week later, Sarah, Clairin, and their pilot, a nephew of the pioneer balloonist Eugène Godard, climbed into the gondola of the *Doña Sol*, a splendid orange balloon named for the intrepid actress. It was an incongruous, Labiche-like sight. Sarah had got herself up in a long, trailing cashmere dress, a jacket trimmed in marabou, a filmy silk scarf, and a small ribboned hat. A slender cane and a pair of highly polished riding boots, in case of an emergency landing, completed her flying gear. Clairin in his smart suit and top hat seemed ready for a stroll down the rue de la Paix. Only young Godard appeared in what he considered proper flight clothes: a floor-length, many-pocketed coat and what looked like an alchemist's skullcap. Supplies included a telescope, a well-stocked picnic hamper, and, for Clairin, a sketch pad.

As the *Doña Sol* rose, a group of sporting enthusiasts gathered round to raise their hats and place their bets, while Sarah's friends shouted: "Be careful! Come back! Don't let her be killed!" Soon the balloon drifted away from the Tuileries, over the Place de la Bastille and the Père-Lachaise cemetery, where Sarah, armed with flowers, released a shower of petals in the direction of Youle's and Régine's graves. At last the limitless sky above and the verdant countryside below were all that could be seen.

"It was splendid, it was stupefying," Sarah remembered. "I left Paris in fog; now I saw a radiant sun. Opaque mountains of clouds crested with iridescent color surrounded us. Not a sound, not a breath. It was a magical sight. Enormous orange curtains fringed with violet descended from the heavens to lose themselves in a carpet of mist." In her euphoria, Sarah recited Musset's adaptations of medieval verse, then joined Clairin in Breton folk songs. At dusk Sarah made foie gras sandwiches and Clairin uncorked a bottle of champagne. Glasses were raised to the glorious day, to the future of aviation, and to all artists, past and present. At twenty-six hundred meters, Sarah complained of a nosebleed and a ringing in her ears. As night was falling, Godard told the rapturous couple to prepare for the descent. Hissing valves were opened, and guide ropes were cast overboard as the *Doña Sol* approached the ground. At five hundred meters Godard blew a deafening blast on his horn. A shrill whistle answered his call. The balloon was hovering over a small railway station miles from anywhere. Moments later, five men caught the ropes and pulled the *Doña Sol* toward the earth. Sarah looked up at the sky, but all she could see was the underside of the balloon. Its taut, rounded beauty gone, it had collapsed into a crumpled bag of varnished silk. As they climbed out of the wicker gondola it began to rain heavily. The adventure was over. Someone offered Sarah an umbrella. That was unnecessary, she said; she was so thin she could slip between the raindrops. After a tedious wait in the station, the trio caught a train for Paris. It was the middle of the night when Sarah got into her bed, where her maid handed her a note from Perrin, asking her to see him in the morning. As the *Doña Sol* passed overhead, he had run into Robert de Montesquiou. "Look," the poet said, "there goes your star." "Which star?" the dour director asked. "Why, Sarah Bernhardt, of course," said the poet, at which Perrin muttered: "Another of her tricks. She'll pay for this." The following day, Perrin gave Sarah a thorough drubbing; she was ill-tempered, capricious, and eccentric. Furthermore, she had broken one of the rules of the house by leaving Paris without permission from the management. She would have to pay a fine. Years before, Sarah would have reacted with tears. Now she laughed with studied condescension, told Perrin it was all too boring to discuss, and offered to resign. But by now, the Comédie Française without Bernhardt was unthinkable. Apologies were made, the fine was forgotten, and soon she was back at work.

Like many famous performers, Sarah claimed that she never read the press, particularly when it was about herself. It was another of her "little white lies," for that year she responded to an article which, it would seem, she studied with considerable care.

"In Paris and in all fashionable circles there is talk only of the actions and gestures of Mlle Sarah Bernhardt," it read. "Even the question of Bosnia has receded into the background. The chief editors of the Paris papers forget everything in order to concentrate on Mlle Bernhardt and her recent ascent in M Giffard's balloon. She is a goddess, aerial and ideal, a creature of dreams, a spirit who aspires to the azure. Her slenderness is the result of the dissolution of matter. . . . She cannot breathe until she is above the towers of Notre Dame."

Had Sarah stopped there, she might have accepted the journalist's description with complacent grace, but the writer was not set on flattery. On the contrary, he was among the futile who imagine they can change the course of stars and show them where and how to twinkle. He believed that Mademoiselle Bernhardt was surrounded by clumsy people who, with their instinct for advertisement and the stories they peddle, end by injuring their favorite artistes. No one appreciated more than he the graces, the wit, the education, and the noble aspirations of the young actress. Why did some of her courtiers insist on spoiling that image by saying that she was strange and eccentric, a reputation, he hoped, she did not care for. In the end they would have Sarah Bernhardt the balloonist, Sarah Bernhardt the sculptress, Sarah Bernhardt and her eleven fathers. He, Albert Millhaud, thought none of these worthy of the Sarah Bernhardt he applauded in her great stage appearances.

Sarah did not take this lying down. Some days later *Le Figaro* published her response:

> Your good will toward the artist prompts me to defend the woman. It is not my clumsy friends who throw me in the face of the public; it is my clever enemies. . . . I had great fun going up in a balloon. . . . But I want to assure you that I have never skinned dogs alive, or burned cats. And I regret that I cannot prove that I am naturally blond. It is thought that my thinness is eccentric. I should very much prefer to be deliciously ripe. . . . I am accused of trying to do everything except act: sculpture, painting, playing the piano. Who does that disturb if my work at the Théâtre Français does not suffer?

As though to give further proof of her versatility, Bernhardt wrote a delightful book about her balloon ascension called *Dans Les Nuages. Impressions d'Une Chaise. Recit Recueilli Par Sarah Bernhardt (In the Clouds: A Chair's Impressions, as Told to Sarah Bernhardt)*. Profusely illustrated by Clairin, it not only prospered, but it gave her an opportunity to make fun of her critics by exaggerating their ridiculous claims to a preposterous degree. "They say of Doña Sol," the chair reported, "that she feasts on dainties made of lizard tails, eats peacock's brains sautéed in monkey fat, and plays croquet with human skulls topped by Louis XIV wigs." The unpretentious, playful book intended chiefly for children amused almost everyone except Gustave Flaubert.

His editor, Charpentier, he wrote, "who has promised again and again to issue a new and luxurious edition of my *Saint Julian*, is neglecting my literature for Sarah's trash." But what irritated him even more was a piece in Charpentier's periodical, *La Vie Moderne*, which compared Bernhardt's acting favorably to George Sand's writing. "Where," Flaubert raged, "will this stupidity end?" Had he seen Sarah in the revival of Victor Hugo's *Ruy Blas* (the great writer had given up the theatre years before), he might have had second thoughts, for while acting and literature are things apart, a great performance arouses emotions as profound and as memorable as a great novel. Sarah gave just such pleasure in Hugo's *Hernani*. At the Odéon seven years before, she had thrilled an audience unprepared for her fresh young talent. Now, in her mid-thirties, she was the complete actress, able to give the sum of her artistry: the gift of her voice, her body, and her unique understanding of Romantic poetry. Beyond that, she gave what Sarcey, in speechless admiration, called her *je ne sais quoi*: that indefinable quality which is remembered long after the play has dimmed in memory.

Traditionally, the Comédie Française was open every day of the year, but in 1879 an exceptional announcement was made: The theatre would be closed in June and July as it was badly in need of repair. Perrin immediately received an offer from the managers of the Gaiety Theatre in London, Messrs. Hollingshead and Mayer. A contract was signed which would bring the entire company to London for six weeks, from 2 June to 12 July. Perrin was delighted to have a London season, as it would help pay for the restoration of his theatre. Besides, he was tempted to show the English the wonders he had accomplished in his eight-year reign. He had every reason to be proud of what Henry James described as the Comédie's "peculiar perfection: something consecrated, historical, academic. . . ." Never had the cautious critic seen anything "so harmonious, so artistic, so complete—dramatic effort refined to a point with which the English stage is unacquainted."

Perrin sent Hollingshead a carefully worked out schedule of programs and casts, leaving Sarah out of the opening-night program. In return, he received a telegram from Hollingshead stating that half the tickets had been sold on the strength of Bernhardt's name, therefore it was essential that she appear on the first night. As Perrin could not offend the actors already scheduled for the first program, he decided to add the second act of *Phèdre* especially for her. It is quite probable that Perrin and Croizette had come to resent Sarah's box-office popularity, and enjoyed the idea of taking her down a peg or two.

Sarah took advantage of the situation to say that she would not go to London at all unless she were promoted to *sociétaire à part entière*, the highest rank in the company's hierarchy. At first, the committee balked, but its members came around, and both Sarah and Sophie Croizette were promoted and would henceforth receive a larger share of the company's profits. But this was just the beginning of what would prove to be a spectacular change in Bernhardt's life.

 F E W   D A Y S   before their departure, an unexpected visitor appeared at Bernhardt's studio, an American theatrical agent with offices in New York, Paris, and London named Edward Jarrett.

"He was very tall," Sarah wrote, "with piercing blue eyes, silvery white hair, and a well-trimmed beard. He excused himself very politely, and, without introducing himself, spent ten minutes admiring my paintings and sculpture. When I asked him to sit down and tell me the purpose of his visit, he said with a strong accent, 'I am Mr. Jarrett, the impresario. I can make your fortune if you would like to come to America.'

" 'Never!' I cried. 'Never!'

" 'All right. Don't get angry. Here's my card. Don't lose it.' "

Just as Jarrett was leaving, he asked if she would like to make a "small fortune" in London.

"How?" asked Sarah, who needed more than a small fortune to keep her debtors at bay.

"By giving private performances in London's smart drawing rooms," Jarrett said.

In a matter of minutes a contract was signed, and a week later the following announcement appeared in *The Times* of London:

Drawing-room Comedies of Mlle. Sarah Bernhardt, under the management of Sir Benedict:

The répertoire of Mlle. Sarah Bernhardt is composed of comedies, sketches, one-act plays and monologues, written especially for her and one or two artistes of the Comédie Française. These comedies are played without accessories or scenery, and can be adapted both in London and Paris to the *matinées* and *soirées* of the best society. For all details and conditions please communicate with Mr. Jarrett (Secretary of Mlle. Sarah Bernhardt) at His Majesty's Theatre.

Perrin was aghast when he saw *The Times*. He could hardly believe that any member of the austere Comédie Française would stoop to such cheap commercialism. Well within her legal rights (others in the company had given private performances), Sarah would not back down. The quarrel soon became public, and Perrin eventually had to admit to the press that the actors of France's national theatre could do whatever they wished with their free time.

Bernhardt thought she was prepared for all emergencies when she boarded the ferry at Le Havre. Wrapped in a heavy cloak despite the warm weather, she was provided with lozenges for seasickness, sedatives for headache, tissue paper to protect her back, plaster compresses to put on her stomach, and waterproof cork soles to put in her shoes to keep her feet from getting cold. A young admirer who was concerned about the dangers his idol might face added to these precautions when he rushed up the gangplank with a life preserver he had invented especially for her. It was a bulky object hung with twelve egg-sized bladders. Eleven were filled with air and lumps of sugar. The twelfth contained brandy. As soon as the ferry was under way, Sarah gave way to one of her famous *fou-rires* and had it thrown overboard.

A sight I shall never forget [Sarah recalled in her memoirs] was our landing at Folkestone. There were thousands of people, and it was the first time I ever heard the cry, "*Vive Sarah Bernhardt!*" I turned my head and saw before me a pale young man, his face ideal for Hamlet. He presented me with a gardenia. This embarrassed me slightly, but I was delighted all the same. . . .

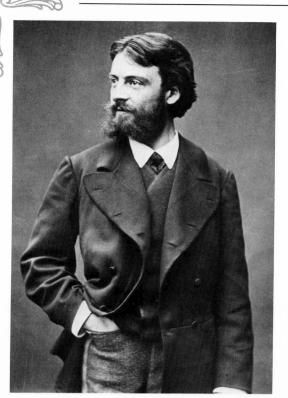

28, 29. LEFT: Mounet-Sully, Sarah's co-star, and the most exigent of her lovers. BELOW: The painter, sculptor, and engraver Gustave Doré was Sarah's professor of sculpture—and her lover.

30. Edouard de Max, often called "the Sarah Bernhardt of actors"

31, 32. LEFT: Sarah and Clairin at lunch. BELOW: Georges Clairin, Sarah's court painter, lover, and closest lifelong friend, in a studio pose

33–35. LEFT: Jean Richepin. Sarah commissioned him to write a new translation of Shakespeare's *Macbeth* for her. BELOW, LEFT: Louise Abbéma, a gifted painter, was Sarah's closest woman friend to the end of her days. RIGHT: Aristidis Damala was a Greek diplomat and notorious ladies' man who became, at Sarah's insistence, her lover, leading man (under the name Jacques Damala), and husband.

36, 37. R I G H T : Sarah toured America in a luxurious private railway train known as the "Sarah Bernhardt Special." B E L O W : Nevil's sketch of Sarah being interviewed by the press upon her arrival in New York

38, 39. RIGHT: Sarah (seated, fourth from right) and her company at Niagara Falls. BELOW: Sarah performed at Convention Hall, which seated 5,000, in Kansas City, Missouri.

40. Sarah tours America. Here she is (center) with her troupe in the Garden
of the Gods, Colorado, enjoying an outing between performances.

41. Sarah in front of the circus tent in which she performed for 2,000 people in Kansas City, Missouri

"Soon they'll make you a carpet of flowers," a spiteful colleague muttered.

"Here is one!" a young man shouted as he threw an armful of lilies on the ground before me. I stopped short, rather confused, not daring to trample the flowers, but the crowd pushed me forward. . . .

"Hip, hip, hurrah! and a cheer for Sarah Bernhardt!" the impetuous young man cried. His head towered above the others. With his luminous eyes and long hair he looked like a German student, but he was an English poet, and one of the greatest of this century, a poet of genius who, alas, was to be tortured, and finally vanquished for his folly. It was Oscar Wilde.

The ecstatic welcome Sarah received did not endear her to her fellow actors, who suspected that, once again, she was up to her tricks. They were mistaken, according to John Hollingshead, who recalled: "It was not a Barnum-organized crowd but a perfectly spontaneous and enthusiastic mob who had come to see Sarah Bernhardt. The attendant photographers watched for Sarah Bernhardt; the chroniclers and 'special correspondents' made a special feature of Sarah Bernhardt. Before the curtain rose on the first night the great British public had made Sarah Bernhardt a star—a star of the first magnitude."

As might be expected of someone with her temperament, such premature attention played havoc with Sarah's nerves. To be singled out among the superb ensemble players of the Comédie Française was flattering but terrifying, as it put her in a peculiarly vulnerable position. Her first moments at Victoria Station gave her a feeling of neglect. Instead of the glorious crowds at Folkestone, only two of Hollingshead's businesslike henchmen were there to meet the boat train and show the actors to their hotels. A stretch of red carpet raised her hopes for a moment. Was it for them? No, she was told, it had been put down for the Prince and Princess of Wales, who had just left for France. Why, she pouted, had they left? Because they had engagements in Paris. Then they would not be in London for the first night? No, but the Duke of Connaught would be in the royal box.

"I was in despair . . ." Sarah wrote. "I don't know why, but I felt that everything would end badly. I crossed London sick at heart."

Bernhardt's first sight of grimy Victorian London did not restore her spirits.

In her depression, the charming house in Chester Square that she had taken for her six-week stay struck her as gloomy, as did the masses of

flowers from Parisian friends. Even the immense bouquet of roses from Sir
Henry Irving, England's foremost actor, seemed ominous. Everything—the
house, the flowers, and the thirty-seven journalists who interviewed her the
next day—seemed to say: "You are about to perform before an alien public.
Now prove you are as great as they say you are."

On 2 June 1879, the Comédie Française gave its first performance,
a gala occasion, as it was one of the rare times that the entire company had
journeyed to foreign shores. Great applause broke out when the curtain rose
to reveal its fifty-odd members, each costumed for the role he would play.
Busts of Shakespeare and Molière graced the sides of the stage, and a poem
to the treasured poets was declaimed by the dean of the company, Edmond
Got. When the ceremony ended, Sarah went to her dressing room, moved
by the welcome, but unnerved by the responsibility of her coming task.
Three times she put on her make-up, and three times she sponged it off.
Her voice, when she tested it, sounded hoarse at the bottom and shrill at
the top:

> I wept with rage, and just then I was told that *Phèdre* was about to
> begin. I hadn't put on my veil and my cameo-belt was still unfastened.
> . . . Everyone was alarmed by my nervous state. I heard Edmond Got
> whisper: "She's going mad. . . ." Once I was on the stage I still had stage-
> fright, not the kind that paralyzes, but the kind that drives one wild. That
> was bad enough, but better than the other sort. It makes one do too much,
> but at any rate one does something. As the public applauded my entrance,
> I said to myself, "Yes, yes—you'll see—I shall give you my blood, my
> life, my soul." But when I began to speak I pitched my voice too high
> and could not bring it down.
>
> I suffered, I wept, I cried out—and it all rang true. . . . My tears
> flowed, scorching and bitter. I implored Hippolyte for the love that was
> killing me, and the arms I stretched out to Mounet-Sully were the arms
> of Phèdre, writhing in cruel longing for his embrace. The gods were with
> me. When the curtain fell, Mounet carried my inert body to my dressing
> room.

When the curtain rose for bows, the public was treated to a spectacle almost
as compelling as the performance itself. Bernhardt—beautiful, ravaged, and
visibly faint—stood supported by Mounet. Heads held high, they faced the

standing, cheering crowd with the grave dignity of ancient statues. There
was an ovation such as England had seldom seen. Engulfed by the waves
of admiration that flooded over the footlights, Sarah sensed that she had
taken her place among the idols of the theatre.

But even idols have problems. The following evening, Sarah played
L'Etrangère in such a state of exhaustion that she left out two hundred lines
of the speech she was making to Croizette. The monologue was essential to
the plot, if not to Sarah, who found herself improvising: "The reason I sent
for you, Madame, is that I wished to tell you why I have acted as I have"
(long hesitation), "but I have thought it over, and I have decided not to tell
you today" (quick exit). Sophie Croizette, left high and dry, crept off the
stage, while the brave Coquelin marched on to finish the act as best he
could. The awkward episode provided a story all three dined out on for
years. One can imagine the special charm with which each of them told his
own side-splitting version of Sarah's historic gaffe.

There was no mention of Sarah's memory lapse in the London papers,
perhaps because the critics, along with the public, had fallen blindly, un-
reservedly in love with the new Rachel. As Henry James wrote: "It would
require some ingenuity to give an idea of the intensity, the ecstasy, the
insanity, as some people would say, of curiosity and enthusiasm provoked
by Mlle. Bernhardt."

No one in the opening-night audience was more intensely enthusiastic
than the young Oscar Wilde, who said: "It was not until I heard Sarah
Bernhardt in *Phèdre* that I realised the sweetness of the music of Racine."
He wrote a sonnet to her which was published in *The World* on 11 June,
plied her with flowers and invitations, and generally made himself useful.
Bernhardt said of him: "Most men who are civil to actresses and render them
services have an ulterior motive. It is not so with Oscar Wilde. He was a
devoted attendant, and did much to make things pleasant and easy for me
in London, but he never appeared to pay court." Of course, Sarah was
worldly enough to know that if Wilde did have an ulterior motive, it was not
the usual one of "paying court," but rather some vague ambition to write a
play for her. (Wilde's ambition would be fulfilled, however unsatisfactorily,
when, some twelve years later, Bernhardt returned to London to rehearse
the *Salomé* he had written with her in mind.) London lionized Bernhardt in
ways somewhat different from those she had known before. Paris had accustomed her to the homage—and flattery—of writers and artists, and from

time to time she was happy to share their beds, read their plays, and pose for their paintings. But when a French man about town, a Rothschild or a Polignac, appeared backstage, it was almost inevitably an overture to an affair. Certainly there was no thought of inviting her to dine with the wife and family. She was, after all, an actress. Titled Londoners might have behaved in the same way, but for one thing: the Prince of Wales had taken to Sarah. His royal attentions gave the cue to the smart set. The doors of Mayfair flew open. Soon Sarah was seen riding with Lord Dudley in Hyde Park and dining at the Duchess T.'s, the Marchioness R.'s, and other irreproachable ladies of the court. Yet there was some stiff-necked resistance. Lady Cavendish, for one, confided to her diary: "London has gone mad over the principal actress of the Comédie Française. Sarah Bernhardt, a woman of notorious, shameless character. Not content with being run after on the stage, this woman is asked to respectable houses to act, and even to luncheon and dinner; and all the world goes. It is an outrageous scandal."

Sarah was of two minds about invitations from the rich and mighty. Although she found her English hosts "charming, witty, the most hospitable people in the world," she could be as cavalier as the loftiest among them. She knew her behavior was "perfectly odious," but when the time came to keep an engagement, she resisted, bored with writing to excuse herself, bored with those who did not speak French, bored with herself for not speaking English, even bored at the thought that she might attract more attention by her absence than by her presence. From the very beginning it was clear that London preferred Bernhardt to any other attraction the Comédie Française had to offer. When she was on the playbill, the box-office receipts rose to five hundred pounds or more; when she was not, they dropped to four hundred pounds or less. The French considered these figures a sad commentary on English taste and resented a public that so visibly preferred Bernhardt's accomplishments to those of distinguished, older members of the company. Yet it was not that the English failed to appreciate the superb ensemble acting of the troupe, but rather that its formal declamatory style— like a great wine that does not travel—was somehow out of place at the Gaiety. *The Truth*, a London weekly, found that "apart from Bernhardt and Coquelin, each phrase the actors pronounced was accompanied by a gesture which one supposes was conventionally thought appropriate. This gesture is held, not only during a speech, but a minute after its completion. True, the tone is varied, but it always has something of the theatrical or declamatory in it."

On the third Saturday of the run, Sarah did not feel well, and, since she was listed for two performances that day, she asked to be excused from the matinee. Edmond Got, in charge of such matters, took the news calmly. Surely a good replacement, bolstered by a brilliant cast, would compensate for one ailing actress. But he had not reckoned with Sarah's box-office appeal. The moment Bernhardt's cancellation was announced, the public stormed the theatre for refunds. Of course Sarah gloated, while her colleagues felt that she had betrayed not only the Comédie Française, but France itself.

As though to irritate them further, Sarah announced an exhibition of her paintings and sculpture at a fashionable gallery in Piccadilly. Gossip had it that the Prince of Wales would be present, for by this time it was an open secret that Sarah had done more than curtsy to the future king of England. If there was any doubt, it would be dispelled by a letter she sent to the dean of the company:

> I have just returned from a visit with the Prince of Wales. It is 1:20 and I cannot rehearse at this hour. The Prince kept me from eleven o'clock on. I beg your forgiveness, dear Monsieur Got, and shall make amends tomorrow by knowing my role.

Bernhardt's "command performance," with conjecture concerning its duration, was perfect backstage material, both for the ribald actors of the company and the envious actresses who told each other that Sarah's behavior was beneath contempt. Nonetheless, they, along with hundreds of others, turned up at her *vernissage* to ogle Prince Edward and Princess Alexandra; Prince Leopold, later Leopold II of Belgium; the prime minister, Mr. Gladstone; the painters Everett Millais and Lord Leighton; and—not least of all—the actress herself. A marble version of *Après la Tempête* was sold, along with most of her other works. At the opening of the exhibition, champagne was served, a rather daring innovation, and Sarah was as engaging as only she could be. Dressed in an elegantly simple costume, one hand resting on a precious cane the Prince of Wales had given her, she exchanged views with Mr. Gladstone on the moral lessons to be learned from *Phèdre* and the evils of capital punishment. Needless to say, Sarah found a way to spend the money the sales brought her. In fact, she claimed that the only reason she had arranged an exhibition was to enable her to buy some animals. On a free day, she went up to Liverpool to the menagerie of a certain Mr. Cross. Why Sarah, who already had three dogs, Minuccio, Bull, and Fly; a parrot named Bizibouzou, and a monkey named Darwin, felt the need for more pets is anyone's guess. All the same, when she got back to Chester Square, she was the proud owner of a cheetah, a wolfhound, and six boggle-eyed chameleons, one of which was fastened to her dress by a gold chain. Gustave Doré, Georges Clairin, Louise Abbéma, and Madame Guérard, all of whom had come to London to hold Sarah's hand, were on the doorstep to greet her when she drove up. At the sight of the new menagerie, Sarah's butler recoiled in terror and Madame Guérard fled, screaming, to her room. But it was the malevolent-looking cheetah who stole the show, when, released from his cage, he scampered, snarling and hissing, up the nearest tree. The dogs howled, the parrot shrieked, Darwin rattled his cage, and Sarah's friends, always delighted by her gift for the unexpected, shook with laughter. Staid Chester Square had never seen the like.

"All the windows opened and more than twenty faces appeared over my garden wall," Sarah remembered, "all of them inquisitive, alarmed, or furious."

The following day, London talked of nothing but the bedlam at Chester Square. (Could it be that the sign "No Noise Permitted After 10 p.m.," which one now sees in that quiet square, was put there as a result of Bernhardt's undomesticated behavior?) Monsieur Got warned Sarah that if she continued to behave like a madwoman the press would be against her. The French correspondents, resenting the way she had managed to upstage the entire Comédie Française, were on the warpath. They claimed that for a shilling anyone could see Bernhardt dressed like a man, that she smoked huge cigars on the balcony of her London house, that she used her maid as an acting partner at her private performances, that she practiced fencing in a Pierrot costume, that she had broken two of her boxing professor's teeth. Even her old friend Francisque Sarcey, who had attached himself to the Comédie Française for its season in London, was writing poisonous articles about Bernhardt, partly, perhaps, because the English made it clear that they found her enchanting while Sarcey, who, for impressive fees, lectured them before the performances on the vast superiority of French theatre to English theatre, was thought pretentious and patronizing.

Sarah might have risen above all this nonsense, but then she would not have been Sarah. Instead, she wrote an open letter to Albert Wolff, her chief detractor at *Le Figaro*, asking how he could believe such inanities. If the slander printed about her annoyed her compatriots, and if they took it into their heads to receive her unkindly, she would resign from the Comédie

Française. As for the English, if they were tired of all the fuss and were to show her ill will instead of the warm appreciation they had heaped on her till then, she would leave England in order to spare the company further embarrassment. Sarah's fellow actors were sympathetic when they read her letter. To her great surprise, many of them took her aside to say that she must not think of leaving the Comédie Française.

Despite her strong stand, Sarah was uneasy when she returned to Paris after her unprecedented triumph. She had sailed to London on a wave of popularity. Now she was drowning in a sea of disapproval. What crime had she committed? True, she had outshone the entire Comédie Française, but not by performing differently than she had in Paris. She had been preferred to Croizette, but was she to blame because the British found that actress too stout and more than a little vulgar? She had sold her art works, but then she was the only member of the Comédie Française who made works of art.

Emile Zola was the one person who came to her defense. As might be expected, his was a more tolerant view than either Sarcey's or Wolff's. Why, he asked in an article in *Le Voltaire*, had the press declared war on Madame Sarah Bernhardt? Why did her painting, sculpture, and writing raise the hackles of Parisian journalists? What made them think she produced art for the sake of publicity or that she should not sell her canvasses and statues as other artists did? Their relentless, banal quips about her thinness were more vulgar than anything she had done. They attacked her for wanting to see her name in print, but it was they, not she, who invented diabolical stories to feed the press. Surely they did not believe she had exhibited herself in London dressed as a man for a penny a peek or that she roasted monkeys and slept with skeletons. Even if their ridiculous tales had been true it was her affair, not theirs. The vicious hullabaloo about the actress they had adored only yesterday was their doing. It was they who created the scandal, not the great artist whose talents should be allowed to speak for themselves.

Bernhardt's first opportunity to face the French public came with the annual tribute to Molière. Perrin initially advised her not to appear at the ceremony as there might be a public demonstration against her. A threatening letter Sarah showed him justified his concern:

My poor skeleton, you would do well not to show your horrible Jewish nose at the opening ceremony. I fear it would serve as a target for all the potatoes that are now being cooked especially for you in your kind city of

Paris. Have some notices put in the papers to the effect that you have been spitting blood, and stay in bed to think about the consequences of excessive publicity.

Perrin pushed the letter aside in disgust. There were others, Sarah told him, too coarse for anyone to see. In that case, the outraged Perrin said, she *must* take part in the Molière evening.

An impressive audience turned out to honor the playwright and to welcome their actors back to Paris. As was the custom, they advanced, two by two, to lay palm fronds on the bust of Molière, but when Sarah's turn came there was a sudden hush, for she had stepped forward alone.

"I strode to the footlights," she recalled, "but instead of bowing, as my comrades had done, I stood erect and gazed into the eyes turned toward me. I had been warned of a battle, a battle I had no wish to provoke, but one I was determined to face. I waited in silence for a minute, stirred by the nervous tremors of emotion that filled the house. Then, suddenly the whole audience burst into a fanfare of bravos and applause. It was one of the most beautiful moments of my career."

There were many other beautiful moments during the 1879–1880 season, notably in performances of two of her finest roles: the Queen in *Ruy Blas* and Doña Sol in *Hernani*. To celebrate the fiftieth anniversary of Victor Hugo's history-making drama, on 25 February 1880 there was a fête at which Bernhardt gave an extraordinarily fiery reading of Coppée's poem "La Bataille d'Hernani." This was followed by a banquet at the Hôtel Continental. Paris's literary and political luminaries were there to pay homage to the great Victor Hugo. He, in turn, paid homage to his great Doña Sol by seating her at his right.

Bernhardt was back, but not for long. In the spring, Perrin insisted that she perform in Emile Augier's *L'Aventurière* (*The Adventuress*), a play she detested by a playwright she despised. As a rule, she worked hard and carefully, whether she liked a role or not. This time she turned suspiciously skittish, neglecting rehearsals and failing to turn up for costume fittings. The day before the première she developed what Perrin suspected was a convenient attack of laryngitis and begged him to postpone the opening. He refused. Reluctantly, Sarah went on, looking, as she said, "like an English teapot" and acting, the critic Vitu wrote, like a vulgar tart in a Zola novel. Vitu's accusation of vulgarity provided Sarah with a perfect pretext to do what she wanted to do. And so, as she said: "I threw my laurels and floral tributes to the four winds, and brutally broke the contract that bound me to the Comédie Française, and thus to Paris." On 18 April 1880 she wrote Perrin:

Monsieur l'Administrateur,

You gave me only eight rehearsals onstage, and the play received only three full run-throughs. I felt that I should not appear before the public but you absolutely demanded it. What I predicted has happened. . . . It is my first failure at the Comédie, and it shall be my last. I warned you the day of the dress rehearsal, but you paid no attention. I always keep my word. By the time you receive this letter I shall have left Paris. Kindly accept my immediate resignation.

To avoid any further discussion with Perrin or the governing committee of the Comédie Française, Bernhardt sent copies of her letter to *Le Figaro* and *Le Gaulois*. The next day found her in Sainte-Adresse, near Le Havre, where she spent a rainy afternoon walking on the beach to think things over. Her resignation, she had told the committee, was due to the shabby way the management and the press had treated her. What she kept back, and what was to be revealed in the lawsuit the Comédie Française filed against her, was that, although she had claimed to be too sick to attend rehearsals of *L'Aventurière*, she had, in fact, been assembling a troupe of her own to take to London's Gaiety Theatre to fulfill a contract she had signed with Messrs. Hollingshead and Mayer without notifying the Comédie Française. (As it turned out, Bernhardt would be performing in London with her new company when the case was tried in Paris.) Worse still, Maître Allou, the Comédie's advocate, said she had broken a house rule which stated that no actor could take a leave of absence without the permission of the committee. This calculating woman, he went on to say, had seduced the English public with her superb artistry, her feminine elegance, her talent for sculpture, and her literary accomplishments. But was it worthy of such a woman to sign a contract (again without notifying the Comédie Française!) with an American Barnum in order to go to the United States? She would be punished for such an action. "There in England and America," he proclaimed, "she will perform surrounded by second-rate actors and no one will understand a word she says. She can take her grand reputation overseas like an exotic cargo, but as her fortune grows her reputation will diminish."

The result of the suit was that Bernhardt would have to give up the forty-three thousand francs she would have received as a *sociétaire*'s pension had she remained at the theatre for twenty years and left it amicably. In addition, she was fined a hundred thousand francs for damages. She never paid the fine. Instead, some years later, when the Comédie Française was damaged by fire, she gave them the use of her own theatre free of charge.

At the end of May 1880, about a month after her break with the French national theatre, Sarah returned to London's Gaiety Theatre. It was a re-engagement, and like all re-engagements it was a challenge. She knew she must outshine her previous efforts and knew, too, that the audience, though kindly disposed, expected to see their admiration justified. Sarah came through with flying colors. Furthermore, she behaved like an angel.

Hollingshead, who had not enjoyed his dealings with the Comédie Française, had nothing but praise for her honesty, reliability, and willingness to oblige. But it was her energy—she gave twenty-eight performances in thirty days—that he found truly remarkable. Just as remarkable in its way was the presence of the critics Sarcey, Vitu, and Lapommeray in London. All three critics had slaughtered her the year before, and Sarah could only imagine that they had followed her in the hope of seeing her fail. To her relief, they found her more seductive than ever. It had been just a lover's quarrel, after all. "Bernhardt was prodigious," Sarcey wired to Paris after she opened her first independent season on 24 May. "Never has an audience been so moved. What a pity it was that she had taken it into her head to resign. . . . Nothing at the Comédie Française could equal her last act in *Adrienne Lecouvreur*. How much better it would be if she had stayed at the Comédie! Our loss is as great as hers. What a pity! What a pity!" A week later, Sarcey wrote about her enormous success in Meilhac and Halévy's *Froufrou*: "I do not think there has ever been emotion more poignant in any theatre. There were exceptional moments during which the artists were transported beyond themselves, above themselves. After the performance I said to Sarah Bernhardt: 'This is an evening that will re-open the doors of the Comédie Française, if you wish it.' 'Let's not discuss that again,' she said to me. 'Let's not talk about it any further.' So be it. But what a pity!"

During her stay in London, Edmond Got paid her an official visit. The Comédie was willing to take her back, even if she persisted in going to

America first. She must realize that America would destroy her, that if there was anything left of her she might be very glad to be taken in by the Comédie Française, which would not be getting the better part of the bargain. Bernhardt found these words unacceptable. With her pockets filled to overflowing (her take at the Gaiety box office was higher than that of the Comédie Française itself the year before), her pride in her work restored, and her vanity gratified, Sarah refused. She was more than happy to rest on laurels she had gathered on her own, she told Monsieur Got. Besides she was able to sleep better.

"Sleeping better, I began to eat better," she remembered, "and great was the astonishment of my little court when they saw their idol come back to Paris, round and rosy."

PA R I S did not see Sarah for long. After a few days there to see how her house was progressing, the new actress-manager was off to Brussels and Copenhagen to help pay for it. If her four-day stop at the Théâtre de la Monnaie in Brussels was like a solid success in the provinces, Copenhagen was a revelation, for it was there that she realized she was an international star. As the train pulled into the station, she leaned out the window and heard "a hurrah so overwhelming" that it frightened her. Two thousand Danes lined the streets from the station to her hotel, cast flowers at her feet, blew kisses, tossed their hats into the air, and shouted, "*Vive Sarah Bernhardt.*" She felt she could never come up to their expectations, but that evening at the Royal Theatre she proved deserving of her reputation. It was with no little satisfaction that she would read in *Le Figaro* of 16 August that her performance of *Adrienne Lecouvreur* was an immense success before a magnificent public: the Danish King and Queen; their daughter Alexandra, Princess of Wales; and their son, who had been made King George I of Greece with his Russian Queen, Olga; that the royal ladies had "thrown their bouquets to the French artiste amidst the thunderous applause of a delirious public. An unprecedented triumph."

King Christian IX presented Sarah with the diamond-studded Order
of Merit and lent her the royal yacht for an excursion to Elsinore. The future
Hamlet was a romantic, and the sad little column said to mark Prince
Hamlet's grave depressed her.

On the way back, Bernhardt leaned on the ship's rail and gazed at
the water. To her surprise, she saw rose petals drifting by:

> There seemed to be thousands, and in the mysterious sunset I heard, like
> a distant fanfare, the melodious voices of the sons of the North. Before
> us, riding the wind, was a pretty boat in full sail. A score of young men
> was scattering armfuls of roses, and chanting the legends of centuries past.
> All this was for me: all the roses, all the love, all the poetry of music.
> The sun itself, I felt, was setting for me. In that fleeting moment, which
> brought me life in all its beauty, I felt very close to God.

Apparently Sarah felt closer to the devil when she attended a huge supper
party in her honor. All went smoothly until Baron Magnus, the Prussian
ambassador, made a toast. "I drink to France," he roared, turning to Sarah,
"which has given us such great artists; to France, the country everyone
loves." Bernhardt, who was still smarting over the loss of Alsace and Lorraine
at the end of the Franco-Prussian War, rose to her feet, pale and nervous.
"Yes," she cried out in her most Racinian tones, "let us drink to France,
but to the whole of France, Your Excellency, the Ambassador of Prussia."
At this the orchestra struck up *La Marseillaise*. Sarah's patriotic gaffe did
her no harm. When she left Copenhagen in the midst of fervent cries of
"Vive la France!" she felt an enthusiasm directed not only to her but to her
country as well.

Before Sarah left for America, Félix Duquesnel, who had forgiven her
defection from the Odéon, arranged a tour of France that would take her to
twenty-five cities in twenty-eight days—a far cry from the Comédie Française,
where she had performed once or twice a week. Nothing could have suited
her better. She enjoyed the constant activity, the handsome fees, and the
chance to polish *Adrienne Lecouvreur* and *Froufrou* for New York. Her friends
planned to join her at the various towns where Duquesnel had organized
excursions and fêtes in her honor. Only one thing stood in the way of her
pleasure. In his desire to keep her happy, he had also arranged for dignitaries
in each city to show her the sights. But the very thought of churches bored

her. "I can't help it," she confided. "The idea of entering those cold spaces while someone explains their absurd and interminable history, of looking up at the ceiling with craning neck, of being obliged to admire the restoration of the left wing—it would have been better to let it crumble!—to have to exclaim at the depth of some moat which was once filled with water . . . all that makes me want to howl! I have always detested houses, castles, churches, towers, and all buildings higher than a mill. I have nothing against the Pyramids, but I would a hundred times rather they had never been built."

Sarah, as we know, had a mind of her own, which was all to the good. Now that she was no longer under orders from Perrin, she was responsible for her own taste, judgment, and decisions. Of prime importance was the repertory for the American tour. With her sure instinct for what suited her, she chose plays that would show the best aspects of her talent: *Phèdre*, *Adrienne Lecouvreur*, *Hernani*, *Froufrou*, and one she had never played before: Dumas *fils' La Dame aux Camélias*. Next, she must dazzle with her costumes, a task that came easily to her. A master of dress design and a student of period costume, she could draw and sew, knew what was most becoming to her, and had a regal disdain for expense. She had special silks woven in Lyon, ordered velvets from Italy and sables and chinchilla from Russia. Her costumes glittered with rare crystal beads, mother-of-pearl inserts, and handmade satin tea roses. And there was no hesitation when she was billed ten thousand francs (then about twenty-five thousand dollars) for the ball gown she would wear as Marguerite, the Lady of the Camellias.

Alas, the Bernhardt costumes outshone the Bernhardt troupe. But there she had little choice. In 1880, the French were reluctant to go to America unless it was to seek their fortunes or escape the law. They found excitement in the books of James Fenimore Cooper, but were not foolish enough to want to share such adventures. And so Sarah had to make do with a leading man named Edouard Angelo, a handsome, if not very gifted actor who had been in and out of her bed since the Odéon days. "As strong as Hercules," and almost as courageous, Angelo would be a reassuring watchdog in case of danger and a reassuring lover should time hang heavy on her hands. Her sister, Jeanne, was recruited for supporting roles, but a few days before the company sailed, she took an overdose of drugs and was sent to a sanitorium. With no one else to turn to, Sarah asked Marie Colombier to take Jeanne's place. It was an awkward situation. When they were girls together, Marie had thought of herself as Sarah's equal. Now Sarah was inconceivably famous, and Marie was just another disappointed actress, too stout, too distracted, too spiteful, and too clever for her own good.

Marie remembered her "best friend," as she called Sarah, throwing herself on her neck and asking her to pack her bags. Why? Marie asked, am I going somewhere?

"To America," was Sarah's reply. "I'm asking you because you're the only person who would do me such a favor on such short notice. I know you still love me in spite of our silly quarrels." But what about her costumes, Marie asked. When could she learn her roles? All that could be arranged, Sarah said. To her relief, Colombier agreed to go. All the while, the newspapers predicted every possible disaster, including shipwreck. Remember Rachel's failure in America, they warned. Think of all those savages who did not understand a word of French. Circus elephants were more to their taste. Real wealth could not be counted in American dollars, but rather in the appreciation and applause of the only civilized people in the world, the French. Sarah, "thrilled by the adventures that lay ahead, thrilled at the thought of stepping off the edge of the world," ignored the dire prophecies.

On 15 October 1880, at 6:00 a.m., Bernhardt, up to her ears in ermine, made her way up the gangplank of *L'Amérique*, a decrepit old tub, half sailing ship, half steamer, that would carry her to New York. A crowd of friends and admirers stood on the quai to cheer her on. Seeing her off on board were Clairin, Abbéma, Duquesnel, and others of her court. She was sad to leave her friends and sadder still to leave her fifteen-year-old son, who kept rushing ashore, then rushing back for tearful farewells. At last the gangplank was raised, cannons boomed, whistles blew, and the *Amérique* slowly moved out of the harbor and into the channel. There was no turning back. Sarah was off to see the New World.

PART FIVE

ENGLAND AND AMERICA

Fédora, 1882

SARAH'S ocean crossing marked a new chapter in her artistic development. Until then, despite her originality, she had been an unmistakable product of the Conservatoire and the Comédie Française. Now, as an actress-manager, she was free to expand her horizons and form a theatre in her own image. To her credit, those who worked with her were in awe of her judgment, her knowledge of stagecraft, and her ability to demonstrate and illumine the thornier passages in anything from *Phèdre* to *Froufrou*. The stormy North Atlantic was hardly the place to exercise her directorial gifts, however. She spent the first few days confined to her cabin, in "utter despair," as she put it, "weeping bitter tears, tears that scalded my cheeks. Then my will power asserted itself and triumphed over my grief." Less dramatically put, she was seasick, as well as homesick, and nothing, not even the tender ministrations of Guérard and her maid, Félicie, could induce her to leave her bed. At last the ship's doctor prescribed a brisk walk in the open air. On deck she found Marie Colombier flirting with the captain. At the very idea of being upstaged, Sarah revived, raised her arms to the heavens, and delivered a paean to the wind and the waves. Then, after a seductive glance at the captain, she fixed her eyes on Colombier's ample waist and added that there was nothing like thinness to prevent *mal de mer*. At that moment the ship, as malicious as Sarah herself, climbed a gigantic wave, hesitated in mid-air, and, shuddering, plunged downward. No one saw Sarah for the rest of the day, but once she was up and about, there was no stopping her. She went over her scenes with Angelo, called company rehearsals, consulted her manager, spent hours studying her roles, and tried to reassure Marie, who, not unreasonably, felt uneasy without a written contract.

Sarah's memories of the voyage as recorded in her memoirs are as picturesque as Doré engravings: *L'Amérique* foundering in an epic storm, *L'Amérique* a ghostly galleon blanketed in snow while an ermine-clad figure—Bernhardt herself, of course—gazes on in an ecstasy of wonder, Sarah assisting at the birth of an immigrant child, a band of cutthroats threatening to finish off the first-class passengers. Most compelling was her meeting with a veiled lady whom she saved from falling down a flight of stairs when the ship suddenly lurched.

"You might have been killed," Sarah said.

"Yes," the stranger replied, "but it was not God's will." Then, with a distracted look at her savior, she asked her name. Sarah Bernhardt was the answer. "And I," said the woman, "am Mary Todd Lincoln."

"A thrill of anguish ran through me," Sarah recalled, "for it seems I had done the unhappy creature a disservice. President Lincoln had been assassinated by an actor, [John Wilkes] Booth, and now an actress had prevented his widow from joining her beloved husband."

During her eleven days at sea, Sarah and her impresario were inseparable. "The terrible Mr. Jarrett," as she called him, was cool, hardheaded, and unshakably tough. His tales were proof of that. One day Sarah asked about the scar on his cheek. It was the result, he explained, of a fight with another manager over a contract for Jenny Lind.

"Look at this eye, sir," he had said to his rival. "It can read in your mind all the facts you are trying to conceal."

"Then it doesn't know how to read," his adversary growled, as he fired a revolver at Jarrett's head.

"A poor shot! Here's the way to shut an eye," Jarrett muttered, as he shot his assailant dead.

Needless to say, Sarah found Jarrett's tall stories enthralling. She was always to speak of him as an honest, chivalrous gentleman—a rare tribute from a performer to a manager. Fortunately, the paternal Jarrett was not merely chivalrous and honest. A brilliant agent, and a fanatic admirer of Sarah's talent, he arranged hundreds of appearances at unheard-of fees and made certain that his precious cargo would enjoy every comfort. This, then, was the man who introduced Bernhardt to America. For several months in advance he had fed the press with extravagant reports of the actress's triumphs and eccentricities. Thus, when *L'Amérique* dropped anchor in New York Harbor, boatloads of newspapermen and French officials clambered aboard to meet La Bernhardt in the main salon. Their first impression was hardly what they had been led to expect. Here was no man-eating *femme fatale* from the city of fashion and vice. Instead they saw an extravagantly pale young woman of grace and distinction, who listened to the French consul's welcoming speech with becoming modesty, stood at rapt attention while *La Marseillaise* was played, and smiled an aesthete's smile as she buried her face in the flowers presented to her. An endless line of enthusiastic celebrity seekers pressed in to gush over Sarah and pump her hand until her rings cut into her fingers. Tired of what she called "*le handshake*," and with no English at her command, she felt an utter fool when she heard herself muttering: "Oh! Combien je suis charmée!" Finally, her nerves gave way.

"I feared I would lose my temper, and burst into tears," she remembered. "And so I pretended to faint. I made a movement with my hand as though it wanted to go on but could not. Then I opened my mouth, closed my eyes, and fell into Jarrett's arms." A specialist at playing dead, Bernhardt lay back on a sofa and listened to the babble of excitement around her until a doctor appeared and ordered the visitors to leave. The moment they were gone, she jumped to her feet, flung her arms around Jarrett, and waltzed him around the room. But her gaiety turned to despair when he told her that he had invited all the reporters to come to her hotel later in the day.

Publicity-loving Sarah's attitude might seem out of character, but it is understandable when one remembers that Europeans had not yet adopted the American way of attacking celebrities en masse. If Sarah was upset by the prospect of reporters, she was terrified when she saw the rowdy mob waiting for her on the pier. There were no poetic, lily-bearing Englishmen or respectful Danes ready to clear a path for an idol of the stage. No, this crowd stood its ground, gaping and grinning as though she were the circus come to town. Indeed it took the combined efforts of Jarrett, his associate, Henry Abbey, whom she henceforth addressed as Monsieur l'Abbé, and a formidable Pinkerton detective to clear the way for their frail charge. A closed carriage took them to the Albemarle, a fashionable hotel on lower Fifth Avenue. (Curious to think that, had they proceeded northward, they would have been in open farmland in a very short time.)

The rooms Abbey had taken pleased Sarah, as well they might. Monsieur Knoedler, the art dealer, had sent busts of Molière, Racine, and Victor Hugo to make her feel at home. The parlor was an imitation of her Paris drawing room with its bear rugs, Turkish ottomans, potted palms, and a divan piled with satin cushions, backed by a Persian hanging. There was

only one drawback: fifty reporters were milling about waiting to inspect her.
At the sight of them she slipped into the adjoining room, pushed a piece of
furniture against the door, lay down on a rug, and proceeded to fall asleep,
deaf to the knocking on the door and Jarrett's angry warnings. Her defiant
gesture was more newsworthy than the questions she was asked when she
finally deigned to appear: What size were her shoes? Her waist? What did
she eat for breakfast? Did she really feed her pet lion cub live quails? How
did she like New York? How much were her jewels and dresses worth? All
the while a young man was busily sketching. A fellow artist, Sarah thought,
and asked to see what he had done.

"Perfectly unabashed," she remembered, "he handed me a horrible
drawing of a skeleton with a curly wig on its skull. I tore it up and threw
the pieces in his face. The next day an identical horror was printed in the
newspapers, complete with an unpleasant caption." During her stay in America Bernhardt was the subject of endless caricatures: a paper-thin virago
kicking a reporter, a skeleton being dressed and painted for the stage, a
cane topped with a sponge, a slinky boa constrictor, a writhing rope tying
itself into emotional knots. Jarrett and Abbey—who were avid believers in
publicity—jumped on the bandwagon with blaring announcements, fabri-
cated or not, about Sarah's tempestuous whims and ways. Cheap and noisy,
theirs was the first publicity campaign to invent, popularize, and launch a
star. Sarah's reaction was a philosophic "Nothing kills but death." Yet, like
Oscar Wilde, she felt that "there is only one thing worse than being talked
about, and that is *not* being talked about."

Two days after her arrival, Bernhardt was taken to see the Booth
Theatre at Twenty-third Street and Sixth Avenue where she would perform.
There is a special pleasure for actors in going through the stage door, *their*
door, to find the quiet gloom of an empty auditorium. Sarah was not granted
that pleasure. To her horror, she found a horde of dirty-fingered, cigar-
smoking customs inspectors, rifling through the forty-two trunks of costumes
and dresses she had sent on ahead. On hand, too, were a couple of "hideous
dressmakers," there to estimate the value of each item. How much did you
pay for this? asked one of the ladies, holding up Sarah's pearl-embroidered
costume for *La Dame aux Camélias*.

"I ground my teeth together," the actress remembered, "and refused
to answer. By the time they had finished it was half-past five. My feet were
frozen, and I was half dead from fatigue and suppressed anger. At last the

band of ugly men offered to put it all back into the trunks, but I refused to allow that." Instead, Sarah sent for five hundred yards of muslin to cover the mountain of clothes that littered the stage and left her maid Félicie's husband there with a revolver to see that nothing was stolen. Then, in need of relaxation, she went to see "the miracle of Manhattan," the partially completed Brooklyn Bridge. If she felt violated by the customs men to whom she eventually had to pay enormous duties, she was seduced by the new structure, "so mad, so admirable, so imposing, that it made one feel proud of the human mind."

Sarah's pride in the human mind was somewhat diminished when she saw Clara Morris, New York's favorite actress, in *Alix*, a cleaned-up version of a slightly risqué French play: *La Comtesse de Sommerive*, by Théodore Barrière. Abbey had announced to the press that Sarah insisted on applauding her great American colleague before she could even think of appearing on the New York stage. Naturally the theatre was packed.

Marie Colombier's description of the evening indicates that she was no kinder to other actresses than she was to Sarah:

> 8 o'clock: The house is packed. Sarah arrives at nine, in time for the second act, accompanied by Jarrett and Abbey. The orchestra strikes up *La Marseillaise* as they settle into their stage-box which was hung with French flags. Wild applause. Sarah acknowledges the public with gestures worthy of a queen. The curtain parts to reveal Clara Morris. Imagine a woman so thin she makes Sarah look buxom. . . . She could never have been beautiful. Or if she was, it was a long, long time ago. Her mouth is a black hole, her teeth as dark as cloves. And they say America is the home of dentistry! Visibly moved, she clings to the curtain and blows Sarah a kiss. More applause. Not to be outdone, Sarah removes her corsage of white roses and casts it at the actress's feet. Cries and bravos from both artistes! To be fair, I must admit that Sarah was laughing up her sleeve. And furthermore, that on their way back to the hotel, Jarrett must have given his protégée high marks for good behavior.

On 8 November 1880, Bernhardt made her American debut at Booth's Temple of Dramatic Art in *Adrienne Lecouvreur*, originally written for Rachel by Ernest Legouvé and Eugène Scribe. One of the most successful plays of the time, it is about the tragic love of the illustrious eighteenth-century actress for her roving paramour, the Baron de Saxe. A virtuoso piece, it begins on a note of tender frivolity and includes recitations from La Fontaine and Racine as well as a venomous confrontation between Adrienne and her rival, the Princesse de Bouillon. It ends on a climactic note of betrayal and death by poisoning. The action, and there is a good deal of it, is accomplished amid a flurry of Louis XV finery, which in Bernhardt's production was a spectacle in itself. And a good thing, too, as most of the audience did not understand French and were grateful for visual diversion when they stopped reading the synopsis long enough to look at the stage.

The evening held its amusements for Sarah. To begin with, a play that schoolchildren flocked to in Paris as part of their education was forbidden to American youth since the tale of an unmarried actress's affair with a rakish aristocrat was considered unsuitable for virgin ears. Then someone came backstage to tell her that an irate theatre-goer demanded a refund because Bernhardt did not appear in the first act. What amused her most were the delightfully inappropriate Offenbach cancans and xylophone solos which the orchestra played between the acts. No, decidedly Booth's Temple of Dramatic Art was not the Comédie Française. Still the evening had its rewards. Sarah was delighted by the twenty-seven curtain calls, the gigantic baskets of flowers the ushers carried down the aisles, and the wreath with a gold-lettered message: "For our Sarah from the artists and sculptors of Paris." And, of course, she was moved by the crowds of admirers waiting in the bitter cold to applaud her and shout: "Good night, Sarah!"

New York's enthusiasm did not stop there. At the Albemarle hundreds were gathered under her balcony, which American ingenuity had illuminated with a powerful electric beam. A brass band played *La Marseillaise* as the actress stepped out to blow kisses to the multitude below. At the festive reception that followed, an American friend assured her that the emperor of Brazil had not created such a stir. Yes, said another, but *he* was only an emperor. If Sarah was in need of further praise, and she always was, the critics provided it. The *New York Times* thought her Adrienne "finer and more natural than Rachel's." Another paper observed that situations which Clara Morris "would moisten with copious tears, or tear to tatters with vehemence of declamation, Sarah Bernhardt illumines with a simple gesture, a trifling inflection, a look." But it was the *New York Herald*'s William Winter who struck the most gratifying note when he wrote of her passionate abandon that "set free the soul of humanity, and redeemed the commonness of the mortal world."

Sarah did not rest on her laurels. During her stay in New York she gave twenty-seven performances in as many days, and, more impressive still, played seven demanding roles, two of which were new to her. It was a feat few actors would attempt today. Her efforts were amply rewarded. After her debut, three-dollar seats went for fifteen dollars and sixty-dollar season tickets for a hundred and twenty. Jarrett and Abbey were quick to exploit her success. At their behest, Sarah was paid to endorse candies, perfumes, gloves, dresses, hair curlers, and even cigars. The women's pages were filled with sketches of her Paris gowns, the story of her life, descriptions of her home, and her opinions on everything from make-up to Molière.

Success of this kind often provokes wit of one sort or another, as jingles about Bernhardt proved. One poked fun at her extravagant wardrobe:

> *Fancy the hussy's dress,*
> *"Expressly made" no less,*
> *Embroidered, festooned satins, laced to kill.*
> *They say that every gown*
> *She wore about the town*
> *Would cost a dry-goods merchant his till.*

Another spoke of her impressive earnings:

> *When "Ta-ta," I say to this country*
> *I know I'll be blinded by tears;*
> *But then I'll bear off many dollars,*
> *The sweetest of all souvenirs.*

These little rhymes were love pats compared to the wrath of a fire-and-brimstone preacher named Dr. Crosby. Sarah Bernhardt, he wrote, was a harlot sent to destroy the morals of American citizens. A religious journal, *The Methodist*, took another tack when it criticized the English for opening their doors to a sinful actress, a corrupt courtesan who flaunted her illegitimate son. As for her repertory, it stood for something forbidden, alien, and evil. Society, too, took care to ostracize the visiting artiste. James Stebbins, a rich, respected man about town was a case in point. The gentleman, if gentleman he was, had raised heaven and earth to meet Bernhardt in Paris and, when he finally succeeded, showered her with flattery and ostentatious gifts. Now, he refused to see her, saying this was New York, not Paris.

Sarah wryly agreed. James Gordon Bennett, the owner of the *New York Herald*, displayed equal insensitivity when he gave a dinner party at Delmonico's in Sarah's honor and invited his friends to come without their wives.

Such behavior seemed barbaric to a woman who counted George Sand, Victor Hugo, Flaubert, Doré, and the Prince of Wales among her friends. In an attempt to improve the situation, Jarrett arranged an exhibition of Sarah's art works at the exclusive Union Club. Once again there were no women allowed, and once again the anthropologist in Sarah pondered the tribal customs of these starched, decorous males who felt it dangerous to expose their mates to a French actress.

If the *grandes dames* of New York avoided Sarah as a social pariah, they were only too eager to be present when she sinned and suffered as Marguerite in *La Dame aux Camélias*. Not that *Camille*, as they called it, was entirely new to them. They had bravely attended *Heart's-Ease*, a tidied-up version of the Dumas play in which Marguerite was a harmless flirt and Armand a proper, if wayward youth who jilted her so callously that she lay down and died. Sarah's performance was not only the first time New York saw Dumas' original drama, it was the first time Sarah took on the role. And what a role, what theatrical riches Dumas provided in his fable of a capricious woman's love, sacrifice, and death! Henry James described it, as he might have said, "beautifully":

> *Camille* remains an astonishing piece of work. The play has been blown about the world at a fearful rate. But the story has never lost its youthful juvenility, a charm that nothing can vulgarize. It is all champagne and tears—fresh perversity, fresh credulity, fresh passion, fresh pain. . . . [It has] a great place among the love stories of the world.

Generous words from a man who did not admire Dumas *fils*. Yet there is more to the piece than champagne and tears, perversity and passion. There is the role of Marguerite, an inspired creation for those elect divas who have the power to play on our nerves, awaken our senses, dim our critical faculties, and leave us spent with emotion. It would be a gross understatement to say that Sarah had success as Marguerite. She *was* Marguerite, and for thirty years, no actress, try as she might, could alter that fact. As Sarcey wrote: "Only a beautiful, worldly woman, born and bred in Paris, only a master at transforming prose into poetry could combine restraint, feverish gaiety, and a tragic yearning for love with the infinite cynicism and careless insolence that was the product of a courtesan's life."

Sarah ended her New York season with a gala matinée of *La Dame aux Camélias*. By then she had been hailed as "the most popular girl in town," a fact made painfully evident when she arrived at the backstage entrance of the theatre to find hundreds of worshippers waiting to bid her good-bye. It was thrilling until she realized that her shouting admirers had no intention of making a passage to the stage door. Instead, they fought to get near her, to shake her hand and touch her furs, to tell her they loved her and hoped she would come back. One wild-eyed woman almost knocked her over in her eagerness to pin a brooch on her coat. Another cut a feather from her hat. Then someone had the idea, new to Sarah, of asking for her autograph. The notion caught on, and soon a "band of young ruffians" elbowed their way up, thrust their hands in her face, and begged her to sign her name on their shirt cuffs. Adulation—or whatever it is that impels people to molest celebrities—gave way to hysteria. Sarah was in helpless tears when the police arrived to rough up the crowd and push her "with as little ceremony" into the safety of the theatre. Half an hour later she was on the stage, a shimmering vision in her Lady of the Camellias' costume. Oddly enough, Marguerite's first lines are in response to an admirer who asks if it is his fault that he loves her. "My dear man" is her reply, "if I had to pay attention to everyone who loves me, I wouldn't even have time for meals," a riposte Sarah may have delivered with special emphasis after her unsettling experience in the alleyway of the theatre.

After a glorious performance and many emotional curtain calls Sarah was on the verge of collapse. But she was told that thousands of people were standing behind the theatre in the hope of catching a glimpse of her. In that case, she said, she would lock herself up in her dressing room and throw the key away. Henry Abbey, more creative than Jarrett when it came to publicity, proposed a less dramatic solution. Sarah's sister, Jeanne, who had been ill when the company left Paris, had just arrived in New York. Why not take advantage of the family resemblance and let her wave to the stage-door Johnnys while Sarah slipped out the front entrance? Later that afternoon, Jeanne, dishevelled but happy, appeared at the Albemarle. She had had the time of her life impersonating her famous sister through a screen of boas, veils, and bouquets. It may well have been the finest performance of her career.

That same evening, Jarrett, always eager for headlines, took Sarah to meet Thomas Alva Edison at his home in Menlo Park, New Jersey. It was an unlikely encounter. Sarah knew as little about duplex telegraphy and telephone transmitters as Edison knew about La Fontaine or Racine. For her, the inventor was a wizard, a Yankee Cagliostro. For him, if the purple blush that came to his face was any indication, the actress was a fairy-tale figure who had appeared out of the snowy night, silken-gowned and satin-slippered. The visit began somewhat stiffly, with "The King of Light" looking shy and the actress wondering how to brighten the atmosphere.

"At last his wonderful blue eyes, more luminous than his own incandescent lamps, enabled me to read his mind," she recalled. "I knew I must win him over, and instinctively I exerted all my powers of fascination to vanquish the delightful, if bashful savant." Edison, fully "vanquished," took Sarah's arm and gave her a guided tour of his laboratory. It was an astonishing sight: furnaces glowed, immense wheels clanked and labored, as lights flashed—green and sputtering—like serpentine trails of fire. Edison, as canny a showman as Bernhardt herself, had saved the best for the last. With no word of explanation, he stood at his recent invention, the phonograph, and sang "John Brown's Body." Moments later, his voice came back like a magic echo. Sarah could hardly wait for her turn. And so, miles from anywhere, the actress made her first recording: some lines from *Phèdre*. The historic session ended with Edison, his shyness forgotten, singing a foot-tapping rendition of "Yankee Doodle Dandy." On the way back to New York, Sarah roared with laughter at the thought of Racine's incestuous heroine meeting the puritan Yankee Doodle in the frozen wilds of New Jersey. The following day the troupe went on to Boston. But not before they saw headlines that read: THE MOST FAMOUS MAN IN THE UNITED STATES MEETS THE MOST FAMOUS WOMAN IN FRANCE.

Sarah was relieved to be in Boston after her hectic weeks in New York. She was not alone. Many foreign visitors saw the latter city as a place of American boastfulness, philistinism, and greed and found its citizens suspicious of Europeans, uncultivated, and obsessed by money, power, and social position. Boston, they felt, had other, more elevated values. As Mark Twain put it, "In New York they ask: 'How much is he worth?' In Boston they ask, 'How much does he know?' "

Boston discovered that Bernhardt "knew" a good deal, more perhaps than any actress they had ever seen, when she opened her two-week engagement with Victor Hugo's *Hernani*. The critics were awed; they spoke of her acting as "perfection that defied analysis." Sarah was grateful, but then she was grateful for all the pleasures Boston offered. First—and of incalculable importance to touring artists—there was the comfort of her suite at the Hotel Vendome. More than comfortable, it was filled with works of art, rare porcelains, and masses of carpets sent by welcoming Brahmins who left invitations along with their calling cards. Good manners and generosity were not their only virtues. They had a tradition of learning and a love of beauty that allowed them to perceive Bernhardt, not as a scandalous personality, but as a supreme practitioner of her art. Sarah, in turn, was captivated by what she called the "Bostonian race," particularly by the sisterhood of spinsters who she felt knew everything, understood everything, were independent, earnest, and blessedly reserved compared to the strident women of New York. And they all seemed to speak French! Sarah's approval was returned tenfold. In the years to come the cultivated ladies of Boston rushed to her every performance. And if the Divine Sarah smiled, they were, like handmaidens of Terpsichore, happy to attend to her slightest wish. Colombier, on the other hand, thought the adoring acolytes rather pitiful examples of womanhood: unfeminine, bookish, and frustrated. But even Marie had to admit that they were largely responsible for Boston's tolerant attitude toward Sarah.

There were those who took Sarah's charms more lightly. One of the most interesting was Lillie Moulton, who had lived in Paris during the Second Empire. An exceptionally gifted amateur singer, she had caught the eye of Napoleon III while ice skating in the Bois de Boulogne, and from then on she "knew everyone" and, rare for an American, was much sought after by European aristocrats. Her letters give lively descriptions of the emperor, his court, and the entertainments at Compiègne.

To Mrs. Moulton, Sarah was just another of the many celebrities who crossed her crowded path. One May evening in Paris, Lillie took her little daughter Nina to see Bernhardt perform. With them were Mrs. Bradley, a Boston dowager, and her son George, an immaculately proper young gentleman. During the second act, Mrs. Moulton put Nina in the front of the box so that the child could see.

"Observe how virtue is rewarded!" Mrs. Moulton wrote in her collected letters. "An *ouvreuse* came in and begged to *parler à Monsieur*. Imagine the chaste George's feelings when he was told that the famous Sarah wished to speak to him, and, moreover, desired him to come behind the scenes to her dressing room. What a situation! His red hair blushed to the very roots, and his yellow face became a sunset. However, one is or is not a man. He proved himself to be one who could face danger when the time came. Trembling at the thought of Boston, the virtuous hearing of it, he saw in his mind's eye the height the Puritan brows of his most distinguished family would reach when the news would be spread over the town, and a certain biblical scene passed before his mental vision. He gave his lemon-colored moustache a final, fascinating twist, and, humming to himself 'Hail the conquering hero comes!' he buckled on his sword and went—all his colors flying."

Sarah, as it turned out, had no sinister designs on the gallant young Bostonian. She simply wondered whether Mrs. Moulton could be tempted to allow her to make a bust of her pretty child. Mrs. Moulton was more than tempted; she was delighted. A few days later she described the sittings in a letter to her mother:

It was enchanting to watch the artist at work. She was dressed like a man; she wore white trousers and jacket, and a white *foulard* tied artistically about her head. . . . She smoked cigarettes all the time she was working. . . . To keep the child quiet, sometimes she would rehearse her roles in the voice they speak of as golden, because it coins gold for her, I suppose; but what kept Nina most quiet was when Sarah told her of the album she was making for her. Every artist she knew was working at some offering, and when it would be finished Nina was to have it. Meissonier, for instance, was painting a scene of the Franco-Prussian war. Then Gounod was writing a bit of music dedicated to *le charmant modèle*, and so forth.

At every sitting Nina would say, "*Et mon album?*" But it never came forth. It only existed in Madame Bernhardt's fertile brain. It had no other object than to keep the model still. It seemed cruel to deceive the child. Even to the last, when Nina had said for the last time, "And shall I have my album today?" Sarah answered that it was not *quite* ready, as the binding was not satisfactory, and other tales, which, if not true, had the desired effect, and she finished the bust. It was not a very good likeness, but a very pretty artistic effort, and was sent to the next Exposition, receiving "honorable mention," perhaps more honorable than we mentioned her at home.

Nina, of course, never received the mythical album, but Sarah gave her mother a terra-cotta copy of the bust.

Mrs. Moulton happened to be back in Boston visiting family and friends when Bernhardt played there early in January 1881:

I went to see her at her hotel. She looked enchanting, and was dressed in her most characteristic manner, in a white dress with a border of fur. . . . This is her first visit. She said she was surprised to see how many people in America spoke French. "Really?" I answered. "It did not strike me so the other evening when I heard you in *La Dame aux Camélias.*" "I don't mean the public," she replied. "It understands very little, and the turning of the leaves of the librettos distracts me so much that I sometimes forget my role. At any rate, I wait until the pages have stopped rustling. . . ."

When I got up to leave she said, "Chère Madame, you know Mr. Longfellow?"

"Yes," I replied, "very well."

"Could you not arrange that I might make his bust? You can tell him that you know my work, and that I *can* do it if he will let me."

I told her that I would try. She was profuse in her thanks, but, alas! Mr. Longfellow when I spoke to him, turned a cold shoulder on the idea. He begged me to assure Sarah Bernhardt that nothing would have given him more pleasure, but, he added with a playful wink, "I am leaving for Portland in a few days, and I am afraid she will have left Boston when I come back. . . ." Evidently regretting his curtness, he said, "Tell her if she is at liberty tomorrow I will offer her a cup of tea." Then he added, "You must come and chaperone me. It would not do to leave me alone with such a dangerous and captivating visitor."

He invited Mr. [William Dean] Howells and Oliver Wendell Holmes to meet her. . . . The next afternoon I met Sarah at Mr. Longfellow's. When we were drinking our tea she said, "*Cher* Monsieur Longfellow, I would like so much to have made your bust, but I am so occupied that I really have not the time." And he answered her in the most suave manner, "I would have been delighted to sit for you, but, unfortunately, I am leaving for the country tomorrow." How clever people are!

Mr. Longfellow speaks French like a native. He said, "I saw you the other evening in *Phèdre*. I saw Rachel in it fifty years ago, but you surpass

her. You are magnificent, for you are more vivid, *plus vivante*. . . . I wish
I could make you feel what I felt."

"You can," she said, "and you do—by your poetry."

"Can you read my poetry?"

"Yes. I read your 'He-a-vatere.' "

"My—Oh yes—'Hiawatha.' But you surely do not understand that?"

"Yes, yes, indeed I do," she said, "*chaque mot.*"

"You are wonderful," he said, and fearing that she might be tempted
to recite "each word" of his "Hiawatha," he hastened to present Holmes
who was all attention. At last the tea-party came to an end. We all accompanied her to her carriage, and as she was about to get in, she turned
with a sudden impulse, threw her arms round Mister Longfellow's neck,
and said, "*Vous êtes adorable*," and kissed him on the cheek. He did not
seem displeased, but as she drove away, he turned to me, and said, "You
see, I did need a chaperone."

It would be difficult to say who was more amused: Bernhardt, at the thought
of the aging poet protecting himself from her wiles, or the bearded Longfellow
at the thought of his narrow escape.

Despite Bernhardt's feeling that Boston was infinitely more refined
than New York, it was in Boston that she became involved in what was
probably the most vulgar publicity stunt of her career. She was approached
by a Mr. Henry Smith, the owner of a fleet of fishing boats, one of whose
men had succeeded in harpooning a whale and bringing it alive to Boston
Harbor. Unfortunately, Mr. Smith persuaded the adventurous Sarah to see
the whale, which lay suspiciously still, and then to take a walk on its back.
From that moment on she was haunted by a kind of publicity over which
she had no control.

After an exquisite last performance of *La Dame aux Camélias*, Sarah,
with her company, left for New Haven and then went on to Hartford. To her
horror, the whale, heavily salted (it was clearly no longer alive), was traveling
on a railway flatcar, following the same itinerary as hers. It was accompanied
by large placards that read:

COME AND SEE THE ENORMOUS CETACEAN, KILLED BY
SARAH BERNHARDT, WHO PULLED OUT ITS FINS TO BE
USED AS WHALEBONES FOR HER CORSETS

Mr. Smith was standing by to take orders from any woman who wanted to buy corsets made with whalebones from Sarah's favorite whale. Sarah, of course, was outraged, but there was no way to stop him, and Jarrett advised her never to discourage publicity no matter how bad it smelled. There was another unfortunate episode in Hartford. At a performance of *Froufrou*, the members of the audience received the English translation of *Phèdre* by mistake. Wonderfully enough, they spent the evening in utter contentment, apparently not aware that while they followed the text of one play, they were seeing another.

"Oh well!" said Marie. "They paid. They cried. What more could one ask?"

The answer lay in French-speaking Montreal, the next stop on the tour. *La Presse* described Sarah's arrival:

Yesterday a deputation of leading French citizens left in a special train to meet Sarah Bernhardt at St. Albans on the Canadian Border. Shortly after it reached St. Albans [the train] of the famous artist steamed in from the United States. Mr. Louis Frechetta, poet-laureate of Quebec's Académie Française, read a poem addressed to the celebrated actress. The Divine Sarah wore a cloak of blue-green plush trimmed with fur over a dress of varied shades of the same color. Her sealskin hat was decorated with what appeared to be a bat.

The trip from St. Albans to Montreal was without incident except for the fact that Madame Colombier graced the special car with her presence, conversing and joking with the gentlemen from Montreal. At the depot an immense crowd had assembled, and, as the train rolled in, the inspiriting strains of *La Marseillaise* were played by the city band. Meanwhile the crowd grew impatient. At length the object of their admiration appeared and was greeted with enthusiastic cheers of *Vive la Bernhardt! Vive la France!*, everyone pressing around her to such an extent that it was with the greatest difficulty that a passage for her was effected.

So great was the throng that Mlle Bernhardt, worn out by her journey and the weakness consequent on hard work, nearly fainted, and once gave way to tears. After considerable trouble the great actress and her escorts, the Messrs Jarrett and Abbey, made their way through the mob, which, with those who lined the tops of the out-going train, numbered at least five thousand, and, entering a sleigh, drove to the Windsor Hotel. A great many people here gathered at the corner of Bonaventura and Cathedral streets to cheer her as she passed.

The Canadian city was not all cheers. For weeks the Bishop of Montreal had threatened to excommunicate any of his flock who attended the evil actress's performances. Not content with that, he extended his excommunications to include Sarah, her company, and Scribe and Legouvé, the authors of the "heinous" *Adrienne Lecouvreur*—distinctly a case of overkill, since Scribe had already gone to his heavenly rest, or hellish torment, some years before. A rhymester at the magazine *Chic* summed up the situation:

> *A Bishop—this is no canard—*
> *His parishioners put on their guard:*
> *Said he, "If you go*
> *To Sarah B.'s show*
> *In the world that's to come you'll burn hard.*
> *His flock at the prospect was sad,*
> *For a moment, but then it got mad,*
> *And when Sarah did act*
> *The hall was so packed*
> *That standing room couldn't be had.*
> *And Sarah remarked, "Bless his eyes,*
> *In my bosom no malice there lies*
> *The Bishop knew not,*
> *When he launched that curse hot,*
> *That me he would just advertise!"*
> *And the Bishop did gloomily say,*
> *"Were this Torquemada's good day,*
> *And that girl I could catch*
> *With stake, faggot, and match,*
> *I'd get up an auto-da-fé!"*

Bernhardt's presence in Montreal created more than theatrical excitement. It was a signal for French Canadians to show that while they were subject to British rule, their hearts belonged to France. On Sarah's opening night a choir of two hundred gave a sonorous performance of *La Marseillaise*. Ovation followed ovation throughout the evening. The public applauded the text, the star, the supporting artists, and the Louis XIV costumes—reminders of the

42. In François Coppée's *Le Passant* (1869), the first of her early triumphs

43–45. THIS PAGE AND OPPOSITE: In Dumas *fils' La Dame aux Camélias* (1880), Bernhardt's greatest romantic role

46–48. LEFT: As the Queen of Spain, Doña Maria de Neuborg, in Victor Hugo's *Ruy Blas*. BELOW: Mounet-Sully as *Hernani*. OPPOSITE: As Doña Sol in Victor Hugo's *Hernani* (1877), with Mounet-Sully in the title role

49. *Froufrou* (1880), Meilhac and Halévy's drama of a frivolous woman

50. *Fédora* (1882), Sardou's Russian melodrama of nihilism

51, 52. The Empress of Byzantium in Sardou's *Théodora* was one
of Bernhardt's most spectacular successes.

53. *La Tosca* was written for Bernhardt by Victorien Sardou long before Puccini turned it into an opera.

54. *La Tosca*

55. With de Max in Sardou's *Gismonda* (1894)

56. In Jules Barbier's *Jeanne d'Arc*

57. *Izéïl*, by Eugène Morand and Armand Sylvestre

58. As Cordelia in *King Lear*

59. As *Hamlet*, one of Sarah's most controversial roles

60. As Cleopatra in Shakespeare's *Antony and Cleopatra*

61–64. THIS PAGE: As Lady
Macbeth in Jean Richepin's
translation of Shakespeare's
Macbeth. OPPOSITE: As Lady
Macbeth, in her "thistle of
Scotland" robe

65, 66. As *Phèdre*

67, 68. L E F T : As Pierrot in Jean Richepin's pantomime *Pierrot Assassin.* B E L O W : As Pierrot, with Réjane as Colombine

69. With Lillie Langtry, who, to Sarah's chagrin, received a higher fee for this postcard than Sarah did

70. As Pelléas, to Mrs. Patrick Campbell's Mélisande

71. As L'Aiglon

past glories of a distant ancestral home. The roars of the crowd continued unabated during the curtain calls. White doves were released, baskets of flowers floated down from the ceiling, and a great laurel wreath bearing the French flag was presented. Reverential and smiling, Sarah pressed it to her lips, then held it aloft to wave high in the air. That night, and each succeeding night, a group of students waited outside in the Christmas cold to carry *"Notre Sarah"* to her sleigh, wrap her in furs, and pull her up the icy hill to the Windsor Hotel.

After Montreal the company played in Springfield, Massachusetts, where Sarah spent the afternoon buying a silver-filigreed pistol to protect her from the perils of the Wild West. The weapon remained in its case, as Sarah discovered that it was not needed during her four days in Baltimore, a city that surprised her by its frigid weather, indoors and out, and by its air of worldly opulence. Indeed, when the company performed on New Year's Eve they were startled to find that southern ladies were equal to Europeans when it came to a display of diamonds and décolletages. To celebrate the arrival of the New Year, Sarah invited Marie, Jeanne, and two French embassy men from Washington to join her for supper. "For a moment," Marie recalled, "we forgot America and its dollars. What a pleasure to talk of home and Parisian friends!" That night Sarah wept. She had been gone for two months, and the idea of celebrating New Year's Eve, "far from everyone and everything" she loved, depressed her terribly.

The following day Marie asked permission to go to New York for some shopping. Sarah agreed, knowing that her friend had left Paris on such short notice that she had had no time to prepare for what began to seem an endless tour. And so Marie set off with the promise that she would join the company in Philadelphia where she was to play the Princesse de Bouillon, the second lead in *Adrienne Lecouvreur*, on opening night. All went according to plan until the train that was taking her to the Quaker City stopped and, after an interminable pause, began to roll backward. Marie asked what was happening. The explanation came as a shock. There was a train wreck ahead, and it would be hours before the rails were cleared. Marie looked at her watch. It was 6:30.

"Fear seized me," she wrote. "What would happen to the show? And I had the first speech! What to do?"

At last a Frenchman on board offered to send a telegram from a nearby station. The wire read: "Train accident. Change tonight's play."

By the time Marie arrived at the theatre, Sarah, as Phèdre, was onstage. "As soon as she saw me," Marie wrote, "No! I cannot describe her fury. God, the saints, Heaven and Hell were invoked with such tragic force that I could not get a word in edgewise."

" 'You're not even dead,' she screamed. 'You can't even show me a broken arm or leg. You are . . . unforgivable!' "

Colombier told this story in her *Les Voyages de Sarah Bernhardt en Amérique*, a collection of pieces she sent in installments to the Paris journal *L'Evénement*. When published as a book it had a great success and marked the beginning of her literary career. Arsène Houssaye, one of the cleverest men in Paris, lent prestige to her work by supplying a preface. He had been the director of the Comédie Française from 1849 to 1856 and was a notorious hedonist, a fine memoirist, and a friend of everyone from Morny and Rachel to Marie and Sarah. His foreword contains kind words about Colombier's gifts and an uninhibited introduction to the lady herself:

Marie [he wrote in a sideswipe at Sarah] has enjoyed every possible adventure, every possible fortune. But she has not become a millionaire like some other actresses who can afford expensive houses in Paris. Not so stupid, for if she did run a grand establishment, she would be obliged to live in it. And then goodbye to escapades! Her life would be as neat as a page of music. She could not tear up her contracts when she felt like it. Instead she would be forced to be one of those respectable ladies who act the classics at the Odéon. No, no, she prefers to live from day to day, playing out the games of love and chance. That is why Marie Colombier rushed out impromptu to see the New World with her friend Sarah Bernhardt. I say friend but perhaps I should say enemy. Two such ardent creatures cannot exist in the sweet passivity of friendship. They both live for storms and prefer to hurl thunderbolts at one another. Fortunately there are rainbows as well. I have known them during their darkest and lightest days, and I must admit they are always charming—even in their rages.

In one of her more affectionate moods, Marie had her publisher use a Clairin drawing of Sarah as a frontispiece. The inscription read: "From Sarah Bernhardt to her best friend Marie Colombier." Then Marie arranged for a portrait of herself by Edouard Manet to be put on the title page.

BERNHARDT'S next engagement took her to Chicago for two weeks. There she enjoyed a success that "surpassed all expectations." The theatre was packed and the press notices worshipful, despite the fact that the Bishop of Chicago, like the Bishop of Montreal, preached violent sermons against Bernhardt and the danger of seeing her performances. The sermons provided such powerful advertisement that Henry Abbey wrote a letter, copies of which he sent to the Chicago newspapers:

> Monsignor:
> It is my custom when I come to your city to spend five hundred dollars on publicity. But as you have done it for me, allow me to send you two hundred and fifty dollars for your poor.

Harsh warnings from the Church did not prevent society matrons from vying with one another to entertain Sarah. At her final performance they joined forces to present her with a magnificent diamond choker entwined with camellias. To add to her pleasure, an aristocratic young gentleman had come all the way from England to be at her side. Together they discovered Chicago, in Sarah's opinion, "the most American of American cities." To begin with there was "the vitality of the metropolis in which men pass each other without stopping, with knitted brows, and with only one thought in mind: to attain their goal." Then there were the elevated trains—juggernauts that rushed and roared above the crowd, belching smoke and dropping fire. Tall buildings lost themselves in the swirling snow. Banks, as massive as the Louvre, lined the streets. The air reeked of coal fumes, and Lake Michigan was a sea of ice. Even Sarah's hotel, the Palmer House, came as a surprise. Never had she expected to see a hotel that contained tailor's shops, shoe stores, restaurants, ornate public rooms, a pharmacy, and elevators large enough for ten. Sarah's suite was a pharaoh's fantasy of Egyptian sofas, lamps supported by massive bronze sphinxes, clocks mounted on marble pyramids, and pictures of lazy days on the Nile. Like all visitors, Sarah and her English beau were urged to see the stockyards. The sight, of course, was disgusting, and she was unable to bear the wholesale slaughter, the nauseating stench, and the nightmare cries that went with the dismembering and disembowelling of helpless animals.

That evening, still shaken by the experience, she fainted during the performance of *Phèdre*. The curtain was lowered temporarily, but when she regained consciousness and entered the stage to take up the role again, it was too late. The audience had mistaken her fainting fit for the end of the play and was on its way out.

Sarah did not look forward to appearing in thirty more towns where very few would understand a word she uttered. Yet she was bound to go on: not by contracts, those could be broken; not by a sense of responsibility to her company, she had earned more than enough to pay them off; but because, like many who struck it rich in America, she had discovered a gold mine, a vein she could always exploit when her prodigious extravagance emptied her purse. And so, desperately homesick, she forced herself to continue.

There was one consolation, however. Jarrett and Abbey, knowing that the smaller cities she was to appear in had nothing but primitive lodgings to offer, had hired a magnificent private train to take her and her company across the country. The Bernhardt Special was worthy of a royal progress. As the player-queen, Sarah was given the Palace Car, a rolling parlor fitted with inlaid wood, stained glass, brass lamps, Turkish carpets, zebra skins, chaises longues, a piano, and, to the discomfort of everyone except Sarah, a wood stove that was kept blazing even in the warmest weather. An added pleasure was the observation car, with its open platform, where Bernhardt, muffled in furs and veils, could contemplate the ever-receding landscape.

The dining car was equally regal, with a table for ten and linen, dishes, and silver decorated with Sarah's *"quand même."* Adjoining her private dining room was a kitchen where two black cooks introduced her to the arcane mysteries of American cuisine. Her sleeping quarters left little to be desired, with a bed wide enough for herself and the ever-willing Angelo, a mahogany dressing table, a gilded pier glass, and a ribboned basket for the inevitable dog, in this instance an unpleasant, and presumably melancholy griffon named Hamlet. Beyond this splendor lay a room for Guérard and a double compartment for Jarrett and Abbey.

"Three pullman cars," Marie wrote, "were reserved for mortals like me," adding that the accommodations were far more posh than any she had seen in Europe. Sarah, faced with such locomotive grandeur, felt a ceremony was in order. Before leaving Chicago she called for the engineer, shook his hand, gave him her most winning smile, and asked after his wife, his children, and his health. Assured of her future safety, she presented him with a handsome tip and presents for his family.

Marie Colombier described life on board the Sarah Bernhardt Special:

"We read, we talk, we argue. The more erudite translate the American papers, the gamblers play *baccarat* and *piquet* with a vengeance, the conscientious study their roles, and more than one letter to far-off family or friend is scratched out on small tables the black waiters set up as if by magic. From time to time someone tells a joke and the whole car rocks with laughter. Sarah looks in occasionally. But usually she shuts herself in with Angelo with whom she rehearses endlessly."

At other times Sarah invited the company to her quarters for a party. Then there were music-hall turns, songs, charades, and all the good-natured rowdiness actors have always enjoyed. Still, the tour was hardly a round of parties. When they were in luck, the actors arrived an hour before curtain time, rushed to the theatre, where they changed into their costumes, galloped through the play and returned for a night's sleep while the train rolled on to the next town. When they were not so fortunate, the train arrived late, and the players, sooty and unwashed, performed on empty stomachs. Then to their horror (they were French, after all) they were forced to make do with crackers and sardines and bits of fruit they had saved for just such occasions.

Of course, there were incidents along the way. One was an attempt to rob Sarah of the jewels she had put on display in St. Louis with the idea that they would attract paying customers to the box office. Instead, they attracted a gang of thieves. Bernhardt made a good, if melodramatic case of it in her memoirs: "a veritable giant" of a man riding the rods beneath the train, his plan to meet his accomplices after disengaging Bernhardt's car from the rest, the hanging of the chief culprit, the guilt she suffered because she had tempted him by exhibiting her gems in the first place.

Marie Colombier sent her version of the "holdup" to *L'Evénement*:

Some hours out of the city [she wrote] I noticed to my astonishment that revolvers were being distributed to the men in the troupe. What is this?

I wondered. Is Sarah about to rehearse a new military play? No, it is funnier than that. The Chief of Police in Cincinnati has wired Abbey that a gang was about to attack our train somewhere in the wilds, empty our safe, and make off with the diamonds Sarah had put on exhibit. Abbey engaged a detective who stayed with us for the remainder of the trip. Well there we are, armed to the teeth, and I must say we look divinely savage. Those who had not been given guns are handed the kind of truncheons carried by policemen in New York and Chicago. Sarah is holding a magnificent revolver. I myself am given one that holds six bullets. Suddenly we come to a halt in the middle of a forest to practice shooting. What a shame there are no prizes! We would all get medals. We get back on the train. It's ten at night, and still no sign of brigands. It's really irritating. Then we begin to go faster and faster, waiting to be robbed. The train stops. Here are the pirates at last!! Alas, it is only the baggage car that is slightly on fire. We go to sleep. Night gives way to dawn. There is no robbery. The train keeps chugging on and on. Then it stops. We are in the station in Mobile. A welcoming committee led by the consul is there to greet us. At the sight of them, Sarah's nerves give way: "Tell them I'm not here, that I'm sick—better still, that I'm dead. Dear, dear Jarrett, tell them anything so long as I don't have to see them." By this time some roughnecks were knocking on the train and calling for Bernhardt. This was too much for Sarah who threw up her window and poured a jugful of water on their heads.

From this point on, the tour became much more tiring for the indefatigable Bernhardt as, in addition to the large cities, there were many small-town one-night stands. The company performed in Atlanta, Nashville, Memphis, Louisville, Columbus, Dayton, Indianapolis, St. Joseph, Leavenworth, Quincy, Springfield, Milwaukee, Detroit, Cleveland, Pittsburgh, Toledo, Erie, Toronto, Buffalo, Rochester, Utica, Albany, and Troy before returning to Boston (four months after her first visit) where she could "rest" by giving six consecutive performances, ending with her first attempt at Alexandre Dumas *fils*'s *La Princesse Georges*, a work she had learned and rehearsed during the tour. She hardly had time to notice how enthusiastically it was received before they were off again to play Worcester, Providence, Newark, Washington, and, in return engagements, Baltimore and Philadelphia.

Finally, Bernhardt returned to New York for a series of farewell performances, beginning with *La Princesse Georges* and ending, on 3 May 1881, with *The Lady of the Camellias*. Both plays were received with ovations and cries from the audience of "Come back, Sarah! Come back!"

Bernhardt would, in fact, come back to America for several more tours, the next in 1886–1887 and the last in 1916–1918, during World War I. In the six and a half months of this first American tour, she earned what was approximately the equivalent today of a million dollars, which she safely tucked away in the metal coffer she always kept at her side. She had given one hundred and fifty performances in fifty-one cities, large and small.

Like many seasoned artists who tour the provinces she found it more amusing to dwell on the mishaps and adventures connected with her travels than on the evenings spent wooing an undiscriminating audience. Georgia was where she was fined a dollar and a half for shooting game on a Sunday. And New Orleans was where she insisted that the train's engineer speed over a bridge weakened by the floodwaters of the Mississippi, only to have the bridge collapse the moment they had crossed it. While in Louisiana she bought a small alligator she called Ali Gaga, which had the unfortunate habit of creeping into her bed. Angelo, her regular bed partner, must have been a happier man when Ali Gaga sickened and died, perhaps because its indulgent mistress insisted on feeding it nothing but milk and champagne.

At Niagara Falls, Sarah, along with Marie and other intrepid members of the company, clambered up a hill of ice to get closer to the roaring waters and then were forced to slide down on their backsides, much to the hilarity of all.

Bernhardt's daredevil love of adventure was one thing, her ability to hold an American audience spellbound another. After all she did not have the advantage of a Patti or a Melba, who sang familiar melodies with the support of a large orchestra—in itself an attraction. Nor could she be compared to a Pavlova, who spoke the mute, yet comprehensible language of the dance. True, a Bernhardt production offered a rich display of costumes and jewels, as well as English translations and synopses of her plays. But these alone would not have kept the public enthralled in lesser hands. The answer lay in what Oscar Wilde referred to as "the glamor of her personality" and her hypnotic power to communicate emotion through the occult chemistry of her presence, the beauty of her speaking voice, the expressivity of her gestures, and the grace of her movements.

Her financial success did not please everyone. A case in point was a caricature in *Puck* magazine which showed Bernhardt with a bestial, hooked nose, standing in a shower of gold coins. The caption read: "The Jewish Danae." Nonetheless, when she returned to New York she invited the actors and artists of the city to be her guests at a farewell matinée of *La Dame aux Camélias*. It was an emotional afternoon. Sarah received more than a hundred bouquets from her admirers. The audience, and there is none warmer or more understanding than one composed of fellow actors, stood up to cheer. Tommaso Salvini—in Bernhardt's opinion the greatest living actor—strode onto the stage to present her with a jewel box of lapis lazuli. And a shy, pretty girl called Mary Anderson, who was to become an actress of distinction herself, ran on to give the departing star a turquoise brooch trimmed with forget-me-nots, emblem of fidelity and friendship.

Two days later, on 5 May, Sarah sailed for France. The trip seemed endless, the rough seas an affront, the future uncertain, for she was fully aware that her enemies, and they were many, had been waging a war in her absence. She was "finished," they said, "penniless, a has-been." Even *Le Figaro* had printed a tasteless attack by the widely read J. J. Weiss:

> Poor Sarah Bernhardt, poor passionate lover of fame! If she sinned by loving publicity too much, she is paying for her sins in America. She imagined that the drawing-rooms of New York and Washington would vie for the honor of receiving her. But the United States has not yet reached the lack of social decorum that we have in Paris. In the theatre her noisily announced performances were given to half-empty houses. It was for this pitiable result that she threw her contract with the Comédie Française in Perrin's face. Poor, poor Sarah Bernhardt!

"Poor Sarah Bernhardt" was naturally offended by the lies and worried about the reception awaiting her in France. But when she received a cablegram from the *Société des Sauveteurs du Havre*, asking her to give a performance upon her return for the benefit of those who manned the lifeboats of Le Havre, she saw a welcoming ray of light at the end of the tunnel.

"It was with an indescribable joy that I accepted," she wrote, "for I would, in returning to my beloved country, be able to make the gesture that dries tears." Sarah spent the rest of the voyage with a "light heart and a smiling face, disdainful of the horrible discomfort" the crossing caused her.

When after a twelve-day voyage the ship was in sight of land, a small boat pulled up alongside. Maurice and Clairin, too impatient to wait on the pier, had come to welcome her.

Marie witnessed the scene: Sarah sobbing and clinging to her son, holding him at arm's length to exclaim how tall he had become. To add to her joy, hundreds of people were gathered on the quai to celebrate her homecoming. A touching passage in Colombier's book recalled the moment:

> Suddenly my heart beats faster. I lean over the ship's rail to examine the crowd. I think I see my mother and sister. I cry out to Sarah. Then I'm choked with sobs. Alas, it is only a dream. It's Louise Abbéma and *her* mother. Sarah grasps the situation at once. Tenderly she takes me in her arms, and whispers: "I do love you, you poor darling." It is just such bursts of heartfelt generosity that explain why she is forgiven everything.

When a few days later Sarah gave *La Dame aux Camélias* in Le Havre to raise money for the lifeboatmen, Abbéma, Clairin, and many other friends who had come up from Paris were there to see it. It was the first time she played it in France, and everyone was curious to see how it would go. Would she, as some feared, exaggerate her effects as she must have done in America? Or was she still capable of restraint, subtlety, and total immersion in a role? There was no need for worry. Sarah was at her best. The audience roared its approval, and even Marie, who was not in the final scene, stood in the wings watching the death scene and "crying like a baby." During the curtain calls Sarah was presented with a medal and a Life-Saver's Certificate. Her response was vintage Bernhardt. Raising her arms in a universal embrace, she cried out: "I shall save someone! I promise to save someone! It's true that I cannot swim, but that doesn't matter. I shall learn!"

If Sarah was not quite prepared to save the drowning, she was determined to save herself. Fortunately, she liked nothing better than a good scrap, especially when she thought she could win. In addition to the points she had made by helping the courageous boatmen who risked their lives in the rough waters of the Atlantic to rescue fishing boats in trouble, she had other tricks up her sleeve. London was one. In no time she arranged a three-week season at the Shaftesbury Theatre, where she would present the two plays of Dumas *fils* which she had done in America with such success: *La Princesse Georges* and *La Dame aux Camélias*. The latter had been banned in England until then, and it was through the good offices of the Prince of Wales that Sarah was allowed to give it. London, unlike Paris, did not resent her trip to America. Dickens, Thackeray, and Trollope had all been there, Henry Irving and Ellen Terry were planning to go, and young Oscar Wilde was soon to bring Beauty to the raw New Land. Indeed, the British attitude to its rebellious offspring was brisk and businesslike. Why not profit from a rich country in dire need of some civilizing influence? As for Sarah she could do no wrong. London society found her amusing, the young made a fetish of her, and the actors adored her. Ellen Terry, who became her friend, teased her affectionately, and called her "Sally B," would in later years recall her impressions of Bernhardt in the early 1880s.

"How wonderful she looked in those days! She was as transparent as an azalea, only more so; like a cloud, only not so thick. Smoke from a burning paper describes her more nearly! She was hollow-eyed, almost consumptive-looking. Her body was not the prisoner of her soul, but its shadow. She is always a miracle."

Sarah liked to say that she attracted all the eccentrics of the world, particularly in England. It was hardly an exaggeration. Women knelt at her feet as she left the theatre. Young girls pasted her photographs and press notices in scrapbooks. Aspiring actresses memorized her roles and aped her manner and her peculiarly nasal delivery in their unmistakably British accents. One elderly spinster built an altar to the Divine Sarah heaped with postcards and such relics as Bernhardt's gloves, combs, and hairpins. When told about it, Sarah said: "You shouldn't make fun of her. I love her dearly." Then, after a moment's thought, she laughed and added: "She must be a drunk."

 F T E R   weeks of basking in British warmth, Sarah returned to France, only to be accused once again of being a traitor to her country and her art. She was neither, but how could she prove it? At last an opportunity arose. There was to be an official gala at the Opéra on the tenth anniversary of that happy day in 1871 when the Prussian army relinquished the French territory it had captured. The president of the republic, Jules Grévy, would be there, along with Gambetta and other key figures of *le grand monde*. The program consisted of three acts of Meyerbeer's *Robert le Diable*, recitations and scenes played by actors of the Comédie Française, and, at the end, a recitation of *La Marseillaise* by Sarah's old friend, Agar, the first Silvia to her Zanetto in *Le Passant*.

As it happened, Agar's dresser, Hortense, was very fond of Madame Bernhardt and was always ready to serve her. With this in mind Sarah sent for her. Would she do her a favor, she asked, and tell Agar that her latest lover, a cavalry captain stationed in Tours, had broken his leg in a fall from his horse. Hortense was delighted to be Sarah's accomplice. Agar rushed off to be with her loved one, telling Hortense to notify the Opéra of her sudden departure. But, following Sarah's instructions, Hortense said nothing, with the result that no substitute was called in. There was panic backstage that evening when Agar failed to turn up. Mounet-Sully was coming to the end of his declamation of a Victor Hugo poem when, to everyone's astonishment, Sarah appeared, enveloped in a hooded cloak. As Mounet left the stage, Sarah handed him her cloak, then marched out to face the public. Dressed in a flowing white gown, a red, white, and blue sash around her waist, she waited for the orchestra to begin. At the first notes of the national anthem, the president and all the magnificent assembly rose to their feet, stirred by the occasion, but dumbfounded by the apparition of the uninvited renegade. Bernhardt began *"Allons enfants de la patrie"* with quiet intensity. Gradually, her voice rose in a crescendo of emotion. As she chanted the last lines, she unfurled a large tricolor flag. Motionless, her head held high, her eyes blazing, she was patriotic France incarnate. The effect was electrifying. Men reached for their handkerchiefs while women wept openly. President Grévy applauded without pause, and Gambetta shouted until he was hoarse. People shook their heads in wonder, saying they had never been so moved, that Bernhardt was prodigious, unique, a miracle. Sarah had won yet another battle. She had come home to defeat and turned it into triumph. Agar, it was reported, took her friend's betrayal with her usual good nature. At her age she had seen enough backstage maneuvering to know that moral rectitude was not the chief ingredient in the making of a star.

PART SIX

HUSBANDS AND LOVERS

Marguerite Gautier in Dumas *fils' La Dame aux Camélias* was Sarah's most popular role.

E A R L Y in 1882, Sarah met a young Greek called Aristidis Damala. He was twenty-five, twelve years younger than she. Damala was born in Piraeus, the port city where his father had made a fortune in shipping. When he was still a boy, the family moved to Marseille. There he graduated from the Lycée Louis-le-Grand. Then, eager for action, he went back to Greece to join the army. Athens knew him as one of the most attractive cavalry officers in town: generous, handsome, and as pleased with himself as Narcissus. A year later, having had more than his share of dueling, gambling, and Greek women, he moved on to Paris to work at his country's legation. But diplomacy requires discretion, a quality Damala sadly lacked. Scandal, in fact, was more in his line. He was addicted to morphine, wrecked the lives of several highborn French-women, and was said to have an eye for the boys as well. How this Byronic corsair, condescending, arrogant, and infinitely indifferent to the feelings of others entered Sarah's life is open to question. Some claimed that her sister, Jeanne, who moved in morphine circles, brought them together. Others said that Damala had dreams of becoming an actor and came to Sarah for advice. However that may be, it was generally agreed that Sarah lost her head the moment he first bent to kiss her hand. Not that she was in need of admirers. The post brought passionate declarations daily. Angelo hoped to marry her. Philippe Garnier, another splendid-looking actor in her troupe, and a finer one, was deeply in love with her. But they were too easily managed. What she yearned for, if Damala is any indication, was conquest and the excitement that goes with uncertainty. She was soon to have more than enough of the latter.

At the time Bernhardt and Damala met, she and her company were about to embark on a grand tour: the French provinces, Italy, Greece,

Hungary, Austria, Sweden, England, Spain, Portugal, Belgium, and Holland. Damala too was about to leave Paris. The Greek government, appalled by his notorious behavior, had posted him to faraway Saint Petersburg. Sarah acted quickly when her corsair said he would like to see her in Russia. Telegrams flew across Europe, dates were juggled and engagements cancelled. When everything was arranged, she told Damala she would meet him in Saint Petersburg, where she was engaged for the month of March.

Bernhardt swept through Europe like a conquering hero. The press was rhapsodic, the public paid double to see her, and the story of her life, scrubbed clean and glamorized, preceded her in bursts of publicity. But without her knowledge storm clouds were gathering.

In Turin, a promising actress of twenty-four called Eleonora Duse saw, or rather experienced, Bernhardt's performances. Sarah chose *La Dame aux Camélias* for her opening night. As was often the case, she not only gave herself to the part, but took the audience into her confidence. During the first act someone carelessly—or deliberately—tore a hole in the paper door which served for her entrances and exits. It was the kind of thing another actress might have pretended to ignore. But Sarah was not just another actress. As she left the stage she put her hand through the hole and ripped the paper down with a savage gesture. Nothing could have pleased the Turin public more. Here was a tempestuous tigress, a prima donna to warm Italian hearts. Duse recalled that during Sarah's stay "no one spoke of anyone but her, that evening and every other evening—in the salons and in the theatre. One woman had accomplished that! My reaction was to feel liberated, to feel I had the right to do whatever I wished. . . . I went to every performance to listen and to weep. Here is a woman who elevates the profession, who induces the audience to respect the Beautiful, and leads it to bow before Art."

At that time no one suspected that the provincial little Italian would one day challenge Bernhardt's supremacy in the realm of Beauty and Artistry. But that was in the future. In 1882 Bernhardt was treated like a visiting monarch. Royalty paid homage to her, gave grand soirées in her honor, and plied her with gifts. King Umberto of Italy presented her with an exquisite Venetian fan. Alfonso XII of Spain gave her a diamond brooch. The Austrian emperor, Franz Joseph, asked for the privilege of placing an antique cameo necklace around her neck after a performance of *Phèdre*, and Archduke Friedrich insisted that while in Vienna she must stay in one of his palaces since queens did not stop at hotels. What these royals received in return for their generosity is a matter for speculation, but it is generally thought that an exchange of favors was traditional. As Sarah respected tradition and loved adventure, it is not unimaginable that these illustrious names were added to her private list of *souvenirs de voyage*.

On a less exalted plane, but perhaps more moving, the citizens of one Scandinavian village petitioned her train's engineer to slow down so that they might bow to her. And everywhere, those who could not afford to buy theatre tickets would stand outside her hotel for hours in the hope of catching a glimpse of her.

It was Russia that Sarah looked forward to most as it presented two challenges: not only would Damala be there, but it was there that Rachel had triumphed years before.

La Vie Parisenne published a drawing of Sarah crossing the steppes in an imperial carriage, accompanied by an escort of fierce Cossacks. What was intended as irony was close to the truth. In Saint Petersburg liveried servants unrolled an immense red carpet to protect Sarah's feet from the snow, as, smothered in furs, she made her way from her troika to the stage door. The imperial family and the court applauded Bernhardt night after night. For a command performance at the Winter Palace, she played *Le Passant*, the death scene from *Adrienne Lecouvreur*, and two acts of *Phèdre*. At the end of the evening Tsar Alexander III, deeply moved, stepped forward to congratulate her. Bernhardt sank to the floor in the deepest of curtsies. "No, no," the Emperor of All the Russias protested, "It is *We* who must bow to you." The Grand Duke Vladimir did not treat her with equal elegance. He sent his equerry to summon Sarah to a different kind of command performance—an intimate supper for two after the theatre. Sarah accepted on condition that Monsieur Damala would also be invited. A short time later, the equerry returned with a message of regret from His Imperial Highness, who had suddenly remembered a previous engagement.

In the old days, Sarah might have thought a midnight tête à tête with a grand duke enticing, an amusing way to arouse a lover's jealousy. Now the situation was reversed: it was Damala who was playing Sarah's game and Sarah who was miserably jealous. And with good reason, since her "real male," as Colombier described him, did little to hide the fact that he was sleeping with a younger actress in the company. Sarah lost her balance and with it her artistic judgment. Aristidis Damala, she decided, had the makings of an actor. She gave him the leading roles that Philippe Garnier had played until then—both offstage and on. As a result, Garnier, enraged, left the company, and Damala, with only a glimmer of talent, changed "Aristidis" to "Jacques" and was seen emoting along with La Divine Sarah. Hers was a desperate maneuver, engendered perhaps by the hope that memorizing his lines and nightly performances would limit his opportunities to stray.

There were other tensions. In Odessa and Kiev, riffraff hurled stones and anti-Semitic insults at Bernhardt as she passed in her carriage. In Moscow, a poor, twenty-one-year-old medical student named Anton Chekhov attacked her in other ways—not that his voice carried much weight. He was a beginner with unfashionable ideas who wrote articles for a comic paper that specialized in taking pot shots at local dignitaries and visiting celebrities. Certainly his words were ineffectual compared to the dithyrambs Sarah received when she opened at the Bolshoi Theatre on 26 November 1881 with *La Dame aux Camélias*. "Yesterday," *Russkie Vedomosti* benignly declared "instead of a pompous heroine we saw the living image of a deeply loving, deeply suffering woman from a notorious milieu—who grappled to herself the audience's sympathy and attention with irresistible force." The review went on to praise Bernhardt's technique, voice, diction, and attention to detail. Another critic, after granting that Bernhardt's Marguerite Gautier had something of the eternal feminine about her, said she was nevertheless "a *Parisienne* from head to toe." Since Marguerite *was* a *Parisienne*, one wonders if the critic, like one of his unfortunate colleagues in America, had been following the libretto of another play by mistake.

It was left to Chekhov to do what is called "a job" on Bernhardt. Even before her arrival, the budding author resented the "frightful amount" of publicity she had received. He wrote, "If we were to pile together everything that has been written about her and were to sell it by the ton (at 150 rubles per ton), and if we were to dedicate the receipts from the sale to the "Society for the Protection of Animals," then—we swear by our quills!—we could at least give dinner and supper to the horses and dogs at [the fashionable restaurant] Olivier's, or at [that dump of a place] Tatar's." To end the article Chekhov made great fun of Bernhardt's American adventures, her meeting with Edison and her extravagant earnings which he could not believe she deserved. With a chip on his shoulder, he wrote: "We shall compliment her as a guest and criticize her up and down as stringently as we can as an actress."

Chekhov kept to his word. "What the hell is going on?" he asked after seeing her for the first time. "O Sarah Bernhardt! All this folderol will end with our straining our reportorial nerves to the maximum. . . ." It seems he was not exaggerating the state of his nerves when he complained that Sarah's image conjured up "the Bois de Boulogne, the Champs-Elysées, the Trocadero, Daudet with his long hair, Zola with his round beard, [and] our own Turgenev. . . ." These, after all, were splendors not to be sneezed at. As the young critic went on, the reason for his resentment became clear: his was the distaste Slavophiles felt for what they considered the decadent, superficial French.

When Rachel came to Russia in 1853, the critic Pavel Annenkov had condemned her to the flames. Now Chekhov took up the torch. He thought Bernhardt was clever, tasteful, deeply read in the human heart and "whatever you please," but in the end she was still all artifice and the product of study. "We envy and most respectfully kow-tow to her hard work. We have no objection to advising our first- and second-rate artistes to learn how to work from our guest. Our artistes, no offense meant, are dreadfully lazy. For them, study is harsher than horseradish!" Like a terrier, Chekhov could not let go: Bernhardt did not pursue the natural, he complained, but looked for the extraordinary, the "ultra sensational." "We watched"—here he relented a little, saying—"we watched Sarah Bernhardt and derived indescribable pleasure from her hard work. There were brief passages in her acting which moved us almost to tears. But the tears failed to well up only because all the enchantment is smothered in artifice. Were it not for that scurvy artifice, that premeditated tricksiness, that over-emphasis, honest to goodness, we would have burst into tears."

In a letter to a friend, Turgenev was equally violent: "I am cross with my fellow countrymen who are making such fools of themselves over the unbearable Sarah Bernhardt, who has nothing except a wonderful voice—everything else about her is false, cold and affected—together with the most repulsive Parisian chic."

Chekhov's final piece on Bernhardt ended with "Tomorrow, back to Sarah Bernhardt. . . . Ugh! However, I won't write any more about her even if the editor pays me 50 kopeks a line. I'm written out! I quit!" Chekhov rarely wrote again on the object of his disdain. But his youthful words foretold the future. Russian actors were not to follow the French school, nor did they produce a Rachel or a Bernhardt. Yet they were to produce equally great actors of their own and develop a magnificent school of acting that illumined the poetry of everyday life, a poetry as foreign to France's foremost actress as French grandeur was to Russia's greatest playwright.

During her stay in Russia, Sarah was obsessed by an uncontrollable urge to dominate and domesticate her wild Greek lover. It was a hopeless task. He was conspicuously unfaithful, persisted in taking drugs, gambled away large sums of her money, and failed to show up for performances. To make matters worse, he had a careless contempt for women, a love-them-and-leave-them attitude that spelt humiliation and future disaster. For Sarah, who was used to being pursued, Damala was a challenge. At last, in Naples, she asked him to marry her. It was a flattering proposal from the queen of players, and Damala accepted. Sarah struck while the iron was hot. As she was Roman Catholic and he was Greek Orthodox, it was almost impossible to get a marriage license in Italy or in France, where their next engagements were set. And so they left for Protestant England. Theirs was a tight schedule: Leave Naples Saturday morning, 2 April; arrive London early Monday, 4 April; wedding ceremony that morning at St. Andrew's; immediate departure for Nice; performance upon arrival.

Like everything connected with their union, the trip was hectic: sixty hours by train there, thirty-six hours back. The train to London was hours late. Damala (was he resisting?) forgot the marriage papers and had to cross the city to get them. Sarah lost the performance in Nice because of the delay, but she had won Damala. The news of their marriage spread quickly. No one took it well. Clairin, Abbéma, and the rest of Sarah's court thought she had lost her mind. Sardou, who was writing a new play for her, felt he had lost his leading lady. Maurice, cut to the quick, said: "Now we have a *Monsieur* Sarah Bernhardt." And the press had a field day poking fun at the ties that bound the ill-matched couple.

On 26 May 1882 Paris was given the opportunity of seeing "Monsieur Sarah Bernhardt" make love to Madame Sarah Bernhardt in *La Dame aux Camélias*. The evening was charged with excitement. Two years had gone by since Sarah last played in her native city, and the mean-spirited were eager to assess the damage her talent had suffered while she, the venal, publicity-mad truant, enjoyed her triumphs abroad. Besides, her impertinence in foisting an amateur actor on the public irritated them. Sarah was aware of the dragons in the audience when she stepped out onto the stage of the Théâtre de la Gaîté, so aware, that her voice gave way and her nerves along with it. Report had it that she sounded like a frightened child during the first two acts. But when she caught fire and played as only she could, there was no resisting her. At the final curtain her apprehensive friends were beaming through their tears, and even her enemies' handkerchiefs were damp.

Damala, however, did not fare too well, according to Edmond Stoullig, the critic for *Le Rappel*:

As may be imagined, the sight of Bernhardt's husband was one of the attractions. His entrance created a sensation. Damala! There he is! Then opera-glasses were turned on the handsome dark-eyed fellow who had the honor of being selected by the great artist to the office of husband in the eyes of the law. While he, as Armand Duval, conquered all hearts from a physical point of view, the same could not be said from an artistic standpoint. His lack of experience was colossal; his voice so deep it was indistinct; his speech handicapped by a pronounced foreign accent, while his bearing was uniformly sad and fearful. In the fourth act he struck a few moving and sincere notes. If he works hard, he may possibly become an actor. Certainly his teacher, Madame Bernhardt, could be helpful to him.

His teacher, in fact, was so helpful that Damala began to be recognized by some as an actor of quality. But not by Victorien Sardou, who—despite Sarah's insistence that her husband play opposite her—refused to allow him to come anywhere near *Fédora*, a play set in Russia and written expressly for her.

Sardou's description of his heroine is a portrait of Bernhardt herself:

She is femininity personified—with all her sudden changes of mood, with all her contrasts! . . . Now caressing and tender, now coaxing and feline! With her supple grace, like the serpentine movements of an adder! All the treachery and all the devotion! A combination of masculine mind and childish superstition. Eyes so deep they make one dizzy. A voice that stirs unknown vibrations in us; the languor of the oriental linked indissolubly with the grace of the Parisian. An exquisite woman. Of that there can be no doubt!

To set his heroine in motion, Sardou tailored a crafty melodrama, thick with intrigue, tension, and unexpected revelations. The Princess Fédora is led to believe that her beloved fiancé was assassinated by a handsome Nihilist. In her desire for revenge, she sets out to win the assassin's love in order to deliver him into the hands of the secret police. But she becomes enamored of Loris Ipanoff, the dread murderer. Lo and behold, it turns out that Loris is not the killer, but a fine, upright fellow. Furthermore, Fédora learns that her fiancé was really an unfaithful cad. Overcome by her discovery, she swallows poison and is given the opportunity to play a magnificent death scene. As the curtain slowly falls, Loris raises her inert body for a final kiss, then faints away in her arms.

Sarah longed to sink her teeth into the tasty, if gory concoction. As did Pierre Berton, her Loris Ipanoff, who in addition to his great gifts as an actor, had enjoyed a long affair with Sarah during her Odéon days. While Bernhardt was hard at work rehearsing *Fédora*, Damala sulked at home. He was not to be envied. Three months earlier, he had married the world's most famous actress in the hope of sharing her triumphs. Instead, the critics pounced on him, his wife's friends looked down on him, and his stepson despised him. Only Sarah seemed to love him—and then only in her spare time. He did not realize how generous she was in her concern. One day she showed him a play by her old friend, the poet and critic Catulle Mendès. It was called *Les Mères Ennemies (Warring Mothers)* and had a part guaranteed to make her husband a star. Did he like it? she asked. Damala grudgingly admitted that he did. His response triggered one of Bernhardt's wilder extravagances. She leased the dingy Ambigu Theatre, redecorated it at vast expense, and then, to pacify her seventeen-year-old son, put it in his name and made him the manager. There was one stipulation: Maurice must share that position with Auguste Simon, who, she gently explained, might know more about the business end of theatre than he.

Mendès' play, directed by Sarah Bernhardt and starring Damala and Agar, was scheduled for December 1882. In that way, Sarah, who had thought of everything, could claim that her husband had turned down Sardou's play because of a previous commitment. Sarah worked with Damala until she uncovered the talent she alone was convinced he had. As a result, when *Les Mères Ennemies* opened, no one could say that Bernhardt's young husband did not belong to the profession. Unfortunately, such left-handed praise was not enough to mollify Damala's wounded ego.

Fédora, on the other hand, was one of Sarah's great triumphs. With it she turned a sharp corner in her career. Three years before, she had been the queen of the Comédie Française. Now she became the queen of the commercial theatre. She owed much of this to Sardou, who, if he had written a second-rate play, had created a first-class melodrama, alive with explosive action, inquisitorial police, sadism, and death. A superb director, he had grasped a certain aspect of Bernhardt's talent and made it tell on the stage. She had always listened with uncanny concentration. In *Fédora* she not only listened, but was asked to fill long moments with pantomimic reactions and gestures which she was able to make more potent than speech itself. Even her harshest critic, Vitu, was forced to admit that "her silences were supreme art." As for the rest, he added: "She could plunge emotion like a knife into the innermost being of the spectator," which was rather how Sarah's great success affected her unhappy husband. Vengeful and bitter, he baited her by calling her a "long-nosed Jewess," bought jewelry for his mistresses and sent the bills to her, and took offense when none was intended. When Sarah fought back, he maddened her by assuming the air of a man above petty details and other feminine nonsense.

One day, with no warning, he bought a red-caped uniform, gave notice to the Ambigu, and left Paris to join the spahi troops in Algeria. His abrupt departure meant the end of the successful run of *Les Mères Ennemies* and the beginning of a series of dismal failures in the theatre his wife had bought to make him happy. Sarah, obliged to fill the Ambigu, went in search of crowd pleasers. But of the five plays she produced, only one gave satisfaction: a powerful work by the poet-playwright Jean Richepin called *La Glu* (*The Trap*). It starred Réjane, a new and brilliant young actress who lit up the gray skies of Paris with her ineffable charm and pathos. The piece had a certain success, but its grim realism frightened the public, and it too was forced to close. If the production contributed to Sarah's financial ruin, it enriched her life. Réjane became her adored and lifelong friend, and Richepin her adored, but short-term lover.

By February 1883, Bernhardt had lost close to half a million francs and, afraid she would lose her house, put her jewels up for auction. The Hôtel des Ventes was crowded for three successive days with collectors, society people, actresses, and demimondaines, all outbidding one another for the privilege of owning Bernhardt's pearls and diamonds. To help recoup her losses, Sarah took her company on a lucrative tour of Scandinavia and

Britain. Richepin went along, as was duly noted in a letter by Ibsen's friend, the Danish critic Georg Brandes: "Sarah the Divine was here in Copenhagen with her shadow, the poet Jean Richepin. She was with him constantly, dined and slept with him." The gossip continued in London, where Sarah proudly flaunted her lover between highly acclaimed performances of *Fédora*.

If Bernhardt had reason to regret her marriage, she had every right to be proud of her new liaison. Five years younger than she, Richepin was quite a different specimen from the usual run of men in her "menagerie." The son of an army doctor, he was born in Algeria and brought up in Paris, where he graduated from the Ecole Normale. In 1870 he served as a sharpshooter in the Franco-Prussian War. A life of adventure followed. At various times he worked as a sailor, a stevedore, a wrestler, and a boxer. Then he went on to join a circus as a tumbler and weight lifter. Perhaps with this in mind, Goncourt was to describe him as a "powerful, smiling personality— an acrobat taking his bows after performing a prodigious feat."

In 1876 he wrote a book of inflammatory verse in defense of the forgotten poor, the tramps and the homeless, called *La Chanson des Gueux* (*The Song of the Vagabonds*). It earned him an instant literary reputation, and—for his severe criticism of the government's neglect of the poor—several months in jail. When Sarah met him, he was a hippie *avant la lettre*: a handsome, bearded faun, a bohemian who sped around Paris on that new two-wheeled craze, the bicycle, dressed in a skin-tight jersey that showed off his bulging muscles and his disdain for convention.

Sarah took him on as a lover when Damala left her for army life in North Africa. But it appears that soldiering was less to her husband's taste than a life of indolence and the pleasures of mistreating his wife, for when Sarah returned from her tour, she found him lying in her bed, calmly reading the papers. The sight must have had its attractions, for she not only asked him to stay on, but dismissed Richepin—and with him her happiness. It was a dark passage in her life. Damala had always taken morphine, but now he was hopelessly addicted. He gave himself injection after injection and thought nothing of plunging the needle through the cloth of his trousers when his need was overpowering. Sarah thrashed her sister, Jeanne, with a riding crop for smuggling drugs into the house. But violence was futile. At her wit's end, she asked for a legal separation, sent her unfortunate husband to a clinic, and went back to Richepin. Six months later, Damala was back under her roof. Richepin, understandably jealous, was told to be patient, to remember that she loved him, not Damala, whom she kept on only to save him from himself. To show her determination, she went to Damala's pharmacy and broke an umbrella over the drug-dealing pharmacist's head, which accomplished nothing except to leave her with one umbrella less.

During this unhappy period, Sarah leased the Porte Saint-Martin, a huge, eighteen-hundred-seat theatre. There, as actress-manager, she produced and performed in *Froufrou* and *La Dame aux Camélias*. It might be thought she was safe from domestic troubles while working. But Damala had an unnerving way of watching from the wings. With the thick-headed insolence of the amateur—his vast knowledge of acting was based on five months' experience—he took it upon himself to offer suggestions, criticism, and ridicule. Of course Sarah flew into a temper, blasted him with invective, and had him thrown out of the theatre. The gossip sheets were delighted. *L'Evénement* revelled in the "clamorous and battling *ménage* of the avenue de Villiers." Another frivolous journal printed a caricature of Damala lying grief-stricken on Sarah's divan, with the caption: "La Damala aux camélias."

While Damala lolled about, Richepin was at work on a play for Sarah. It was not the first piece he had written expressly for her. On 28 April 1883 she had appeared at the Trocadéro, as Pierrot, with Réjane as Colombine, in his *Pierrot Assassin*, a macabre pantomime that made a lasting impression despite its short run. *Pierrot* was short-lived, but it gave Nadar one of his most moving photographs: Sarah as a white-faced clown doomed to play out the harsh comedy of love and intrigue. Richepin's new drama attempted to depict the dramatic events in the India of 1857, during the native uprisings against British rule. Unfortunately, the French public saw it as an exotic spectacle that dealt with unlikely people doing unlikely things in filmy costumes. *Nana Sahib*, as it was called, opened at the Porte Saint-Martin on 20 December. It enhanced no one's career, Richepin's least of all, for when the leading man became sick, Richepin took over the role, only to prove that his acting was no better than his ill-considered orientalia.

While *Nana Sahib* faltered, Damala unexpectedly rose from his torpor to give a good account of himself in Georges Ohnet's *Le Maître de Forges* (*The Master Blacksmith*). Success did not improve his manners, however. One matinee he seated himself in the front row of the Porte Saint-Martin to see Sarah and Richepin perform. The house was half empty and the audience half asleep. Damala soon took care of that. Each time his wife neared the footlights, he shook his head commiseratingly and very audibly moaned:

"Poor Sarah." When he left the theatre, Richepin caught him in a deadly grip, beat him within an inch of his life, and warned him that the world was too small for both of them. And indeed it was. Before long Damala was back in the clinic, and Richepin had Sarah to himself, or so he was led to believe. But to believe in her, or at least to believe in her fidelity, was to undergo the agonies Mounet-Sully had suffered ten years earlier. Richepin was not Mounet and would have none of it. Instead he disappeared whenever Sarah kicked up her restless heels.

A letter from Bernhardt, reminiscent of those she had written Mounet and Doré, yet infinitely more erotic, describes the situation:

My adored, my maddening master, I ask you to pardon me. Oh yes! A great pardon. What I said to you must have been unspeakably vile since you write me in such a howling rage. I am completely stunned. Your words pierce me to the heart, and echo in all my being. I read the eight pages of your letter, each more insulting than the last. I am exhausted by all your reproaches, and still I am yours more than ever. I need you. I cannot exist without you. Come back, I beg you, come back, for I was born to be yours. I swear to you, adored *seigneur*, that I am not capable of deceiving you. Yes, I know that I like to deceive, that I am made of evil thoughts and betrayals. I deserve every bad name you choose to call me. I am all those things, but I behaved badly only because I felt superior to all who surround me. That is over. You appeared. You blew your powerful breath on my lies, and my equivocal "maybes" and "becauses" were blown away. I drank the truth of love from your lips, and, quivering in your arms, I felt the real, the wild sensations of the body's ecstasy, and I saw in your eyes the absolute supremacy of your being. I gave myself to you completely—and completely new—for I brought you a being that belonged to you and you alone. I did not invent anything about myself. Indeed, I rediscovered myself in you.

Jean, you must forgive my foul temper. You left me without giving me time to think, while I was still moist from your arms, still perfumed by the intoxicating scent of your body. I looked at our bed, thought of our night together, our awakening, our embraces, our——. All right, all right, let us pass over that. I ask your pardon with my arms about your neck, suffering for having cried aloud. Ah! Jean, hold me close, very close. Carry me off into the blue skies of tender loves, roll me in dark clouds, trample me with your thunderstorms, break me in your angry rages. But love me, my adored lover.

However strong my claws, they cannot leave a very deep mark in your heart, since your heart is made of love. Destroy my stupid letter, and tell me that you know I do not deceive you, that I am incapable of deceiving you. It would be cowardly, stupid, foolish.

I uttered a cry of vengeance—and you believed it! It was nothing but rage and pain. What you do not realize, my idol, my master, is that you are always near me, looking at me with your golden glance. Calm yourself, take pity, from the heights where you dwell, on my sad folly. I was sick. I was in the wrong. I submit to your will, and swallow my pride. It would be an unbearable punishment, if you refused to let me kiss your lips. Write me a sweet letter; the last one hurt me so. You aren't scowling any longer, are you? Your sardonic smile has disappeared, hasn't it? I gently kiss your small, beautiful feet.

Let us resume our flight! Never again will I stop its mad course. If you make me suffer too much, I shall simply throw myself from the heights, my love, and—I swear—I shall kill myself in the fall.

I fondle your adored body, I kiss your every hair—and my lips demand that your lips forgive me a thousand times.

Richepin forgave Sarah more than once, only to put an end to their affair the following year. But, unlike Mounet, who turned against her in hatred, in later years he accepted the fact that while she could not be a faithful lover, she could be a faithful friend.

DECEMBER of 1883 saw the publication of *The Memoirs of Sarah Barnum*. It was Colombier's second book about Bernhardt. The first, *Sarah Bernhardt in America*, did not seem to offend its heroine despite its irreverent tone and caustic jibes. *Sarah Barnum* was another story, and a devastating one. What prompted

Marie's cruelty? If we are to believe her, the fault lay with Sarah, who refused to pay her more than a pittance for the months she spent in America. Envy provides an additional explanation for Marie's spleen. The two actresses had begun as equals. Talented, ambitious girls, they acted together, shared their secrets, joked about their many conquests, and dreamt of future glory. Now the future had caught up with them, leaving Colombier far behind her famous comrade in arms. Except that she had become stout, and had more or less given up acting, Marie was much the same as she had been fifteen years before. She was still the irrepressible Second Empire cocotte who cooked delicious dinners for her friends, knew all the latest gossip, travelled in racy circles, and changed lovers as often as she changed the color of her hair. It would have taken a far more saintly creature than she to accept without resentment the extraordinary position Sarah had achieved. There was another, more pressing consideration. Marie needed money and hoped to earn a good deal if the book caught on. It was Sarah who unwittingly made that happen. Colombier's *Barnum* caused barely a ripple when it first appeared. The press shunned it, as it smelled dangerously of dirty linen and libel suits. It was Octave Mirbeau, a recent addition to Sarah's menagerie, who brought the book to public notice. There was nothing the fiery writer enjoyed more than a good fight. Indeed, he was almost irrational in his attack on *Barnum* in the satirical journal *Les Grimaces*. "If I were Maurice Bernhardt," he wrote, "I would take a hammer and break the head of M. Bonnetain. Then I would drag Marie Colombier into a public square. There I would turn up her skirts, show her old, contaminated derrière to the crowd, and give her a bloody beating."

Marie's current lover, Paul Bonnetain, was the author of *Charlot s'Amuse*, a novel about the dangers of excessive masturbation, and Mirbeau accused him of being the co-author of *The Memoirs of Sarah Barnum* as well. Although he very probably was, Bonnetain took offense and challenged the offender to a duel. Mirbeau accepted on one condition: Bonnetain must swear that he had nothing to do with the book. Bonnetain swore, the duel was fought, and Mirbeau was declared the winner after drawing blood from what he hoped was his opponent's writing hand. While the combatants parried and thrusted, another violent scene was taking place. Maurice, accompanied by his friend Jean Stevens,* burst into Colombier's apartment, where they

---

*In the early 1880s Sarah studied painting with Jean's father, the Belgian artist Alfred Stevens, who not surprisingly became her lover and made a beautiful portrait of her as well.

found her calmly drinking tea with a journalist named Jehan Soudan. She was a whore, Maurice shouted. And he, Marie laughed, was a son of a— Sarah Bernhardt. At this effrontery, Maurice snatched a picture of Marie from the wall, threw it to the floor, and stamped on it. Then he left, his honor satisfied. A few moments later, Sarah, armed with a whip and a dagger, and Richepin, brandishing a carving knife, roared into the room. By this time Marie had had the good sense to disappear. In no time at all her apartment was a shambles. The next day the London *Morning News* reported: "M. Soudan was attacked by M. Richepin who was in a state of great excitement. Madame Bernhardt lashed up sofa cushions and hangings and broke a considerable amount of porcelain. Monsieur Richepin offered the maid a thousand francs to tell him where her mistress was hidden, but without success. The party then rushed out."

News of the scandal spread quickly. In New York the *Herald* published an interminable article and the *Police Gazette* celebrated the incident with a lurid two-penny drawing of Sarah and Richepin, their eyes blazing, their nostrils distended, in the act of vengeful pillage. Shortly afterwards Sarah sued Marie for libel. If Marie paid for her sins—she was fined two thousand francs and condemned to three months in prison with a suspended sentence— the book paid for Marie. Ten thousand copies of *The Memoirs of Sarah Barnum* were sold in the next weeks, making her richer than she had ever been. The cynical did not take the episode at face value. Some felt that Sarah had stormed Marie's apartment for the publicity. Others went so far as to claim that she and Marie had put their heads together to stage a scene that would stimulate the sale of Marie's book and, at the same time, stir up interest at the box office for Richepin's *Nana Sahib*, which had just opened to rather discouraging reviews. The critic Albert Wolff offered his belated advice: "Certainly Sarah Bernhardt would have done better to stay at home for the sake of her dignity as an artist, and allow public disdain to take care of the abominable book."

During the winter of 1884, Parisians flocked to the Porte Saint-Martin to see Bernhardt in *La Dame aux Camélias*. The impression she made was beyond description. Sarcey tried, but his attempt to portray her character- ization through analysis of her technique merely hints at her powers. One can only imagine that her Marguerite stirred the sensations one has felt, when, profoundly moved, one experiences the hypnotic magic of a unique artist. Her success in *La Dame aux Camélias* brought Sarah a good deal of happiness and a certain relief from her financial problems. The money that poured into the box office enabled her—though not without a sigh—to pay her son's imposing gambling debts and reimbursed her for some of the vast sums she had squandered on her lover's *Nana Sahib*.

But Sarah had bright plans for the future. She had always longed to stage *Macbeth*. Now she asked Richepin to translate it, a noble idea that, alas, did not prosper. The play closed in less than a month. In June Bernhardt stubbornly took it on a tour of Scotland, then on to London. If Parisians disliked it despite her fine notices as Lady Macbeth, Londoners, for the most part, liked it even less.

Oscar Wilde was a notable exception. He and his wife, Constance, had come to Paris on their honeymoon. On 9 June 1884, Oscar was interviewed in their rooms at the Hotel Wagram overlooking the Tuileries. After indicating to the reporter from the *Morning News* that he was very easily bored, he changed his tune and said:

It is not easy to exhaust the message of Paris, especially when Sarah Bernhardt is playing. I have seen *Macbeth* over and over again. There is nothing like it on our stage, and it is her finest creation. I say her creation deliberately, because to my mind it is utterly impertinent to talk of Shakespeare's *Macbeth* or Shakespeare's *Othello*. Shakespeare is only one of the parties. The second is the artiste through whose mind it passes. When the two together combine to give me an acceptable hero, that is all I ask. Shakespeare's intentions were his own secret: all we can form an opinion about is what is actually before us. . . .

There is absolutely no one like Sarah Bernhardt. She brings all her fine intelligence to the part, all her instinctive and acquired knowledge of the stage. Her influence over Macbeth's mind is just as much influence of womanly charm as of will—with us they only accentuate the last. She holds him under a spell: he sins because he loves her: his ambition is quite a secondary motive. How can he help loving her? She binds him by every tie, even by the tie of coquetry. Look at her dress—the tight-fitting tunic, and the statuesque folds of the robe below. The whole piece is admirably done.

Wilde went on to praise Richepin's prose translation, which Bernhardt's Swiss biographer, Ernest Pronier, described as "very literary, unafraid of plain, coarse language, extremely vivid, and very close to the original," qualities which were not necessarily appreciated by the French public when it came to the great Shakespeare.

Sarah spent a very gloomy summer in her seaside villa at Sainte-Adresse, feeling sick and brooding about the failure of *Macbeth*. The fact that Richepin had literally disappeared and had made his friends promise not to tell her where he was did not help.

Jean,

My despondent letters have been sent everywhere I thought you might be. No doubt not one of them has reached you. Will this one have the same fate? I do not know. I shall write all the same, and your friend Ponchon has taken it upon himself to bring it to you. I beg you on bended knee . . . to send me a word.

I am mad with grief. I cannot live in the deadly silence around me. I am suffering, Jean, suffering. Where are you going, what are you doing, and if you are hurt, and if—My God, I have done nothing to deserve such torture. Yes, yes, I was bad the other day. Oh, how I weep for that badness in me. How I regret having spoken evil words that you think of now that you are alone. Oh, my adored lover, my beloved idol, my seigneur, think only of the sweet, tender words I've said to you, my prince, of my absolute passion, my adoration, my devotion. I no longer have any pride. I am tamed! I am at your feet, submissive and repentant. Never, never again will I be bad; my wild love lives only to love you, to listen to you. My God, Jean, what have I done to deserve such treatment?

But then, you cannot know the anguish I feel since your departure. When I received your note, I collapsed, and I haven't left my bed since. Ponchon will tell you that only he can calm me . . . for with him I can speak of you. . . .

Listen! Since you know so well how to hide, and since no one knows where you are, would you like me to join you? Nothing is important to me, not the theatre, not Maurice, nothing but you. I want you. I shall never look back. I shall be cowardly, I shall be despicable, but I shall be at your feet. Or tell me to kill myself, that you have had enough of me, that you no longer love me, that my love is a burden to you.

Seriously now, did you think that I could wait in silence? Have you never looked at me, never understood me when I made love to you? I weep, that's all, I weep and weeping makes me ugly. If you wanted to destroy my pride, subdue my will, force me to see that you are clearly the master, it is done. . . . I fully realize that your will is stronger than mine since it allows you to make me suffer so. . . . I no longer take pride in anything except loving you. Make me your slave, your possession, but keep your love for me. What dreadful nights I spend! I look for you, I pound your pillow, then I kiss it and beg it to confide in me, to tell me your last thoughts, the ones that carried you so far from me. How enormous the space is that separates us! The pillow does not answer, and I weep alone.

Pity! Have pity, my master. I beg you for mercy. I cannot go on. Everything has crumbled around me and those with me, stupefied and desolate, watch me dying of love for you. None of that matters. . . . But what if you no longer love me. Tell me that you permit me to come and look at you. I shall say nothing to you, nothing. I shall kiss your lips, and, in a spasm of love, I shall gently kill myself with your ivory knife. And you will throw your mistress's body into the street. And no one will know, and then you will show them this letter, and you will say, "You see, she was mad." And Ponchon, when he shows them the insane things I've written to him, will also say, "She was mad."

You see, Jean, that would be for the best, since I cannot go on suffering. It is too much! I am suffocating. Perhaps to live is not all-important, when I should have died in order to soften your heart. Oh, my lover, let yourself be touched. You have tortured me so much that you cannot do more. I beg you, take pity on your slave, your mistress. I do not dare to kiss your lips if you do not wish it.

I love you.

At last Sarah received a reply from Richepin, but a letter she wrote to their mutual friend, the poet Raoul Ponchon, would indicate that she must give up all hope of his coming back to her:

. . . Jean wrote me a letter so monstrous that I am filled with despair. He accused me of such infamy that I cannot defend myself. His letter has left me sick, disoriented, stupefied, outraged . . . Ah! How evil it is, and how badly he has behaved. I swear to you, my dear Ponchon, I couldn't write. My arms are reduced to a pulp, and my eyes are black and blue. I was afraid that if I wrote him, he would be upset beyond all measure, and my gullibility makes me fear that he would come running. Ah! Poor me, whom he does not love at all! I adore him, I love him, I weep, I suffer, for I am wounded to the depths of my soul, wounded in my dignity as a lover, wounded in my pride as a woman, wounded in the idealism of my love.

I do not want to write him ever again unless he should ask me to forget his infamous accusations. Write to me, pity me, I'm so unhappy I could kill myself. If you knew—Ah! if you knew what he said to me. And I who had only one thought: Him, and the fear of becoming ugly, and no longer able to please him. Ah! What a poor, abominable nature Jean has.

What is he not capable of doing, he who thinks in that way? I am sad, Ponchon, sad, and with no hope for the future.

Despite her letter's hysterical, abject, masochistic tone, Sarah was not exaggerating. Richepin's disappearance had made her truly ill.

Madame Guérard who, as always, was at Sarah's side was alarmed by her condition and sent a note to Duquesnel:

Saint-Adresse

Madame has had a very high fever for days. The doctor has been here. He thinks there is great danger that she may have galloping consumption. Please try to come here to see her. She is very low.

That September Félix Duquesnel took over the management of the Porte Saint-Martin Theatre. At Sarah's insistence—and against his better judgment—he agreed to revive Richepin's version of *Macbeth*. This time it ran for only two weeks. Richepin was to have great success with his plays in later years, but his collaborations with Sarah were doomed to failure. Deeply depressed by the breakup of their affair, she looked forward to *Théodora*, a new work by Victorien Sardou. The play had all the earmarks of a hit. Set in sixth-century Istanbul, the spectacle was written in broad, bloodthirsty strokes that reek of sadism, lust, and violence. The production under the guidance of Duquesnel was a revelation in stagecraft. "It was the greatest achievement," Emile Perrin said, "of *mise-en-scène* in the nineteenth century." In the opinion of many, the décor and costumes, conceived by the leading designers of the Opéra and the Comédie Française, were more solidly constructed than the play itself. The great spaces of the stage glowed with Byzantine splendor. One set, a palace room of massive pillars and soaring arches, was filled with Oriental draperies, friezes and mosaics, statues and fantastic furniture overlaid with silver and precious stones. The backdrop revealed the imperial gardens and the golden domes of the city. Another set boasted a plane tree whose branches reached out to cover the entire stage, behind it a painted forest and the distant blue of the Bosporus. Yet another was all gold and jewelled ornaments.

Sarah, of course, played Théodora, the whorish dancing girl who rose from a life of debauchery to become the empress of Byzantium. The play was magnificent hokum. Yet, like the films of Cecil B. DeMille, it fascinated the public and amused the knowing. And, like those epics of the silver screen, it provided the kind of role actresses kill for. Bernhardt and her playwright did not take the exotic melodrama lightly. Sardou, a stickler for authenticity—and a past master at twisting it to his purposes—pored over history books day and night. And Sarah travelled all the way to Ravenna to study the mosaic portrait of Théodora until its saturnine spirit entered her very soul. This occult mission accomplished, she made detailed drawings of the empress's robes, rushed back to Paris, and ordered a crown and costumes encrusted with thousands of semiprecious stones: a heavy weight she would bear on the stage with imperial grace.

The plot of *Théodora* is as tortuous as the intrigue that flourished at the court of the emperor Justinian. With all its twists and turns, it gave Sarah an opportunity to display her infinite store of virtuoso tricks. How skillfully Sardou provided them! The first act begins slowly, a device that allows the audience to sit back and admire the set. Suddenly a great blast, an explosion of Massenet's organ music, heralds the entrance of Théodora, who appears upstage, followed by her attendants and eunuchs. She is in a golden gown embroidered with angel heads, over which is thrown a bright satin cloak shot with gold thread and gleaming with topazes. A jewelled crown completes her costume. Hieratic and mysterious, she moves to the center of the stage and poses, icon-like, as the entire court sinks to its knees. Then she descends to her peacock divan and extends a hand to be kissed, and then, yes, a foot! Her regal presence established, the action takes Sarah, or rather Théodora—they are one to the audience—into the shadowy streets of Istanbul, where, dressed as the lascivious slave girl she was in her youth, she meets and falls in love with Andréas, the man who is plotting to overthrow the emperor. The story line thickens as do Théodora's chances to show off a vast wardrobe and an even vaster range of emotion.

In the end, having gone through more than anyone ever deserves to suffer, she poisons her lover by mistake. Crazed by her act, she falls on his prostrate body. A sinister executioner, holding a red silk cord, walks slowly toward her.

"Come then," she sobs, "I am ready." The curtain falls as she is about to be strangled with the scarlet loop.

At the première on 26 December 1884, the melodrama, the production, and, above all, Bernhardt herself were rewarded with one of the most thunderous ovations in theatre history. Sarah kept *Théodora* on the boards all through 1885. It was performed three hundred times in Paris and more than a hundred times in London. In the summer months she took it to Brussels, Geneva, and the French provinces. All this despite the critics, who found the plot unlikely, the historical background hazy, and the romantic fantasy hollow. Yet with all their complaints they were ready to admit that even hokum could be glorious in the hands of a Bernhardt. For the critic Jules Lemaître she was "a Salomé, a Salammbô: a distant chimerical creature, sacred and serpentine with a fascination both mystic and sensual."

Most theatre-goers were content to be dazzled by Sarah and to leave it at that. But there were those who had a feverish longing to become close to her, to find out what she was made of. The novelist Pierre Loti was one. Born Julien Viaud in 1850 in Rochefort-sur-Mer, a sober little seaport on France's Atlantic coast, Loti was brought up in an atmosphere of strict Protestantism by a household of women who liked nothing better than to spoil him. As a boy he played the piano and made a museum of the snake skins, butterflies, shells, and feathers his seafaring uncle brought back from the tropics. Such quiet occupations did not prevent him from responding to the rough sailor life he watched from his bedroom window. It was perhaps that siren call combined with the nautical adventures his brother told that led him to the naval academy. After three years he was a midshipman on a schooner headed for Tahiti and the Easter Islands.

Pierre was no ordinary sailor. He had a need to express himself and in his early twenties began to send articles and drawings to *L'Illustration* and *Le Monde Illustré*. He was twenty-five when he met Sarah, and she was thirty-one. By then he had travelled the world, engaged in heated friendships, both male and female, and was obsessed by the exotic, forbidden pleasures of native life.

Loti first saw Bernhardt from a front-row orchestra seat at the Comédie

Française. "I shall never forget," he confided to his journal, "the moment she walked to the footlights and fixed me with those great somber eyes, her head thrust forward like an angel of evil. Twice I met those eyes. . . ."

Young Loti took a more playful tone when he described the event in a letter to his shipmate, Lucien Jousselin. (The "Pierre" he refers to is, of course, himself):

Just imagine . . . in the middle of June, I fell into the strange clutches of Sarah Bernhardt. On a certain evening topman Pierre, who had never given a thought to milady S.B., decided to go in his modest blue sailor suit to the Comédie Française, and get himself a good seat. . . . The beautiful Doña Sol, who was already onstage, gave him her most gracious smile, to the great astonishment of the audience.

The next day, seaman Pierre went to the house of milady S.B., who welcomed him most charmingly, gave him a rose, accepted the portrait he had sketched of her, and bade him *au revoir*. The following day, Loti, dressed in his most heavily embroidered and gilded Turkish costume, paid milady S.B. a second visit. It lasted four hours, fours hours in which many mad things were said and done. The house was thoroughly inspected, and Loti was introduced to the staff, a monkey, and various wolfhounds and Great Danes. Two very curious hours were spent on a certain couch, during which time milady S.B. behaved in a most extraordinary, nervous fashion. Loti naively took his leave at dinner time and left for Rochefort.

Nevermore did poor Loti hear a word from *La Belle Dame Sans Merci*. He sent her crates of roses, handsome drawings, and beautiful letters aflame with love. But the lady was indifferent and failed to respond. Loti had shown a lack of courage and daring; he committed the unpardonable when he allowed the psychological moment to escape—that moment which never returns. The inevitable consequence and moral: Loti, who had hardly given milady S.B. a thought, is now under the creature's spell, and, contrary to all expectations, desires her in the maddest way. . . .

Loti once said that he was not his own physical type. Nor was he Sarah's. Her weakness for great strapping fellows like Mounet and Richepin was well known, and Loti was anything but that. A doe-eyed slip of a man, he wore heavy make-up, sported high heels, and was committed to what he called "the sins of Sodom." Sarah ignored him after his first visit as he seemed to be just another of her many queer, besotted fans. But she was mistaken. One day a large carpet was delivered to her house by two burly men who unrolled it to reveal Loti, as impish and as seductive as Cleopatra when she had herself smuggled into Caesar's presence. Loti's trick seems to have amused Sarah, for soon the two were intimate friends.

Before long, Loti felt confident enough to send Sarah a photograph of a naked sailor. And when *Aziyadé*, his first novel, was published, he dedicated it to her. "Madame": he wrote, "The very obscure boy whom you call *'Pierre le fou'* humbly dedicates this story to you, you who shine so brilliantly among the intelligent of this world. Your name will lend poetry and charm to these sad pages." Alas, his publisher informed "Pierre the Mad" that it was too late to include the dedication as the book was already in galleys. The omission was of little consequence as, with or without her name, Sarah found *Aziyadé* admirable. Her reaction was not surprising. If Loti was a minor master, he was a major talent whose tales glow with rapturous pictures of the sea, of sailors, of primitive people and what it is to love them. Touched by Sarah's appreciation of his work, Loti wrote: "She understands them to their very limits." Once their friendship was under way, Loti discovered that Sarah was even more extraordinary than he had realized. In another letter to his friend Jousselin he describes her bedroom:

A large room, sumptuous and funereal: the walls, ceiling, doors, and windows are all hung with heavy black Chinese satin embroidered with bats and mythical monsters. There is a large dais decorated with the same black drapery under which, partially hidden, lies a coffin made of fragrant, precious wood, lined with tufted white satin. A massive ebony four-poster bed with black curtains; and a coverlet embroidered with a large Chinese-red dragon with gold wings and claws. In one corner a full-length mirror framed in black velvet; perched on the frame, a stuffed vampire bat, a real one, its hairy wings outstretched. In the midst of all this mortuary splendor, three figures stand gazing at themselves in the mirror, hand-in-hand. One, "the skeleton of a handsome young man who died of love," a skeleton called Lazarus whose white bones are as polished as ivory, a masterpiece of anatomical craftsmanship which can stand erect, and knows how to strike poses. In the center, facing the mirror, a young woman in a white satin dress with a long train, a young, deliciously pretty woman with large somber eyes, graceful, distinctive, supremely charming, a strange creature: Sarah Bernhardt. The third personage, a young man dressed in a gold-embroidered oriental costume as if for a fête in Istanbul: Pierre Loti, or even Ali Nyssim—as you wish. How many insanities we three exchanged in this courtesan's room, a room unique in the world!

An entry in Loti's journal shows us Bernhardt at home shortly before her first trip to London with the Comédie Française:

28 May 1879

At 4 o'clock I present myself to Sarah, dressed in my sailor's blues. She is in the grand salon-atelier, more cluttered than ever with strange, precious oriental objects; bouquets of roses and rare flowers everywhere. She is dressed in black with a corsage of red roses. Present is a whole crowd of artists and men of letters in whose midst my sailor's costume makes a singular impression. Sarah Bernhardt approaches and gives me her hand with perfect grace. She compliments me on my book which she has circulated among her entourage who praised it as "the work of a poet." From the moment I arrive, her attentions place me on the same level as those who surround me and look me over with such curiosity. I ask if I can see her alone tomorrow. She agrees. She counts the hours on her fingers, rapidly going through her appointments for the next day and fixes 1:30 p.m. for our tête-à-tête. On leaving I hold her hand a little too long, with more emotion than should be shown in public. The thought of our rendezvous disturbs me.

At precisely 1:30 I ring the bell at the house in the avenue de Villiers. A smiling chambermaid leads the poor sailor Pierre into the bizarre salon. Madame appears with a dreamy air, still dressed in black. A cablegram has arrived advancing her departure for England by one day. Her visitors—princes, marquesses, writers, and artists—arrive in droves to say goodbye. I can still see the scene: a group of artists and prominent women, the painter Jules Bastien-Lepage, Mlle Abbéma, Mlle [Jeanne] Samary, the old *dame de compagnie* [Guérard], the chambermaids, the Great Dane, and the large wolfhound painted by Clairin. Everyone is occupied with preparations for the voyage; indescribable disorder. Sarah Bernhardt, extremely calm, gives orders seated at her desk on the tall gothic chair which bears her motto *Quand même*. In the midst of this turmoil, a great many letters and farewell cards are brought in. Graciously rising, Sarah gives

me her photograph as Doña Maria de Neubourg [the queen of Spain in
Ruy Blas].

"Write to me in London," she says, "77 Chester Square—and don't
forget me!"

There was little danger of that. Loti, unknown and new to Paris, was more
than intrigued to be a part of Sarah's court, and quite uneasy about his
position among her famous friends. His relative anonymity, however, was
not to last very long. On 9 July 1879 he wrote her as follows:

It seems to me a change has taken place in my life: that I attained
something unhoped for and impossible when you so openly accepted me
as your friend. From time to time I'll write you from the far countries to
which I soon return. I shall speak of my existence, so far from yours. I'll
send you my impressions of solitude. . . . When my letters reach you,
you will not even look at them. You will give them to the skeleton, Lazarus,
who will read them aloud to the bat.

I am still under the spell of those few moments I spent with you. But
I tremble at the thought that I must have seemed ridiculous, especially in
my Turkish costume. . . . I'd rather you remembered Pierre the seaman,
who late that night amused you for a moment. I never wished to flatter
you; besides, you receive so much flattery that it would be banal. Let me
say, once and for all, that for me, you are an ideal, placed very high, a
being exquisite and delicious soaring far above other women; that you
have the mysterious attraction of an enigma; that a certain dark side of
your nature attracts me as much, perhaps, as your charm.

My irrational dream would be to take you with me, to sail the seas on
a ship under my command, with my friends as the crew. By my friends,
I mean a band of pirates who know no fear, and stop at nothing, except
at my command. How well you would fit in with us, and how many wonders
we should see! Please excuse this senseless letter.

Eight months later, in his journal of 29 March 1880, Loti is still brooding
about his failure to carry his seduction of Sarah to its expected conclusion.

Chez Alphonse Daudet. There's a man who charms me completely.
There is something unique about him. He says that in these last years he

has not seen anything in French literature as good as [my book] *Le Mariage de Loti.*

Chez Sarah Bernhardt at 3 o'clock. She is sick. Her door is closed to everyone, but I am allowed in. I am led into the large salon and asked to wait; an old lady, talkative and witty—an actress no doubt—is sent to keep me company. She is an endless explosion of witticisms. A chambermaid appears, and gives me permission to go up to Sarah's bedroom. Sarah is in her monumental bed with its black satin curtains, in her monumental black-lined mortuary chamber. She is buried in white satin quilts bordered with swans. I have never seen her looking so young, so rested, with such sparkling eyes. She has the air of someone playing sick.

The skeleton is there, seated near her. The witty old woman is even more embarrassingly in the way than he. S.B. is in a charming mood. She gives me her hand to kiss with an exquisite grace—as in the second act of *Ruy Blas*—nonetheless her tone is no longer what it was two years ago, when I visited her as a Turk. My moment in the sun has passed, never to return. The old duenna has been instructed not to leave us alone; it is she who sees me out, very politely, with many compliments—and a certain ironic air that is killingly funny.

An entry in Pierre Loti's journal of 1884 reveals that he has completed the journey from anonymity to fame:

Ten very exciting days in Paris. I am now a celebrity, surrounded and fêted as never before.* Yet I still dream of the ravishing Scandinavian creature whom, no doubt, I shall never see again. [And who, given the ambivalent nature of Loti's sexuality, is most probably a man.]

I feel newly attracted to Sarah Bernhardt, especially one evening when I visit her dressing room during the entr'actes of *La Dame aux Camélias.* While she dresses for the first act, still in her "chemise," Madame Guérard and the *femme de chambre* tell me, at her orders, to come in backwards

*Snobbish Parisians who, in the late seventies, had wondered what the miniature sailor lad was doing in Sarah's salon were now proud to know the author of the Polynesian idyl *Le Mariage de Loti* and *Mon Frère Yves*, his novel of a sailor's travels round the world, published in 1883. That year Loti, as a French naval officer, took part in the battle of Tonking Bay in that part of French Indochina that is now called Vietnam, and sent highly controversial articles to *Le Figaro*, exposing a series of scandals following the fall of Hué.

with my eyes closed. The voice that answers is seductive and somewhat excited. Her dressing room, hung with white Chinese satin embroidered with imps and devils, is exquisitely perfumed.

"Tonight," she says "I shall play for Renan [Ernest Renan, author of *The Life of Jesus*], and for you because you are back from Tonking. You will see how good it will be." In fact, she was incomparable. How amusing her enthusiasm for Renan is!

"It's all the same to me that he smells bad," she says, "that he looks like a toad; no matter what they say, I admire him."

"I do the best I can," she replies modestly to a whole court come to praise her after the performance. To leave the theatre that evening she simply puts a long fox fur over her sleeveless batiste chemise, and there she is, ready to climb into her large landau while extending her hand to me, between the two rows of obscure admirers waiting to see her come out.

There was no sexual ambivalence in the case of the poet Comte Robert de Montesquiou, another of Sarah's literary attachments. Flamboyantly homosexual, thin as his poems, grand as his name, precious as the gray pearl he wore in his cravat, Montesquiou was perhaps the rarest orchid in all of Paris. Sarah fawned over him and called him "my brother, my soul mate, my alter ego forever." She went even farther. She seduced him, an act that caused the poor count to lose his dinner. That ordeal behind them, Sarah continued on a more spiritual plane.

"I love you with a sweet, infinite tenderness," she gushed, "I love you with a divine maternal passion, and I am certain that my life is bound to yours."

In celebration of their platonic love, they posed for an amusing photograph: Bernhardt as Coppée's *Le Passant*, the ardent young troubadour, Zanetto, and Montesquiou in an identical costume. The poet-count was perhaps the most affected man of his generation, an attribute the highly stylized Bernhardt relished to the full. Indeed, it was pure theatre to watch the actress, arms outstretched, her eyes shining with admiration, as she advanced on her "*poète adoré*," while he, doubled over in a spasm of *fin-de-siècle* ecstasy, kissed her bejewelled fingers as he appraised her silver gown embroidered with garlands of irises. Even more theatrical was the spectacle of Bernhardt, artfully propped against the mantelpiece of some aristocratic salon, reciting Montesquiou's latest poems while he, in rapt attention, assumed the pose of Rodin's *The Thinker* (*Le Penseur*).

Such parlor games were put into perspective when on 22 May 1885 Victor Hugo died at the age of eighty-three. His death was a profound blow to Bernhardt. The great poet was her youth; his plays her first taste of glory. Now her old friend was gone and, with him, the romantic fervor that had nurtured her art. Two million people followed the pauper's hearse the writer had requested. Amid the surge of humanity that made its way on foot from the Étoile to the Pantheon was Sarah—an anonymous, veiled figure in black. As she walked along the crepe-lined boulevards, she was recognized, and the crowds fell back to create a space around her: Doña Sol in mourning for her lost creator. In his honor she revived *Marion Delorme* at the end of the year. Sadly enough, Parisians were quicker to follow their national hero to his grave than to buy tickets for his play.

At the end of February 1886, to please Philippe Garnier, the lover she had dismissed in Russia when she decided to make an actor of Damala, she agreed to play Ophelia to his Hamlet. The result was disastrous. For the ten days of the run he was hissed and booed. Although she was applauded and praised for her Ophelia, Sarah did not fare much better—worse, in fact, since it was she who paid the bills at the Porte Saint-Martin. Desperately in need of money, she put her possessions up for auction, sold her luxurious house in the avenue de Villiers, and rented a sparsely furnished flat in the rue Saint-Georges as a *pied-à-terre*.

In April 1886, she set out on a fourteen-month tour of Britain and North and South America. Before leaving Paris, she revived Sardou's sure-fire *Fédora* for a limited run. One evening an unexpected caller appeared at her dressing-room door. It was the Prince de Ligne. Twenty years had passed since she had borne his child, unpredictable years in which Sarah had risen to unforeseen heights, while Ligne remained what he had always been: the scion of a rich and noble house. The next day, after lunch with Sarah and Maurice, he offered to recognize his son and settle a certain amount of money on him. Maurice refused, gracefully but firmly, saying that as his mother had brought him up by herself, often with great difficulty, he owed everything to her and, in his gratitude, preferred to keep her name.

In his aristocratic way, Maurice, never one to worry about how his endless supply of money was earned, overlooked the possibility that he might better express his gratitude to his mother—at forty-one, in humiliatingly conspicuous financial difficulties—by allowing his father to relieve her of the burden of supporting him. Indeed, it is highly likely that the Prince de Ligne reappeared in order to help Sarah, only to be put off by his handsome but arrogant son.

That afternoon Maurice saw his long-lost father off to Brussels. The Gare du Nord was packed, and Ligne, afraid he might miss his train, asked a station attendant to put him ahead of the crowd. By way of encouragement, he pressed a coin into his hand and muttered his princely name. As neither had any effect, Maurice stepped in. He was the son of Sarah Bernhardt, he announced. Couldn't something be done? At the mention of the magic name, they were whisked through the throng and shown to the prince's compartment. As father and son shook hands, Maurice could not resist a parting shot: "You see," he said, "it's not so bad to be a Bernhardt." True words, at least from Maurice's point of view. At twenty-one he was Sarah's "dauphin," her spoilt darling. When he proved to be inept at theatre management, she shrugged her shoulders and forgave him. When he gambled away vast sums of her money, she wished him better luck next time. When he squandered large sums on clothes, carriages, and horses, she thought it his birthright as the son of a prince and smiled proudly at the sight of her handsome, extravagant young dandy trotting off to the Bois de Boulogne. In a word, she was the unconditionally loving mother, always ready to pamper her child in return for his devotion. And, one must add, Maurice was always ready to show his devotion in exchange for his pampered existence.

AT THE END of April 1886, Bernhardt and her troupe embarked at Bordeaux for Rio de Janeiro, where she was engaged for the month of June. On her first trip to America, she had left her fifteen-year-old son with Aunt Henriette and Uncle Faure. Now that Maurice was twenty-one, she was delighted to take him along for the first part of the tour. To provide him with companions of his own age, she invited his friend Jean Stevens to join them. Sarah also engaged her sister Jeanne's daughter, Saryta, to come along as one of her company. (Saryta's father was Oscar Planat, one of the "lions" of Paris who moved in the same circles as Charles Haas and the Prince de Ligne. A gifted actress, Sarah's niece was to have a career at the Comédie Française using the name Saryta Bernhardt.)

Sarah's first visit to Brazil was one long triumph. She was pleased that the emperor, Dom Pedro II, came to each of her plays, although her letters imply that he was not as lavish with gifts as some of the European monarchs she had known.

To follow Bernhardt from Brazil through Argentina, Uruguay, Chile, Peru, Cuba, and Mexico, and then from Texas across the United States to New York would be almost as exhausting as making the trip. However, for Sarah, the homesickness, the backbreaking work, and the thousands of miles of uncomfortable travel were balanced by red carpets, fêtes, and honors; precious gifts, exotic rulers, and imposing fees.

This tour of the Americas is not described in *My Double Life* as that book ends in 1881 with her return to France after her first trip to the United States. But she did describe it in letters that differ from her memoirs in much the way that intimate conversation differs from public speaking.

The chief recipients of her letters were her son and Raoul Ponchon. Ponchon might have been a character in Murger's or Puccini's *La Bohème*. A close friend not only of Richepin but of Paul Bourget, he haunted the Latin Quarter, wrote a book of verse called *The Muse of the Cabaret*, and, like Richepin, prided himself on his affection for the street people of Paris. For Sarah he was the ideal *petit ami*, the cozy confidant to whom she could speak openly about Richepin, who, she tried to delude herself into thinking, would forgive her infidelities and come back to her.

The following letters are from Bernhardt to Ponchon:

Aboard ship, 4 May 1886
. . . Despite the pain, the shame, and the sorrow my *liaison amoureuse* with Jean caused me . . . I still carry one grateful memory: that of knowing you and of knowing that you are in my heart forever. I love you profoundly; you are part of my dreams for the future. Dear friend, always remain my friend, keep intact the place I occupy in your heart. I feel so well there. . . .

Rio de Janeiro, 27 May 1886

My dear Ponchon, my Ponchinot,

Here I am at last, after 22 days at sea. What a superb voyage, and what an enchanting country! . . . But each joy has its sorrow. If the country is remarkable, the climate is dreadful. The fabulous vegetation is due to extreme heat and horrifying humidity. . . . Everyone feels somewhat sick. . . . I'll write you after the first performance. . . .

I embrace you with all my soul,

. . . Poor Berthier, one of our group, nearly died of yellow fever and Jarrett is not at all well. Maurice has been spitting blood. The doctors here tell me it's heart trouble. But, alas, if it's his heart rather than his lungs, that doesn't make me feel any better. We leave in a few days for a small place called São Paulo, fourteen hours from Rio. They call it the Switzerland of Brazil, and say it's extremely cold there.

What murderous thieves live here! Ah! If only yellow fever would carry them off. I wouldn't shed a tear. . . . On Monday I play Phèdre, yes Phèdre. Of course they won't understand anything at all. . . . My travelling companion is Marie Jullien [one of the actresses in the company]. We have meals together and sleep in adjoining rooms. We leave the connecting door open and talk until we fall asleep. What do women usually talk about? Clothes. But we, we speak of love. She adores her captain, her lover of six years. Happy girl, she trusts him and he trusts her! I listen in envy. And while she confides in me, I think of my beloved Richepin, and of Ponchon, the sad clown who never laughs.

Life here is sad and ugly—oh so ugly. Not that people aren't charming, and my success enormous. But what a theatre! Rats and mice everywhere. Lights so dim the morning scenes look as though they were taking place at midnight. No props but a couch hard enough to break my back, and a carpet so small it could be a stagehand's scarf, spread out to dry his tobacco. Still I've laughed a lot. I've given some good performances, and now we'll be leaving soon.

A big hug, a kiss, and all my heart,

. . . His Majesty, the Emperor of Brazil seems to be too poor to buy a subscription. Each night he arrives at the theatre in a carriage pulled by four wheezing mules. And what a carriage! It's as mad as his threadbare guardsmen. They all seem to be playing, these gallant Brazilians. They play at building houses, they play at making roads, at putting out fires, at being enthusiastic.

There is a magnificent place, quite high up, a virgin forest in all its splendor with paths bordered by bamboo as thick as your legs and magnificent banana trees covered with fruit. And yuccas as big as oaks, and camellias with gigantic twisted trunks. Just opposite is a mountain covered with various flowering trees and masses of camellias, and waterfalls amid the rarest plants. Hummingbirds as small as butterflies wheel about one's head. Herons with golden crests, rails with enormous red beaks, and rose-colored ibis: the effect is magical.

In order to go hunting in the lagoons of the region, one must get into a small pirogue carved from the trunk of a single tree. A black boatman stands in the front and the hunter sits in the middle. A sudden fearful motion, or a sneeze, and the pirogue capsizes. I haven't yet navigated in this way, but I shall the next time we go there. . . . How interesting it would be to make this trip with you. I hug you with all my strength, and I love you very much.

Write to me at the Hôtel de la Paix in Buenos Aires.

Buenos Aires, 17 August 1886

Listen, lord Ponchinot, at the present hour, this 17th of August at four in the afternoon, I have two hundred thousand francs. All my expenses are paid, my dresses, Maurice's bills—everything! Congratulate me, and tell Richepin who I know will be pleased. In fact I'll be bringing back a tidy million. Complete. With all this great success, I have to admit I work like a slave, and long to leave Argentina for Chile—even though the twelve-day crossing is atrociously dangerous. Write care of my uncle, Hôtel Colon, Valparaiso.

My Maurice is very well, and returns to Europe in October. Since my arrival, photographs of Jean Richepin are on sale next to mine. This is somewhat irritating, but that kind of boring nuisance will be with me for life, and I must get used to it. But then he's so ugly in his photographs that *that* irritates me further. When one of my local adorers says with flaring nostrils and emotion-filled voice: "Your photograph is in such and such a shop next to Richepin's," I reply; "Yes, but he's so much better looking than that."

I have two admirers here. Both are madly in love with me. One is twenty-two, very elegant, very flirtatious, very strong, and, I believe, very depraved. He is so wildly passionate that every other day leeches have to be placed behind his ears to draw out some of his hot blood! Blinded by desire, and fatuous beyond belief, he cannot be discouraged. The other is all of twenty-four. He is sincere, with the eyes and mouth of a sentimental woman. He is discreet, ardent, and ready to be completely devoted. The first is an important lawyer, and a political enemy of the second, who is the President's private secretary. I think I'd better leave town before the trouble begins. Since my arrival there have been nothing but duels fought over me because they all think they're in love with me. Oh, dear Ponchinot, how I prefer your sweet tenderness!

I'm astonished by those infamous French newspapers. Never have I seen such cowardly lies, or such obvious glee, as when they report that I am ruined and sick. What miserable creatures! What filthy fools! There is no truth in what they say, except, I admit, in the story of the madwoman who assaulted me, and whom I struck with my riding crop. . . .

Before making the dangerous trip around the southern tip of South America, Sarah sent her son and his friend to New York where, she wrote Ponchon, "Maurice is having a wildly amusing time. The lion of the day, and the darling of both society and the demimonde, he's as proud as a peacock." And as self-centered, we learn from a letter she was to send from London, the last stop of her strenuous thirteen-month tour:

If you see Maurice, dear Ponchon, tell him I'm bored to death, and it would be an act of charity if he were to spend a few days with me. He says he's coming on the 18th, but I don't believe him. Please write him in this vein, but *don't scold him or force him to come.*

Sarah described her trip from Argentina to Chile in a letter to Maurice in which she reveals yet another of her selves: the intrepid world traveller far removed from the decadent, hothouse creature Pierre Loti wrote of in his journals:

On board the Cotopaxi, 11 August 1886

My dear, beloved Maurice,

I just received your telegram announcing your arrival in Paris . . . Oh, how far apart we are, my dear son, and how painful it is for me to count the hours that separate us! While your ship sailed toward France, mine carried me farther and farther away from you. . . .

The first two days of the voyage were stormy, but then the sun came out, and we entered the Straits of Magellan easily under our own steam. The captain was all smiles when—boom!—one splendid morning, in calm seas, the ship lurched, went over on one side, then, righting itself violently, ran aground. . . . Through the porthole I could see a white house within shooting distance, and—almost touching the ship—cattle somewhat frightened by this big machine. Had the sea been rough, I swear on my honor we would have crashed into the house. This habitation belongs to two Englishmen who live quite alone on this strange barren island, with no hills, no trees, with nothing but coarse yellow grass. They came aboard to see who their unexpected visitors were. On learning that Madame, your mother, was one of them, they told me they had made a four-day trip to Montevideo just to see me perform. They invited me to stay with them and hunt the puma one could see on the low sand dunes in the distance, but the captain begged me not to disembark. I stayed on board, not without regrets. We played baccarat all day, and I won a thousand francs which I deducted from what you owe Grau.* I shot at seagulls with Garnier's Winchester, but only managed to damage a buoy. At four o'clock a large German ship appeared on the horizon. It stopped a mile away. Then the German captain came up to us in a launch. . . . Our Captain Hayes seemed very nervous. He took me aside and said: "The German commandant has offered to tow us out to sea, but it's possible he won't succeed. What do you think? Are you afraid of being stranded, or do you have confidence in me?"

"Ah, captain," I said, "I beg you to send him away. I have confidence in you, and in my lucky star," and I touched the good-luck medal you gave me, the one I wear on a chain around my neck. The captain, visibly moved, uttered his open-hearted thanks. That evening at dinner, we drank to his health, and to the tides on which our fate depends. The next day, after hours of hard labor on the part of the engine and the crew, the vessel righted itself, and we cast off. There my darling, you have the story of my little odyssey.

---

*Sarah was terribly saddened when her impresario, Edward Jarrett, who had taken ill in Brazil, died on the way from Rio to Buenos Aires. Her secretary, Maurice Grau, replaced him, and would manage all her tours for the next twenty years. He would also manage New York's Metropolitan Opera Company in its "golden years."

12 August 1886

. . . This morning I take up the story of our voyage. The Straits of
Magellan provided a superb spectacle: a chain of mountains covered with
vegetation and snow. At times one seems to be closed in. . . . but one
passes through, squeezed on both sides by the magisterial, awesome Great
Cordillera of the Andes. Ah! How I thought of you, my dear little Maurice,
especially when some Patagonians came up to us. They stopped their
pirogue at the foot of our ship. There were three men and four women,
one with a small infant on her back. The women had red skin and shaved
heads with a tuft of thick, black hair. Their wide bony faces were smiling
and full of charm. They wore cloaks of guanaco* or sealskin. One man
was nude to the waist with breeches of fine black cloth; another wore a
short, checked English jacket. Yet another had on women's stockings, a
pair of chestnut-colored men's underpants cut above the knee, and a flannel
waistcoat. The women asked for biscuits in their sweet voices, saying:
"Gayetta! Gayetta!" They also like to repeat an English phrase which throws
the entire crew into wild fits of laughter. No one would translate it for me,
as it was taught them by sailors and is very naughty.

The first mate climbed down to their boat and traded the captain's
visored casquette for two necklaces made of bones which the captain
presented to me. One is for you. Finally I asked one of the women if she
would give me what she was wearing, an ostrich skin fastened by two
thongs. She stood up, laughing, and with no false modesty, took it off and
gave it to me. She was very pretty too: strong, young legs, small breasts,
and extraordinarily large feet, from which, of course, comes the name,
Patagons.

At last we resumed our voyage. At twilight the following day the ship
came to a stop. We were about to round the perilous Cape Silas. We could
see two grounded vessels, one with its prow in the air, the other with its
main mast out of the water. Our arrival at Cape Silas was horrible: four
days and nights fighting a raging wind. The noise was infernal; the whole
ship creaked; and everyone clung to the walls.

We sighted Lota at four in the morning, five days late. A launch covered
with flowers was sent out to meet us. As soon as I set foot in it, music
was heard: *La Marseillaise* followed by the national anthem of Chile. The

---

*Guanaco: a brown, woolly animal related to the camel, but without humps. Along with the
ostrich, it was the chief means of subsistence for the natives who hunted them on horseback
with the help of dogs.

gardens of Lota are enchanting: cascades, bridges, grottoes, mountains, a superb château and a magnificent Government House with the sea and rocks as a backdrop. Far in the distance, we see a mining village, crushed and brutish.

After lunch, to which we did full honors, we were transported to the mines in a freight car decorated with ribbons, flowers, and French flags. When we arrived, a motley crowd of miners, both women and men, were waiting for us. The two-hundred-foot descent into the underground is very dramatic, much like the descriptions in Zola's *Germinal.* Once in the mine, I was overcome with emotion. The miners were lined up in their shabby work-clothes, lamps attached to their foreheads. One of them presented me with palm fronds. Sweet, plaintive music could be heard. It was so poignant that we all began to weep. Oh, that beautiful day in which nothing was lacking except your sweet presence. But I feel that way every time something gives me pleasure. I hope you do not have that same sadness. . . .

At Valparaiso Sarah was met by her Uncle Edouard (Youle's brother), her aunt, and numerous cousins, some of whom had visited her in France. Then, after a day in one of the hotels owned by her prosperous uncle, she went on to Santiago:

But what am I to do? [she continued in her epic letter to Maurice] People storm the train, among them my cousins, Edouard and Jeanne, who climb on board to greet me. But I must get off the train! As soon as I set foot on the ground there are deafening cries and a terrifying crush. Edouard, Garnier, Decori [one of the actors in her troupe], and a Frenchman I don't know join hands to form a circle around me. Cousin Jeanne takes me by one arm, Grau by the other. Thirty minutes to go thirty metres. I am pushed about, and am ready to faint. Garnier and Decori are outraged, my cousin Edouard lashes out with his fists, and Grau shouts: "Calm yourself, they're just a bunch of savages!" Eventually I am rescued, but poor Decori's arm is badly sprained. . . .

I arrive at the hotel. When Saryta finally gets there, her watch has been stolen. She was able to stop the thief who still had the chain in his hands. He has now been condemned to two years in prison. . . .

I made my debut in *Fédora.* Immense success and wonderful receipts, although not as good as Buenos Aires. I am exhausted by this letter . . . and must leave you, and that is hard. Don't forget to send me your photograph to Havana. The twenty-third is my birthday. Can I count on a little telegram from you, my beloved? . . . I've agreed to play the two towns, Valparaiso and Santiago, twice each week. It takes four hours to get from one to the other.

The reviews here are excellent, but what new infamous things are they saying about me in that beautiful country called France? Ah, how I love you, my son! I dream of you constantly. Say hello to Jean Richepin if you see him. Ingratitude is man's most common quality! I love *you.*

As the Bernhardt troupe made its way up the west coast of South America, life became more and more primitive. Yellow fever threatened. "Filthy dangerous beasts" crawled up dining tables and scurried across theatre stages. Hotel accommodations were scarce, and Sarah was forced to share mosquito-infested rooms with four travelling companions. Still she thrived on travel and adventure, as a letter she sent Ponchon from Ecuador indicates:

I was amused to go hunting for crocodiles. The river is superb, twenty times wider than the Marne and teeming with great reptiles. We took two boats. The natives are careful not to allow the beasts to snap off their oars. We killed quite a few, two of which, my dear Ponchon, I shall bring back. . . .

Midway through her letter, Sarah's thoughts turned to home. If only Richepin, Maurice, and her dear Ponchon were there in place of Guérard, Saryta, and the rest, how exquisite that would be! Would Ponchon send her Monsieur Edouard Drumont's book on the Jews? She was anxious to see what that anti-Semitic devil had to say about her. She might extend her trip by six months and go on to Australia, India, and Egypt, as that would make her financially independent. Besides, she had no desire to play in Paris ever again. She had had more than enough of its malicious tongues and its insidious press.

Sarah did not venture as far as the Orient, however. Instead, she continued her tour of the Western Hemisphere, entered Texas via Mexico, crossed the United States in a tour of large cities and small towns as she had done five years earlier, and reached New York in April. In May she was in London. From there she made her first tour of England, Ireland, and Scotland.

Wherever she went she was triumphant. In his book *Les Contemporains*

(*Our Contemporaries*), Jules Lemaître wrote: "More than any other, she will have known immense glory, concrete, intoxicating, maddening, the glory of the conquerors and the Caesars. In every country in the world she has been accorded receptions which are not given to kings. She has had what the princes of the mind will never have."

Shortly after her return to Paris that summer, the Comédie Française invited her to come back to the fold. In September she was in Belle-Ile, thinking it over. It was a tempting offer, as Perrin had died two years before and Jules Claretie, always one of Bernhardt's most ardent admirers, was now in charge, but the idea of losing her freedom, of suffocating in the rigidly controlled House of Molière did not appeal to her. Furthermore, she was not prepared to live on the hundred and fifty thousand francs a year offered her, when she could earn the same amount in a month on her own.

Her refusal provoked a new kind of punishment from the press. "At forty-three," *Le Gaulois* wrote, she is "a greedy has-been, too old to play anything but *confidentes* and mothers." Bernhardt had her revenge. On 24 November, as fresh and youthful as ever, she appeared in *La Tosca*, the third melodrama Sardou had fashioned in her image. Once again the critics were confounded, and once again the young rushed to their diaries to record their emotions.

"Ah, Sarah! Sarah!" the enraptured eighteen-year-old poet Pierre Louÿs wrote, "Sarah is grace, youth, divinity! I am beside myself. My God, what a woman! . . . When shall I see you again, my Sarah? I weep, I tremble, I grow mad! Sarah, I love you!"

The English critic Clement Scott was no less carried away when he wrote, "Bernhardt, knife in hand over the dying Scarpia, is the nearest thing to great tragedy ever seen in modern times."

Puccini's opera *Tosca* was first performed in 1900, thirteen years after Sardou's première. With time the opera eclipsed the play on which it is based, but it did not eclipse Sarah's performance. On the contrary, the sopranos of the day copied her every effect and passed them on to their pupils. Thus, what we see in the opera house today is often Bernhardt's way of fixing Baron Scarpia with her eyes while fumbling for the knife that lies on a desk behind her; of setting candles around his corpse and placing a crucifix on his silenced heart; of creeping from the murder chamber while her sinuous train, as snake-like as crime itself, follows in her wake while

she melts into the shadows. Bernhardt's was a characterization so powerful
that she was still able to thrill her public with it at the age of sixty-five.

In the summer of 1887, when Sarah had returned to Paris after her American-
British tour, she was, as she boasted to Ponchon, a millionaire. She bought
a house at 56 boulevard Péreire, which was to be hers for life. Photographs
and drawings tell something of its atmosphere and, perhaps more arresting,
how she had changed. Gone was the coquettish salon of her courtesan days.
Gone too was the macabre bat-infested bedroom that intrigued Loti. In their
place she created a setting that spoke of journey and adventure. In this, she
was a creature apart. Few of her friends ventured farther than Normandy
and Brittany, or the south of France, and so they were fascinated by her
two-story, glass-roofed salon, its red walls crowded with memorabilia: primitive masks, Indian sabers, South American daggers, silver cups from Mexico, gilded mirrors from Venice, bas-reliefs from Greece, and Clairin's and
Abbéma's portraits of Sarah, Maurice, and the dogs. Palm trees reached up
to touch the skylight. Bursts of luxuriant roses, lilacs, orchids, and tuberoses
were everywhere in the overheated room. And when their scent began to
fade, Sarah, always one to gild the lily, would spray them heavily with
appropriate perfumes. In one corner stood a large cage. Once the home of
her pet lion cubs, Scarpia and Justinian, it now housed dozens of exotic
birds. Opposite was a low divan. Immense and somewhat disconcerting, it
was laden with furs and skins, outlandish trophies of the hunt: tiger, jaguar,
beaver, buffalo, and crocodile.

    To relieve the barbaric effect, silk cushions were profusely strewn
about. A tall silk canopy, supported by dragon-head poles, filtered the light
from above. At the foot of the divan lay a snarling bear rug. No one dared
question Sarah when she claimed to have shot it in the dizzying heights of
the Andes. The rest of the room was chockablock with Renaissance furniture,
vases, Buddhas, Japanese monsters, marble stands, Oriental carpets, and
vitrines to hold the overflow. If the clutter seems oppressive to purists of
today, it seemed the latest thing to Parisians of yesterday. Fortunately there
was Sarah to lighten the hothouse atmosphere, Sarah, with her easy laughter,
her ferocious wit, her killing imitations, and her more or less conscious
gaffes: "Have you seen my latest?" she would say, pointing to a handsome
newcomer. Or "They tell me you've just divorced" (this to a couple she had
invited to lunch). "I've seated you side by side as you must have so much

to talk about." One guest explained that he had not turned up the day before because he had been at the cemetery to visit his wife's tomb. "What!" Sarah cried. "Your wife is dead, and you never told me, *me*, your oldest friend! It's incredible."

"But my dear Sarah, she died three years ago, don't you remember? You were at the funeral."

"I know, I know," was her answer, "but I still can't believe it."

Bernhardt's new establishment was run by an extraordinary character, an ex-violinist named Pitou. A man of middle height with lifeless black hair, bulging eyes, and a blue serge suit that had seen better days, Pitou scurried about the house making himself indispensable. He copied out plays, poetry, and music, read all the other parts when Madame was learning a role, took charge of the servants, paid the household bills, and ran about delivering letters by hand since his mistress, it seems, preferred that to stamps. Perhaps because he was obsequious, or because he was always in the right, or because he bit his nails and wore a pencil behind his ear, he drove Sarah wild. She threw dishes at him, which he dodged without seeming to move; screamed curses, which he pretended not to hear; and at midnight, when he came to her room haggard with exhaustion to ask if there was anything she needed, he meekly hung his head while she accused him of being a lazy good-for-nothing. His masochism gratified, the poor man would go to his room, take up his violin, and console himself with a melancholy tune. Pitou never thought of leaving her. Devotion itself, he considered himself privileged to be associated with a great artist and played out his tragicomedy to the end.

A month after her triumph as Tosca, Sarah was to know another kind of triumph, for on December 29 her son married Princess Marie-Thérèse Jablonowska in the fashionable church of Saint-Honoré d'Eylau. From Sarah's point of view it was a brilliant match. The pretty bride was the daughter of a very distinguished Polish family. And Maurice, just twenty-four, was what Sarah had brought him up to be: the charming, if ineffectual son of a rich and famous actress, a dandy with beautiful manners, a sportsman, and a gambler. He was educated first by tutors, then in boarding schools. As Sarah put special emphasis on fencing lessons, he became one of the more skillful duellists in Paris—all to the good, since he was quick to challenge anyone who made what he considered offensive remarks about his mother.

Although Maurice was undoubtedly the great love of Sarah's life, she rarely had much time to give him. Curiously enough, his early years were not unlike hers. The words that she chose to begin her memoirs, "My mother adored travelling. She would go from Spain to England; from London to Paris; from Paris . . . to Christiania; then come back to give me a kiss, and leave again," could just as easily have been said by Maurice. Maternal neglect affected them in different ways, however. Sarah escaped from Youle and found her lifework in the theatre, whereas Maurice was content to live his entire life in his mother's protective shadow. Her friends did not approve. Louise Abbéma said she must stop spoiling her son; Georges Clairin was more specific. He begged her not to pay her son's gambling debts and to hold on to her hard-earned money. Naturally, she paid no attention. Maurice was her "Dauphin," she told them, and they were childless egotists, barren wretches unable to understand that a mother's sacrifices are her greatest joy.

Le Tout-Paris, or rather Bernhardt's Tout-Paris, came to Maurice's wedding: the Prince de Sagan and the Comtesse de Béthune, Dumas *fils*, Sardou, Duquesnel, Alfred Stevens, Whistler, and other artists and actors of the day, including, of course, Clairin and Abbéma.

An English friend recalled Bernhardt's late entrance "amid the general craning of necks and whispers of 'There she is, there's Sarah.' " In fact, Maurice and Terka, as his bride was always called, seemed almost redundant when the actress walked up the aisle "in a cloak of gray velvet over a dress of soft pink faille. Her face was blurred at the edges by the maribou of her coat. Her reddened lips drew back over her teeth in that smile that is part of the daily toilette of the Frenchwoman."

Sarah's smile was indeed official. In private, she wept over the loss of her son until she realized that despite his marriage vows and the fact that he no longer lived under her roof, Maurice, for better or for worse, would always be his mama's boy and come to see her every day.

Bernhardt performed *La Tosca* for a month before Maurice's wedding, and for four months afterward; then, even though the house was always packed, she took it to London, where she was received even more rapturously than in Paris. But that was almost to be expected from the British, who had launched her international career eight years before. In the course of those years Sarah made many English friends. Of these, W. Graham Robertson was closest to her heart.

Many homosexuals are drawn to actresses, perhaps because they admire and envy their power to attract men, their stylish indifference to convention, and their open promiscuity. Or perhaps because they identify with the heroines they portray. Sarah, for whatever reasons (her love of eccentricity might be one, her unsuccessful love affairs and her unwillingness to commit herself another), was a friend of some of the best-known homosexuals of the day: Oscar Wilde, Robert de Montesquiou, Reynaldo Hahn, Jean Lorrain, and Graham Robertson, himself.

In 1931 Robertson was to write *Time Was* (called *Life Was Worth Living* in the American edition), a discreet memoir about indiscreet people. His restraint was not a matter of unawareness. As he said, he knew that a "really interesting book compiled from my omissions would be a best seller," and he knew, proper Edwardian that he was, that it would be improper to divulge his scandalous secrets or those of his friends.

Graham first met Sarah in London's Metropole Hotel when he was twenty.

"I well remember her coming to me across the great empty room," he wrote, "her russet hair loosely wisped up, her long robe of cream-colored velvet falling over an underdress of mauve silk gathered into a silver girdle." On his first visit to her in Paris he found her

in dejection in her studio before a huge mass of clay out of which she had been trying to evolve Love doing something or other—Triumphing, I think. Death was also somewhere about, and a few other rather unconvincing allegories. . . . For a moment Sarah looked murderously at the wobbly lop-sided Love, then seizing a strong wire, she sliced off a considerable portion of its anatomy.

With Robertson's help Love was soon reduced to an "innocent-looking mud pie" and thrown out the window. That same day he asked about an empty cage in the salon:

"I kept a lion there once," said Sarah.
"And—and it died?"
"No," said Sarah, "he didn't die," and her tone implied that there were worse things than death.
I afterwards learned from Mme Guérard that the lion had been one of Sarah's failures.
"I am going to keep a lion," she had announced.

"Yes, yes, of course, a lion," her friends had agreed, knowing the futility of argument, "but doesn't he—won't he——?"

"Won't he what?" asked Sarah.

"Won't he—perhaps—smell a little?"

" 'Smell?' cried Sarah. "Smell? The lion, the King of Beasts? No, of course he won't smell."

So the lion came—and he smelt. Sarah bore it bravely, and made no sign, but gradually the smell crept from the studio to the dining room, from the dining room to the bedrooms. Sarah became pensive, but no one ventured to make a suggestion, until, at last, one morning she descended, took one final and comprehensive sniff, and exclaimed: "He smells; take him away."

Soon after, Robertson wrote: "Sarah bought a tiger cub that was sometimes allowed to walk about the dinner table, which excited and made him fractious, and I was always rather relieved when he tottered snarling past my plate without paying me any marked attentions."

Graham, almost as fond of animals as Sarah herself, paid his respects to Sarah's pet lynx: "The mysterious white-robed figure of Sarah coming down the steps into her studio with the lynx gliding noiselessly beside her was so suggestive of Circe that one looked about for the pigs."

As their friendship grew, he made several portraits of Sarah while she made drawings of him. At one sitting, he watched her rehearse the death scene from *La Dame aux Camélias* and was dazzled by the "absolute precision with which she built up her apparently spontaneous effects."

"I know," she told him, "that I'll break my neck some day. If Armand does not keep tight hold of my hand as I swing around, I'm done for."

Her art [Robertson wrote] made for beauty. Many actresses agonize through the last moments of *La Dame* with heart-rending fits of coughing and sick-room symptoms in full play. Sarah passed lightly and mercifully over these details and struck an infinitely deeper and more touching note by the portrayal of an overwhelming happiness. I have often watched it from the wings, at about four yards distance, but it was no trick of the stage. A quick look at the bearer of the news [of Armand's arrival], then the haggard face began to glow, the skin tightened, giving an effect of transparency lit from within, the pupils of the eyes dilated, nearly covering the iris and darkly shining, the rigid lips relaxed and took soft childish curves, while from them came a cry that close at hand sounded no louder than a breath, yet could be heard in the uttermost corner of the theatre. The frail body seemed to consume before our eyes in the flame of an unbearable joy, and to set free the glorified and transfigured spirit.

One day Sarah took Robertson along when she went to be photographed as Tosca. "Several times," he wrote, "she fell into the pose of horror and triumph after the murder of Scarpia, but always seemed dissatisfied."

"Come here, Graham," she cried. "Come here, and let me kill you." Now, I had, on more than one occasion, figured as the corpse in *Fédora* [The Prince of Wales also thought it amusing to play this undemanding role], and found the sensation of being wailed over by the distraught heroine thrilling, so I advanced cheerfully and with confidence. But when those awful eyes of Floria Tosca—full of terror and deadly purpose—blazed into mine at such close quarters, I became uneasy, and finally, as she seized me with her left hand and caught up the knife with her right, I disgraced myself.

"Madame Sarah," I yelped, "do remember that you've got a *real* knife and not one that shuts up into the handle!"

At Bernhardt's request, Robertson took her to visit his friend, the painter Edward Burne-Jones, whose pre-Raphaelite musings had made a deep impression on her, so deep that she decided to commission a portrait of herself as Théodora. A letter she sent Robertson asked for his help:

My dear Graham,
Would you do me a great favor? I should like to have my portrait painted by Burne-Jones. Would you ask him how much it would cost me? It will give me very great pleasure to have it and to leave a work of genius to my son. I rely on you for this delicate mission.

Robertson approached Burne-Jones, but the painter did not want to take Sarah on. The portrait, alas, was never painted. A few sardonic notes from Burne-Jones to Robertson are all that remain of the negotiations. A few fragments give the tone:

Tell me how long *She* stays and how long she is to be seen and worshipped in this new play—for go I must, although I shall be ill for a month
after it.

Even if I were free tomorrow I don't think I could meet her at lunch. I
cannot speak French even to a waiter and what could I say to her?

No, come with Her and gently interpret what She says to me and I will
gape open-mouthed and be quite happy. . . . On no account is She to be
bored or tired, but to have everything Her own lovely way and at a minute's
notice.

ON 1 MARCH 1889, after a tour that took her as
far as Egypt and Turkey, Sarah returned to Paris and went
at once to see Damala, who was said to be ill. She found him
in a dingy flat littered with drugs and the sad remnants of his former life: a
battered Greek flag, a saber from one of his plays, and a gold crown from
another. Sarah sent him to a sanitarium, and six weeks later he was well
enough to see her in *Léna*, a play written by Pierre Berton. The evening did
not improve his spirits, partly because he resented Berton, an ex-lover of
Sarah's who had gone on to glory as her leading man, which Damala had
naïvely thought he would do.

One of Sarah's last gestures to Damala was strangely touching. Aware
that he did not have long to live, she asked him to appear with her in *La
Dame aux Camélias*, an invitation he accepted eagerly even though he was
in no condition to perform. The revival began on 18 May and ended on 30
June. As always, Sarah was triumphant in the role, but as one critic said:
"Alas, where is the handsome Armand Duval whom we saw for the first time
only a few years ago?"

Damala had lost his looks, his voice, and his strength, and at the age
of forty-two he lost his life to morphine. Defeated and grief-stricken, Sarah

sent his body back to Greece, along with a bust she had made for his tomb. She did not forget him. For some years she would sign her letters "the widow Damala." And whenever she found herself in Athens, she called on his mother and visited his grave to cover it with flowers and weep over a marriage that had so quickly turned to ashes.

PART SEVEN

ZENITH

In 1897 the magazine *La Plume* honored Sarah with an issue devoted entirely to her. The design was by Alphonse Mucha.

IN NOVEMBER 1889, a letter appeared in *Le Gaulois* addressed to its theatre critic and signed by fifty well-known Parisians: "Could you tell Sarah Bernhardt that many women and young girls would like to applaud her, but the kind of play she performs prevents them from going to her theatre. Sometimes she plays a vicious queen, sometimes a strumpet, sometimes a great lady of doubtful morality. How many of us would acclaim her with enthusiasm if she were to play a pure heroine in a moral work!"

Sarah replied that she had always longed to play Joan of Arc and had recently received from the poet Jules Barbier just the play she dreamed of. (What Barbier had sent her was the libretto for an opera with music by Gounod in the hope that it could be adapted for her use.) She hoped to satisfy their wishes by asking her friend Duquesnel to produce it. "Besides," she added, "I cannot wait much longer. Soon I shall be too old to play Jeanne d'Arc. After all I am a grandmother!" (Bernhardt was forty-five; Maurice and Terka's first child, Simone, was just a few months old.) Grandmother or not, when on opening night (3 January 1890) Bernhardt, as Joan, was asked to state her age in the trial scene, she slowly turned from her inquisitors to face the audience and proudly proclaimed: "Nineteen!" Needless to say, she brought down the house. It was a *coup de théâtre* she would repeat to even greater effect almost twenty years later on 25 November 1909, in Emile Moreau's *Le Procès de Jeanne d'Arc* (*The Trial of Joan of Arc*). Each night, when the astonishingly youthful sixty-five-year-old great-grandmother (Simone had produced a child) announced to the inquisitors that she was nineteen, the audience's enthusiasm knew no bounds.

The 1890 *Joan of Arc* was one of Duquesnel's grand spectacles with reconstructions of the old market square in Rheims and the sacristy of the cathedral, all heightened by Gounod's choral and orchestral interludes. At forty-five, Bernhardt managed to look like the Maid of Orleans, but the role cost her a good deal of pain, as it repeatedly called for her to fall to her knees. Her right knee became so inflamed that she was forced to close the play after sixteen tortured weeks. During the run, even the skeptical Anatole France fell under her spell.

"She is poetry itself," he wrote. "She bears upon her face that afterglow of stained glass which the visitations of the saints had left on Joan of Arc, the fanatical visionary of Domremy. She is legend come to life. If her voice seems too weak at times, it is the fault of the libretto. She should not have had to force her voice in vibrant tirades. Joan of Arc never declaimed."

What Anatole France does not say is that from time to time Bernhardt declaimed Barbier's text while the orchestra played Gounod's music. Most of Sarah's more elaborate productions were given with orchestral accompaniment, what the French call "mélodrame," a sensational or romantic drama with incidental background music. The well-trained actors of the period did not need microphones in order to be heard, but their voices were sometimes covered by the music when the conductor got carried away.

On 5 April Bernhardt, Philippe Garnier, and an actor named Léon Brémont gave a reading at the Cirque d'Hiver of Edmond Haraucourt's adaptation of the Passion Play. Sarah longed to stage the play with herself as the Virgin Mary. To prevent her from doing so the Minister of Fine Arts had to invoke a decree from the time of Henri IV which forbade impersonations of the Holy Family. Perhaps it was just as well since Bernhardt as the Holy Virgin was not exactly typecasting.

In mid-April her doctor ordered two months of bed rest since her knee had become dangerously inflamed. By June she had recovered enough to take *Jeanne d'Arc* to London for her annual month-long London season. In October Sarah turned from saintliness to Sardou and sin. This time he put her in Egyptian costume and called her *Cléopâtre*. But even he could not fool those Parisians who were amused to find that Cleopatra, Queen of the Nile, was none other than Théodora, Empress of Byzantium, in disguise. Yvette Guilbert, that tart and saucy *diseuse*, added to their amusement when, in her *café-concerts*, she sang a song called "Sarah's Little Serpent." It tells the story of a hungry asp which Sardou brings to the theatre for Cleopatra's death scene. At the sight of slender, serpentine Sarah, it cries out: "I know her, she's my mother!" In the end, with nothing to feed on but Sarah's small

72. Clairin's poster for Sardou's *Théodora*

73. Georges Clairin's portrait of Sarah in Hugo's *Ruy Blas*

74–76. ABOVE, RIGHT: Portrait of Sarah
by Louise Abbéma. CENTER: Philippe
Parrot, *Sarah Bernhardt* (1875). LEFT:
Gustave Doré, *The Young Sarah Bernhardt*

77. Alphonse Mucha, *La Dame aux Camélias*
(1896)

Mucha, *Lorenzaccio* (1896)

78. Mucha, *La Samaritaine* (1897)

Mucha, *Medée* (1898)

79. From the popular French comic strip *Lucky Luke*

12me ANNÉE. — N° 612   PARIS ET DÉPARTEMENTS : 15 CENTIMES LE NUMÉRO   31 Décembre 1882.

LE GRELOT

REDACTION
5, Cité Bergère, 5
PARIS

ABONNEMENTS
PARIS ET DÉPARTEMENTS

Un an...... 8 fr. »
Six mois..... 4 »
Trois mois... 2 »

ADRESSER
Lettres et mandats à M. Madre
directeur-gérant
5, Cité Bergère, 5.

ADMINISTRATION
5, Cité Bergère, 5
PARIS

ABONNEMENTS
PAYS DE L'UNION POSTALE

Un an...... 10 fr. »
Six mois..... 5 »
Trois mois... 2 50

L'Agence Ewig, rue d'Amboise
est seule chargée
de recevoir les annonces
pour le journal.

LA POULE AUX ŒUFS D'OR

80. The "tart" that laid the golden eggs, 1882

81, 82. LEFT: Cartoon by Orens, *Hamlet*.
BELOW: André Gill, cartoon of
Bernhardt

83, 84. LEFT: *Grotesque*, sculpture by Sarah. BELOW: Sarah's bas-relief of Ophelia drowning

85, 86. ABOVE: Georges Clairin, *La Vièrge d'Avila* (*The Virgin of Avila*).
The inscription reads, "à Sarah Bernhardt, son ami G. Clairin."
BELOW: Clairin, *Théodora*

87. Sarah in the role of *Izéïl*, in her dressing room

88. Alfred Stevens's portrait of Sarah as *Fédora* (1882)

breasts, it dies of malnutrition. According to Yvette Guilbert, Bernhardt laughed until she cried when she came to hear it, then never forgave her for singing it.

Victorian London's reaction was somewhat different. After watching Sarah as Cleopatra, lasciviously entwined in her lover's arms, an elderly dowager was heard to say: "How unlike, how *very* unlike the home life of our own dear queen!"

After her London season, Sarah spent three months at Belle-Ile-en-Mer off the coast of Brittany to prepare for strenuous days ahead. In September she appeared in Paris in a revival of *La Tosca* with Berton, and in October she revived *Théodora* with Garnier.

In January 1891, the international press announced that Madame Sarah Bernhardt was about to embark on a world tour that would last almost three years. Was she sorry to leave Paris? one journalist asked. Not a bit was the reply. It was as easy as going to the Bois de Boulogne or up to Normandy. She adored travel, never tired of it. Of course she would be returning to North and South America (she was to include two tours of the United States this time) and perform in many places in Europe where she had already played, but how exciting it would be to see the Sandwich Islands and Honolulu. Then, think of it, she would go to Greece and Turkey, even to Australia and New Zealand. And she would begin and end this marathon tour in London. After that, Paris would seem a mere nothing.

Sarah displayed less enthusiasm in her letters to Ponchon. She felt stale, she complained, sick of trying to please the Parisian public, sick of vicious reviews, sick of her friends, her enemies, and her idiotic lovers.

There were other considerations that she failed to mention. To remain in Paris was to gamble on expensive new productions which might or might not fill the Porte Saint-Martin, whereas if she took her tried-and-true repertory abroad, she was guaranteed success, both artistic and financial. Moreover, there was a certain satisfaction in knowing that she would be received, not as one of several important actresses, as she was in Paris, but as the queen of them all.

Her feelings were justified. In Bucharest, her acting reduced the exiled Queen Natalie of Serbia to such violent sobbing that the performance "commanded" by the Queen of Romania had to be interrupted. In Australia her arrival was greeted with booming cannons, flags, red carpets, official receptions, and more renditions of *La Marseillaise* than she perhaps cared to hear. To the Australians, she was "the greatest actress who ever lived, *la belle Frangsay*," who had come to camp on their shores with fifty-five trunks, one hundred and thirty-two pieces of luggage, a Great Dane, a miniature pug, and countless dresses, shoes, and hats straight from gay Paree.

Journalists could not get enough of her. Soon after her arrival she invited the actress Myra Kemble to lunch. "Nothing surprising eventuated," it was reported, "except that Bernhardt's pets—she has already acquired a 'possum, a koala bear, and a wallaby—were presented, like children, at dessert time. The 'possum climbed into Myra's lap and ate the heads of the roses she was wearing in her corsage. Bernhardt's comment? 'How I envy zat leettle thing's *appétit!*' "

Another reporter asked Sarah whether her leading man objected to her falling on him when she died as Cleopatra. "I tell him," she explained, "zat ze art ees above consideration of ze *avoirdupois*. It ees ze art to flop— and I flop."

In May 1892 Sarah and her troupe were back in Paris, and the next month they were in London. A note from Oscar Wilde to the French poet and novelist Pierre Louÿs explains her presence there:

> You've heard the news, haven't you? Sarah is going to play *Salomé*!!!
> We rehearse today.

The rehearsals were for a production at the Palace Theatre of Wilde's *Salomé*, which he had written in French with Bernhardt in mind. The handsome French actor Albert Darmont was to play Herod, and Graham Robertson would design the costumes. Sarah had plunged into rehearsal with great enthusiasm as she loved to play biblical figures. Alas, the Examiner of Plays for the Lord Chamberlain, a Mr. Edward Pigott, whom Shaw was to describe as "a walking compendium of vulgar insular prejudice," banned *Salomé* precisely because it dealt with a biblical subject. To justify his decision, he too had to invoke an ancient statute. Both Sarah and Oscar were bitterly disappointed. After all, he had created the perfect role for the actress he admired above all others.

Wilde announced that he would move to France as he could not continue to live in such an unenlightened country as England. If only he had done so, he might have been spared the horrors of his trials, imprisonment, and exile, when he was forced to leave England under infinitely more painful and humiliating circumstances.

On 23 February 1893, *The Times* of London reviewed *Salomé*, which had just been published in the original French:

> This is the play, written for Mme Sarah Bernhardt, which the Lord Chamberlain declined to license for performance in this country. It is an arrangement in blood and ferocity, morbid, bizarre, repulsive, and very offensive in its adaptation of scriptural phraseology to situations the reverse of sacred. It is not ill-suited to some of the less attractive phases of Mme Bernhardt's genius. . . . As a whole it does credit to Mr Wilde's command of the French language. . . .

Oscar was offended and wrote a letter to *The Times* "simply to correct a misstatement":

> The fact that the greatest tragic actress of any stage now living saw in my play such beauty that she was anxious to produce it, to take herself the part of the heroine, to lend the entire poem the glamour of her personality . . . will always be a source of pride and pleasure to me, and I look forward with delight to seeing Mme Bernhardt present my play in Paris, that vivid centre of art, where religious dramas are often performed. But my play was in no sense of the words written for this great actress. I have never written a play for any actor or actress, nor shall I ever do so. Such work is for the artisan in literature, not for the artist.

This letter is often quoted to prove that Wilde did not write *Salomé* for Bernhardt, but from statements he made later on when he had every reason to resent her, it is clear that he thought of her as the ideal, the only Salomé.

In April 1895, when he was in Holloway Prison desperately in need of money, he wrote to R. H. Sherard asking him to try to sell Sarah the rights. Sherard, in his *Oscar Wilde: The Story of an Unhappy Friendship*, would describe how Sarah received him graciously, wept at the thought of Wilde's plight, and said she could not buy *Salomé* but would lend Wilde some money. She made a series of appointments with Sherard, but kept none of them and sent Wilde nothing. It is a pity from all points of view that

Sarah did not buy the rights. It would have helped Wilde when he needed her help; it might have encouraged her to put the play on herself; and, had she but known it, the rights to *Salomé* were to turn into a valuable property.

In Posillipo in 1897 Wilde wrote: "Eleonora Duse is now reading *Salomé*. There is a chance of her playing it. She is a fascinating artist, though nothing [compared] to Sarah."

While on the Riviera in January 1899, Wilde went to Nice to see Sarah in *La Tosca* and wrote to his friend Robert Ross: "I went round to see Sarah and she embraced me and wept, and I wept, and the whole evening was wonderful."

From Paris in September 1900, he wrote to another friend: "What has age to do with acting? The only person in the world who could act Salomé is Sarah Bernhardt, that 'serpent of old Nile,' older than the Pyramids."

In the end, his play would receive its first performance in 1896 at Lugné-Poë's Théâtre de l'Oeuvre with Lina Munte as Salomé, de Max as John the Baptist, Suzanne Després as the Page, and Lugné himself as Herod.

In 1893 Bernhardt sold the Porte Saint-Martin Theatre and arranged through her impresario, Maurice Grau, to buy the Théâtre de la Renaissance, a small theatre decorated in the rococo style. Then to help pay for it she went on to Budapest, Vienna, Athens, and Istanbul.

After so many years of trains, ships, and hotels, of performance after performance in theatres makeshift or grand, Bernhardt returned to France the richest and most publicized actress of the day. Still there were problems. Before leaving on her marathon tour, she had said that Paris would seem a mere nothing compared to the wide world. But that was bravado. The truth was that, for her, Paris was the omniscient arbiter of all that was civilized on earth. Like most Parisians, she felt no other city could boast of such urbanity, such wealth of talent, such tolerant attitudes to pleasure, innocent or vicious, such elegant, if arrogant manners among the rich, such apparent gaiety among the poor.

All this was admirable in her eyes, but it held the challenge she always faced after a long absence: the need to reaffirm her position. This she accomplished on November 6, when she opened the refurbished Théâtre de la Renaissance with *Les Rois* by Jules Lemaître. An interesting play about the mysterious deaths of the Austrian Archduke Rudolph and his mistress, Baroness Vetsera, it won the respect of thoughtful Parisians. Unfortunately, it bored the general public and closed after thirty performances, although

Bernhardt won high praise for her work as manager, director, and leading lady, functions she would fulfill in her productions for the next five years.

Lemaître became her lover, friend, and literary adviser. She could not have done better. At forty, he was an illustrious critic and essayist respected in academic, social, and theatrical circles. Moreover, he had a calming effect on Sarah, who, since she was not in love with him, felt no urge to torment him with infidelities and anguished scenes. And then, although she looked astonishingly youthful, she was approaching fifty.

Bernhardt had rarely performed with great actors since her days at the Comédie Française. Now, for *Les Rois* and for succeeding productions, she engaged Edouard de Max and Lucien Guitry, both of whom were to become shining lights of their generation. At thirty-three, Guitry was not without experience. Born in 1860, he had left the Conservatoire at seventeen, played leading parts at the Gymnase, and appeared in London with Sarah's troupe in 1882. Then, tempted by a lucrative offer from the Mikhailovsky Theatre, the French theatre in Saint Petersburg, the young actor signed a nine-year contract and took his pretty young wife off to Russia. There he enjoyed immense success, both on the stage and in the boudoirs of many a Slavic Madame Bovary. If his efforts pleased the ladies, they did not please his wife, who went back to Paris to sue for divorce, taking their two sons, Sacha and Jean, with her.

Sacha, of course, was to become the wittiest, most amusing actor of his generation. One of France's most prolific playwrights, he would write, direct, and star in over one hundred and twenty plays and more than thirty films.

Even at four he was remarkable, at least to his father, who went to Paris, wrapped him in the folds of his greatcoat, and spirited him back to Russia. Not too many years later, Lucien and Sacha had a falling out after Sacha, like his father a precocious womanizer, made off with one of his father's mistresses. They did not speak to one another for years, but they both remained close to Sarah, so close that whenever either of them married— which was often—she was asked to be present at the ceremony. Thus, she was a witness at the first of Lucien's many weddings, in 1882, and played the same role thirty-seven years later when Sacha took Yvonne Printemps as the second of *his* many wives.

Lucien Guitry, like Jean Mounet-Sully, was an ideal foil for Bernhardt. Yet how different they were! Mounet was a devouring fire, Guitry a mesmeric flame; Mounet was classically beautiful, Guitry ruggedly handsome. Sarah preferred to share the stage with Guitry. This was made clear when in later years she rehearsed a young man in *Ruy Blas*. The actor Roger Gaillard recorded the scene in his memoirs:

"Bloody idiot! Murderer!" she screamed. "Are you trying to imitate Mounet, that imbecile of a genius? That house-bound cyclone! That roaring lion! He almost broke my hands during *Hernani*. He pulled my hair and pinched me black and blue. What a dangerous madman, but what a beauty, the brute! You know he took an hour to swallow the poison in *Ruy Blas*. He gargled and gargled. But what a genius he was! You, my child are not a genius, and if you think you can become one by imitating Mounet, you might just as well give up now."

Sarah could hardly accuse the debonair Guitry of such excess. Onstage he was a master of the minimal effect and offstage a model of unruffled affection. Sacha followed suit, even as a child:

For ten years [Sacha remembered] we went to kiss Madame Sarah as others go to mass—piously. For my brother and myself she was familiar and magical at one and the same time. We would walk into her drawing room with bouquets of roses or violets in our hands. We knew she was not a queen, but understood she was a sovereign.

The Christmas tree at Madame Sarah's was an absolute marvel. It rose very high in the middle of her studio, lit by a thousand candles and hung with fifty gifts for the fifty children gathered round. Each toy was numbered, and when it came time to distribute them Madame Sarah would stand with a large velvet bag, from which we each drew a number by chance. But Sarah and "chance" always saw to it that the most wonderful gift fell to her son's little daughter, Simone. Dressed like a fairy-tale princess, adored and caressed, Simone Bernhardt seemed a very rare creature. We even had the feeling that we had all been invited in order to bear witness that she was the happiest child in the world.

With true familial loyalty, Sacha felt that while it was all right for him to point out Madame Sarah's foibles, it was impertinent in others. It was not that he took offense at "witty and delicate descriptions of her house and meals, her astounding way of welcoming people, her whims, eccentricities, and extraordinary lies. But when I hear anyone trying to compare her with

other actresses, it is not merely odious to me, it is something I cannot bear.
Jules Renard once said: 'Those who do not love Victor Hugo are a bore to
read, even when they are not writing about him.' I feel that way about certain
young actors who are foolish enough to wonder what would happen if Sarah
Bernhardt were to come back. They think she was an actress of *her* time.
What stupidity! Can't they understand she would be an actress of *our* time?"

Both Sacha and his father belonged to that race of actors who are
more stylish than the merely fashionable, more extravagant than the rich,
and more knowing than the worldly. Edouard de Max was of another school.
The son of a Jewish doctor and a self-styled princess, he was born in Romania
in 1869. At sixteen he entered the Paris Conservatoire under the name of
"Edouard de Maxembourg, Prince Sakala." It was an extravagant example
of gilding the lily, for it was his rare talent, not his fake title, that became
his passport to success. Like Sarah, he was an actor-poet, a creature outside
reality. The stage was his life and Bernhardt his inspiration.

"I have spent my entire existence," he once said, "trying to free
myself from her influence. But whenever I see her I am carried away by the
madness of her madnesses, and the splendor of her splendors." That was
not always the case, however. One day, during a rehearsal, Sarah complained
that he was standing too close to her, that they looked like two concierges
having a gossip. Would he kindly step back? De Max refused. Then he could
leave the theatre, Sarah shrieked. At this the young actor sank to his knees
and addressed her in his most honeyed tones: "Madame Sarah, I have infinite
respect for you as a woman. I have a mad passion for you as an actress.
But," he added, springing to his feet, "as a director—you stink."

Such scenes did not prevent Sarah from asking de Max to play a
leading role in *Phèdre*, her next production. Her decision to play the Racine
heroine came as a surprise to those aesthetes who, in their categorical way,
had pigeonholed her as the tainted queen of commercial melodrama. But
they were wide of the mark. During her years at the Comédie Française,
Bernhardt had been given few opportunities to play her finest classic role.
Now she was prepared to give it for three weeks at the risk of losing a good
deal of money. Her gamble paid off. Parisians rushed to the Théâtre de la
Renaissance to listen to Racine's mighty lines and to clap until their hands
ached.

Among the most fervent was the young Marcel Proust. In *Remembrance
of Things Past*, he examined the art of Bernhardt, or Berma, as he named

her, like a jeweler appraising a diamond: for its value, its weight, and its possible flaws. The flaws came first. "Unfortunately," he wrote, "for some years now, since she had abandoned the serious stage to throw in her lot with a commercial theatre where she was the 'star', she had ceased to appear in classic parts."

Proust's alter ego, the narrator Marcel, speaks of seeing Berma in *Phèdre* at two points in his life. The first time, as a stage-struck child who expects too much of the actress and is left in a "state of agitation," disappointment, and disillusion. The second time, as a cultivated, precocious young man who finds Berma-Bernhardt "a window opening upon a great work of art. . . . Her stage presence, her poses, which she had gradually built up, which she was to modify yet further, and which were based upon reasonings altogether more profound than those of which traces could be seen in the gestures of her fellow-actors. . . . had melted into a sort of radiance whereby they sent throbbing, round the person of the heroine, rich and complex elements which the fascinated spectator nevertheless took not for a triumph of dramatic artistry but for a manifestation of life; those white veils themselves, which, tenuous and clinging, seemed to be of a living substance and to have been woven by the suffering, half-pagan, half-Jansenist around which they drew themselves like a frail and shrinking cocoon—all these, voice, posture, gestures, veils. . . . were. . . . [like Berma's interpretation] a second work quickened also by the breath of genius."

Certainly Proust was beyond melodrama, but not when it was in the hands of the great Bernhardt. "Thus," he wrote, "into the prose sentences of the modern playwright, . . . Berma contrived to introduce those vast images of grief, nobility, passion, which were the masterpieces of her own personal art."

Proust and Bernhardt met in 1903 at a party in her honor. It was an auspicious occasion: the first of the magnificent garden parties Comte Robert de Montesquiou gave at his Pavillon des Muses in Neuilly. At the time, Proust was an obscure young man, while the other guests were, to him, and to themselves, the most fascinating members of Parisian society. Frolicsome aesthetes, one and all, their charms were not wasted on the budding author. Twenty years later they appeared in roles which brought them a legendary fame they would never have achieved had he not given them a place in his novel. Thus the Comtesse Greffulhe inspired his beautiful, insensitive Duchesse de Guermantes and Montesquiou his fascinating, overbearing, but pathetic Baron de Charlus. (Incidentally, both Jules Lemaître and Anatole France served as sources for Proust's great writer, Bergotte.) Although Proust had access to the details of Bernhardt's private life through his friend and ex-lover, the composer Reynaldo Hahn, he chose to describe her art rather than her personal life, perhaps because by the time he wrote *Remembrance of Things Past*, five novelists had devoted themselves to that task.

Sarah added a spicy note to the Montesquiou fête when she introduced Yon Nibor, a handsome young sailor who entertained the company with sad songs about his native Brittany and the sea monsters that haunt its shores. One wonders if the infinitely elegant ladies and their foppish escorts felt a twinge of envy when Sarah, dressed in a glittering silk sheath with garlands of irises, swept out on the arm of her nautical protégé.

When Nibor pulled up anchor and sailed away, there were others who were eager to take his place. One was the seventeen-year-old Suzanne Seylor, who would become Bernhardt's lady in waiting after Madame Guérard died in the early nineties. The two first met in Brest, where Sarah stopped for a single performance of *Phèdre*. The next morning, dazzled, and in love, Seylor packed her bags, kissed her parents good-bye, and left for Paris to be with her idol. A tiny creature, as colorless as the faded ribbon in her hair, Suzanne was to travel with Sarah, perform in her plays, and keep her company wherever and whenever she was wanted. Her devotion had its rewards. Like others who live in the shadow of celebrity, she saw countries she would never have seen, met people she would never have met, and enjoyed the immense satisfaction of knowing that the world's leading tragedienne depended on her.

Sardou's *Gismonda*, which opened at the Théâtre de la Renaissance in October 1894, was the fifth melodrama he wrote with Bernhardt in mind and the first to be produced and directed by the actress herself. Like all Sardou's work, it called for pictorial imagination, a gift for deploying large groups of actors, and the ability to focus attention on the plot and the principal characters, in spite of the eye-catching pageantry that threatened to swamp them. A cruel fable set in twelfth-century Greece, *Gismonda* is the story of an Athenian princess (Bernhardt) who loves a commoner (Guitry) and, to everyone's surprise, succeeds in marrying him and living happily ever after. But not before the audience is terrorized by a heinous priest (de Max), an ax murder (committed by Bernhardt), a bloody massacre, and the grisly spectacle of a child being thrown to a ravenous tiger. Such heart-stopping moments were almost incidental in a production that offered impassioned speeches, the elaborately wrought splendors of a Byzantine church, processions of flower-clad maidens, and, as a finale, a wedding complete with pealing church bells, choral hosannas, and triumphal organ music. With all this, the show belonged to Bernhardt, an *art nouveau* vision in serpentine robes and a headdress of rare orchids.

Gismonda did nothing to add to Sarah's fame—that would hardly have been possible—but it did a lot to launch an unknown Czechoslovakian artist named Alphonse Mucha. Mucha had left Prague for Paris when he was twenty-seven. There, after studying at the Académie Julian, he joined the ranks of those obscure artists who illustrate calendars and cheap novels. After six years of hack work, one day he was asked by a fellow worker to complete a poster advertising *Gismonda*. Mucha not only obliged, he scrapped the original design and produced a new one worthy of the great actress. His life changed the moment Bernhardt saw it.

"Ah! How beautiful!" he remembered her saying. "From now on you will work for me, close to me. I love you already." True to her word, she gave him a five-year contract. Her instinct was sound, independent too, in a city where Toulouse-Lautrec, Bonnard, Vallotton, and Chéret were all available. But brilliant though their *affiches* were, their ironic, playful visions were not well suited to Bernhardt as the muse of tragedy. Mucha, on the other hand, caught her tone with a chaste, yet sensuous image that turned her into an *art nouveau* icon. In the next few years, Mucha made seven memorable *affiches* of Sarah for the Théâtre de la Renaissance. His duties did not stop there, however. He helped with sets and costumes, designed her jewelry, and served as her general artistic adviser.

Advice was hardly needed when on 6 February 1895, Bernhardt presented Molière's *Amphytrion*, with Constant Coquelin—who had left the Comédie Française—his brother Ernest, and Lucien Guitry as her prestigious co-stars. Here was a rare gift to the public: an opportunity to see four virtuoso players, wonderfully at home in their roles, and crystal-clear in their diction, disport themselves in a masterpiece close to their hearts. For those were the halcyon days when great actors knew what to do, and how to do it, without benefit of a director's concepts or proddings. Besides, if Bernhardt was in need of direction, who better to turn to than Coquelin, and if Guitry was in need of direction, who better to turn to than Bernhardt?

An amusing feature of this revival was the casting of the Coquelin brothers—one as Mercure, messenger of the gods, the other as Sosie, his earthly twin—superbly convincing in the scenes of mistaken identity. There were those, however, who felt that Lucien Guitry, wonderful though he was as Jupiter, could not efface the memory of Mounet-Sully's Olympian majesty in the role.

On 13 February Sarah presented *Magda*, a translation of Hermann Sudermann's *Heimat (Home)*. Unfortunately, Parisians had little patience with its Ibsenesque theme, and it came and went in short order. The play offered touching roles, dramatic confrontations, and cogent thoughts about women and their new place in society. The plot concerns the unmarried Magda, who was banished from her provincial home when she became pregnant and has become an internationally famous opera singer. The action begins when Magda finds herself in her native town, where, against her better judgment, she decides to visit her family. Defiant and experienced in the ways of the world, she confronts her narrow-minded father and manages to win his sympathy. After several harrowing scenes, some highly improbable, the play ends with the father's death and Magda's crying out: "My home-coming cost him his life! May I not stay here now?" to which the village priest replies: "No one will stop you from praying on his grave."

It was said that Sudermann modelled his flamboyant, tenderhearted heroine after Bernhardt. Certainly there are strong resemblances, since Magda is a "brilliantly dressed" performer of explosive temperament and decisive opinion who, like Sarah, is the proud, loving mother of an illegitimate child.

In June 1895 Bernhardt took *Magda* to London. Her desire to show England a new production would have been natural under normal circumstances, but the circumstances were far from normal. Eleonora Duse, the rising Italian star, was about to make her London debut and had chosen to play *Magda* the day after Bernhardt was scheduled to perform it. The coincidence, if coincidence it was, gave the signal for the critics to sharpen their quills and go forth into battle: Max Beerbohm for Bernhardt, George Bernard Shaw for Duse. It cannot be said that the fracas led to victory on either side, as the careers of both actresses were left undamaged and the opinions of their followers unchanged. Yet, if anyone had the edge, it was Shaw, since it was he who led future generations to think of Sarah as a moneygrubbing queen of melodrama and Duse as an otherworldly priestess of high art. Shaw, as we all know, was an extremely clever man, clever enough to disarm his opponents by confessing his shortcomings:

> I have, I think, always been a puritan in my attitude towards Art. I am as fond of fine music and handsome buildings as Milton was, or Cromwell or Bunyan; but if I found that they were becoming the instruments of systematic idolatry of sensuousness, I would hold it good statesmanship to blow every cathedral in the world to pieces with dynamite, organ and all, without the least heed to the screams of the art critics and cultural voluptuaries.

Shaw's aesthetic terrorism suggests that Sarah—an "instrument of idolatry of sensuousness" if ever there was one—was in danger of being blown sky-high. Indeed, he had already set his time bomb when he saw her as Fédora and described her as an "outdated ex-actress who had left [France's] National Theatre to travel around the world pretending to kill people with hatchets and hatpins, and making heaps of money doing it."

Of course Sarah made a fortune with Sardou and found excitement and release in portraying the bejewelled, sensuous, decadent *femmes fatales* he created in her image. But melodrama was not her sole interest. At fifty-one she could look back at a life devoted to Racine, the Romantics, and all that was superior in the French drama of her time.

Duse had won Shaw's respect by playing Ibsen's *A Doll's House*, but he chose to ignore the fact that her repertory was largely the same as Bernhardt's; that she too had hatcheted and hat-pinned hapless victims in plays by Sardou, both in Italy and on tours of Europe and South America; and, it might be added, played them without the bravura or the visual allure that Sarah alone could bring to them.

In Shaw's article about the two great actresses, dated 15 June 1895, he wrote:

> This week began with the relapse of Sarah Bernhardt into her old profession of serious actress. She played Magda in Sudermann's *Heimat* at Daly's Theatre on Tuesday and was promptly challenged by Duse in the same part at the Drury Lane on Wednesday. The contrast between the two Magdas is as extreme as any contrast could possibly be. . . . Madame Bernhardt

has the charm of a jolly maturity, rather spoilt and petulant, perhaps, but always ready with a sunshine-through-the-clouds smile if only she is made much of. Her dresses and diamonds, if not exactly splendid, are at least splendacious; her figure, far too scantily upholstered in the old days, is at its best; and her complexion shows that she has not studied modern art in vain. Those charming roseate effects which French painters produce by giving flesh the pretty color of strawberries and cream, and painting the shadows pink and crimson are cunningly reproduced by Madame Bernhardt. . . . She paints her ears crimson, and allows them to peep enchantingly through a few loose braids of her auburn hair. Every dimple has its dab of pink. . . . Her lips are like a newly painted pillar box; her cheeks, right up to the languid lashes, have the bloom and surface of a peach; she is beautiful with the beauty of her school, and entirely inhuman and increditable. . . . The dress, the title of the play, the order of the words may vary; but the woman is always the same. She does not enter into the leading character; she substitutes herself for it.

All this is precisely what does not happen in the case of Duse, whose every part is a separate creation. . . . In *La Dame aux Camélias* it is easy for an intense actress to harrow us with her sorrows and paroxysms of phthisis, leaving us with a liberal pennyworth of sensation, not fundamentally distinguishable from that offered by a public execution. . . . As different from this as light from darkness is the method of the actress who shows us how human sorrow can express itself only in its appeal for the sympathy it needs, whilst striving by strong endurance to shield others from the infection of its torment. That is the charm of Duse's interpretation of the stage poem of Marguerite Gautier. It is unspeakably touching because it is exquisitely considerate; that is, exquisitely sympathetic. No physical charm is noble as well as beautiful unless it is the expression of a moral charm; and it is because Duse's range includes these moral high notes . . . that her compass . . . so immeasurably dwarfs the poor little octave and a half on which Sarah Bernhardt plays such pretty canzonets and stirring marches.

Amusingly enough, Max Beerbohm, Shaw's successor at the *Saturday Review*, was in total disagreement. For him, Bernhardt was "majesty, awe and wonder," while Duse had no conception of the roles she played. "She treats them," he wrote, "as so many large vehicles for expression of absolute self. From first to last she is the same in *Fédora* as she is in *Magda*. . . . 'Io son' Io,' in fact, throughout. Her unpainted face [Duse disdained make-up], the unhidden grey of her hair . . . are symbolic of her attitude. . . . Am I overwhelmed by the personality of Duse? . . . The wretched fact remains that I am not. True, I see the power and nobility in her face, and the little shrill soft voice . . . has a certain charm for me. But my prevailing emotion is hostile to her. I cannot surrender myself and see in her the 'incarnate womanhood' and 'the very spirit of the world's tears' and all those other things which other critics see in her. My prevailing impression is of a great egoistic force; of a woman overriding, with an air of somber unconcern, plays, mimes, critics, and public."

From these diametrically opposing views, it appears that Beerbohm and Shaw, like play-goers everywhere, based their opinions on personal appeal rather than impartial judgment. Beerbohm, a fantasist and lover of all things feminine, adored Bernhardt for the melting tenderness and prowling sexuality she brought to her roles. Shaw, on the other hand, more comfortable with ideas than with passion, more dedicated to Anglo-Saxon matter than to Gallic manner, was unable to accept the sensuous thrust of Bernhardt's presence. Indeed, one suspects that the man who made love chiefly through the mails could not find attraction in a woman who, had she been Eve, might have devoured the snake along with the apple.

There was another factor Shaw failed to consider. When Duse and Bernhardt were playing Dumas' Marguerite Gautier, they were not playing the Virgin Mary; they were playing a successful courtesan who confronts the world with a thousand feminine wiles—and always in her best finery. Sarah, of all people, knew this, and knew that to appear as self-centered splendor itself in the first act would heighten the poignancy of her sacrifice and downfall. Duse, no doubt, understood the shape of Dumas' drama as well as Bernhardt. Yet she chose to portray Marguerite as a noble, somewhat dowdy victim. Shaw felt her decision was born of intellect, but a reading of the play makes one wonder. Marguerite is not a ladylike character who spares herself, or the audience, what he called the "infection of torment." She is an abandoned demimondaine, imperious, ironic, and promiscuous, who makes the fatal mistake of falling in love.

Duse was able to reduce her audience to tears with her portrayal. But it was not her intellect that was operating, it was the innocence of an autodidact, a genius who had spent her life in provincial Italian theatres without the benefits—and disadvantages—of *conservatoire* training. In a word, she was freshness itself, a new, natural, deeply expressive voice in a world accustomed to the stylized brilliance of French acting.

The American writer Willa Cather became the drama critic of the Lincoln, Nebraska, *Journal* while still in her third year at college. She had gone once to Omaha to see Bernhardt in *La Tosca* and never saw Duse at all, but she studied everything the New York papers wrote about them and summed it up neatly: "Art is Bernhardt's dissipation, a sort of Bacchic orgy. It is Duse's consecration, her religion, her martyrdom." To put it another way, one might say that Sarah Bernhardt was the last great actress of the nineteenth century, Eleonora Duse, the first great actress of the twentieth.

BEFORE coming to London, Bernhardt had produced *La Princesse Lointaine*, a play in verse by the young Edmond Rostand. A *succès d'estime*, it left her two hundred thousand francs in debt. This came as no surprise. She had already told the press: "It is conceivable that I won't make a *sou*. That means nothing to me. I think it superb, and shall put it on for my own pleasure."

Her enthusiasm was justified. At twenty-seven, Rostand was a man of immense promise, a talent worthy of Sarah's extravagance. The two had not met by chance. One day Sarah received a letter and a bulky manuscript from Madame Rostand, asking if she could find time to read her husband's first full-length play. As Madame Bernhardt might recall, his one-act play *Les Romanesques* had been well received at the Comédie Française the year before. Sarah, who received dozens of similar requests, was inclined to throw both letter and manuscript into the nearest wastebasket. But somehow—was it the fine note paper or the fashionable address in the rue Fortuny?—she settled down to the play. After a quick reading her decision was made. The following day the Rostands were ushered into the presence. It was a rapturous moment. Bernhardt pronounced Rostand the new Victor Hugo and his wife, the poet Rosemonde Gérard, the most adorable creature on earth. They were, in fact, made for Sarah: mannered enough to be amusing, worldly enough to be reassuring, talented enough to be respected. Besides, they were a handsome pair. Rosemonde was a slender beauty, blond and exquisitely dressed. As for Rostand, he was theatrical elegance itself, from his natty gray suit, his boutonniere, and monocle to his bristling waxed mustache, as pointed as the rhymes he invented.

The première of *La Princesse Lointaine* took place on 5 April 1895. The story of a medieval princess torn between spiritual dreams and fleshly desires, it gave Bernhardt, de Max, and Guitry endless opportunities to spout high-flown verses, strike pre-Raphaelite poses, and languish after one another in Swinburne fashion, all to the sound of Gabriel Pierné's fluttering flutes and sweeping harp arpeggios. Despite praise from the critics and bravos from the aesthetes, *La Princesse* bored the Paris public and closed after thirty-one performances.

Sarah refused to abandon it, however. With stubborn resolve, she took it to London, where, in the land of Dante Gabriel Rossetti and Burne-Jones, she hoped for a more sensitive response. Instead, she received another thrashing from Shaw, who insisted that her "nervous power" was not to be confused with talent, that the public was right to laugh at the precious goings-on, and—here he came a cropper—that French verse was not verse at all.

Sarah had been thrashed before. Contemptuous of the criticism and the laughter, she rushed to Rostand's defense, not only with words of praise, but with a commission to write another play. Then, as had become her custom, she went off on a tour of America, where she earned more than enough money to indulge in a long-dreamt-of luxury: the first staging of Alfred de Musset's *Lorenzaccio*. The play, written in 1834 when the poet was twenty-four, had always been thought unplayable—quite understandable, when one considers its impractical length, its confusing subplots, and its profusion of characters. Even after cuts were made, Sarah's production provided a full evening in the theatre. Cut or uncut, the play glowed with romantic intensity. Byronic in spirit, Shakespearean in scope, *Lorenzaccio* tells the story of Lorenzino de' Medici, a cultivated Renaissance Florentine nobleman who, in search of truth and justice, falls prey to the corruption and debauchery he set out to destroy.

Sarah was at her splendid best in the Hamlet-like title role. Even Jules de Tillet, one of her harshest critics, came round. "The talent of

Madame Bernhardt has often disturbed rather than charmed me," he wrote
in the *Revue Bleue*, "but this time her success is unbounded and deserved.
Beyond the summit of her art, she gave full life to the part of Lorenzaccio,
a part no one dared approach before her. I have never seen anything equal
to what she gave."

In a scholarly article Anatole France wrote for the *Revue de Paris*,
he recounted the historical events on which the play is based. About the
performance, he said:

Madame Sarah Bernhardt, who, in the lovely course of her career, has
created so many charming portraits, and presented her contemporaries
with images equal . . . to the dreams of poets, has now shown us that
grace in art is a happy aspect of strength.

Strength is the most striking characteristic of her latest creation. Madame Bernhardt has built the figure of Lorenzaccio with a perfectly sure
hand. She has modeled and shaped her own person into a Cellini bronze,
a high-strung Perseus.

We know what a work of art this great actress can make of herself. All
the same, in her latest transformation, she is astonishing. She has formed
her very substance into a melancholy youth, truthful and poetic. She has
created a living masterpiece by her sureness of gesture, the tragic beauty
of her pose and glance, the increased power in the timbre of her voice,
and the suppleness and breadth of her diction—through her gifts, in the
end, for mystery and terror.

The chorus of praise notwithstanding, Musset's play lasted only two
months and cost Sarah thousands. But the financial loss was a mere drop
in the bucket for the actress-manager, who, in her eagerness to give the
public theatre pieces of quality, was to lose two million gold francs in her
six years at the Renaissance.

Bernhardt's long life in the theatre had brought her many foreign decorations,
but no formal recognition from her own country. The situation was remedied
by those best qualified to appreciate her gifts. In the fall of 1896, a group
of actors and writers organized a banquet in her honor. As the day drew
near, Jules Huret of *Le Figaro* asked her to "revive the memories of her

emotions, struggles, and triumphs" for its readers. Her response was published in the form of a letter:

> My dear friend, you ask me for nothing less than a full confession. . . . I am proud and happy at the prospect of the fête. You ask whether I feel I deserve the honor. If my answer is Yes, you will think me conceited. If my answer is No, you will accuse me of false modesty. I should rather tell you why I feel so proud and happy. For twenty-nine years I have given the public the vibrations of my soul, the pulsations of my heart, the tears of my eyes. I have played one hundred and twelve roles, and created thirty-eight new characters, sixteen the work of poets. . . . I have ardently longed to climb the top-most pinnacle of my art. I have not yet reached it. By far the larger part of my life is behind me, but what does it matter? . . . . The hours that have flown away with my youth have left me courageous and cheerful, for my goal is unchanged, and I am marching towards it.
>
> I have journeyed across the ocean, carrying my artistic ideals with me, and the genius of my nation has triumphed. I have planted the dramatic literature of France in foreign hearts. That is my proudest achievement.
>
> If there are any carping critics who feel the fête about to be given in my honor is out of proportion to my talents, tell them I am the militant *doyenne* of a grand, inspiring, elevated form of art. Tell them, too, that French courtesy was never more manifest than when—to honor the art of interpretation and raise the interpreter to the level of other creative artists— it chose, as its symbol, a woman.

At noon on 9 December 1896, five hundred guests in full evening dress met in the Salle du Zodiaque of the Grand Hôtel. Bernhardt's entrance was dazzling. All eyes were raised when she appeared at the top of the winding staircase that led to the flower-decked banquet room below. Dressed in a trailing white gown embroidered in gold and bordered with chinchilla, she was outrageously wonderful as she made her way down in a series of poses that brought the cheering crowd to its feet.

"At every turn," Huret recalled, "she bent over the railing, one arm entwined around the velvet pillar, and paused to acknowledge the thunderous applause. Her feet seemed scarcely to touch the ground. It was as though she floated towards us in a halo of glory."

"Sarah Bernhardt Day" was bathed in love and memories. Old friends, Coppée and Coquelin, Sardou and Halévy, Montesquiou, Clairin and Ab-

béma, spoke nostalgically of the never-to-be-forgotten beauty she had brought
to *Andromaque* and *Le Passant, Ruy Blas*, and *Hernani* and recalled too her
foibles, her little lies, and her gift for friendship. The young, Rostand and
Léon Daudet, among others, exchanged anecdotes about the fabled creature
they were so proud to know. The menus were designed by Louise Abbéma,
Jules Chéret, and Alphonse Mucha. At the end of the banquet, Sardou
saluted Bernhardt. She was, he said, "the acknowledged sovereign of dramatic art, as everyone on earth knew. But, while it had been given to them
all to see the actress, few were fortunate enough to have known the good
will, the generosity, the exquisite kindness of the woman. In conclusion,"
he said, "I ask you all to drink to the health of our great and good Sarah."
More applause followed as Sardou reached for his handkerchief to wipe the
tears from his eyes. Then Bernhardt arose, her arms outstretched: "To all
of you, dear friends, I say thank you, thank you from the bottom of my
heart."

   The festivities ended with a "Hymn to Sarah Bernhardt" with words
by Armand Sylvestre and music by Gabriel Pierné, performed by the Colonne
Concerts Choir. Everyone then moved on to the Théâtre de la Renaissance,
where mounted police held back the crowds assembled to watch the guests'
arrival. That afternoon Bernhardt outdid herself in the first act of *Phèdre*
and the fourth act of Parodi's *Rome Vaincue* before a house overflowing with
le grand monde as well as celebrities from the worlds of art and literature.
As the finale, five poets read sonnets written in Bernhardt's honor. When
the curtain rose, the audience was treated to a *tableau vivant* that could
have existed only in those days and in that theatre. Dressed in the diaphanous
veils of Phèdre, Sarah was seated on a throne of multicolored flowers under
an arched canopy of palms intertwined with orchids, her face framed by
camellias. The actresses of her company, in white robes, crowned with roses,
gazed at their goddess in adoration. Of all the paeans of praise, it was the
sonnet of Rostand, Sarah's *"poète chéri,"* that stole the show:

> *En ce temps sans beauté, seule encore tu nous restes,*
> *Sachant descendre, pâle, un grand escalier clair,*
> *Ceindre un bandeau, porter un lys, brandir un fer.*
> *Reine de l'attitude et Princesse des gestes.*
>
> *En ce temps sans folie, ardente, tu protestes!*
> *Tu dis des vers. Tu meurs d'amour. Ton vol se perd.*

Tu tends tes bras de rêve, et puis tes bras de chair.
Et, quand Phèdre paraît, nous sommes tous incestes.

Avide de souffrir, tu t'ajoutes des coeurs;
Nous avons vu couler, car ils coulent, tes pleurs!
Toutes les larmes de nos âmes sur tes joues . . .

Mais aussi tu sais bien, Sarah, que quelquefois
Tu sens furtivement se poser, quand tu joues,
Les lèvres de Shakespeare aux bagues de tes doigts.

In this unlovely age, who but you knows
How to descend a staircase, bind your brow,
Carry a lily, draw a flashing sword—
Princess of gesture, and pale queen of pose!

In this dim age, you light a torch for us:
You speak verse; die for love; expiring stretch
Arms of pure dream out, and then arms of flesh.
Your Phèdre turns us all incestuous.

Avid for pain, you win hearts. We have seen
Flowing down your cheeks—for ah, you weep!—
The tears of our souls' inmost sufferings . . .

But, Sarah, you well know, during a scene,
You've sometimes felt the touch of Shakespeare's lips
Bestow a furtive kiss upon your rings.*

Sarah was visibly moved. In Huret's words:

She stood with heaving breast, pale as the camellias about her. Her trembling lips tried to shape themselves into a smile, but the tears gathered
in her eyes. Her hands were clasped over her heart as if to keep it from
bursting.

And so she stood, overwhelmed and vanquished by the power of a few
lines of poetry delivered before these fifteen hundred enthusiastic auditors.

*Translation by James Merrill.

Flowers from the topmost gallery fell onto the stage, and, with long-sustained cheers, *La Journée de Sarah Bernhardt* came to an end.

Bernhardt canonized was one thing, Bernhardt the day-to-day woman another, as is charmingly evident in *La Grande Sarah*, a lively, touching memoir in the form of a journal by Reynaldo Hahn. Born in Venezuela, Hahn was an astonishing child prodigy who left Caracas for Paris at an early age in order to study composition with Massenet. He was only twenty when Sarah took him up, but he had been "a young Mozart," a pet of Parisian society from the age of fourteen, when he would sing and play his song *"Si mes vers avaient des ailes"** in aristocratic salons to the swooning delight of his listeners. It was not his precocious musical gifts alone that endeared him to the ladies and gentlemen of the *faubourg*. Added to these was a sparkling wit and a nature as seductive as his music.

When Hahn first met Sarah, he was Proust's lover. In fact, Reynaldo took Marcel on an excursion to Belle-Ile, where Sarah had bought a house a few years earlier. Unfortunately, "the pilgrimage to the habitation made glorious by Sarah Bernhardt," as Proust put it, did not include an opportunity for Hahn to present his friend to the great actress. Unfortunately, for if it had, Proust might have portrayed her in depth, whereas Hahn, in *La Grande Sarah*, confined himself for the most part to descriptions of Bernhardt, relaxed and at home, surrounded by friends. Yet even he could not resist certain judgments. He saw that "frightful fame" had made her egotistical and proud. "Not that she showed it in an unpleasant or hostile fashion," he wrote. "No, it was far from that. Still with all her smiling charm, there was a kind of defensive armor, an indifference to praise, or, to put it another way, an impassive, slightly disdainful acceptance of the adoration she received."

Here Hahn showed a certain lack of sympathy. As he himself must have known, it is difficult to handle the feverish flattery and ignorant gushing that celebrated stars are made to suffer. Another of her flaws, he continued, was her weakness for the mediocre hangers-on who swarmed around her. They, he felt, created an atmosphere of nightmarish lies and cheap intrigue. But the main blemish in her life was her son. There, said Hahn, was the real cancer. The rest was nothing in comparison. Having voiced

---

**If My Verses Had Wings.* Of all Hahn's exquisitely perfumed songs, it is still the one most frequently performed.

these negative opinions, Hahn went on to describe the Sarah he loved.

On 18 June 1896 he went with Bernhardt and her troupe to London. A week later he noted in his journal:

A sitting this morning at the photographer, Downey's. Everyone in the studio is waiting joyfully but impatiently. As it is raining we fear she may not turn up. However at 11:30 Sarah arrives with Clairin, Seylor and her maid, Marie, in tow. Always sensitive to cold, she complains of the "freezing weather." Actually it is hot. A hearty, affectionate hello to Downey, whom she has known for twenty years. "Always young," she says in English as she pats him on the shoulder. The old man, a true artist, is beaming. We go up a narrow black stairway to the studio. Sarah is very awkward going up and down stairs; she likes to be given a hand or a shoulder to lean on. She is in a very good mood. She takes off her pretty Leghorn travelling hat and, in front of the mirror, rumples her hair with abrupt little movements of her forefinger. She raises her eyebrows slightly, and looking radiantly youthful, goes to take her place before the camera. First she poses . . . with her new dog Jack at her side. . . . After various changes of costume and pose, I tell her how becoming her skirts are; it is a style she invented and continues to wear in spite of changing fashions, a form that clings to her legs and ends in a swirling-out about the ankles. An undulating line is the chief characteristic of the Sarah Bernhardt silhouette.

As we leave she strokes Downey's bald head, and calls him "dahrrling." We get into the carriage. [Sarah always called Clairin Jojotte instead of Georges and he called her "Dame Jolie."]

"Jojotte," she says to Clairin, "you're lunching with us?"

"No," he answers.

"But, Jojotte, you are a swine. You might have told your family (his sister and his niece) that you would be lunching with me."

A gay ride home. . . . Sarah claims that I'm a nuisance. "But we forgive you because you're amusing." I accept the compliment gracefully. She tells us about a maid she once had who deceived her husband with the coachman. The said husband came to Sarah in tears.

"A coachman," he cried, "just a coachman! The least she could have done was to betray me with one of Madame's friends!"

When we reach the hotel, Sarah does a little dance—very distinguished—in the corridor!

Hahn was endlessly amused by Sarah's view of other actors. What did she think of Duse, he asked.

"What a lovely head!" was her reply. "That disdainful mouth, those white teeth, those eyes, smiling and wretched. And what charm! A great actress." A pregnant pause, and then: "What a pity she is so pretentious!"

Sarah was even less kind about her old rival, Madame Favart:

Absolutely no talent. None. Don't talk to me about that horrible, dark, long-nosed creature. Long in the waist, short legs, hideous hands. Even her fingers were fat. Dreadful.

Lucien Guitry she admired without reservation. As for Mounet-Sully:

"He was amazingly beautiful, but what a character! He could be absolutely vile. About one of her old teachers, Regnier: "He always believed in me, God knows why. I must have been a detestable pupil."

When Bernhardt read Hahn's *La Grande Sarah* in manuscript, she wrote him that she found it a faithful portrait and added: "Thanks to your journal and Rostand's sonnet I shall be able to embark with ease on the great, final voyage."

NO H O U S E Bernhardt ever had gave her as much pleasure as Le Fortin in Belle-Ile-en-Mer, a small fort she and Clairin had discovered when they were on holiday together. Brittany spelled nostalgia—for Sarah, because it was the scene of her earliest childhood, for Clairin, because of a memorable walking trip he had made in his youth with the composer Camille Saint-Saëns and the painter Henri Regnault. Nostalgia went overboard when Sarah and her Jojotte came upon

the small fortress standing high above the wild Atlantic. The moment Sarah
saw the "For Sale" sign she knew it must be hers. That was in 1893. Two
years later Sarah, Maurice, and Terka with their daughter, Simone; Abbéma
and Clairin; Sarah's friend and private secretary, Emile Geoffroy; and a
small army of servants and pets spent their first summer in the "Beautiful
Island in the Sea." During those two years Sarah had spent a fortune turning
the gloomy barracks into a welcoming home. Narrow slits in the thick walls
were replaced by large sunlit windows overlooking the sea. The vast space
that had once housed a garrison of thirty soldiers was transformed into
comfortable living quarters: cheerful salons, an ample dining room, five
bedrooms, and—an eccentric extravagance at the time—a luxurious bath-
room for the chatelaine. This was just a beginning. In the next years, Sarah
added Reynaldo Hahn and Dr. Samuel Pozzi to the list of regular visitors,
enlarged Le Fortin, bought a good deal of property near it, including a farm,
built studios for Abbéma and Clairin, and a separate house for Maurice and
his family, which now included a second daughter, Lysiane, who would be
baptized at Belle-Ile in the summer of 1897.

If life on the island was different from life in Paris, the atmosphere
was much the same. Pitou, who had arranged the purchase of the property,
was still in charge, still driving Sarah mad with his "I've got to put things
in order," to which Sarah would growl: "You wretch, you want me to kill
you, but you won't get off that easily." Then she would tell him to have her
horses, Vermouth and Cassis, brought round so that she could take Clairin
and the children to visit a garden nearby.

The daily ritual at Belle-Ile was centered around lunch followed by
a siesta in the "Sarahtorium," a sun-drenched enclosure of chaises longues
and rustic tables. A strange siesta, Hahn tells us,

during which everyone talks without stop, discussing the articles in the
newspapers and magazines the postman has just delivered, swatting in-
sects, and jumping up to glare at the hated tourists on a knoll in the
distance, who, armed with spy-glasses, try to get a glimpse of Sarah
Bernhardt! All this time, Sarah seemed to be asleep. But no, even then
she could not resist calling attention to herself.

"I'm asleep, I'm asleep," she would mutter through the thick veils that
protected her from the sun. In the afternoon, Sarah, refreshed and full of
energy, would go fishing or play tennis. The game was an ordeal for her

opponents as it was their duty to place the ball where she could reach it easily, for although she had a good serve and a strong return, it did not amuse her to run about as she had problems with her right knee. Maurice, who was a marvellous player, was a past-master at this. Clairin and Geoffroy managed fairly well, but their frequent lapses elicited furious curses from Sarah.

At dinner one night passionate discussions about nothing. Dominoes. Then I go to the piano and play the gypsy song from *Carmen*. Maurice tries a Spanish dance; his daughters imitate him. I speed up the tempo. Suddenly, Sarah's friend, old Geoffroy, in knickerbockers and a Norfolk jacket, leaps up and improvises a mad fandango. With unbelievable "go," he executes dizzying twists and turns, back-bends and cart-wheels, shaking the lamps and knocking the chairs over. . . . I fall to the ground convulsed with laughter. We all laugh until it hurts. Sarah, her head in her hands, laughs till she weeps, sobs, and hiccoughs. Gasping for air, she leans back, her eyes closed. Then, just as she calms down, she bursts out all over again.

More serious matters awaited her in Paris. After her great *succès d'estime* in Musset's *Lorenzaccio*, Bernhardt turned to Sardou, now in his sixty-seventh year, and in February 1897 put on his *Spiritisme* (*Spiritualism*) about an unfaithful wife who stages her own "death," then reappears as a "ghost" to beg her husband's forgiveness for her infidelity. "It was a play so weak," wrote Gustave Kahn, "that nothing could save it." Bernhardt hurriedly took it off and substituted Sardou's sure-fire success, *La Tosca*.

During Holy Week, she presented several matinée performances of Rostand's second full-length drama, a gospel play called *La Samaritaine*. He had provided it with fine passages inspired by the biblical sonorities of the Song of Songs, large doses of evangelical uplift, and the chance to watch Bernhardt being saved from sin and debauchery by the good Lord Jesus Himself. When asked by a journalist to describe it, the young author told him to imagine "a courtesan like Liane de Pougy meeting Christ, then going back to Paris to preach the Holy Gospel to her depraved friends."

A noted courtesan of the Belle Epoque, Liane de Pougy had many of the same friends as Sarah. In her memoirs, *Mes Cahiers Bleus* (*My Blue Notebooks*), she writes that she and Reynaldo Hahn "were very fond of one another," that for years he was the sweetest thing in her life, and describes him as "prodigiously beautiful, a dream of beauty . . . the beauty of intelligence, of mystery, of cultivation, of sensibility." But when she renounced her enormously successful dissolute life to marry the Romanian prince Georges Ghika and broke the good news to her dear Reynaldo, he said, "Adieu, Liane, I detest married couples" and dropped her completely. She also writes that she was completely faithful to Prince Ghika, even as she describes hours in bed with her lesbian admirers, who were allowed to make love to her "only from the waist up," as from the waist down she "belonged to her husband," who enjoyed sitting at the foot of her bed to watch the girls at play.

Although she says she is attracted by beautiful women and finds most men disgusting, she is openly disapproving of the Duc de Morny's daughter, "Missy," for smoking cigars and dressing like a man and of Sarah's beautiful niece, Saryta, who has the same inclinations and "lives off other women."

"Saryta, too, smokes cigars," Liane wrote, "but at least she wears skirts, and only 'masculinizes' the upper part of her clothes."

"Sarah Bernhardt," Liane continues, "tried several times to make her niece change her milieu and her habits. She reasoned with her, paid her expenses, took her to America, made her an actress. Nothing helped. . . . She died quite young of intestinal tuberculosis after atrocious suffering, alone in a clinic where her famous aunt had put her."

At the end of her life, Liane de Pougy became a tertiary sister of the Dominican Order, which may explain why Rostand thought of her in connection with *La Samaritaine*. In the preface to her memoirs, her spiritual adviser, Father Rzewuski, recounts an event from the time she was considered by many to be the "most beautiful of all courtesans." When she was offered a contract at the French Theatre in Saint Petersburg, as her only previous stage experience had been at the Folies-Bergère, she asked Sarah Bernhardt to coach her. After five or six "exceedingly expensive lessons," Sarah said: "My dear, there's not much I can do with you. Display your beauty, but once you are on the stage you had better keep your pretty mouth shut."

As Sarah longed to play biblical figures, *La Samaritaine* became one of her favorite roles. She was to present it during Holy Week almost every year as late as 1912.

In April 1897 it was announced that the great Italian actress Eleonora Duse would give a series of performances—her first in Paris—at the end of the spring season and that her impresario, Joseph Schurmann, was negotiating with several theatres in the French capital. When Bernhardt heard this, she offered to give her theatre, free of charge, to her rival. This meant that the box-office receipts would go to La Duse instead of being shared with the Renaissance as was customary whenever Bernhardt let her theatre to a foreign company. The two divas—Duse, at thirty-eight, fifteen years younger than Sarah—signed a contract stating that she would give ten performances in the first two weeks of June and would send a list of the plays in which she would appear well in advance.

When in mid-May the list arrived, Sarah could not believe her eyes. The plays Duse had chosen after consulting her lover, Gabriele D'Annunzio, and her friend Comte Giuseppe Primoli were Dumas *fils*'s *La Dame aux Camélias* and *La Femme de Claude* and Sudermann's *Magda*, as well as Verga's *Cavalleria Rusticana* and a double bill consisting of Goldoni's *La Locandiera* and D'Annunzio's *Il Sogno d'un Mattino di Primavera* (*A Spring Morning's Dream*). In short, the first three of the six plays proposed were in Bernhardt's own repertory. Sarah was outraged that Ibsen's *A Doll's House*, which Duse introduced to Italy, Russia, and Austria was not included and that *La Dame aux Camélias*, for years considered to "belong" to Bernhardt, was. Suspicious theatre-goers wondered what lay behind Bernhardt's generosity. Had she invited her rival into the lion's den in order to gobble her up? Was it her way of proving that she was Duse's superior? Or was it simply her way of publicizing herself and her theatre? That La Duse accepted Bernhardt's hospitality was also endlessly discussed. Of course, she would save a lot of money. Perhaps the explanation lay with D'Annunzio, the great love of Duse's life, a man as Machiavellian as he was talented. Or perhaps it was Duse's dream to be on an equal footing with the idol of her youth. Or, and this is quite likely, because Duse was as competitive, as fired with ambition as Sarah herself—this despite her reputation as a spiritual creature whose conversation, *Le Figaro* reported, consisted mainly of passionate utterances about "goodness, the soul, and the meaning of life."

Duse's stay in Paris had its amusing moments. The Comte de Montesquiou remembered introducing the ladies to one another: "It was more like a collision than a meeting. The two women grasped each other so tightly that it looked like a mad wrestling match." That afternoon Bernhardt invited Duse to sit in her loge for a performance of *La Samaritaine*. Duse did not sit for long. At each of Sarah's entrances she jumped to her feet and remained standing as long as Bernhardt was on the stage. Her bobbing up and down had the expected result. It ruined Sarah's scenes, as the distracted members of the audience looked from one to the other as if they were at a tennis match. There was little Sarah could do but smile her most gracious smile in the direction of her overheated admirer.

This farce was enacted in reverse on Duse's opening night in *La Dame aux Camélias*. At that performance Bernhardt sat in the stage box, her chin cupped in her hand, her eyes fixed on her rival. Sarah, covered with jewels and magnificently dressed, with a wreath of roses entwined in her freshly dyed red hair, was Dumas' Parisian heroine come to life—in sharp contrast to Duse, who wore little or no make-up onstage or off and cared little for stylish clothes. During the intermission, *le Tout-Paris* came to pay their respects to Bernhardt and to ask what she thought of the Italian actress. "One of the best" was her cheerful reply, knowing that Duse, frightened and nervous, was at her worst that night.

Sarah was even more cheerful when she read Sarcey's notice. "La Duse," he wrote, "either because she thinks of the character in that way, or because she cannot play it in any other, suggests a good little soul who ruins her lovers by making them buy macaroni for her. Yet," he conceded, "she excels in expressing tenderness, and the way she offers a flower to Armand, though quite absurd if one follows the text, is in itself exquisitely graceful." These words from France's leading critic were small change for an actress who had been showered with the highest praise in Germany and Russia, as well as in Italy. If Duse was discouraged, she did not show it when she appeared as Magda, a part, some critics felt, in which her performance was greater than Bernhardt's. Even Sarcey came round. At the end of her stay, he wrote: "La Duse leaves victorious; from the general point of view of the theatre, she leaves behind her an example which it would be well for all to profit by. . . . She has won us over by the sheer power of truth."

Sarah handled the unwelcome news with Parisian guile. On 14 June a gala benefit was to be held in her theatre, the proceeds to go toward the completion of a monument in memory of Dumas *fils*, who had died two years earlier. Why not invite her guest to participate? Duse could do Acts II and III of *La Dame aux Camélias* and Sarah Acts IV and V. But Duse was too clever to be lured into a battle she might lose. Instead, she proposed to do a scene from *La Femme de Claude*, Dumas' somewhat Ibsenesque play, in which she knew she would shine. Her proposal was accepted, and the contest was on. It was the only time that Bernhardt and Duse would appear on the same stage. As added attractions, the evening's program listed *L'Aveu* (*The Confession*), a one-act melodrama of adultery written and performed by Bernhardt herself some years before, recitations by Coquelin and Yvette Guilbert, arias sung by members of the Paris Opéra, and, as the finale, Rostand's "Homage to Alexandre Dumas from Marguerite Gautier," to be declaimed by none other than Sarah Bernhardt.

Everyone seemed happy with the gala performance, particularly La Duse, who, in an inspired half hour onstage, convinced the audience that she could hold her own, even with La Divine Sarah. Unfortunately, Sarah had one last surprising card up her sleeve: Duse's lover. A flamboyant poet, novelist, and playwright, D'Annunzio was a dark, if seductive character, ruthless, untrustworthy, and exceedingly full of himself. These qualities were on display when he first called on Bernhardt at her house in the boulevard Péreire. "You are sublime," he cried, as he bent to kiss her hand. "Yes, Madame, you are positively D'Annunzian!" What was meant to flatter her did not go down well, for Sarah, with a rather healthy ego of her own, preferred to think of herself as Bernhardtian. Still there was business to discuss. He had sent her *La Ville Morte*, a French translation of his play *La Città Morta* (*The Dead City*), and she liked it, not only for its theme of incest and its antique Grecian setting, but because the play, inspired by, and written for his mistress, was now offered to Bernhardt to play in Paris before Duse did it in Italy. D'Annunzio's unscrupulous behavior gave Sarah immense satisfaction. First, because in giving her his play, he made it clear that he thought her even more "sublime" (one of his favorite words) than the actress he claimed to love. Then too because Sarah felt Duse had misused her abominably—which she complained about in a letter to Montesquiou, the man who first brought them together:

You introduced me to Duse. I was extremely courteous and polite to her. She was supposed to perform ten times in eleven days; instead she performed ten times in thirty days. [It is true that La Duse often postponed and cancelled performances.]

This cost me a good deal of money since I kept my theatre open although it was due to be closed. I also paid my staff more than usual since they were entitled to a holiday. All that was done without a word to anyone. You are aware of all the pettiness and infamy I have been exposed to since

La Duse's arrival. I have had my apotheosis, my "*Journée Sarah Bernhardt.*" Now they want to bury me. All this is bad, including *La* Duse
who has played a shrewd role—Oh how shamelessly shrewd! It's all ugly,
despicable. The Italian artiste is an underhanded, ignoble creature. Imagine, she didn't even write to thank me or bid me farewell! It makes me
feel sick at heart. . . .

La Duse could very well have used the same words, "shamelessly shrewd,
ugly, despicable, underhanded, ignoble," to describe Bernhardt's blatantly
seductive behavior in regard to D'Annunzio.

No one got much pleasure from Sarah's production of what the cast
called "The Deadly City." Duse was heartbroken by her lover's callous
betrayal. D'Annunzio was furious when a critic described his play as "a
relentless flood of words." And Sarah's revenge on Duse backfired. She was
forced to close *The Dead City* soon after it opened, as the public thought it
as "deadly" as the cast did. Duse was to have her revenge when she appeared
in the play in Italy and had a great success, but by that time Sarah and
D'Annunzio had had a brief affair which neither of them took seriously, and
Duse's heart was permanently broken.

As is often the case after a theatrical failure, each person involved
claimed that the others had behaved with malicious intent, and each deluded
himself into thinking that he was the only one who had behaved well.

T H E tangled, rather nasty situation at the Renaissance Theatre was as nothing compared to the shameful affair which
shook France in those years. Although it was called *L'Affaire
Dreyfus*, its repercussions went beyond the forged documents used to convict
the innocent Jewish captain Alfred Dreyfus and far beyond his condemnation
to life imprisonment on Devil's Island. Volumes have been filled with anal-
yses of the legal entanglements, the false accusations, the racist hatreds,
and the political opportunism that were part of the Dreyfus case. The French,

so proud of their past glory, of their ideals of freedom, equality, and broth-erhood, were at one another's throats once again. Their behavior, sad to say, gives substance to the words of the historian J. E. C. Bradley: "There is a nation to the members of which Frenchmen are more revengeful than to Germans, more irascible than to Italians, more unjust than to the English. It is to the French that Frenchmen display animosity more savage, more incessant, and more inequitable than to people of any other nation."

Bradley's statement would be more complete had it included the rabid anti-Semitism that arose in the wake of the *Affaire*. "Jews are contaminating the nation" was the cry of the anti-Dreyfusards. They were "pimps, chancres, thieves, synagogue lice" who deserved vivisection or deportation. Above all, they were not Frenchmen, but traitors to France.

Incredibly enough, the brutal reaction to Jews was condoned by such refined spirits as Jules Lemaître, Alphonse and Léon Daudet, François Coppée, and the majority of social and church notables in Paris. Fortunately for Dreyfus, and for France, there were humanists and social reformers, intellectuals and scientists—and Jews—who came to the realization that Dreyfus was the innocent victim of prejudice and military corruption.

Sarah was passionately pro-Dreyfus, and with good reason. How in-deed could she not be? Disfiguring anti-Semitic caricatures of her had ap-peared world-wide for years. She had been met with stones and racist insults in Russia and in Canada. Marie Colombier had written about her "vile Jewish habits" in *The Memoirs of Sarah Barnum*. There were, in fact, no end of ugly allusions to her "Hebrew blood." But there was more than private suffering at stake. Like Octave Mirbeau, Sardou, Rostand, Hahn, Clairin, Lucien Guitry, and many others of her circle, she felt more and more certain that Dreyfus was the victim of a sinister plot. Sad for Sarah, her beloved son did not agree. Openly anti-Semitic despite his portion of Jewish blood and convinced that the army, the Catholic Church, and the smart set could do no wrong, he fought bitterly with his mother. Unable to stand up to her and her friends, he took his family to Monte Carlo, and for many painful months Maurice and Sarah were not on speaking terms. But, of course, they were just one of the many French families torn apart by *L'Affaire Dreyfus*. When he finally returned to Paris, Maurice would be as devoted, as loving, and as financially dependent as ever, and from then on the Dreyfus case was never to be mentioned between them.

In October 1897, Bernhardt toured Belgium while, in *her* Renaissance

Theatre, Lucien Guitry appeared in *Secret Service* by the popular American actor-playwright William Gillette as adapted by Pierre Decourcelle. Alas, it was not at all popular in Paris, and Sarah had to pull her theatre out of debt. At the beginning of November, she gave the first of fifty superb—and money-making—performances of *La Dame aux Camélias* and rehearsed a new play by Mirbeau, *Les Mauvais Bergers (The Evil Shepherds)*. Mirbeau was one of the more violent of the Dreyfusards and spent most of the rehearsal time convincing Sarah that something must be done to prove Dreyfus's innocence.

In later years, Louis Verneuil claimed that Sarah told him that it was after one of these rehearsals that she went to see Zola and present him with Mirbeau's views and thus was instrumental in rallying Zola to the cause. And that it was at her suggestion that Zola published the article for *Le Figaro* in defense of Dreyfus which ended with the celebrated phrase: "Truth is on the march, and nothing will stop it."

Furthermore, Verneuil claimed that Bernhardt was present that day in January 1898, when *J'Accuse* was published and a threatening crowd marched up to Zola's small house in the rue de Bruxelles shouting: "Death to Zola!" Suddenly, Verneuil remembered being told, a French window on the second floor opened, but instead of Zola, Bernhardt appeared. She had come to congratulate him on his courageous campaign, a campaign she had initiated two months before. At the sight of Sarah, the mob quieted down and was dispersed with the help of the police.

The next morning the anti-Dreyfusard papers printed headlines: SARAH BERNHARDT AT ZOLA'S. THE GREAT ACTRESS IS WITH THE JEWS AGAINST THE ARMY. For the next week there were angry demonstrations outside the Renaissance Theatre and Bernhardt was asked by the prefect of police to suspend the performances and close the theatre to avoid further trouble.

In all likelihood Verneuil—or Sarah—was exaggerating. But if she was, and even if she wanted the world to think she played a larger part in the rehabilitation of Captain Dreyfus than she actually did, one must admit that her heart was in the right place.

In December Zola had published his *Lettres à la Jeunesse*, urging the young to fight injustice. It created enormous excitement. It was just at that time that Sarah launched *Les Mauvais Bergers*. The title refers to greedy factory owners who exploit their workers. Each time there was a speech referring to injustice, the audience presumed it to be a reference to the

Dreyfus case and burst into angry shouts, pro and con. Lucien Guitry was impressive as one of the workers killed in a bloody strike, and, when in the last scene Sarah, as his loved one, finds him dead on a stretcher, her acting was so painfully realistic that there were shouts in the audience of "Enough! Enough!"

As the world knows, Emile Zola became the hero of the Dreyfusards when in January his inflammatory "*J'Accuse*: A Letter to the President of the Republic" was published in *L'Aurore*. In it Zola named and accused high army officers of distortion of facts, monstrous partiality, and blindness to justice:

It is a crime to seek support from the gutter press, to allow ourselves to be defended by the riff-raff of Paris in such a way that it is now the riff-raff who insolently parade their victory over law and simple decency.

It is a crime to poison the meek and the humble, to exasperate the passions of reaction and intolerance while seeking shelter behind an odious anti-Semitism from which the great liberal France of the Rights of Man will die if it is not cured.

It is a crime to exploit patriotism for works of hatred, and it is, finally, a crime to make the sword the god of modern times when all human science is laboring towards the future work of truth and justice.

Even if Bernhardt did not go to Zola's house when *J'Accuse* appeared, she did write to its author:

Cher Grand Maître,

Allow me to speak of the inexpressible emotion I felt when I read your cry for justice. As a woman I have no influence. But I am anguished, haunted by the situation, and the beautiful words you wrote yesterday brought tremendous relief to my great suffering.

I thought of writing to thank Scheurer-Kestner [vice president of the Senate and an ardent Dreyfusard] but knowing that everything that admirable man does is considered criminally suspect, I thought that if an *artiste*—what am I saying?—an *actress* was known to admire his courageous deeds, that discovery would be used to crush him. To you whom I have loved so long, I say thank you with all the strength of a melancholy instinct which cries out to me: "It's a crime! A crime!"

Thank you, Emile Zola. Thank you, beloved master. Thank you in the name of eternal justice.

A S   T H E   century drew to a close, Sarah began to think that the Théâtre de la Renaissance was under a curse. She had lost millions of francs in her five years as directrice and would have faced bankruptcy many times had she not gone off on foreign tours. Besides, the backstage was cramped, the stage itself too small, and— a prime concern—at fifty-four, she felt the time had come when a greater distance between herself and the public might spare her a certain embarrassment—and a good deal of make-up. With such thoughts in mind she asked Maurice Grau to sell her lease on the Renaissance and to find her a larger theatre.

After her success as Lorenzaccio, Sarah felt she must play the title role in *Hamlet*. As she did not like the official French adaptation used by the Comédie Française, and probably could not get permission to use it, she commissioned Eugène Morand and Marcel Schwob to write a prose version that would follow Shakespeare's text faithfully. She took it with her when she went to Belle-Ile in June and studied it carefully with the idea of doing it in her new theatre.

For her farewell to the Théâtre de la Renaissance, on 18 November 1898, she revived *La Dame aux Camélias* and, as Marguerite Gautier, died on that stage for the last time on 11 December. Meanwhile, she had signed a twenty-five-year lease, to begin on 1 January 1899, for the Théâtre des Nations, which was owned by the City of Paris. Located on the Place du Châtelet, it had been the home of the Opéra-Comique under the name Théâtre Lyrique. It was to be the only theatre in Paris in which she performed during the last twenty-three years of her life.

It was a practical, if ambitious move. As an experienced actress-manager, Sarah knew that the Théâtre des Nations, with seventeen hundred seats, could bring in almost twice as much at the box office as the Renaissance, which had only nine hundred seats. And then, what scope there was in the immense stage, what satisfaction for a repertory company to know there was room enough to store sets for four or five different productions, and what comfort could be enjoyed when the decrepit old dressing rooms were done over. But, eager to begin, she decided to postpone the lengthy work of renovation until the summer, renamed her imposing new playhouse the Théâtre Sarah Bernhardt, and announced that it would open on 21 January with a revival of *La Tosca.*

Posters were put up, the box office was opened, and the crowds poured in. Three hundred performances later—a record run for the Sardou play—Sarah was a richer and happier woman. At last she could breathe, she told her friends. How had she ever managed to put up with that bird cage, that ridiculous Renaissance, where she couldn't even spread her arms without bumping into the scenery?

In the summer and fall of 1898, the Sarah Bernhardt Theatre was renewed from top to bottom. The results were worthy of its proud owner, who had promised it would be the most beautiful theatre in the world. The once crumbling walls were now covered with yellow velvet, as were the seats, a startling innovation since red interiors were traditional in French theatres. The lofty boxes gleamed with ivory-colored paint. The seats in the orchestra were wide and comfortable. Immense chandeliers shed their soft light everywhere. The foyer, spacious and welcoming, was lined with portraits of Bernhardt in her various roles as seen by Mucha, Clairin, and Abbéma. And finally, after years of musty changing rooms, Sarah treated herself to a luxurious dressing room that was literally a five-room duplex apartment. First, there was a large antechamber (where backstage visitors could wait for her) separated from the stage by a double door and a few steps. Next was a large drawing room hung with yellow satin where Sarah received, seated on a huge divan. All done up in Empire style, with a boost from Lalique, it was furnished with magnificent pieces of the period. The dressing room proper was large enough to hold fifty costumes, a tall dressing table equipped with the latest in electric bulbs, a gigantic mirror with three panels, a monumental washstand, and a bathtub, the first ever installed in a theatre. These three communicating rooms were on the second floor of the theatre. From the antechamber, a spiral staircase led down to the ground floor, to a dining room large enough to seat twelve comfortably. Adjoining was a small kitchen with pantry. On Sundays Sarah would give dinner parties for *le Tout-Paris Théâtral* between her matinée and evening performances.

In this atmosphere of confidence and success, Bernhardt chose to follow *La Tosca* with a revival of *Dalila*, the mediocre Feuillet play no one had liked her in twenty-six years before when she played it at the Comédie Française. If it had not suited her in 1873, it suited her even less in 1899. As a result, the theatre which had been packed with cheering crowds for *La Tosca* was a sea of empty seats for the next two weeks. This dismal mistake was followed by warmly received revivals of *La Samaritaine* and *La Dame aux Camélias* with occasional matinées of *Phèdre*.

But Sarah was only marking time. On 20 May 1899 she strode out onto the stage in cape and sword to play her first Hamlet. Her performance in the part was to prove more controversial than any in her long career. There is a certain stigma attached to actresses who take on men's roles. First, because one is never quite convinced by the voice, the gait or the manner, and, second, because they have the double task of impersonating an actor who, in turn, is portraying another man. Under the circumstances Sarah did spectacularly well. *Hamlet* ran for months, despite the fact that the production lasted more than four hours. Learned critics admired the truth and intelligence she brought to Shakespeare's lines. The poet Catulle Mendès was so overcome that he fought a duel with a fellow journalist who had the effrontery to say that Bernhardt's wig was the wrong color. Even Mounet-Sully, who had become the reigning Hamlet at the Comédie Française, went to see Sarah's Prince of Denmark over and over again. Her former lover had not changed. As tenacious as ever, he argued every point of her reading. Why did she do her soliloquy, "To be, or not to be," sitting down? And why did she show fear in the scene with Rosencrantz and Guildenstern when at that point Hamlet does not know that the king means to kill him? But he does know, Sarah answered. He senses danger in the scene with the players. It is then that he is convinced that the Ghost speaks the truth. That, Mounet argued, was too subtle. But Hamlet *is* subtle was Sarah's reply. Their discussions, Bernhardt remembered, continued far into the night. And just as in the old days, Sarah was convinced that she was right and Jean lost his temper.

Bernhardt ran *Hamlet* for a fortnight, then closed the theatre for renovations, while she took the play on a six-month tour, beginning in London, where she played it for another fortnight.

English reaction was mixed. The writer Maurice Baring had no reservations. He felt that it was not until the French public saw Sarah's interpretation that it got an exact idea of what Shakespeare's play was. For him Sarah was "a marvel, a tiger, natural, easy, lifelike, and princely." In certain speeches he seemed to be "overhearing Shakespeare himself." Each scene, each mood was part of a whole, "like clouds that chase one another but belong to one sky, and not like the separate slides of a magic-lantern."

Max Beerbohm disagreed violently in an article entitled "Hamlet, Princess of Denmark":

I do, while there is still yet time, earnestly hope that Sarah's example in playing Hamlet will not create a precedent among women. . . . No doubt, Hamlet, in the complexity of his nature, had traces of femininity. . . . This, I take it, would be Sarah's own excuse for having essayed the part. She would not, of course attempt to play Othello—at least, I risk the assumption that she would not, dangerous though it is to assume what she might *not* do—any more than her distinguished countryman, Mounet-Sully, would attempt to play Desdemona. . . . Mounet-Sully could be no more acceptable as Lady Macbeth than as Desdemona. He would be absurd in it, though, (this is my point) not one whit more absurd than Sarah is as Hamlet. Sarah ought not to have supposed that Hamlet's weakness set him in any possible relation to her own feminine mind and body. Her friends ought to have restrained her. The native critics ought not to have encouraged her. The custom-house officials at Charing Cross ought to have confiscated her sable doublet and hose. I, lover of her incomparable art, am even more distressed than amused when I think of her aberration at the Adelphi. For once even her voice was not beautiful. . . . The best that can be said for her performance is that she acted (as she always does) with that dignity of demeanour which is the result of self-possession. Her perfect self-possession was one of the most delicious elements in the evening's comedy, but one could not help being genuinely impressed by her dignity. One felt that Hamlet, as portrayed by her, was, albeit neither melancholy nor a dreamer, at least a person of consequence and unmistakably "thoro'bred." Yes! the only compliment one can conscientiously pay her is that her Hamlet was, from first to last, *très grande dame.*

Bernhardt defended her conception of the role in a letter to an anonymous critic who felt Shakespeare could only be understood by the English and found her interpretation of Hamlet too manly:

I am reproached for being too active, too virile. It appears that in England Hamlet must be portrayed as a sad German professor. . . . They say that my acting is not traditional. But what is tradition? Each actor brings his own traditions. . . . In the scene in the chapel Hamlet decides not to kill the king who is praying, not because he is irresolute and cowardly; but because he is intelligent and tenacious; he wants to kill him when the king is sinning, not when he is in a state of repentance, for he wants him to go to hell, not to heaven. There are those who are absolutely determined to see in Hamlet a woman's soul, weak and indecisive; but I see the soul of a resolute, sensible man. When Hamlet sees his father's spirit and learns of his murder, he resolves to avenge him, but he is the opposite of Othello, who acts without thinking; Hamlet thinks before he acts, a sign of great strength and a powerful soul.

Hamlet loves Ophelia, but he renounces love, he renounces his studies, he renounces everything in order to achieve his goal, and he does: he kills the king when he finds him in a state of the blackest, most criminal sin. . . .

In closing, Monsieur, permit me to say that Shakespeare, by his colossal genius, belongs to the universe, and that a French, German, or Russian mind has the right to admire him and understand him. . . .

If Sarah read Max Beerbohm's review, or if anyone dared read it to her, she was consoled by an invitation to bring *Hamlet* to Stratford-upon-Avon. From there she went on to Edinburgh. How one would have enjoyed reading Beerbohm had he followed her to Scotland! There, because her costume failed to arrive on time, she played the melancholy Dane in Scottish kilts to the stupefaction of the audience.*

On leaving Britain, Sarah played Hamlet in the French provinces, Switzerland, Austria, and Hungary, returning to Paris in time to reopen her beautiful new theatre on 16 December with the first of fifty more performances of—*Hamlet*.

*The story of Bernhardt's ingenious, if startling, costume was told to us by Madame Annette Vaillant, whose mother, Marthe Mellot, was a moving Ophelia to Sarah's Hamlet. Bernhardt herself is possibly the only great actress who played both Ophelia and Hamlet.

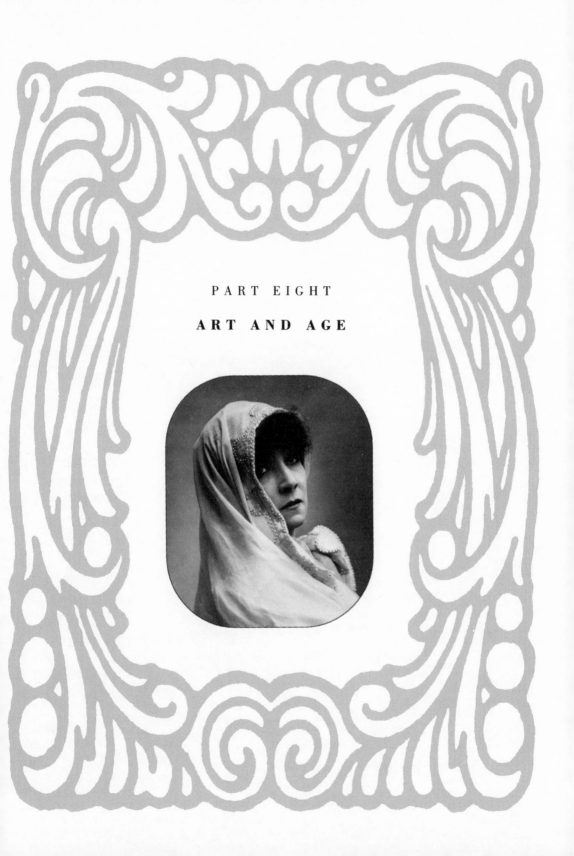

PART EIGHT

ART AND AGE

Sarah in the title role of Racine's *Phèdre*

IN THE fall of 1899 Bernhardt and Rostand made a trip to Austria. It was not only a love tryst as many supposed.* Sarah had engagements in Brünn (now Brno), near Vienna. Together they planned to visit Schönbrunn, the eighteenth-century castle that was to be the setting for *L'Aiglon*, the play he was writing for his "adored Sarah." It was an engrossing time for both: for Rostand, because he had almost completed his verse drama and was eager to verify the details described in his stage directions; for Sarah, because she had studied the play with passionate interest and lived for the moment when she could transform herself into Napoleon's seventeen-year-old son, the ill-fated Duc de Reichstadt.

Rostand was no longer the obscure versifier whose pen dripped mystical, some thought half-baked effusions about princesses and evangelists. Two years before, he had swept the Symbolist cobwebs away and produced his scintillating and immensely popular *Cyrano de Bergerac*. Success had not gone to his head. On the contrary, he was still the quiet young dreamer who worshiped the aging Bernhardt and took vicarious pleasure in her prima-donna ways. Proof of that is found in his fond recollections of Sarah in Austria.

After the first performance in Brno, they took Bernhardt's private train back to Vienna. On the way Sarah noticed a sign that read Wagram. She was thunderstruck. Out there in the dark were the very plains where Napoleon brought Austria to its knees, the plains that were the scene of the fifth act

*When we asked the French ambassador to the United States, Robert de Margerie (who is Rostand's great-nephew), if he thought their affair was a serious one, he replied: "*Je dirais plutôt que c'était une étape sur la route de l'amitié*" ("I should say it was more a wayside stop on the road of friendship").

of *L'Aiglon*. Here was an opportunity for historical research, a chance to soak up atmosphere for the play. A torchlit pilgrimage must be arranged at once. The following morning Bernhardt's Austrian manager, an obsequious white-haired gentleman with an infinite distrust of actresses, was summoned to her hotel suite.

Rostand remembered that the poor fellow turned deathly pale when Sarah told him her plan:

"To Wagram? Organize a pilgrimage to Wagram? You cannot be serious, Madame," he lisped, making negative gestures with his plump little hands. "There is nothing of interest in that dreary hole."

"I don't give a damn," said Sarah in a tone that suggested contempt for all the practical businessmen she had had the misfortune to meet. The manager persisted. The place was miles from the station. Furthermore, where would he find horses, carriages, lights, and all the other equipment they would need? These, replied Sarah, were insignificant details.

"Most divine of living beings, you are demanding the impossible. There is nothing to see but beetroots and potatoes."

"That will be quite enough," said Sarah, coloring her golden voice with a glint of steel. "Arrange it any way you like, but arrange it as soon as possible."

A week later Bernhardt and Rostand were on their way from Brno to Vienna once again, when, suddenly, the train faltered, heaved, and came to a screeching stop. They were in Wagram, but an unbelievable Wagram. The dreary station had been hung with garlands of paper flowers. Hundreds of flaming torches turned night into day. Soldiers, resplendent in helmets and gold braid, stood at solemn attention. To the sound of a booming cannon, an official stepped forward, clicked his heels, and begged his illustrious visitor to allow him the privilege of showing her the site made sacred by the great Napoleon. And might he be permitted to add that the humble earth would be made even more sacred at the touch of her footstep? Bernhardt stood transfixed, radiant, a gracious queen accepting the homage of a chivalrous subject. But just as she was about to step down from the train her eye caught the station clock. It was two, unmistakably two o'clock in the morning.

"But this is impossible," she gasped. "Do you realize how late it is?

Is something wrong with the clock?" "No, Madame," was the reply. "The clock is in perfect order."

At this Bernhardt, no longer a queen but a weary actress at the end of her strength, turned to the engineer, shouting: "Start the train! *En route! En route!*"

"Oh, the mayor and the officials!" [Rostand wrote]. "I shall never forget their faces when the train began to move, their stupor, their frightened round eyes as Sarah retreated while the mayor was still 'speechifying.' I can still see him, his dignity shattered, surrounded by his committee and those sad paper flowers." As the train gathered speed, Bernhardt sank into her chinchilla coat, and fell asleep as though nothing had happened.

When Rostand first read *L'Aiglon* to Bernhardt and her company, they had been moved to tears. Their response was not surprising as the piece has the patriotic fervor of a national anthem. Moreover, it paints a touching portrait of Napoleon's son, who died in exile at the age of twenty-one. Much of *L'Aiglon* takes place in Schönbrunn Palace, where the duke is kept on a tight, if golden leash by Metternich and his cohorts. It is a situation that lends itself to tea parties, masked balls, and moonlit gardens. Against this background, L'Aiglon and Flambeau, a grizzled veteran of the Napoleonic Wars, hatch a farfetched plot. They plan to raise an army of Bonapartists, march into France, and recapture Napoleon's imperial throne. But L'Aiglon is not the Man of Destiny his father was, not the Imperial Eagle, but a mere eaglet, touching but ineffectual. Still, he has great appeal, and, in the moving last act, as he lies dying, he is seen not only as a pawn on the chessboard of history, but as a tragic figure who prefers to die rather than relinquish his quixotic dreams of glory.

Sarah approached her role with characteristic enthusiasm. For weeks before the opening, she would receive her visitors at home, sword in hand, dressed in the dashing uniform the young Paul Poiret designed for her so that she would learn to feel comfortable in it.

Sacha Guitry, whose gift for amusing, theatrical exaggeration was even greater than Sarah's, described the preparation of *L'Aiglon* in his memoirs, *Si j'ai Bonne Mémoire (If Memory Serves).*

Daily rehearsals were called at one-fifteen for one-thirty. At least, that was what the call-board said, for only the supernumeraries were punctual.

The actors would stroll in, one after the other. My father never appeared before two or two-thirty. Edmond Rostand would turn up at three o'clock, and, at about ten to four Madame Sarah Bernhardt would make her entrance. Everyone stood up, the men removed their hats, and each in turn stepped forward to kiss her hand. As there were no fewer than sixty people on the stage, that took a good half-hour. Immediately after the kissing of the hand, Mme Sarah Bernhardt withdrew to her loge to dress, for in order to feel more at ease she rehearsed *L'Aiglon* in the costume of Lorenzaccio. As soon as she was ready, the rehearsal began. But at five o'clock it was interrupted for Mme Sarah's "cup of tea." The entire company would patiently, affectionately, respectfully watch her drink her tea. Everything this woman did was extraordinary, but those who surrounded her found it perfectly natural that she did nothing but extraordinary things. And here you have the reason *L'Aiglon* was in rehearsal for five or six months!

L'Aiglon was first performed on 15 March 1900. The première was triumphant, some said the most triumphant in theatrical history. Certainly it came at an appropriate moment. The French, for all the brouhaha about the Belle Epoque and the Great Exposition that year, were at a low ebb with the ever disturbing *Affaire Dreyfus*. And here was their Sarah in military uniform uttering speech after cymbal-crashing speech to the glory of France. It was patriotic, unifying, inspiring. People wept openly. Ovation followed ovation.

With *L'Aiglon* Sarah became a folk heroine. Everyone, rich and poor, young and old, Dreyfusard or anti-Dreyfusard, went to the play. Thousands bought picture postcards of her in the role. Buttons and medals bearing her profile were displayed in the shops. Children wore copies of her trim white uniform. And the master chef Escoffier created Pêches L'Aiglon to honor her.

Soon after the première, Rostand came down with pneumonia and moved to a house at Montmorency on the outskirts of Paris, so close that when a breeze came up off the Seine the poet liked to think he could hear "bravos" being wafted all the way from the Théâtre Sarah Bernhardt. That was imagined comfort. His real consolation came with Sarah's daily visits. Rosemonde Rostand remembered her stepping out of her "enchanting carriage, all laughter, dressed in a chinchilla coat and up to her ears in gauzy lace." Rostand was eager to hear the news. How did Guitry do yesterday? Which act went best? How many curtain calls? Who was there? Did Jules

Renard appear backstage? Had Anatole France liked it? And Montesquiou, and Sardou, and the Comtesse Greffulhe, and the Prince Murat? Sarah laughed, imitated them all, and recounted the latest gossip. Then, suddenly realizing it was late, she kissed the Rostands good-bye, presented a bouquet of violets to her pale *poète chéri*, and left, her mind already on the first act.

Bernhardt gave two hundred and fifty performances of *L'Aiglon*. Then, lucrative contracts in hand, she, Coquelin, and a company of thirty left for a six-month tour of the United States. It is heart-warming to think of the well-seasoned troupers going off together to show their wares in America after forty years of friendship. But more than mutual admiration was involved. Coquelin, son of a baker, and Sarah, daughter of a cocotte, had risen to undreamed-of heights. And now, close to sixty, they were the last practitioners of an acting style handed down by performers who had worked with Victor Hugo, Dumas, and Rachel. It was this Romantic heritage, combined with their magnetic personalities, that gave them such grandeur, such authenticity, and such a magisterial sense of themselves as artists. One envies those who saw Sarah during her two-week engagement at New York's Metropolitan Opera House, in a performance that earned her the headline: SARAH BERNHARDT IN L'AIGLON MAKES GREATEST TRIUMPH OF GREAT CAREER. One also envies those fortunate theatre-goers who saw the zestful Coquelin as Cyrano de Bergerac, a portrayal that inspired Henry James to call him "the Balzac of actors."

Despite the praise, or perhaps because of it, they liked to cut up backstage. *"Allons tuer Coq!"* ("Let's kill Coq!") was Sarah's cry when places were called for the murder scene in *La Tosca*. In that same scene, having stabbed Scarpia to death and completed the "business" of placing candles around his corpse, Bernhardt reached for the crucifix she was meant to lay on his heart. To her horror it was nailed to the wall. After a humiliating tug or two, she gave up the struggle, shrugged her shoulders, and, turning to the audience, said: "Oh well, he doesn't deserve it anyway." Dead or not, the corpse could not resist a wink, for it was Coquelin himself who had nailed the cross to the wall. There was every reason for their high spirits. They were earning enormous amounts of money and their press had never been better. Yet Sarah was faced with a nagging problem. The critics insisted on observing, however gallantly, that she was showing signs of her age. Their observations could not have come as a surprise to a woman so concerned about, and so dependent on her beauty. After all, each time she examined herself in the mirror she could see that her waist was thick, her hair dyed, and her face puffy. But that was only what the mirror told her. As soon as she turned away, illusion replaced reality, and she felt she was young, beautiful, vibrant, and seductive. The public too was willing to suspend belief, not because she had retained her youth, but because she had the power to make them think she had. Youth indeed was gone, but maturity had given her ways of supplanting it with the sleight of hand that comes with long years of experience. In December 1903 her success in *La Sorcière* (*The Sorceress*) was proof of this. The seventh and last play Sardou wrote for her, it was another of his melodramatic spectacles, complete with a fiendish villain (de Max) who hounds a helpless victim (Bernhardt, of course) to her death. Set in Toledo at the time of the Inquisition, it tells the blood-curdling tale of a passionate gypsy who loves, suffers, and, suspected of witchcraft, is burned at the stake.

Bernhardt at fifty-nine, and Sardou—who was now seventy-two—took great pains with the piece. Marguerite Moreno, a gifted young member of the cast, remembered the two veterans in rehearsal:

> It was an unforgettable experience to see them fight for their rights with all the cleverness and verve, the energy and endurance they possessed. Suddenly Sardou climbed up on a table. And what a sight he was in his eternal black velvet beret and white silk foulard. First he mimed a scene and Sarah spoke the text. Then they exchanged places and she mimed the scene and he spoke the text. During this exercise Sarah sipped coffee and nibbled a biscuit while Sardou had beer and sandwiches. Their bickering was endless.
>
> Sardou: "I want you to sit still during this scene."
>
> Sarah: "But, adored master, I'll look like a dead fish if I don't move."
>
> Sardou: "Listen, *ma petite*, I'm not an idiot yet, and I tell you that if you move you'll ruin the scene."
>
> Sarah: "I'd rather ruin it than sit still."
>
> Sardou: "Good God, Sarah, you *are* irritating." (Then, turning to the rest of the cast): "All right, ladies and gentlemen, let's take it again."
>
> The rehearsal went on till dawn, and when we left the theatre the streets were empty save for the milk wagons making their morning rounds.

M O S T critics were fully aware of the play's weaknesses and criticized the writer for falling back on old formulas, but some were nostalgically grateful to the old gentleman for creating yet another grand vehicle for Bernhardt. Their thanks were ecstatic: "Sardou succeeds, Sarah triumphs" . . . "Madame Bernhardt is incomparable, prestigious, glamorous" . . . "Never has she been more beautiful . . . Never has her voice been fresher . . . Never has her charm and tragic appeal been more devastating." Rather remarkable reviews for a woman approaching sixty. In her own way Sarah was a sorceress who had bewitched critics and audiences alike, for the old-fashioned melodrama of a Christian who has fallen under the spell of an infidel was to be one of the greatest successes of her later years.

The praise was welcome as Sarah had produced some lackluster plays before doing *La Sorcière*. It was not that she neglected contemporary French geniuses (there were few, if any in the theatre) but rather that she could not see beyond the boundaries of a certain French culture. And it was beyond those boundaries that Strindberg, Björnson, Ibsen, and Chekhov were creating modern drama. That was difficult to accept for an actress who had dedicated her life to the Romantic school and its ideals of beauty. Moreover, the very thought of playing middle-class Norsewomen, provincials shocked by immorality and wracked by neurasthenia, was inconceivable.

Certainly Maeterlinck's *Pelléas and Mélisande* was more to her taste. Sarah first saw it in London in 1898 with Martin Harvey as Pelléas, Johnston Forbes-Robertson as Golaud, and Mrs. Patrick Campbell as the untouchable Mélisande. It is difficult to know which she found more enchanting, the Symbolist play or the ravishing Stella Campbell in a golden gown uttering veiled hints and moving about a moonlit garden to the music of Gabriel Fauré.

Some years later, in 1904, Bernhardt, in London for her usual strenuous summer season there, engaged Mrs. Campbell to play Mélisande to her Pelléas. Sarah was at the Vaudeville playing *La Sorcière*, sometimes twice a day, rehearsing *Pelléas* in the mornings and giving matinées in outlying theatres on her free afternoons. When Graham Robertson suggested to Maurice that Sarah was working rather hard, and that perhaps the extra matinees were tiring, Maurice replied: "Well, what *is* mother to do in the afternoons?"

In her memoirs, *My Life and Some Letters*, Stella Campbell wrote: "At first I was very nervous at the thought of acting in French, but Sarah only laughed at me, saying Mélisande would speak French just as I did, and that she could play Pelléas with no one else. So I ventured—how dared I?" Daring or not the venture was a happy one. "I took over the direction," Mrs. Pat goes on to say, "and the company never smiled as I 'directed!' Sarah altered nothing, but asked my permission to turn her back to the wall of the tower, so that my hair might fall over her face."

Sarah adored Mrs. Campbell and thought her Mélisande was as perfect, pure, and harmonious as Maeterlinck had said it was. And Mrs. Campbell, properly awed at the idea of acting with her "dear Sarah," described her friend as a wonder who "carried her body with such ecstasy and breeding. Her voice was the voice of a youthful melancholy spirit, gradually melting into a tenderness that more than once almost struck me dumb for fear of breaking the spell." A publicity photograph of the actresses in a scene from the play bears witness to their feelings for one another. Pelléas embraces Mélisande tenderly while Mélisande, her splendid head thrown back, her lovely long neck straining upward, closes her eyes and abandons herself to dreams of love. The picture, sensuous and vaguely sapphic, might well have been the cause of a prudish outburst from Max Beerbohm, who refused to see the play. "Sarah is a woman and Mrs. Campbell an English woman," he wrote, "and by these two facts such a performance is ruled out of the sphere of art into the sphere of sensationalism."

Stella Campbell had many kind things to say about Sarah in her memoirs. "At one moment," she recalled, "Sarah was hard pressed for money. Wonderful to relate, I had a hundred pounds in the bank, and I thank heaven that I was able to do her a service. During a performance of *Pelléas and Mélisande*, Sarah Bernhardt returned the hundred pounds to me, in five pound notes, in a little silver casket, before the many people who were in my dressing room. She said how grateful she was to me—the simple graciousness of her act! Did she ever know, I wonder, how my heart almost choked me?

"In July 1905, a year later, on Madame Bernhardt's next visit to London, she and I went to the provinces meaning to give only a few performances of the play. Sarah paid me 240 pounds a week, 35 pounds for each additional performance, and all traveling expenses. I provided the scenery and costumes. We met with such a brilliant success that we played it every day for three weeks." (One Dublin critic took a more somber view. "Mrs. Campbell," he wrote, "played Mélisande, Madame Bernhardt Pelléas. They are both old enough to know better.")

"The most beautiful performance I have ever seen," Mrs. Campbell wrote, "was a performance Sarah gave of Phèdre—she held a crowded house spellbound for over two hours with scarcely a movement or gesture to detract from the lovely alexandrines—the great pulsating passion seemed to wind about the audience like a web—it was magic. The world knows her genius; but not everyone knows the thought and affection she has always ready in her heart for her friends."

It was far easier for Sarah to be considered a sterling character in London, where she was a bird of passage, than in Paris, where she was known less for her kindness and more for her ruthless ambition and overbearing ways. And so it was not surprising that Parisians did not share Mrs. Campbell's wide-eyed enthusiasm.

Among those who saw her clearly was Aurélien Lugné-Poë, the enterprising director who introduced Ibsen's *Rosmersholm* and *The Enemy of the People* to the French as early as 1893. Sarah knew him as a matter of course—knew too that he hobnobbed with strange young writers and painters such as Alfred Jarry, Edouard Vuillard, and Pierre Bonnard, all of whom she thought would come to nothing if they continued to write nonsense and cover canvasses with unintelligible daubs. Still, she was not blind to Lugné-Poë's talents and helped him whenever she could. One day he asked her to see Suzanne Després, the actress who had just made a great stir as the young boy in Jules Renard's *Poil de Carotte* (*Carrot-Top*), a role brilliantly created by Sarah's Ophelia, Marthe Mellot. Sarah could hardly refuse since Renard was a frequent guest at her house and Suzanne was Lugné's mistress.

The Great, the Incomparable, the Divine Sarah [Lugné wrote] was magnificently intuitive and quite—how shall I put it—offhand. Or rather she pretended to be when it suited her purpose. She fascinated others with a flow of songful words that were pure enchantment. Suzanne admired her profoundly and never missed her performances of *Phèdre*. She went to them as to a lesson and returned overwhelmed by the experience.

"You must go backstage and congratulate her," I said. "But she doesn't know me," my shy Suzanne replied. Finally, at my insistence, she got up her courage. The great actress's dressing room was swarming with admirers when Suzanne, still teary-eyed from the performance, was introduced. But the closer she got to Bernhardt, the more uneasy she felt. Not so much because of the Divine One but because the others were staring at her in a most obnoxious way. At last someone—the faithful Pitou no doubt— called out Suzanne's name. And there was the exhausted actress seated in an armchair, receiving compliments with an abstracted air. "Where is she? Where is she?" the tragedienne asked, stressing each syllable in her precise, dental way. "Let me see the little one." This, as though the little one was not standing at her side. "Come closer, closer. There we are." (Imagine the timid, rebellious Suzanne confronting Phèdre-Sarah and managing to smile.)

"Oh," Sarah continued, "look at that charming face—just look—and she is playing a carrot. It is you who are playing a carrot, is it not?" At this point Suzanne could not master the strength to say, not a carrot but *Poil de Carotte*. If only Renard had been there to protect her! Sarah could not stop. "What a pretty smile! You only play character bits, is that it? Nurses and things like that. Where are your breasts? You must join my company. I'll have you play real women, women like me, like the rest of us. Come and see me after the Sunday matinee. I have a ravishing part for you. Enough of those character parts, enough, enough. Just imagine this darling as King Carrot!" Suzanne was skeptical when she went backstage that Sunday, but Sarah recognized her at once. "Yes, yes," she said, "I have a fine role for you. Not a weird character, not a carrot—I myself shall play a *grande amoureuse*, a passionate *femme fatale*. And you, you'll be—a Chinese woman." Suzanne left the dressing room grateful but bewildered. *Poil de Carotte*—in China! And so the little affair ended. I've forgotten who played the Chinese woman.

In 1905 Sarah set out on a long tour of the Americas. It was a courageous undertaking, as her right knee had bothered her for some time and she found it painful to walk. Reynaldo Hahn, who was with her in Belle-Ile the summer before, described her condition:

I watch Sarah walking, leaning on her stick. It upsets me to see how she suffers with each step. From time to time she stops to rest on some pretext or other, pointing out something in the distance or looking at a flower. She chatters and smiles stoically and utters no complaint. Yesterday Clairin whispered to her: "You're in pain."

"Just a bit, Jojotte dear, don't worry."

But sometimes one can see that she is in pain. She is working at a play—*Adrienne Lecouvreur*. It is an odd idea. But she likes the character and does not want to act Scribe's and Legouvé's version any more because she finds it so bad. I say: "It might be mediocre but you had success with it, as did Rachel."

"I don't know how Rachel managed, my darling, but I can't do anything with it."

I remind her of the memorable effects she achieved in it. But nothing will make her change her mind.

As it turned out, neither Sarah's knee nor her new play was any good. *Adrienne Lecouvreur* was a failure. Far more serious, when Sarah arrived in Buenos Aires for her first engagement, her knee was abscessed and she was forced to have an operation. Three months later she had an accident in Rio de Janeiro. It happened at her last performance of *La Tosca*, when the heroine throws herself to her death from the parapet of the Castel Sant'Angelo. Normally, thick mattresses were placed behind the set to cushion the fall. This time there were none, and Sarah landed on the bare boards. Moments later her knee had swollen to twice its size. Ominously enough, it was the same knee she had injured when, as a child, she fell from her nurse's window in her eagerness to catch up with her Aunt Rosine.

Sarah did not stay in Rio, despite urgent pleas from her friends. Instead, she took an ocean liner to New York, where she was due to play in November. As soon as she was carried to her stateroom the ship's doctor came in to examine her. But he had dirty fingernails, and she would not allow him to touch her. Her knee was no better when she got to New York, and her first appearances were cancelled. Finally, it improved, and, good trouper that she was, she decided to go on with what was billed as the "Farewell American Tour of Madame Sarah Bernhardt."

Her good-bye to America was not without drama. In Quebec, religious fanatics threw rotten eggs at the company after the archbishop denounced *La Sorcière* as blasphemy. Their chief target was de Max, who played the

Grand Inquisitor. He received an egg full in the face and, as Sarah said, would have been beaten to within an inch of his life had it not been for some Englishmen who helped him into a nearby café.

A letter from Irma Perrot, one of the minor members of her company, gives the sordid details:

New York 12 October

My dear Gastineau,

First we played a week in Chicago, an immense success for Madame Sarah (as we all now call her). Then a week in Montreal where the success continued in spite of a sermon printed by the Archbishop of Canada blaming those of the faithful who go to the performances of Sarah Bernhardt who is "more pernicious than ever now that she no longer has any talent!" She had scheduled Sardou's *La Sorcière*, which depicts fanatics in a bad light: Inquisition, torture, etc. The all-powerful clergy of Canada is afraid to fall from its pedestal! After that two days in Quebec. There triumph inside the theatre, hostility outside. Two groups. On one side the French Canadians, fanatic Catholics; on the other the English Canadians who are for us. Police, cries of "Kill the Jewess!" (no less!). When we left they threw stones at our carriages and beat us on the head with sticks all the way to the station, shouting "Kill them! Kill them!" One, a girl in my carriage, still has bruise marks on her arms and behind her ears. When we arrived at the station, we had to get our bags off and pay the coachman in a hail of sticks and stones. The coachman took advantage of the situation by making us pay twice the amount agreed on before he would let us have our hand luggage. How can it be possible in the twentieth century that fanatics can attack defenseless women. It's unbelievable. In Ottawa, another Canadian town, but an English one, the governor asked Madame Sarah and her company to forgive the culprits. The first cause of the trouble: the sermon by Archbishop Brusch! The second: An interview with Madame Sarah in which she said that Canadians, so advanced from many points of view, are still Iroquois Indians as far as art is concerned.

In Kansas, Sarah's private train jumped the tracks and she was jolted right out of her bathtub. "Fortunately, I was not hurt," the actress said, "but I would have been, had the train behind not stopped. For just think of it, we were at the edge of a steep cliff."

There were those who thought the cliff a figment of Sarah's imagination

since this was not her only narrow escape. According to her, she might have
been burned alive in the San Francisco fire had the date of their engagement
not been postponed. "Instead," she told the *Echo de Paris*, "I performed
after the catastrophe was over. Only one theater was left standing—a theater
modelled on a Greek temple. It was there I played *Phèdre*, an experience
I shall never forget."

In March 1906 Sarah made more news when she gave *Camille* in a huge
tent in Kansas City, Missouri, and in Dallas and Waco, Texas.

> These two informal presentations [a Dallas paper reported] were an
> outgrowth of the bitter war between the Klaw and Erlanger syndicate and
> the young Shubert brothers for control of American theatres. The struggle
> was so relentless that even the great Bernhardt was forced to bow to its
> consequences. Coming to Texas under the auspices of the Shuberts doomed
> her to whatever hardships any other Shubert attraction had to undergo in
> the syndicate-ruled provinces. In this case it meant performing in a 5000-
> seat tent that was put up in an abandoned cornfield near a bicycle park.
>   Arriving from New Orleans, the French star had a special train of seven
> cars shunted onto specially laid tracks just outside the park. (Here, in-
> cidentally, she tried out a track-inspector's bicycle, mounting it with great
> agility despite her sixty-one years.) She had just gone hunting near New
> Orleans, where after playing matinée and evening performances she rose
> at 4 a.m. for some snipe shooting. She bagged as many as sixteen birds,
> she told us: a tribute to her marksmanship. Despite these exertions she
> seemed quite as young as she did sixteen years ago. The performance
> itself was a fiasco. Only a handful of spectators could see or hear the
> actors, and the stubble of cornstalks underfoot tore the dresses of many
> of the women present. All was confusion. A huge crowd had gathered
> outside the canvas theatre when the management opened the gates. Several
> thousands immediately surged in, sweeping ushers and policemen aside.
> Before order was restored, hundreds more had broken in. They were
> latecomers who had arrived by carriage and trolley car.

   The Waco performance was more orderly. In San Antonio Madame
Bernhardt gave *Camille* in a music-hall saloon. In Houston, the same play
was performed in a skating rink.
   If Sarah was put out by these primitive arrangements, she looked

back at them through rose-colored glasses. Never had she made so much money, she told Louis Verneuil; her name alone had such magic that people travelled for miles to see her. One night a cowboy rode up to her "big tent" and asked for a seat. There were none left, the cashier told him. "But I came three hundred miles on horseback just to see her," he said. Then, to add weight to his argument, he drew his revolver. At this, the cashier produced a standing-room pass and an apology for the partial view. "That's all right as long as I get in," he drawled, adding, "by the way, what does this gal do—sing or dance?"

Before leaving America Sarah played a week's engagement at the Lyric Theatre in New York. Twenty-six years had passed since she first appeared in that city, an explosive young woman out to make her fortune in the New World. Now she was making her final bow and the public was moved. Long lines of admirers queued up for tickets. The young went to see her for the first and last time. The critics found her greater than ever. Society leaders who had shunned her as a loose woman opened their doors to her—often in vain. With all this Sarah might well have thought farewells a good thing. In fact, she was to make three more "farewell tours" of America.

"I come home with fresh élan," Sarah told the press when she arrived at Le Havre. She was not exaggerating. That summer in Belle-Ile she worked on two new plays, supervised the décor and costumes, and put the finishing touches to her memoirs. Her efforts bore fruit—especially in the case of the memoirs, which are in print in France to this day. Max Beerbohm reviewed the book in 1907. His reactions help to explain the fascination Sarah held for the English public.

"Imagine a somnambulist awaking to find himself peering down into the crater of a volcano," Beerbohm wrote, "and you will realize how startling Mme Bernhardt's book has been to me. Hers is a volcanic nature, as we know, and hers has been a volcanic career; and nothing of that volcanicism is lost in her description of it. It has been doubted whether she really wrote the book herself. The vividness of the narration, the sense of what was worth telling and what was not, the sharp, salt vivacity of the style—all these virtues have, to some pedants, seemed incompatible with authenticity. I admit that it is disquieting to find an amateur plunging triumphantly into an art which we others regard as a close concern of our own. When Sarah threw her energies into the art of sculpture, and acquitted herself very well, the professional sculptors were very much surprised and vexed. A similar disquiet was produced by her paintings. Let writers console themselves with the reflection that to Sarah all things are possible. There is no use in pretending that she did not write this book herself—the rushing spontaneity that stamps it is Sarah's own."

One statement in *My Double Life* struck Beerbohm particularly: "I have seen four executions, one in London, one in Spain, and two in Paris." Was Sarah dragged to them by force, he asks. "No, she appears to have gone to them of her own accord."

Indeed, she waited all night on the balcony of a second-floor flat to see the execution of the anarchist Vaillant, whom she had known personally and admired. After the blade had fallen, she mingled with the crowd and was "sick at heart and desperate. There was not a word of gratitude to this man, not a murmur of vengeance or revolt. She felt inclined to cry out: 'Brutes that you are! Kneel down and kiss the stones that the blood of this poor madman has stained for your sakes, for you, because he believed in you!' You, gentle reader, might not care to visit an execution—especially not that of a personal friend. But then, you see, you are not a great tragedian. Emotion for emotion's sake is not the law of your being. It is because that is so immutable, so overwhelmingly the law of Sarah's being that we have in Sarah—yes, even now, for all the tricks she plays with her art,—the greatest of living tragedians. If ever I committed a murder, I should not at all resent her coming to my hanging. I should bow from the scaffold with all the deference due to the genius that has so often thrilled me beyond measure. And never has it thrilled me more than through this unusual medium."

In her memoirs Sarah spoke of various enemies but seldom named them. She did not spare her fellow actors in the same way. In her opinion, Henry Irving was an admirable artist but not an actor. Coquelin was an admirable actor but not an artist. Réjane was both artist and actor, but only when she felt so inclined. Eleonora Duse received special attention. She was "more an actress than an artist. She walks in the path others have laid out for her." (By others, of course, Sarah meant herself.) "To be sure, she does not imitate them. Instead she plants flowers where there are trees and trees where there are flowers. But she has never created a personage one can identify with her and her alone. She wears other people's gloves but puts them on wrong side out. All this is done with infinite grace and an unconscious abandon. She is a great, a very great actress but she is not a great artist."

The criticism was unclear, unjust, and unwarranted, and Duse was offended—so offended that when Sarah again offered her the use of her theatre, she refused to accept it. "At this point," Duse wrote to her onetime idol, "I cannot ignore the judgment you expressed on my art. I cannot ignore it, admit it, or forget it, because one does not like to forget that which sets vibrating in us the most fertile of powers. But—the memory of your artistic judgment must not make me forget your first kindnesses *for each hour in life has its particular value* and at this moment, I prefer to recall the hour when you were perfect and good to me."

Duse was writing from a position of strength. She was about to give a short season at Lugné-Poë's intimate Théâtre de l'Oeuvre and was happy to be associated with that idealistic champion of the avant-garde. Happy too, because she would be playing to a select group of intellectuals, not to the large, often undiscriminating audience that frequented the cavernous Théâtre Sarah Bernhardt. Moreover, Duse was now recognized as the supreme Ibsen player, whereas Bernhardt continued to tread the well-worn path of Romanticism. Not that Sarah ignored Ibsen completely. In 1906, the year of his death, she gave one performance of *The Lady From the Sea* in Geneva. But even the acclaim of public and critics did not encourage her to repeat the experience.

Léon Daudet spoke for Sarah as well as for himself when he wrote: "Ibsen's works have an original, painful beauty. But his laughter is a sneer, his melancholy a congenital cramp, his dialogue a series of mutual reproaches. His characters all seem suicidal. They inhabit dark cellars of bitterness and fruitless lust. One imagines they have never sipped wine or gazed at a sunny landscape. The moment they have a wife, a fiancée, or a *petite amie* they do nothing but interrogate her, scrutinize her, terrify her, wrest her secrets from her, so that they can catch her out later. The women behave just like the men. If that is northern love, then long live Romeo and Juliet, Don Quixote and Dulcinea!" Daudet was one of the most brilliant men of his generation, but his judgment was warped by a mistrust of anyone who was not French, Catholic, and anti-Dreyfusard. Had he looked more closely at his beloved Balzac, he might have noticed that several of Ibsen's characters are related to the vengeful Cousine Bette and the inquisitorial Vautrin.

Sarah's interests lay elsewhere. She was not an intellectual but an actress concerned with extending her gallery of mythical characters: larger-than-life heroines with whom she could take flight, preferably in verse. Ibsen did not fit the bill, nor did Strindberg, or Chekhov, the other great dramatists of the time. Curiously enough, Parisians were to come round to Sarah's view. After 1910, the Scandinavian works were less frequently performed in France. Chekhov, however, remained a favorite, perhaps because the French were more in tune with the Slavic temperament than they were with what Sarah dismissed as "*des norderies*" ("that northern stuff"). It was not long, however, before the French came full circle. What Sarah called "*des norderies*" have for many years been staples of the Parisian theatrical scene.

In 1906, she appeared as Saint Theresa in *La Vierge d'Avila* (*The Virgin of Avila*), a grandiose spectacle by Catulle Mendès. The idea of Sarah playing a virgin saint caused a ripple of amusement. But the title was misleading. Mendès, an old hand at erotica, had written a suggestive piece, a compendium of the sexual ambiguities attributed to nuns. The effect was rather like a wildly overheated version of *Dialogues des Carmélites*, the Bernanos-Poulenc opera, what with Sarah swooning at her beloved Jesus' feet and falling into the arms of her amorous Carmelite sisters. *La Vierge d'Avila* was one of Sarah's "most sublime creations" according to the critic Adolphe Brisson in *L'Illustration*. Mendès too won high praise. "When a poet like Catulle Mendès, disdainful of halfway measures, of convention, of fashion and of the taste of our day, takes us to the highest levels of art, one must respect his noble effort." If the play was shocking, Spanish reaction to it was medieval. The archbishop of Avila ordered his congregation to circle the town walls in prayer to exorcise the sacrilegious effect of a play written by a Jew for a Jewess.

Like many an aging superstar, Sarah had found a successful formula and saw no reason to change it. What change could she make at her age? Her taste and gifts had little in common with the new crop of French plays, many of which were drawing-room melodramas disguised as social realism. But the main difficulty lay in the fact that Bernhardt had become an institution. As G. G. Geller, an early biographer of Sarah, wrote: "Certainly she was successful, always successful. But each triumph was so like the last that they become monotonous. Admiration for Sarah became a commonplace due to a certain snobbishness. It was chic for people to affect a slightly blasé attitude towards the great actress." Geller was thinking of those who had seen Sarah throughout the forty years of her career, who felt she had not outlasted her reign. They still attended her first nights, still went to refresh themselves with the sound of her voice and the beauty of her gestures.

Moreover, they took their offspring to experience the wonder of her acting. The young responded much as their parents had, with this difference: the older generation had seen Sarah as a modern young actress, the new generation saw her as a grand old woman whose adventurous past, lurid, enviable, and triumphant, had become legend. Jean Cocteau spoke for his generation in *Portraits-Souvenirs*:*

In our theatre-mad youth two great figures predominated: Sarah Bernhardt, Edouard de Max. For what had they to do with tact, with restraint, with proportion, with anything *comme-il-faut*, this royalty of the *comme-il-ne-faut-pas*, these tigers who licked themselves and yawned in front of every-one, these forces of artifice at grips with that force of nature, the public? . . . Bernhardt and de Max frequently performed together, and I can never forget our delirium when the golden curtain parted after the play and the tragedienne took her calls, the talons of her left hand thrust between her breasts, her right, at the end of its long stiff arm, leaning on the proscenium arch. Like some Venetian palazzo, Sarah listed under the weight of her chokers and her fatigue, painted, gilded, prosthetized and propped amid a columbarium of applause. *La Sorcière! La Samaritaine! Phèdre! Andro-maque! . . .*

Her body was like that of some splendid rag doll. The broad breastplate, gleaming in the uniform of the Duke of Reichstadt or under the turquoises of Théodora, ended at the thighs with a sash which lashed her together behind and in front gathered itself in a huge knot that trailed down over boots or a train. Endlessly, she bowed: at her entrance, at her exit, at the end of each act; and her sublime acting, which exploded every convention, was one long swoon broken by screams of rage. . . .

Those were spectacles of the theatre inconceivable to our times, when we are so ridiculous as to suppose we have a sense of the ridiculous and take as an insult to ourselves the first unfamiliar sign of greatness. . . .

Madame Sarah Bernhardt presented the phenomenon of living at the extremity of her person in life *and* on the boards. By her extraordinary power of swooning she filled the arms of the world. She was said to be tubercular, doubtless because of the countless handkerchiefs she kneaded and crushed in her mouth, because of the red roses she chewed during her love scenes. And then, all at once, she would break off the swift flow

*Translation by Richard Howard.

of her automaton's voice to emphasize some salient truth all the more striking in that it occurred unrehearsed.

Cocteau met with Bernhardt's disapproval when he was sixteen.

I will tell you about the scandalous incident at the ball given by Robert d'Humières in the Théâtre des Arts, where he was the manager. De Max, the most naive man in the world, had the bizarre idea of arriving with a coterie. Our naivety surpassed his. We thought of his project merely as a chance to go to a costume party. Imagine De Max's pearl-gray electric automobile unloading us at the theatre: De Max wearing an eagle headdress and an Arabian veil, Rocher and Vesperto dressed as Arcadian shepherds and me, got up as a Heliogabalus with red curls, an overwhelming tiara, a train embroidered with pearls, rings on my toes and painted nails. We soon realized we had made a faux pas. Robert d'Humières quickly planted us in a stage-box. Everyone laughed at us. Sarah Bernhardt sent her assistant, Mlle Seylor, to me with a note saying: "If I were your mother, I'd send you right home to bed." I sniffled up my tears but my eyes were smarting and my face was streaked with mascara. De Max realized he had made a terrible gaffe. He led us out, straightened our hair, wiped off our makeup, and dropped us at home.

THE NEXT few years saw changes in Sarah's domestic life. Her elder granddaughter, Simone, married an industrialist, Edgar Gross, and moved to England, where she soon produced a child. In 1910 Maurice's wife, Terka, died and their younger daughter, Lysiane, moved into Bernhardt's house in the boulevard Péreire, where she remained until her marriage to Louis Verneuil on 10 March 1921. There is reason to believe that Verneuil married Lysiane in order to be close to Bernhardt. In any case the Verneuils were divorced in the summer of 1923, shortly after Sarah died. As Verneuil himself wrote: "Suddenly I was deprived of the only object, of the very reason, for all my activity. It took me months to make a new life for myself, which [Sarah Bernhardt] could no longer fill." From then on Lysiane called herself Lysiane Sarah-Bernhardt.

In September 1910 Sarah played an engagement at the Coliseum in London. Her decision to appear on the same bill as Yvette Guilbert and troupes of acrobats and jugglers seemed shameful to the more exigent of her Parisian admirers. Londoners were far more tolerant. "This afternoon Madame Sarah Bernhardt made her debut at the huge Coliseum theatre in London," a reporter wired *Le Figaro*. "She performed the second act of *L'Aiglon*. Always spirited, always full of the energy of genius, she conquered the huge audience. There was an indescribable ovation when she came out for her curtain calls. Madame Bernhardt will always be London's favorite artist. Her month-long stay will be one long triumph." Sarah's success set a precedent. Réjane and Jane Hading, Damala's co-star in *Le Maître de Forges*, were soon to do star turns at the Coliseum. Singers, instrumentalists, and dancers followed, feeling, as Sarah did, that half an hour's work, twice daily, and very well paid for, was worth a little indignity. Besides, the performers were delighted to make their arts known to the masses of people who wanted to see them but could not afford the high-priced tickets of the "legitimate theatre."

On 23 October 1910, her sixty-sixth birthday, Bernhardt left for the United States for her second "farewell tour." With her she brought her usual sure-fire hits, several of her recent productions, and, as her leading man, her handsome twenty-seven-year-old lover, Lou Tellegen. Needless to say, the liaison shocked her friends, her family, and her biographers. As Louis Verneuil wrote in *La Vie Merveilleuse de Sarah Bernhardt (The Fabulous Life of Sarah Bernhardt)*:

I should have preferred not to mention his name in this book. The interest of Sarah Bernhardt, almost seventy years of age, in Lou Tellegen is not a memory which it is agreeable to me to recall. But have I the right to ignore Lou Tellegen's career with her, after it was given such immense publicity in the French and American papers? All the Paris critics discussed and deplored it. Many even thought it their duty to explain to their readers, however discreetly, the reasons for the surprising solicitude of the great artist for this mediocre actor. On December 3, 1911, *The New York Times* announced their marriage, only to retract the statement the following day.

. . . For three years, until June 1913, both on tour and in Paris, he became Sarah's sole partner in the principal men's parts of all her plays.

Verneuil, who obviously loathed and envied Tellegen, went on to describe his good points: "Extraordinarily handsome, tall, thin, and clean-shaven, with a very delicate little head and blond curly hair, beautifully arranged, and the body of a young god, he was greatly in demand by sculptors, posing for Rodin among others."

Lou Tellegen described his first meeting with Bernhardt in his memoirs, *Women Have Been Kind*. Dorothy Parker, in her review of the book for *Vanity Fair*, said its title should have been "Women Have Been Kind But Dumb!" It was also referred to as "Kiss And Tell-Again." The book, as fatuous as its title, reaches rare heights of egotism and banality.

"As I start this chapter about the glorious Madame Sarah Bernhardt," Tellegen wrote:

I wish to emphasize that this will be a description . . . of my personal association with her, starting from the first moment I met her and finishing at the moment I left her four years later. . . . I was alone in her drawing-room [at the Carlton Hotel in London] and I smelled the fragrant roses which were in profusion all over the room. The door opened and there stood in the doorway—a creature from Heaven! Her gown was of white lace; her eyes seemed like stars. Her personality was overwhelming. Yes, I understood now why that gorgeous woman had the power to hold a world spellbound! . . . I had faced almost everything in life—danger, death, horror, murder, love, despair,—but I must admit that, however my emotions had become steeled through all the risks of my perilous existence, my heart seemed to stand still for a moment when I faced that immortal creature.

Then she came toward me and offered me her hand. Only Sarah Bernhardt could so gracefully present her hand to be kissed. Then she spoke, and I realized why she was called "The woman with the golden voice." Only these few words, "Enchantée de faire votre connaissance!" became a Beethoven symphony. I bowed low and kissed her extended hand with reverence. I was rather powerfully built and my legs had steel sinews, but at that moment they were as weak as water. . . . Her conversation was always animated. Underneath the frail frame of that wonderful woman, I sensed a volcano burning. But oh, with what refined touches she displayed her sense of humor! What a command of language, so *choisi* and to the point! I couldn't keep my eyes from her—she was everything—*Life itself*! I could not repress my astonishment . . . that this woman, who was then nearly sixty-nine . . . [Lou was exaggerating] had the spirit, looks, and vivacity of a girl of twenty.

The writer of these delirious lines was born in 1883. His mother was a Greek dancer, his father a Dutch general. At fifteen Lou eloped with his father's mistress. From then on, as the saying goes, he never looked back. He travelled the world, seduced countless women, became a prize fighter, a trapeze artist, a champion fencer, a self-confessed murderer ("when I had to kill to save my hide"), a gambler, and a gigolo. He was jailed in Russia for handing out birth-control pamphlets and in Paris for alleged robbery. Despite his busy life, he found time to study at the Conservatoire with Mounet-Sully's brother, Paul. During this period he worked as a model for Rodin, with whom he lived for a time. According to Tellegen, the great sculptor said little to him beyond "*Déshabillez-vous*" and "*Habillez-vous*" ("Take off your clothes" and "Put your clothes on"), but he did immortalize him in his monumental *Eternel Printemps* (*Eternal Springtime*).

After Tellegen graduated from the Conservatoire, he appeared in small parts at the Odéon, where he went largely unnoticed. Along the way, he met de Max and became part of the sexually ambiguous group of actors and poets who paid court to that "Sarah Bernhardt of actors." In fact it was de Max who sent him to Sarah when, in 1910, bored at the thought of joining her for another American tour, he proposed Tellegen as his replacement. It never occurred to him that Tellegen would soon be playing all his roles, not only at the Studebaker Theatre in Chicago and the Greek Theatre in Oakland, but at the Théâtre Sarah Bernhardt in Paris as well. No one accused Tellegen of being a great actor, but many thought him a great beauty. Sarah was among the dazzled. On the very day they met in the Carlton Hotel, she invited him to return for lunch in an hour and engaged him as her leading man.

"I read the contract," he wrote. "Four years! Earning a salary for two hundred and eight consecutive weeks! Looking at the figure I nearly collapsed. Never had I earned so much money before! A salary? A king's ransom!"

"Now return to Paris," she said. "Go and see my son, and get all the manuscripts and your passage to America. In the ten days before we leave, try to learn as many parts as you can. I'll see you on the boat and we'll have ample time for rehearsals during the crossing."

"And with this," Tellegen recalled, "the divine woman gave me one hundred gold guineas 'as an advance.' Then she smiled and disappeared into her private room."

One can assume that Sarah had plenty to think about after Tellegen left. She knew he was not up to her theatrical standards, but then she had forced Damala on the public and managed to get away with it. She was sixty-six and a great-grandmother; yet who was to say it was too late to play at romance—and with such an attractive fellow? Sarah had not been a courtesan for nothing. She knew that bribery would help keep Tellegen in line. Fortunately for her, the young man understood the rules of the game:

> After about six weeks when we were in some big city in Canada, Madame called me to her private car after the performance. She dismissed the people about her, Miss Seylor her companion, her private physician Dr. Marot, and Eddie Sullivan, the company manager for the impresario William Connor. She told me that she was going to increase my salary, which was already princely. I refused flatly. I told her that our contract must remain as it was—for the first year at least. She argued adorably, in her extremely quick volubility, but I stuck to my guns. "Then at least accept my second offer," she exclaimed! "Like Miss Seylor, Dr. Marot, and Mr. Sullivan, I want you to share part of my private car and travel in comfort. We have one compartment open, so please take it and be my guest."
>
> Of course *that* I couldn't refuse! . . . The next day I moved into my new "home" and from that moment I enjoyed the greatest friendship of my life—the superhuman kindness of that great woman. Of course, the members of the company could have fed me rat poison, but after all, I was now removed beyond the reach of their envy and jealousy.

In a letter to Ponchon, Sarah not only referred to Tellegen as her fiancé but enclosed two photographs to show how irresistible he was. She was more discreet in her letters to her son:

> My adored one: I press you to my heart on this first day of January 1911. I finished my New York performances yesterday amid an indescribable ovation. The box office receipts have been splendid: 530,000

francs for the month. I must say they find me better, more beautiful, and younger than ever. And the letters of love, passion, and madness! It's very amusing when I think of my great-granddaughter, little Terkette, asleep in London. . . .

Sarah may have been exaggerating when she said they found her more beautiful and younger than ever. At least one critic, Channing Pollock, was more realistic: "If Bernhardt's fires are burning out, they are burning out brightly and the departing flare, if it be a departing flare, is something approaching a blaze of glory. She represents the highest reaches of her art, thus far, and perhaps even for all times."

Sarah tended to avoid any mention of her young lover when she wrote to her son. But her discretion stopped there. She appeared on Tellegen's arm at public functions, insisted he share her interviews, fawned over him at company rehearsals, plied him with money, and kept him on a short leash when he showed interest in other, younger women. A photograph of Tellegen as Hippolyte in *Phèdre* shows him wearing Bernhardt's jewel-encrusted gold belt. One can imagine her, maternal and lustful at once, clasping the intimate object around the slim waist of her handsome favorite. The American press was quiet about Sarah's unconventional liaison either out of respect for her age or because it chose to think of Tellegen as her protégé rather than as her lover. This was hardly the case in France, where everyone was appalled, not so much by her unseemly romantic attachment as by her irresponsible obstinacy in giving Tellegen the classic roles that belonged to de Max. Thus, when she revived *Lorenzaccio*, Edmond Stoullig wrote: "Never, perhaps, has the great artist reached such heights. What applause, what curtain calls, what a triumph! But what a pity she is surrounded by such a bad cast! There is an actor in the part of Alessandro de' Medici who is positively worse than mediocre! 'Work hard at your tears,' a certain acting teacher used to say to a young pupil. 'Work hard at your laughs,' one might say to Mr. Lou Tellegen, whose perpetual bursts of laughter are as insufferable as they are unnatural."

The audience at the Théâtre Sarah Bernhardt was crueler still. Hoots of laughter greeted Tellegen's pronounced Dutch accent, groans of disapproval his inept delivery and wooden gestures. Even more painful, when Sarah took her solo bows, the theatre rang with bravos, but when he shared her curtain calls a great silence fell. This hostility did not seem to affect Tellegen, who felt sufficiently rewarded by a handsome salary, leading roles,

89. Sarah recuperating from the amputation of her right leg, 1915

90. World War I: shortly after her leg was amputated, Sarah entertained the
French troops at the front, 1915.

91. Sarah in one of her last films: Tristan Bernard's *Jeanne Doré*

92. Sarah with her great-grandchildren, Terka (left) and Bernard Gross, Nice, 1916

93. Sarah's funeral cortege stopped in front of the theatre bearing her name. It was estimated that 600,000 to 1 million people lined the streets.

and the protection of a loving, if much older mistress. During the season
Sarah directed Emile Moreau's *Queen Elizabeth* with herself as the aging
monarch and Tellegen as Essex, her young lover. The play, as close to her
heart as it was to her life, lasted little more than a week, but fortunately
Sarah had discovered a new way to recoup her losses. In 1900 she had
filmed *Le Duel d'Hamlet*, and in 1906, she had appeared in a film version
of *La Tosca* along with Lucien Guitry, Paul Mounet, and de Max. When she
saw it she recoiled in horror and demanded that the negative be destroyed
but fortunately or unfortunately it still exists. Two years later she was paid
thirty thousand dollars, a vast sum in those days, to play in a film of *La
Dame aux Camélias* with Lou Tellegen as Armand. It was said that she
fainted dead away when she saw it. But if she did, she recovered enough
strength to write to her American manager, William F. Connor, "I have
conquered a new world—that of the photo-play. I never thought, my dear
William, that I would ever be in a film, but now that I am two whole reels
of pictures, I rely for my immortality on these records." (All Bernhardt's
films were silent of course.) If today's movie audiences find *La Dame* absurdly
primitive, Sarah's Marguerite an agitated marionette, and Tellegen inept
beyond description, yesterday's audience was deeply impressed. SARAH THE
DIVINE IN MOTION PICTURES was the headline of a review that read: "Camille
was never more pitifully eloquent than in this mute record. Great genius
that she is, Bernhardt suited herself to her medium and the result is a long
series of photographs that are staccato in their expressiveness. Someone has
said that the pictures fairly crackle with life and project wireless messages
to the spectators. All over Europe the photoplay of *Camille* is a sensation
and Americans are eagerly awaiting the release of these reels which are now
in the control of the French-American Film Company."

Jean Cocteau wrote about this film with a poet's insight: "I recommend
to those who cannot admit the existence of sacred monsters that they go to
New York and see the film of Madame Sarah Bernhardt, preserved at the
Museum of Modern Art. At sixty [Sarah was actually sixty-six] she acts the
part of Marguerite Gautier. One is reminded of a famous Chinese actor who
said at the same age: 'I'm beginning to be able to play ingenues.' What
actress will play the great *amoureuses* better than Sarah in this film? None.
And when it is over, we find ourselves back in modern life, like the diver
who returns to the surface after having come face to face with a giant devil
fish in tropic seas."

Sarah was only one of the leading actors who lent their talents, or rather their flickering images, to the motion pictures. By 1912, the Comédie Française had appeared in excerpts from the classics, Réjane in a two-reeler of Sardou's *Madame Sans-Gêne* and Mounet-Sully in a drastically abridged version of *Oedipus*, one of his noblest stage efforts. The tragedian had not changed his ways. Still reluctant to take direction, he refused to adapt himself to the new medium, with the result that he appears as a mouthing, frenzied madman, a silent parody of Comédie Française declamation. Sarah was a more willing student, just as she had been years before when the two were acting partners. She conferred with the cameraman and paid attention to Louis Mercanton, her director. And so, while *Elisabeth, Reine d'Angleterre* (*Elizabeth, Queen of England*) is primitive and Sarah's performance far from subtle, the film remains a notable contribution to the early cinema.

In 1912 Adolph Zukor, a furrier turned movie magnate, formed a company called Famous Players. ("Famous Players in Famous Plays" was its slogan.) He then proceeded to buy the American rights to the film, paid Sarah the unheard-of sum of $360 a day, plus 10 percent of the gross, and arranged a lavish opening at the Lyceum Theatre in New York. It was reported that the audience stood and cheered at the end of the show. *Elizabeth, Queen of England* was distributed throughout the United States. A four-reeler, it reconciled exhibitors towards the longer film and earned $80,000 for Zukor on an investment of $18,000. With this money Zukor was able to make a distribution deal with Paramount Pictures, which he eventually took over. As for Bernhardt, that most famous of famous players, she added an unexpected feather to her multifeathered hat and became the first international movie star—and that in her late sixties.

In the fall of 1912 Sarah went back to the United States for yet another "farewell tour," taking Lou Tellegen with her. Her stay was unutterably sad. Her knee caused her agonizing pain, and she was reduced to giving half-hour performances on the Keith-Orpheum vaudeville circuit seven days a week. Her final stop was New York. There the press reported that "the French actress avoided standing unaided during the entire action." But there were good days as well. "So long as she can talk, she can act," wrote Burns Mantle in the *New York Times*, "for there is more true dramatic expression in her spoken lines than there is in the entire performance, tricks and all, of many an able and experienced actress a third her age. Her genius will hold her supreme to the end."

The *New York World* did not agree: "The voice that once rose from the depths of woe to the heights of passion now sounds like an echo; the long cat-like step that used to carry Bernhardt across the stage halts at the first table or chair; the sharp staccato, the liquid monotone, the splashing laughter are things of the past. Time has taken its toll."

Sarah's tour ended at the Palace Theatre in New York. "That night in 1913," Tellegen remembered, "was the last night I had the honor to appear beside her in public. At the finish the applause came so endlessly, in such vast tidal waves, that it seemed the public would not let her go. With tears welling in my eyes I held her hand. . . . At last she looked at me wearily, and going into the wings, I found a chair and brought it out to her. She seated herself there, bowing and smiling and weeping, while the applause did not abate for an instant. Although I returned with her to France I left her soon afterward to star alone. She herself said: 'Be wise, my child, learn English. They like you in America. There is your future!'. . . .

"Every moment I worked with her I knew the best that the theatre can give and, remembering the most glorious four years of my life, my eyes fill with tears and my heart again cries out 'Madame! Grande Madame! I am so alone without you!' "

Tellegen took Sarah's advice and went back to America, where he had considerable success as a matinée idol in silent films. In 1916 he married Geraldine Farrar, the beautiful, celebrated opera and movie star. For two years he lived the luxurious life of a Hollywood prince consort, but by 1918 they had gone their separate ways. Sixteen years later, sick, drugged, and penniless, he committed suicide by stabbing himself with a pair of scissors.

On her return to Paris, in December 1913, Sarah gave *Jeanne Doré* by Tristan Bernard. In it she played a humble shopkeeper whose son, Jacques, kills a man who has taken his fiancée from him. Jacques is condemned to death, and his fiancée refuses to see him. The final scene is especially poignant. The night before the execution Jeanne Doré goes to the prison to bid her son a final farewell. In the dark he does not recognize her veiled figure. Instead he takes her for his fiancée and pours out his love. Jeanne listens to his passionate words and longs to reveal her identity, but knowing it is his last moment of happiness she remains silent. Those who saw Bernhardt, pale and radiant in her sacrificial anguish, never forgot her performance. *Jeanne Doré* had a successful run. It was Sarah's last full-length play, and one of her last and finest films, at least as shown at the Cinémathèque in Paris.*

In 1914, Bernhardt was made a Chevalier of the Legion of Honor. It was high time. Hundreds of her admirers wrote to congratulate the selection committee, and the press took the occasion to rap its members over the knuckles.

The stubborn resistance which for so long has put obstacles in the way of decorating Sarah Bernhardt has finally given way [wrote one journalist]. . . . There was not a discordant voice in the joyful chorus. One wonders what objection there could have been in the first place. More than a hundred women [Louise Abbéma and Judith Gautier among them] have already received the rosette. It was not refused to Julia Bartet. I know that as the doyenne of the Comédie Française, that eminent artiste's position entitled her to special consideration. But Madame Bernhardt has other qualities and a prestige that should have been recognized by the committee. We were told they were afraid of setting a dangerous precedent. "After Sarah Bernhardt," they argued, "we will be obliged to decorate Mlle Y., Mlle G. and other actresses, singers—even dancers with influential friends." Their argument does not apply to the present case. Sarah Bernhardt cannot be confused with other women in her profession for she is exceptional, unique. There is only one Sarah, just as there was only one Rachel. She has given her heart and soul to the French drama. She is endlessly active, conquering, Napoleonic. She might have stayed at the Comédie Française, basking in its glory. Instead she formed her own company, toured the world, returned to Paris bringing the fortunes she made in the United States and lavishing them on extravagant productions and the poets who wrote for her to the honor of our theatrical literature. . . . In honoring Madame Sarah Bernhardt the State is honoring the Ambassadress of French poetry.

Sarah did more than lecture on the drama. She held regular acting classes on the stage of her theatre. "We all sat around in a wide semi-

---

*In most early films, whatever one sees in motion appears to be much faster than it actually was. The Cinémathèque has addressed this problem and reduced the speed of some of the films in its archives to what is obviously their "real" speed so that what one sees is no longer ridiculous. In the case of *Jeanne Doré*, Bernhardt's performance on film is a revelation.

circle," a student from England named May Agate remembered. "Madame Sarah was installed behind the producer's table down-stage, protected from draught by a curious tent-like contraption known as *le guignol*. Well, there she reclined in her easy-chair, swathed in her famous chinchilla coat, rug over her knees, elbows on the table, and chin cupped in hand."

In 1935 Miss Agate's brother James, the lively drama critic of the Manchester *Guardian* and later of the *Saturday Review*, asked his sister to add her impressions of Sarah to his autobiography, *Ego*.

The actress who I knew [she wrote] was a lady of infinite dignity. I used to watch her give lessons on the stage of her Paris theatre to pupils who were either artists of repute or humble students. Those who had no capacity were dismissed with a smile; upon such as showed a vestige of talent Sarah would bestow first a scolding, then an infinity of pains. To the younger pupils she was a veritable Mother Superior, and often the theatre took on the aspect of a convent. She played so many Empresses and Queens that towards the end of her life she would throw remarks over her shoulder, addressed to a court that was not there. I remember Sarah, on her seventieth birthday, sitting by the fire in my mother's drawing room, telling stories, and in manner and spirit as young and fresh and radiant as a girl of twenty. I remember the look of affection which she threw to my mother as the carriage rolled away. I remember how we gazed after it, and that presently, from the window, a bunch of flowers was waved.

My "recollections of Sarah" would take *tomes*. I have had in mind a little book of memories of her which, when I am an old lady keeping a wool-shop in Dorking, may get set down.* But in the meantime and in case it should never get done I should like to say something like this: No one has ever said how in *advance of her time* she was. Her flamboyance has been stressed so much that it has taken on the complexion of spuriousness in minds that never knew her. Even people who saw her remember the glamour to the belittlement of her intellect. Now, her personal magnetism was no flashy, calculated effect. You can't blame the sun for shining. She loathed pretentiousness and was regal simply because she couldn't help it. Indeed the words that were most often on her lips were *la pensée, le naturel, la*

---

*May Agate did write her "little book" in 1945. Called *Madame Sarah*, it gives a splendidly detailed description of the Bernhardt method of acting.

sincérité, and *dire juste* [thought, naturalness, sincerity, and intonation].

Truth was the whole secret of her greatness. There was nothing bogus about her—no intellectual vapourings or complicated theories. I never heard her use the word psychology, though God knows she knew more about it than anyone before or since. 'I've never been on the battlefield, but I know it's like that,' was what she said (before 1914) having given the most blood-curdling, hair-raising performance of the battle-field scene in *L'Aiglon*. She was the first person to dare to preach naturalness in the French Theatre (*theatre size*, of course) and to discard tradition. The Conservatoire and the Comédie Française are using methods she threw overboard half a century ago. My outstanding memory of her lessons is of one long outcry against the old school of acting. Their arm-waving and barnstorming must have been grotesque, but nobody saw it until Sarah came along and said it was meaningless. The proof is they are still at it, and not only in the remote provinces.

James Agate wrote that he could not "allow that about 'naturalness' and psychological mastery to pass entirely unchallenged," and the result was a heated meeting over a cold lunch. The next day May wrote a second letter to her brother saying: "I never said Sarah was of the naturalistic school of commonplace realism. She gave you the kernel without the husk. It all depends on how much you demand that acting should be portraiture of the photographic variety. Surely we know that all acting is mental. Her art seemed to me like modern painting or sculpture—she eliminated externals to give you pure thought—a process of simplification. . . . When I said 'psychology' I meant all that an actor need know about the mind and emotions of the character in hand—not text-book stuff."

"And now" James Agate concluded, "on the subject of Sarah, I am sworn to an Iago-like silence. From this time forth I never will speak word." The critic did not keep to his promise. No matter who he praised—Mrs. Patrick Campbell, Duse, Edith Evans, Garbo, Charles Laughton, Olivier, Gielgud, or Richardson—Bernhardt remained his star of stars, his standard of greatness. His reasons for this were strange but plausible. An instance was his comparison of Duse and Bernhardt. "Duse's art at its finest," he wrote, "still seems possible—as all modern acting must. Sarah Bernhardt's is not. It is extravagant, rare, with all that makes for glamour, and with the fascination of the impossible."

ON 3 A U G U S T 1 9 1 4 , Germany declared war on France. It was a death knell for Europe and the beginning of the end for Sarah. Her leg had been giving her excruciating pain and was now in a cast. The Germans were marching on Paris. Her friends were joining the great exodus to Bordeaux and Biarritz, Marseilles and Nice. But Sarah refused to move, or be moved, saying she had remained in Paris during the Franco-Prussian War and would stay there now. It was not stubborn patriotism alone that kept her shut up in the boulevard Péreire reading the grim war communiqués and cursing her age, her immobility, and her discomfort; it was the presence of Dr. Samuel Pozzi, the only surgeon she trusted completely. She had known the handsome, worldly Dr. Pozzi, or *Docteur Dieu* (Dr. God), as she called him, since her days at the Comédie Française, known and loved him. It was Georges Clemenceau, another old friend, who convinced Sarah to leave Paris when he told her she was on the list of hostages who would be shipped to Berlin if the Boches succeeded in taking the French capital. Toward the end of January 1915, Sarah rented a modest villa in Andernos, a fishing village and spa near Bordeaux, where it was hoped that prolonged rest with her leg immobilized would heal it. A letter Sarah sent Dr. Pozzi indicates that she had lost faith in this cure.

4 Feb 1915

My beloved Docteur Dieu: I beg you to take this letter seriously. On February seventh my leg will have been in a plaster cast for six months. I was suffering more than ever and asked the surgeon, Denucé, to remove it. The pain was caused by the cast which had pierced my flesh. It was nothing; it has healed; but it is as painful now as it was before. Listen to me, my adored friend. I beg you, cut off my leg a little above the knee. Do not protest. I have perhaps ten or fifteen years left. Why condemn me to constant suffering? Why condemn me to inactivity? Even with a celluloid cast I shall be handicapped and won't be able to perform. And horror of horrors, I shall always be in pain. My nights will always be anguished for it is then that my knee hurts most, nothing but my knee. With a well-constructed wooden leg I'll be able to give poetry readings and even make lecture tours. I'll be free to come and go without pain. Therefore, I beg you to cut off my leg, or give orders to have it done.

I cannot bear to be useless, confined to a chair as I have been for six months. It's clear to me that my leg will never fuse; I'm not young enough for that. I am not a conservationist by nature and I don't give a hoot for my leg. Let it run about where it wishes. If you refuse me I'll shoot a bullet into my knee and then it will have to be cut off. My friend, don't think I'm hysterical. No, I'm calm and cheerful. But I want to live what life remains to me, or die at once. You understand, my dear Sam, that between one apparatus and the other I prefer a wooden leg. That way I could take it off and bathe every day. That alone would improve my health a hundred percent. I'll give lecture tours, I'll give lessons, and be gay. I don't want to lose my gaiety. At this moment lads of twenty are losing their legs, and their arms, meant for embraces. And you refuse me! No, it's impossible. My leg must be cut off immediately. After a month I'll be free. Don't abandon me in this last painful stage. Be my devoted friend and I'll come running to Paris and give you my leg to cut.

I embrace you with all my loving gratitude

Four days before the operation Sarah sent a wire to Dr. Pozzi: "I spent the night in atrocious pain unable to take any more pills. I beg you to operate one day earlier. It's mad, it's odious. My friend, put an end to this useless torture."

As "one day earlier" was a Sunday, Pozzi was unable to reschedule the operation. In the end, afraid that Sarah might die under his hand, he authorized Denucé, a former student of his, to take his place. Mademoiselle Coignt, the young anesthetist who assisted at the surgery, left a record of the sad event.

At 10 A.M. the great artist was wheeled into the operating room. She was dressed in a white satin peignoir and swathed in pink crepe-de-chine veils. She seemed very calm. She sent for her son Maurice who came to embrace her. During the tender scene she was heard to say "Au revoir, my beloved, my Maurice, au revoir. There, there, I'll be back soon." It was the same voice I had heard in *La Tosca, La Dame aux Camélias, L'Aiglon.* Turning to Denucé she said: "My darling, give me a kiss." Then to me, "Mademoiselle, I'm in your hands. Promise you'll really put me to sleep. Let's go, quickly, quickly." In all this one could not help see the tragedienne putting on an act. I felt I was at the theatre except that I myself had a role in the painful drama. When I placed the ether mask on her face she cried out: "I'm choking, I'm suffocating. Take it off!" Meanwhile the indicator was rising normally. "I'll never fall asleep. Why this ether? Chloroform would have been better." Moments later she muttered, "Ah! That's good. It's working, it's working. I'm going, going, going. I'm gone." Now the illustrious patient was put on the operating table. Professor Arnagon takes her pulse. Professor Denucé, aided by Doctor Robère, makes the first cut. Five minutes later the leg falls off. The ligatures are sewn. The wound is dressed and the great tragedienne, crowned by her peignoir and satin-lined sheepskin, is wheeled back to her room. When she is in bed she screams: "I want my beloved son, my Maurice, my darling child!" He kisses her, saying: "*Maman,* you look just fine, you're all right, all right." "Where is Denucé and the young woman who put me to sleep?" "Madame, I am here," I said. "Ah, darling, you're nice. Come here, I want to see you." I try to leave but she detains me. "Darling," she says, "I like you, stay a bit longer." I tell her to be calm and not to talk. "I'm talking because I must speak a little. Oh, I'm suffering, suffering." The drama continues. One feels she is always acting, playing the role of someone who has just undergone a grave operation. Later that day I found the patient exactly the same as the woman I admired on the stage. Her eyes were made up, her lips painted.

It was a great joy for me to be so close to the actress, who, one might say, has ruled the universe through her art.

That day Denucé wired Pozzi: "Operation completed. Very rapid. No problems. Used minimum ether. All goes well."

Sarah was her old self when she wrote to Pozzi two months later. Gallant, and in a flirtatious, reminiscent mood, she did not mention her disability:

How is it that my infinite love and gratitude over so many years have not taken root and blossomed in your heart??? How is it that I feel the need to tell you again and again that there is no being dearer to me than you?

Can it be, dear friend, that I must open the box of memories we share to
let you breathe the perfume of those flowers we gathered together in the
garden of Life! No, I have not written to you! Why? There is no Why!
There is no Because! I love you tenderly, infinitely. I love you with all
the vital and intellectual force of my being, and nothing, nothing could
change this feeling, greater than Friendship, more divine than Love.

During her next months in Andernos Sarah tried several wooden legs, none
of which suited her. Finally, she solved the problem in her own way. She
had the wooden legs thrown out and ordered a sedan chair in which she
could be carried about. It was an admirable solution, one she managed with
the air of a Byzantine empress. An American admirer remembered her being
held aloft, "her arms full of roses, her mutilated figure a mass of velvets.
She was the personification of undaunted courage."

 Paris agreed when in October 1915 she appeared in *Les Cathédrales*,
a "scenic poem" by Eugène Morand. She was a sad but valiant sight as the
embodiment of the Strasbourg Cathedral, enthroned on a dais, in penumbrous
light. Unable to move, she delivered a long patriotic speech. Then a miracle
occurred. At the end of her tirade, she raised herself to her full height and
cried, "Weep, weep Germany! The German Eagle has fallen into the Rhine."
Never had her compatriots loved her more. Never, that is, until she went to
the front with a group of players from the Comédie Française. Beatrix Dussane, the actress and theatre historian, recorded the venture in her admirable
book *Reines de Théâtre* (*Queens of the Theatre*):

At that time Sarah was more loudly acclaimed than ever. Our generation
reacted badly, perhaps unjustly, to her fame and glory. Indeed, it seemed
monstrous somehow for anyone to have been idolized for so long a time.
"Why doesn't she retire?" we'd say. The young always find it easy to bury
the old.

 In 1916, we formed a group known as the Théâtre des Armées. Few
in number, we worked with humility, happy to provide our soldiers with
a little diversion, anxious not to soil our task with snobbism or publicity.
One day we were told that Sarah wanted to join us. I was to go to her
house to rehearse the cues that would lead into her monologues. I must
confess, I grumbled. What could old, helpless Sarah do under such difficult
circumstances?

The front was not pleasurable or brilliant, it was exhausting. Many of us, in fact, left a part of our young health behind. But Sarah! With her bouquets, her furs, her sovereign luxury—and her fragility, how could she be transported from barn to barn, from makeshift stages to army trucks? What would be left of her prestige after playing in poorly lit places or in blinding sunshine? Playing for men who knew her only as a legendary name? She would fall ill the first day, and that would be the end of the tour.

When I called on Bernhardt I was ushered into her white boudoir. She was seated in the depths of a large armchair. I remember thinking her extraordinary, with her thousand folds of satin and lace, her rumpled red hair, her ageless features, her wrinkles covered with every imaginable kind of makeup. It was upsetting, sad and upsetting. There she was, the great, the radiant Sarah, so small, so weak—a little pile of ashes. Then, like many before me, I witnessed a miracle. For two hours she rehearsed, went back over her lines, made cuts, ordered tea, asked about our trip, was in turn enthusiastic, touched, and amused. She saw everything, understood everything, anticipated everything. All this time the little pile of ashes never stopped throwing off sparks! I realized she had been born like that and would be like that forever! An unextinguishable sun burned under the painted, frilled decrepitude of the old actress.

Here we are en route. Oh, the railway station, that Gare de l'Est crossed by our bizarre procession! Sarah is lost in a floor-length tiger-skin coat, huddled up in her sedan chair. She smiles at everyone who looks at her so that they don't dare pity her. The only civilians on the train, we get off at Toul. The sedan chair reappears. It is painted white and decorated in Louis XV style. It, too, seems to smile as though it were just a caprice, rather than a sad necessity. The townsfolk look on, so moved that they forget to applaud or cheer our tragedienne. An automobile takes us to our first performance, given in an immense covered market-place in Commercy. There is a platform, a ramp and a curtain. The small lean-to assigned to Sarah has an earthen floor. One had to climb ten steps in order to reach the stage. Sarah seemed to like her temporary dressing room. In fact, she was delighted. The curtain was lowered while she was hoisted onto the "stage" and deposited in a shabby armchair. Three thousand young men (many with bandaged wounds) were told they were about to see Sarah Bernhardt. We waited for an ovation but it was long in coming, and even then there were only a few scattered bravos. The men had expected a film. Illustrious names meant nothing to these sturdy farm boys. Sarah sensed this and shuddered. Then she began. Her every word was vibrant, delivered in a pounding rhythm that mounted like a charge into battle. Her speeches evoked those heroic figures who plant flags on conquered soil. With her final cry "*Aux Armes*," the band attacked *La Marseillaise* and three thousand young Frenchman rose to their feet to cheer. Our performances continued: on the terrace of a château, in a hospital waiting room, in a decrepit barn packed to the rafters. I saw the genius of Sarah and I saw her bravery. No, we were not exposed to gunfire. It was not a question of that. It was her courage, her willpower that impressed us. At one moment I helped her dress. She went from chair to table leaning on my arm, or hopping on her poor, seventy-two-year-old leg, saying with that infectious laugh of hers: "Look, I'm just like a guinea-hen." The way she ignored her handicap was beautiful—a victory of the spirit over the failing flesh. One did not pity her, one admired her. I shall always remember her, that old woman of genius clopping along in her sedan chair or on her one leg, ready to give her flaming heart to those brave men who fought and died for us.

Sarah lived up to her motto, *quand même*, when she went to the United States in 1916. Thirty-six years had passed since America had first seen her, a tumultuous young woman eager for money, success, and notoriety. In those days society, or what passed for society, closed its doors to her for fear of being tainted by her old-world depravity, her being a Jew, and her shameless love of publicity. Now they welcomed her as a latter-day saint who had come to them not merely as an entertainer but as an envoy from war-torn France. A born crusader, Sarah spoke at Red Cross rallies, at benefits, and at other public meetings, urging Americans to join the Allies in their fight against "the hated enemy." Even more effective were the short scenes she performed—she could no longer sustain a whole evening—which, like *Les Cathédrales*, were designed to win sympathy for her ravaged country. After eight months of strenuous touring Sarah was forced to undergo a near fatal kidney operation. A few days later she was strong enough to send a reassuring letter to Maurice.

She had thought she would never see him again. Only her infinite love for him had given her the strength to fight, "breath by breath, death rattle for death rattle." Her condition was so grave, she continued, that she had written him a farewell letter in case of disaster. Now she was very well and was happily gorging herself on mussels and crayfish, *tête de veau* and *cassoulet*. She had spent enormous sums of money on doctors and hotel bills, on her staff, and on meals sent in from Delmonico's. To think she would be near him in February. She did not dare to anticipate such joy! This time, she promised, she would never leave him. She had suffered so much that surely her wish would not be denied. A few months later she wrote to Maurice to tell him: "I have donned my mask, my fool's cap and bells, and taken up my wanderings across America once again. How many cities there are, ugly and unknown. Some are fine, some ghastly. For example, here in Jacksonville, Illinois, there are thirteen thousand inhabitants: two hundred in an insane asylum, seven hundred in a house for the deaf and dumb, three hundred in a home for the blind, and three hundred in an orphanage. That makes three thousand who cannot come to the theater. It's idiotic!"

Your daughter [Lysiane was touring with Sarah] has brought me all the happiness and all the sweetness that I'd hoped for. What an adorable child, and how like you she is! At a large ceremony in Chicago I was named godmother to all the children of America. I recited some poems which Lysiane wrote for the occasion. . . . Au revoir, my adored son. How I wish I were arriving in France at this very moment. That would make me mad with joy. A thousand kisses—on your hair, your forehead, your heart. . . ."

In other letters Sarah tells Maurice that he is the son of her soul, the sweetness of her life, the dearest of her pleasures. She owes everything to him: her most elevated thoughts, her kindest acts, her striving after beauty. She has won her modest glory in order to make up for his fatherless state, for his being forced to bear her name. Then, perhaps thinking she had gone too far, she excuses herself, saying she knew he thought her effusions exaggerated. Exaggerated! Little did he realize how she restrained herself for fear of being found ridiculous. "You want me to stifle my feelings," she wrote. "That hurts me because it belittles my love. Oh! Maurice, be gentle with the heart that beats only for you."

FORTUNATELY for her, Sarah's responsibilities kept her from such sad, twilight broodings. She was having "immense success," she wrote, despite her years, her amputation, and her last painful operation. Most observers agreed. "Let it be understood," said a Philadelphia paper, "that she is not in need of the consideration of having been the greatest actress of a former generation. She does not evoke admiration because of her many recent sufferings but purely and simply because she is the greatest living actress." Others, like George Jean Nathan, took a much dimmer view: "To contend that Madame Sarah Bernhardt is still a great actress is to permit chivalry to obscure criticism. Hers is now a glory of memory . . . truly remarkable for a woman of her advanced years, but it is work, not acting. The public goes to the theatre less to venerate Sarah Bernhardt the actress than to see Sarah Bernhardt the freak."

Margaret Mower, a charming young American adjunct of Sarah's company, was to witness what Nathan was talking about. The beautiful, bilingual Miss Mower had been engaged to step out before the curtain and explain in English the plot of the scene that was to follow. She would never forget, she wrote in a short memoir, the night in Montreal when she first appeared with the troupe. Wearing a Fortuny dress bought for the occasion, she appeared backstage before the performance began:

The entire company was standing in a semi-circle awaiting the arrival of Madame Bernhardt. After a brief delay there was a stir, and I saw two men [Pitou and Emile, Sarah's factotum and secretary], carrying a sedan chair by its poles advancing to the center of the stage. . . . There was considerable maneuvering and I could hear impatient orders: "*Non, non, par ici. Doucement.*" (No, no, this way. Gently.) Madame Bernhardt was being installed in the exact position in which she would play *Aux Champs d'Honneur* (*On the Battlefield*), one of her patriotic numbers. That first sight was a decided shock. At that time seventy-two years old, the great actress, dressed as a wounded young soldier in a torn and blood-stained uniform, was stretched out on the floor, leaning against a property tree-stump. She wore a dishevelled blond wig and her makeup was dead white. Her red mouth was wide and her eyes were deeply shadowed with blue kohl. She wore puttees and soldiers' shoes. The effect was miraculously youthful in a macabre, melodramatic way. Now that she was comfortable, the members of the company approached, one by one, bowing and kissing her hand, murmuring *"Bon soir, Madame. Vous allez bien, Madame? Chère madame."*

Madame smiled charmingly, but there was a queenly aloofness about her. It was a queer little ceremony. Sadly enough, Sarah's actors were respectful only in her presence. Behind her back they callously referred to her as the old madwoman, or simply as the old lady.

Pitou, of course, was truly loyal, although, as Miss Mower wrote: "The pride he took in his association with Madame Sarah was colossal to the point of being comic."

Miss Mower's memoir reveals that while Sarah had aged, in some ways she had not changed:

When she performed at the Brooklyn Academy of Music, there was tremendous excitement backstage. I peered through the peep-hole and there in one of the front rows I saw Lou Tellegen and Geraldine Farrar, recently married, both of them handsome and radiant. Even I knew that Tellegen had been one of Madame's greatest favorites. Bernhardt outdid herself that night. She was tireless, radiant, "beyond herself" as one of the actors put it. The evening ended with *Camille*. Never had she looked so beautiful, lying there in her canopied bed with its embroidered sheets, her exquisite nightgown with widths of lace falling softly around her neck and wrists, her pale face and her halo of bright hair. Her cough, her cry for Armand, her joy at his arrival—all tore at the heart. From time to time I peered out at Tellegen who had been her Armand so often. His face was an inscrutable mask. The scene ended with a tremendous crash of applause, and after the curtain calls Madame had herself taken quickly to her dressing room, from which she ordered all visitors except Tellegen be excluded. I shall never forget the wait there behind the scene. All of us waited—and Tellegen did not come. Gradually the lights went out. I dressed sadly, and even Madame, I felt, could not have been more heart-broken than I. She was utterly shameless, during the next days, in revealing that his neglect had cut her to the quick. On several occasions she suddenly murmured, "He didn't come back. Why?" It made no difference that others were there to hear; and the tone of the tortured "Why?" varied from misery to bitterness, with a hint of revenge.

Sarah was full of plans when she returned to France in the fall of 1918, arriving shortly before Armistice Day. Never stop, she would say, otherwise you die. True to her word, she opened the doors of her house, presided at lunch parties, conferred with authors, and even planned future tours. Yet there were many sadnesses to contend with. Pozzi, Sarah's *Docteur Dieu*, had been killed by a madman the year before. Suzanne Seylor, her faithful companion for so many years, had left Sarah after a violent argument, and died six months later. Edmond Rostand perished, a victim of pneumonia, only three weeks after Sarah's return. Perhaps her greatest loss was Clairin, the brother of her heart, who died in 1919. Sarah withstood these and many other such blows with the equanimity of someone accustomed to suffering and the threat of death. Her energy, in fact, was astonishing, as the writer Colette observed in *Dernier Portrait (Last Portrait)*, a touching account of their last meeting:

. . . I had received an invitation which was more like a command. "Madame Bernhardt expects you for lunch on such and such a day." I had never seen her so close. There she was at the end of a long gallery, the *raison d'être* of a somewhat funereal museum, filled with potted palms, sprays of dried flowers, commemorative plaques, and tributes. Her amputation no longer mattered, enveloped as she was in fold upon fold of some dark material. Her white face and small hands still glowed like bruised flowers. I never wearied of looking at her blue eyes which seemed to change color with each lively movement of her small imperious head.

Sarah disappeared just before lunch, whisked away by stage machinery, or simply by faithful arms. We found her on the floor above, seated at table in her gothic throne. She ate, or seemed to eat. She became animated each time the conversation turned to the theatre. Her critical sense, her opinions, and her way of expressing herself were extraordinary. She was mischievously severe about an actress who had just attempted to play

L'Aiglon. "The poor dear isn't man enough to make us forget she's a woman, and not woman enough to be appealing."

She stopped talking theatre only long enough to attend to a large earthenware coffeepot which was brought to the table. She measured out the ground coffee, wet it with boiling water, filled our cups and waited for our well-earned praise.

"Don't I make coffee every bit as well as Catulle Mendès?" she asked as she leaned toward me from the height of her majestic chair.

I record here one of the last gestures of the tragedienne approaching her eightieth year: a delicate faded hand offering a full cup; the cornflower blue of her eyes, so young, caught in a web of wrinkles; the laughing interrogative coquetry of the turn of her head. And that indomitable, endless desire to please, to please again, to please even unto the gates of death.

Colette caught the essence of Bernhardt in those last words, and for the actress "to please" meant to act. Loyal to her *devise*, she performed until her last strength gave out. It was generally thought that she was forced to work because extravagance had left her penniless, and that was more or less true, as extravagance was her way of life. But penniless or not, she went on with her lordly life, maintained eight servants, and supported her spendthrift son, now approaching sixty, in the style to which she had accustomed him. One might say that Sarah did little from the fall of 1918, when she returned to France from the last of her farewell tours of America, to the spring of 1920, if doing little consists of giving readings of Victor Hugo and Fernand Gregh, lecturing and delivering taxing monologues by Rostand in Lyon, Geneva, Montpellier, Pau, and Bordeaux. In April 1920 the seventy-five-year-old actress returned to her own theatre to appear in her new production of Racine's *Athalie.* The classic masterpiece, scheduled for three performances, ran for an unexpected three weeks. Its success was understandable when one considers what Sarah brought to the part. Indeed, who could have resisted the old tragedienne when in the famous "Dream" monologue she speaks of herself as an aging woman, painting her face in an attempt "to repair the irreparable ravages of time"? The audience rose to its feet and cheered when she said these lines, for instead of the traditional anguished cry she whispered them in a hushed and bitter tone. Her novel approach to the role moved the public to what one critic called "wild enthusiasm and frenetic applause. This manifestation," he wrote, "was not only a tribute to her sovereign powers but to the long line of our great classics, to all the Art of immortal France as personified by one woman." The same journalist attended her last performance. There in the theatre he found the crowds of writers, poets, artists, and students who, having seen her *Athalie* once, felt they must see it again. They were rewarded, he said, with an even greater reading, with new psychological insights, new subtleties, new phrasing that did nothing to disturb the grand line of the noble piece. Backstage the critic asked Sarah why she did not prolong the run. Didn't he think she deserved a rest? she answered with a smile. "After all," she continued, "I said I would give three performances and I've given eighteen. Certainly I'm happy that my staging of *Athalie* succeeded so well, for I must confess I approached it with some fear. Now that I see the public is willing to accept me as I am, I'm going to do new things. My next will be Louis Verneuil's *Daniel*, in which I play a morphine addict. Then I'll do *La Gloire* by Maurice Rostand."

"Are you leaving Paris?" the critic asked.

"Yes," Sarah answered. "I'm going to Belle-Ile where I can dream, make future plans, and gather strength for my next season at the Théâtre Sarah Bernhardt."

Miraculously enough, she found the stamina to give both pieces: *Daniel* in 1920, *La Gloire* the following year. According to Verneuil *La Gloire* was sheer drivel and Sarah wasted her time on it only because Maurice was the son of Edmond Rostand, "and because, twenty-five years earlier, she had known him as a child."

Maurice Rostand was equally spiteful: "*Daniel* was unimaginably bad," he wrote. "Furthermore Sarah would never have appeared in it except that Verneuil is about to marry her beloved granddaughter Lysiane. But even Sarah who could talk herself into thinking Sardou a genius could not abide Verneuil's play. 'It's nothing but *merde, merde, merde*,' she repeated in her rage. As spoken by her, the language of the streets sounded like the language of the gods."

The truth is that neither *Daniel* nor *La Gloire* added to the authors' reputations. But at least in the case of *Daniel* it gave Sarah a new role to take to London. Her last trip to England was not easy. Her car broke down between Paris and Boulogne and she was forced to spend a night on the road. Then the channel crossing was so rough that by the time she reached the Savoy Hotel she was in a state of collapse.

All the same she went to a rehearsal where, Sir George Arthur reported, she "startled even those she had ceased to startle by a remarkable impersonation of Daniel, the lovesick youth who seeks to drench disappointment in drugs." Sir George, who wrote a book about Bernhardt, was among those for whom Sarah could do no wrong. There were others, of course, who felt she was a ghost, a shadow of her former self. But for the Sir Georges of the world, she was still vibrantly alive in spite of her disability and her quivering voice.

"There was the makeup," he wrote, "which really produced a young man, diseased and disabled, but with flashes of virile vitality; there were all the resources of technique which forbade the audience to remember that the actress could not move at all; there was a death scene, which for pure beauty has seldom been bettered; and all this from a veteran who was nearer eighty than seventy."

Before leaving London, Bernhardt gave a command performance for Queen Mary. She must take more rest, the queen advised when she saw the depleted actress in her dressing room. "Your Majesty, I shall die on the stage; 'tis my battlefield," cried Sarah in her best *L'Aiglon* manner. But that was more theatrical talk from the woman who had died a thousand deaths onstage only to spring back to life in time for the curtain calls; from a woman who, when she saw another actress obviously much younger than herself, was heard to say with a perfectly straight face: "Think of it, that's the way I'll look ten years from now."

It was business as usual when Sarah returned to Paris. In the fall of 1922 she gave a benefit performance to raise money for Madame Curie's laboratory, acted in *Régine Armand*, another of Verneuil's efforts, and went as far as Turin, where she gave *Daniel*, her last performance on any stage.

That December a wonderful thing happened. Sacha Guitry, her own, her beloved Sacha, asked her to appear in his new play, *Un Sujet de Roman* (*A Subject for a Novel*), along with his father, Lucien, his wife, Yvonne Printemps, and, of course, himself. She was enormously pleased. She would be working with great artists who loved her tenderly, indulgently, wittily, and with true understanding of who and what she was. How could she not feel at home with Sacha, one of the few who was permitted to carry her from stage door to limousine with no hint of discomfort on either side? Or with Lucien, who spoke for her, as well as for himself, when he said: "I love, I adore my profession—I serve it constantly. I never stop acting. I've always acted—always and everywhere, in all sorts of places, at every instant— always, always. I am my own double. I act in restaurants when I ask for more bread. I act when I ask Julia Bartet's husband how his wife is feeling. Blessed work that fills me with drunken joy and peace, how much I owe to you!"

Sarah was her own irrepressible self when she spoke of *Un Sujet de Roman*. The play, she told the press, "is entirely admirable. It's modern, absolutely modern, *cruelly* modern. The subject has never been treated before. It's—Shakespearean!" The play may not have been Shakespearean, but it is one of Sacha Guitry's finer works, towering far above the thin effusions of Louis Verneuil and Maurice Rostand.

A celebrated novelist (Lucien Guitry) has come to detest his success and his ambitious wife (Sarah) who promoted it. The tone of the piece is found in a short speech. "For twenty years," the novelist says, "you've hated me and I have hated you. I loved you because you were beautiful. You loved me because I was famous. Now you're old, and the glory you dreamt of for me is something I never wanted."

René Benjamin, a writer friend of Sacha's, attended one of the first rehearsals. There was no problem of upstaging, he recalled. Sacha deferred to his father, and his father deferred to Sarah, who showed no trace of vanity or pettiness. In fact, she was humble. When she forgot a line, she apologized, saying, "I'm working badly today: it makes me so unhappy. No, don't try to make excuses for me."

Sacha described the dress rehearsal with great emotion:

> Sarah had a long speech in the last act. It was the terrible scene in which the woman confesses that she understands her husband and when he, who despises her, finds it in himself to forgive her. Sarah was at the peak of her powers that day. With no lapse of memory she spoke in a terrifyingly thin, disjointed, magnificent, heart-rending voice. My father was seated at a table opposite her, his hat pulled down over his eyes. When she finished, instead of answering, he reached for her hand and muttered: "Wait a moment." He could not go on. He was weeping. Theatre? But the theatre was their life, their death, their everything. When we finished Sarah asked if she could rest in my dressing room. But towards 7 o'clock she began to choke and we took her home.

Bernhardt never went back to the theatre, any theatre. Three weeks later *Un Sujet de Roman* opened with Harriett Roggers in Sarah's role. That

night, at her request, a stagehand telephoned to tell her when the curtain
was going up. Bedridden and weak, she began to repeat her lines. It was
one of her last performances, for Sarah was in danger of dying of uremia.
But sick as she was, she still made plans for the future. In 1922 she sold
her property in Belle-Ile and bought some land in Garches. Belle-Ile, she
announced, was too cold, too damp, and too far away, ridiculously far away.
Garches, on the other hand, was only fifteen minutes from the boulevard
Péreire, an ideal place to spend her Sundays. Besides, think of the fun of
building a new house.

In the spring of 1923 Mr. Abrams, a Hollywood agent, offered Sarah
the title role in *La Voyante* (*The Fortune Teller*), a film by Sacha Guitry with
Lili Damita, Harry Baur, and the young Mary Marquet, Edmond Rostand's
last mistress and Sarah's protégée. Bernhardt was sick in bed when Abrams
called on her. Was she ill? he asked. No, no, she lied, just a touch of
influenza. But perhaps, she added, it would be wiser to do the filming in
the boulevard Péreire. Mr. Abrams agreed. By 15 March Sarah's atelier had
been transformed into a motion-picture studio, with cameras, scaffolding,
and glaring lamps. Mary Marquet remembered Sarah seated at a table, her
wasted body huddled up, her eyes blinking in the harsh light. Someone put
drops in them from time to time. A small monkey that was part of the plot
lay in her arms. "There was nothing left of her," Mademoiselle Marquet
wrote. "All at once the director shouted Camera! Sarah rose from her torpor;
her face lit up, her neck grew longer, her eyes shone. 'What do I do?' she
demanded in a voice that was young and strong. We were all stupefied. She
had just dropped thirty years." Sarah acted out the scene. But the effort
was such that she collapsed and had to be carried to her room. For the next
two months doctors came and went; the faithful—Maurice and his family,
Louise Abbéma, and Sarah's personal physician, Dr. Marot, took turns at
her bedside. From time to time Sarah felt stronger and insisted on being
dressed and taken down to lunch. One day Mrs. Patrick Campbell came to
share her meal.

Sarah was charm itself, Mrs. Pat remembered, in an antique velvet
cloak, a gift, she fondly boasted, that Sacha had brought all the way from
Venice. But her food remained untouched. Finally, after a good gossip, two
servants appeared with her sedan chair. As they carried her off she blew
her Mélisande a kiss, then, smiling, disappeared. It was the last time they
would meet. As Sarah's condition grew worse, daily bulletins appeared in

newspapers the world over. They were hidden from her, of course, but no one could hide the crowds that stood under her window waiting for her to die.

"Are they journalists?" she asked Maurice. "Some of them are," he said. "Then I'll keep them dangling. They tortured me all my life, now it's my turn to torture them."

These were her last words, said with a smile. On 26 March 1923, Sarah died in Maurice's arms. Minutes later Dr. Marot opened her window to announce that Madame Sarah Bernhardt was no more. That evening the actors of Paris asked their audiences to observe a two-minute silence, then, when the performances were over, those who had been close to her—and there were many—went to the boulevard Péreire to offer the flowers they had received that evening. For three days an unending stream of mourners filed past Sarah's body. Impressive in death as she was in life, she lay in her famous coffin, dressed in white, her head resting on a pillow of violets, a silver cross in her hand, the ribbon of the Legion of Honor on her breast. Overwhelming masses of lilacs, roses, orchids, carnations, and gladiolas filled the room, the staircase, and the foyer. Even more touching were the innumerable bouquets of violets and jonquils, modest tokens of love from the humble who had worshipped her from afar. Thousands of people, young and old, rich and poor, theatre-goers and those who had never been to a theatre, lined the streets, ten deep, to watch the funeral procession make its way from the boulevard Péreire to the Church of Saint François de Sales and from there to Sarah's last resting place in the Père-Lachaise cemetery. No woman in French history and very few men had ever inspired such a spontaneous rush of feeling, such a universal display of love. On its way through the city, the cortege stopped in front of the Théâtre Sarah Bernhardt. In those solemn moments a shower of multicolored petals floated down from the roof of the theatre to light on the coffin below. There were no speeches at Sarah's graveside, but there was one heartfelt cry. It came from a young actress who uttered four words that echoed in the hearts of those present: "Immortals do not die." The grave was marked by a stone simply inscribed:

SARAH BERNHARDT.

Some years later, a statue of the actress was put up in the place Malesherbes. In World War II, when the Germans occupied Paris, a Nazi zealot took it upon himself to smash the nose, an ugly, pathetic gesture for, mutilated or not, the Divine Sarah lives on in the memories of those who cherish the quest for beauty in the service of art.

BIBLIOGRAPHY

Permission has been graciously granted to quote from the books listed below. Unless otherwise stated, all French books were published in Paris and all English books were published in New York. Some of the earlier books were published with no date.

FICTIONAL ACCOUNTS OF EPISODES IN BERNHARDT'S LIFE

Bernhardt, Sarah. *Petite Idole* (Editions Nilsson, 1920).

———. *The Idol of Paris* (The Macaulay Company, 1922).

———. *Jolie Sosie* (Editions Nilsson, n.d.).

Champsaur, Felicien. *Dinah Samuel* (Pierre Douville, n.d.).

Goncourt, Edmond de. *La Faustin* (Ernest Flammarion, 1881).

Lorrain, Jean. *Le Tréteau* (Jean Bosc Editeur, 1906).

BOOKS BY BERNHARDT

Bernhardt, Sarah. *Un Coeur D'Homme* (*Pièce en Quatre Actes*) & *L'Aveu* (*Drame en Un Acte*) (Charpentier et Fasquelle, 1911).

———. *Memories of My Life* (D. Appleton & Company, 1923).

———. *The Art of the Theatre* (London: Geoffrey Bles, 1924).

———. *Ma Double Vie* (Editions des Femmes, 1980). English translation, *My Double Life* (London: Owen, 1977).

———. *L'Art du Théâtre* (Editions Nilsson, n.d.).

BIOGRAPHIES OF SARAH BERNHARDT

Agate, May. *Madame Sarah* (New York / London: Benjamin Blom, 1945, reissued 1969).

Arthur, Sir George. *Sarah Bernhardt* (London: William Heinemann, Ltd., 1923).

Baring, Maurice. *Sarah Bernhardt* (London / New York: D. Appleton-Century, 1934).

Bernhardt, Lysiane. *Sarah Bernhardt, My Grandmother* (London / New York: Hurst & Blackett, Ltd., 1945).

Binet-Valmer. *Sarah Bernhardt* (Flammarion, 1936).

Castelot, Andre. *Ensorcelante Sarah Bernhardt* (Librairie Academique Perrin, 1961).

Colombier, Marie. *Les Voyages de Sarah Bernhardt en Amérique*, preface by Arsene Houssaye (Marpon & Flammarion, 1881).

———. *Les Mémoires de Sarah Barnum*, preface by Paul Bonnetain (1883).

———. *Mémoires* Tome I: *Fin d'Empire*; Tome II: *Fin de Siecle*; Tome III: *Fin de Vie* (Ernest Flammarion, n.d.).

Dupont-Nivet, Jean. *Sarah Bernhardt, Trente Ans de Passion pour Belle-Ile-en-Mer* (Jean Dupont-Nivet, 1973).

Emboden, William. *Sarah Bernhardt* (London: Macmillan, 1974).

Geller, G. G. *Sarah Bernhardt* (Frederick A. Stokes, 1933).

Hahn, Reynaldo. *La Grande Sarah* (Hachette, 1930).

———. *Sarah Bernhardt* (London: Elkin Mathews & Marrot, Ltd., 1932).

Huret, Jules. *Sarah Bernhardt* (London: Chapman & Hall, 1899).

Jullian, Philippe. *Sarah Bernhardt* (Editions Ballard, 1977).

Pierrefeux, Guy de. *Madame Quand Même, Sarah Bernhardt*, edited by D. Chabas (Mont-de-Marsan, 1920).

Richepin, Jean. *La Vie de Marie Pigeonnier.*

Rostand, Maurice. *Sarah Bernhardt* (Calmann-Levy, 1950).

Rueff, Suze. *I Knew Sarah Bernhardt* (London: Frederick Muller, Ltd., 1951).

OTHER WORKS

Agate, James. *Ego: The Autobiography of James Agate* (nine volumes). Various publishers including (London: Hamish Hamilton, 1935; George Harrap & Co., 1949).

———. *An Anthology* (London: Rupert Hart-Davis, 1961).

Andry, Marc. *Edmond Rostand, la Panache et la Gloire* (Plon, 1986).

Anonymous. *An Englishman in Paris* Volume II: *The Empire* (D. Appleton & Company, 1892).

Auerbach, Nina. *Ellen Terry* (W.W. Norton, 1987).

Beerbohm, Max. *Around Theatres* (Alfred A. Knopf, 1930).

———. *More Theatre* (Taplinger Publishing Co., 1969).

Blanch, Lesley. *Pierre Loti* (A Helen & Kurt Wolff Book / Harcourt Brace Jovanovich, 1983).

Campbell, Mrs. Patrick. *My Life and Some Letters* (Dodd, Mead & Company, 1922).

Chevalley, Silvie. *Rachel en Amérique* (La Société d'Histoire du Théâtre, 1957).

Cocteau, Jean. *Portraits-souvenirs* (Bernard Grasset, 1935).

———. *Professional Secrets*, translation by Richard Howard (Farrar, Straus & Giroux, Inc., 1970).

Colette. *Dernier Portrait* (1944). An article in the program of a gala to celebrate the hundredth anniversary of Bernhardt's birth

Coppee, François. *Souvenir d'un Parisien* (Lemerre, 1910).

Daudet, Alphonse, *Pages Inédites de Critique Dramatique 1874–80* (Ernest Flammarion, 1922).

Daudet, Leon. *Paris Vecu* (Gallimard, 1969).

Delluc, Louis. *Chez de Max* (L'Édition, 1918).

Dussane, Beatrix. *Reines de Théâtre* (Lardanchet, 1944).

———. *Dieux des Planches* (Lardanchet, 1964).

Ellmann, Richard. *Oscar Wilde* (Alfred A. Knopf, 1988).

Faure, Paul. *Vingt Ans d'Intimité avec Edmond Rostand* (Plon, 1928).

Gaillard, Roger. *La Vie d'un Joueur* (Calmann-Lévy, 1953).

Genty, Christian. *Histoire du Théâtre de L'Odéon* (Fischbacher, 1981).

Goncourt, Edmond et Jules de. *Journal des Goncourt* (Fasquelle and Flammarion, 1956).

Gosling, Nigel. *Nadar* (Alfred A. Knopf, 1976).

Got, Edmond. *Journal* (Plon, 1910).

Gribble, Francis. *Rachel* (London: Chapman and Hall, Ltd., 1911).

Guilbert, Yvette. *La Chanson de Ma Vie* (Grasset, 1927).

Guitry, Sacha. *Lucien Guitry, Raconté par Son Fils* (Raoul Solar, 1953).

———. *Si J'ai Bonne Mémoire* (Librairie Académique Perrin, 1965). English translation, *If I Remember Right* (London: Methuen, 1935).

Harding, James. *Sacha Guitry* (London: Methuen, 1968).

Hegermann-Lindencrone, Lillie de [Lillie Moulton]. *In the Courts of Memory* (Harper & Brothers, 1912).

———. *The Sunny Side of Diplomatic Life* (Harper & Brothers, 1914).

Hollingshead, John. *Gaiety Chronicles* (London: Westminster Archibald Constable & Company, 1898).

Holroyd, Michael. *Lytton Strachey: The Unknown Years* Volume 1 (Holt, Rinehart and Winston, 1967).

Huret, Jules. *Loges et Coulisses* (Editions de la Revue Blanche, 1901).

James, Henry. *The Scenic Art* (Brunswick, New Jersey: Rutgers University Press, 1948).

———. *Parisian Sketches* (New York University Press, 1957).

———. *The Tragic Muse* (Thomas Y. Crowell, 1975).

Jones, Ernest. *The Life and Work of Sigmund Freud* Volume 1 (Basic Books, Inc., 1953).

Jullian, Philippe. *Robert de Montesquiou, Un Prince 1900* (Librairie Académique Perrin, 1965).

Lugne-Poe, Aurelien. *La Parade: Souvenirs et Impressions de Théâtre.* (Gallimard, 1930–1933).

Marquet, Mary. *Ce Que J'ose Dire* (Jacques Grancher, 1977).

Maurois, Andre. *Olympio ou La Vie de Victor Hugo* (Hachette, 1954).

———. *Victor Hugo* (Jonathan Cape, London, 1956).

———. *Les Trois Dumas* (Hachette, 1957).

Moreno, Marguerite. *Souvenirs de Ma Vie*, preface by Colette (Editions de Flore, 1948).

Mounet-Sully, Jean. *Souvenirs d'un Tragédien* (Editions Pierre Lafutte, 1917).

Mucha, Jiri. *Alphonse Maria Mucha* (London: Academy Editions, 1989).

Olivier, Laurence. *Confessions of an Actor* (Penguin Books, 1982).

Peters, Margot. *Mrs. Pat: The Life of Mrs. Patrick Campbell* (Alfred A. Knopf, 1984).

Porel, Jacques. *Fils de Réjane* (Plon, 1951).

Pougy, Liane de. *Mes Cahiers Bleus* (Plon, 1977). English translation, *My Blue Notebooks* (Harper & Row, 1979).

Pronier, Ernest. *Sarah Bernhardt* (Geneva: Alex Jullien, n.d.).

Proust, Marcel. *Remembrance of Things Past*, translated by C. K. Scott Moncrieff and Terence Kilmartin (Random House, 1981).

Renard, Jules. *Journal* (Gallimard, 1965).

Ripert, Emile. *Edmond Rostand, Sa Vie et Son Oeuvre* (Librairie Hachette, 1968).

Robertson, W. Graham. *Time Was* (London: Hamish Hamilton, 1931).

Robinson, Phyllis C. *Willa: The Life of Willa Cather* (Doubleday & Company, 1983).

Russell, John. *Paris* (Harry N. Abrams, Inc., 1983).

Salmon, Eric. *Bernhardt and the Theatre of Her Time* (Westport, Connecticut / London: Greenwood Press, 1984).

Sarcey, Francisque. *Quarante Ans de Théâtre* (Bibliothéque Des Annales, 1900).

Shaw, George Bernard, *Dramatic Opinions and Essays* Volume I (Brentano, 1909).

Simone. *Sous de Nouveaux Soleils* (Gallimard, 1957).

Skinner, Cornelia Otis. *Madame Sarah* (Boston: Houghton Mifflin Company, 1967).

Symons, Arthur. *Eleonora Duse* (Duffield, 1927).

Taranow, Gerda. *Sarah Bernhardt: The Art Within The Legend* (Princeton, New Jersey: Princeton University Press, 1972).

Tellegen, Lou. *Women Have Been Kind: The Memoirs of Lou Tellegen* (The Vanguard Press, 1931).

Terry, Ellen. *Memoirs* (Victor Gollancz, Ltd., 1933).

Toussaint du Vast, Nicole. *Rachel* (Stock, 1980).

Trollope, Fanny. *Paris and the Parisians* (London: Alan Sutton, 1836, reissued 1985).

Valmy-Baysse, Jean. *Naissance et Vie de la Comédie Française* (Floury, 1945).

Verneuil, Louis. *La Vie Merveilleuse de Sarah Bernhardt* (Brentano, 1942). English translation, *The Fabulous Life of Sarah Bernhardt* (Harper & Brothers, 1942).

Weaver, William. *Duse: A Biography* (Harcourt Brace Jovanovich, 1984).

Wilde, Oscar. *The Letters of Oscar Wilde* (Harcourt, Brace & World, 1962).

———. *Selected Letters of Oscar Wilde* (Oxford University Press, 1979).

Woon, Basil. *The Real Sarah Bernhardt* (Boni & Liveright, 1924).

I N D E X

PERMISSIONS ACKNOWLEDGMENTS

Peters Fraser & Dunlop Group, Ltd.: excerpts from *Ego: The Autobiography of James Agate.* Reprinted by permission of Peters Fraser & Dunlop Group, Ltd. on behalf of the Estate of James Agate.

Laurence Pollinger, Ltd.: excerpts from *Letters of D. H. Lawrence, Volume 1, 1901–1913,* edited by James T. Boulton, Cambridge University Press, 1979. Reprinted by permission of Laurence Pollinger, Ltd. and the Estate of Frieda Lawrence Ravagli.

Random House, Inc. and *Chatto & Windus:* excerpts from *Remembrance of Things Past* by Marcel Proust, translated by C. K. Scott Moncrieff and Terence Kilmartin. Translation copyright © 1981 by Random House, Inc. and Chatto & Windus. Reprinted by permission.

Eva Reichmann: excerpts from *Around Theatres* by Max Beerbohm. Reprinted by permission of Eva Reichmann.

Vanguard Press: excerpts from *Women Have Been Kind* by Lou Tellegen. Copyright 1930 by Lou Tellegen. Reprinted by permission of Vanguard Press, a division of Random House, Inc.

P H O T O G R A P H I C   C R E D I T S
(by figure number)

A NOTE ABOUT THE AUTHORS

Arthur Gold died in 1990, shortly before the completion of this book. With his partner, Robert Fizdale, he formed the celebrated piano duo that gave concerts throughout the world for nearly forty years. They are the authors of *Misia, The Life of Misia Sert*.

A NOTE ON THE TYPE

This book was set in a digitized version of Bodoni Book, so called
after Giambattista Bodoni (1740–1813), son of a printer of Piedmont.
After gaining experience and fame as superintendent of the Press
of the Propaganda in Rome, Bodoni became in 1768 the head of
the ducal printing house of Parma, which he soon made the foremost
of its kind in Europe. His *Manuale Tipografico*, completed by his
widow in 1818, contains 279 pages of specimens of types, including
alphabets of about thirty languages. His editions of Greek, Latin,
Italian, and French classics are celebrated for their typography. In
type designing he was an innovator, making his new faces rounder,
wider, and lighter, with greater openness and delicacy.

Composed by PennSet, Inc., Bloomsburg, Pennsylvania

Printed and bound by Arcata-Halliday Lithographers
West Hanover, Massachusetts

Designed by Iris Weinstein